CLEAN SWEEP

By Teresa Uluiviti

Table of Contents

FOREWORD

HAVE YOU EVER HAD ONE OF THOSE MOMENTS IN YOUR LIFE WHERE EVERYTHING SEEMED TO GO WRONG, AS IF YOU WERE STUCK IN LIMBO OR A TIME WARP SOMEWHERE AND YOU WEREN'T SURE IF YOU'D EVER GET OUT OR WHETHER TO JUST LAUGH OR CRY? THE ANSWER SEEMS LOGICAL, YOU EITHER LAUGH OR YOU CRY. THAT'S THE BEAUTY OF CHOICES I SUPPOSE. MY THINKING, AND THIS IS JUST AN OPINION, THERE ARE TIMES WHEN YOU LAUGH, BECAUSE IF YOU WERE TO CRY YOU MAY NEVER STOP. I'VE BEEN THERE MORE TIMES THAN I CAN COUNT.

MY DESIRE IN WRITING THIS BOOK IS TO BE AN ENCOURAGEMENT TO THOSE WHO FOUND THEMSELVES A VICTIM OF ABUSE, WHETHER IT BE, EMOTIONAL, VERBAL, PHYSICAL, SEXUAL. I BY NO MEANS AM AN EXPERT, NOR HAVE I HAD ANY

SCHOOLING TO BE A COUNSELOR OR PSYCHOLOGIST, BUT WHAT I CAN DO IS SHARE MY PERSONAL EXPERIENCE AND HOW GOD BROUGHT ME THROUGH TO BE THE WOMAN OF GOD I AM TODAY. IT'S ONLY THROUGH GOD THAT I WAS ABLE TO GET THROUGH SOME OF THE THINGS I ENDURED, AND ALTHOUGH THERE ARE MANY, MANY, WORSE CASES OUT THERE, THEN WHAT I ENDURED, EACH ONES SITUATION SEEMS UNBEARABLE AND HARD TO THEM. I BELIEVE FROM HEARING DIFFERENT STORIES OF WHAT ONE WENT THROUGH, HOW THEY OVERCAME, CAN INDEED HELP YOU KNOW THAT YOU ARE NOT ALONE IN THE PAIN YOU BEAR.

I BELIEVE THERE IS NO AMOUNT OF SCHOOLING, OR DEGREES YOU MAY HAVE, ALTHOUGH A GREAT ACHIEVEMENT, CAN EVER COMPARE TO YOUR PERSONAL EXPERIENCE. I MEAN, THINK ABOUT IT FOR A MINUTE IF YOU WILL, WOULD YOU WANT SOMEONE TELLING YOU HOW TO RAISE YOUR CHILD, IF THEY HAD NO CHILDREN THEMSELVES, BUT THEY DID HAPPEN TO HAVE A DEGREE IN CHILD PSYCHOLOGY? SURE, THEIR KNOWLEDGE OR SUGGESTIONS MAY INDEED BE HELPFUL, BUT IF YOU, LET'S SAY, HAVE A HYPERACTIVE CHILD, WHO BEING DIAGNOSED WITH ATTENTION DEFICIT HYPERACTIVITY DISORDER, (ADHD), WHO ALSO HAS OPPOSITIONAL DEFIANT DISORDER, (ODD), FETAL ALCOHOL SYNDROME, AND MILDLY MENTALLY RETARDED, BEING THREE YEARS BEHIND THEIR PEERS, WHO HAS TROUBLE SLEEPING TO THE POINT THEY ARE SO IRRITABLE THAT THEY BANG THEIR HEAD AGAINST THE WALL, EVEN TO THE POINT OF DOING IT SO MUCH, THEY PUT A HOLE IN THE WALL. YES, ALL ONE CHILD, WHO WAS ONCE A

RELATIVE OF MINE. COULD YOU EVEN ACCEPT THE ADVICE FROM ANYONE WHO HAD NO KIDS, OR EXPERIENCED THESE CHALLENGES? I WOULD THINK NOT, YOU'D PROBABLY SEEK THE ADVICE OF OTHER MOTHERS WHO HAD EXPERIENCED SIMILAR CHALLENGES THEMSELVES. SAME WAY WITH ANY SITUATION THAT MAY ARISE, WE WANT TO HEAR FROM SOMEONE WHO HAS EXPERIENCED WHAT EVER SITUATION WE'RE IN, TO FEEL CONNECTED, TO RECEIVE COMFORT AND SUPPORT. I PRAY THIS BOOK WILL OFFER YOU THAT SUPPORT YOU NEED, HOPE, HEALING, AND THE COURAGE TO GO ON, AND FOR YOU TO KNOW YOU ARE INDEED A PERSON OF GREAT WORTH.

I WANT TO POINT THIS OUT TO YOU BEFORE I SHARE MY STORY.

GOD HAS GIVEN EACH OF US MANY GIFTS AND TALENTS, HE HAS FEARFULLY AND WONDERFULLY MADE EACH AND EVERYONE OF US, OUR LIFE MATTERS TO GOD AND IS OF GREAT VALUE TO HIM. HE NEVER MEANT FOR HARDSHIP TO COME, BUT WHEN WE GO THROUGH A THING, IT'S HARD FOR US TO IMAGINE THAT GOD CARES. AM I RIGHT ABOUT IT? BUT, LET ME TELL YOU THAT HE DOES CARE AND HE LOVES US SO MUCH, BUT BECAUSE OF THE FALL OF LUCIFER, WHO IS LISTED IN EZEKIEL 28:12-19, ISAIAH 14:9-23,WE NOW LIVE IN A FALLEN WORLD, RATHER THAN THE PARADISE THAT GOD INTENDED FOR HIS CREATION. WE ARE FACED WITH CHALLENGES, TRIALS, AND ABOVE ALL ELSE CHOICES. LET ME GIVE SOME BACKGROUND ON LUCIFER.

LUCIFER WAS GOD'S MOST BEAUTIFUL ANGEL, MEANING BRIGHT ONE, OR LIGHT BEARER, AND WHEN LUCIFER BECAME PRIDEFUL TO THE POINT HE THOUGHT HE WAS GOD, HE WAS CAST OUT OF HEAVEN, ALONG WITH THE ANGELS WHO SIDED WITH HIM, THEREBY CREATING WHAT WE KNOW AS HELL, OR THE LAKE OF FIRE. WHEN GOD CREATED MAN, FROM THE DUST OF THE EARTH AND BREATHED INTO HIM THE BREATH OF LIFE, AS DESCRIBED IN GENESIS 1 AND 2, GOD THEN FORMED EVE OUT OF A RIB FROM ADAM'S SIDE. LET ME STOP THERE A MINUTE AND EXPLAIN SOMETHING TO YOU.

WOMAN WAS CREATED FROM MAN'S SIDE TO WALK BESIDE HIM, NOT TO DOMINATE ONE ANOTHER, WALK ALL OVER ONE ANOTHER, OR RULE OVER ONE ANOTHER. ALTHOUGH THE BIBLE SAYS, THE MAN IS THE HEAD OF THE HOME, AS CHRIST IS THE HEAD OF THE CHURCH, DOES NOT MEAN WE AS WOMEN SHOULD BE DOMINATED. NEITHER SHOULD A WOMAN TRY AND CONTROL HER MAN, OR GIVE ULTIMATUMS TO GET WHAT SHE WANTS.

THE MAN IS TO LOVE THE WOMAN AS CHRIST LOVED THE CHURCH AND GAVE HIMSELF FOR IT. SAME WAY FOR MEN, THEY ARE TO LOVE THEIR WOMAN, AND BE WILLING TO GIVE HIS LIFE FOR HER. WHEN THE MAN FOLLOWS THIS, THEN THE WOMAN IS TO SUBMIT HERSELF TO HER HUSBAND. ALL COUPLES WILL HAVE STRUGGLES IN THEIR RELATIONSHIP, BUT THERE COMES A POINT WHEN IT GOES SO FAR, AS TO BE BEAT DOWN, WHETHER BY PHYSICAL ENCOUNTERS OR WORDS, AND LADIES? MEN ARE NOT EXEMPT TO THIS

EITHER, THERE ARE MANY MEN ABUSED BY WOMEN AS WELL.

BACK TO THE STORY OF LUCIFER, WHEN LUCIFER WAS CAST OUT OF HEAVEN, HE WAS GIVEN DOMINION OVER THE EARTH. ONE DAY WHEN ADAM AND EVE WERE WALKING IN THE GARDEN, THEY CAME TO THE TREE IN THE CENTER OF THE GARDEN THAT WAS FORBIDDEN FOR THEM TO EAT FROM. ALL OTHER TREES, THEY COULD FREELY EAT FROM, BUT THIS ONE TREE THEY WERE FORBIDDEN, FOR IF THEY DID THEY WOULD SURELY DIE.

LUCIFER, ALSO KNOWN AS, SERPENT, SATAN, THE ENEMY, THE DEVIL, THE FATHER OF LIES AND THE GOD OF THIS WORLD, TEMPTED THEM WITH THE FRUIT OF THAT TREE AND DECEIVED THEM INTO THINKING THAT WAS THE MOST DELICIOUS FRUIT OF ALL THE OTHER TREES THEY HAD TO EAT FROM AND LIED TO THEM SAYING THEY WOULD NOT SURELY DIE. SO EVE ATE OF THAT TREE AND THEN GAVE TO ADAM AND HE ATE, THAT LED TO THE FALL OF ADAM AND EVE, AND THEN SIN ENTERED INTO THE WORLD,GENESIS 3, ROMANS 12: 12,13.

IN 2 CORINTHIANS 4:4, IT EXPLAINS THAT LUCIFER, BECAUSE OF HIS FALL FROM HEAVEN, NOW RULES THIS WORLD, BRINGING HEARTACHE, PAIN AND STRUGGLES, FOR SOME MORE DIFFICULT TO GO THROUGH THAN FOR OTHERS, BUT NEVERTHELESS, HARD FOR US TO FACE. WE ARE NOW IN A BATTLE FOR OUR LIVES, AGAINST GOOD AND THE FORCES OF EVIL. SATAN WANTS TO BLIND THE EYES OF PEOPLE SO WE CAN'T SEE THE GOOD THAT GOD HAS FOR US, AND

DOESN'T WANT TO SEE PEOPLE TOUCHED BY THE LOVE OF GOD BECAUSE SATAN HAS A HATRED FOR GOD AND WANTS TO TAKE AS MANY PEOPLE AWAY FROM GOD AS POSSIBLE.

BUT THE GOOD NEWS IS THAT GOD, SENDING HIS ONE AND ONLY SON, BORN OF A VIRGIN, AS LISTED IN MATTHEW 1: 18-25, AND ONE WHO KNEW NO SIN, BECAME SIN FOR US AND THE ULTIMATE SACRIFICE, BEING CRUCIFIED AND DYING ON CALVARY, BEING BURIED AND ON THE THIRD DAY, RISING AGAIN. HALLELUJAH!!!

2 CORINTHIANS 5:19:21, THIS SCRIPTURE GIVES US HOPE AND THE ASSURANCE OF ETERNAL LIFE TO ALL THOSE WHO ACCEPT JESUS INTO THEIR HEART AS LORD AND SAVIOR, THEREBY BRINGING US BACK INTO RIGHT STANDING WITH GOD, (JOHN 3:16). IF WE WILL PUT OUR TRUST AND HOPE IN HIM, HE PROMISES IN THE BIBLE HE WILL NEVER LEAVE US OR FORSAKE US AND WILL ALWAYS PROVIDE A WAY OF ESCAPE, BUT HE NEVER FORCES HIMSELF ON US OR MAKES US DO ANYTHING, WE HAVE TO CHOOSE FOR OURSELVES. HE DOESN'T WANT TO SEE PEOPLE TRAPPED IN THE CLUTCHES OF SATAN.

WHEN WE BECOME A CHRISTIAN, WE BECOME NEW CREATURES IN CHRIST, THE OLD THINGS OF OUR PAST BEING DEAD, AND ALL THINGS NOW BECOMING NEW, 2 CORINTHIANS 5; 17. HOWEVER, JUST BECAUSE WE BECOME A CHRISTIAN, DOESN'T MEAN WE ARE EXEMPT FROM HARDSHIP. HOWEVER, THROUGH GOD'S WORD, WE HAVE A GUIDE TO HOW WE CAN GET THROUGH THOSE TOUGH TIMES. GOD PROMISES AS WE CAST OUR CARES ON HIM, HE IS FAITHFUL TO

BRING US THROUGH THOSE TOUGH TIMES. HE HAS OVERCOME THE WORLD, JOHN 16:33, DEFEATING DEATH, HELL, AND THE GRAVE THROUGH THE DEATH, BURIAL, AND RESURRECTION OF JESUS. MATTHEW 27:51-66, 28:1-10.

I'M SO THANKFUL THAT GOD GAVE US HIS WRITTEN WORD AS A GUIDE TO ENCOURAGE US AND TO SPEAK TO US, IT'S SORT OF LIKE HAVING A ROAD MAP. YOU'D TAKE A ROAD MAP OR USE A GPS SYSTEM IF YOU WERE TRAVELING SOMEWHERE, SO YOU'D KNOW HOW TO GET THERE. THAT'S WHAT THE BIBLE IS AND AS WE PUT OUR TRUST IN GOD, READ HIS WORD, WE'LL FIND THAT HE WILL HELP CARRY US THROUGH THOSE TRIALS THAT COME OUR WAY, THE WHOLE TIME LEARNING PERSERVERANCE, ENDURANCE, AND STRENGTH, NOT TO MENTION BOOSTING OUR CONFIDENCE AND FAITH IN OURSELVES. HE WILL SHOW US HOW TO BE MORE THAN A CONQUEROR THROUGH HIM, AND TO BE OVERCOMERS OVER THE SCHEMES OF THE DEVIL HIMSELF. WE NEED TO RECOGNIZE THAT WE HAVE AN ENEMY, WHO DOES NOTHING MORE THAN TO COME TO STEAL, KILL, AND TRY AND DESTROY US, JOHN 10:10.

SATAN KNOWS HOW VALUABLE WE ARE TO THE KINGDOM OF GOD, AND HE WILL GO TO GREAT LENGTHS AT TIMES TO SEE THAT WE FAIL, AND KEEP US IN BONDAGE, ENSLAVED TO SIN. BUT GOD COMES TO GIVE LIFE AND LIFE MORE ABUNDANTLY, JOHN 10:10, TO SET US FREE FROM THE TRAPS THE ENEMY HAS LAID OUT FOR US. GOD IS THE POTTER AND WE THE CLAY, ISAIAH 64:8 AND HE WILL TAKE YOUR BEAT DOWN, BROKEN LIFE, AND MAKE SOMETHING

BEAUTIFUL OUT OF IT THAT WILL BRING GLORY TO HIM, AND GIVE YOU A TESTIMONY THAT MAY BE THE VERY THING TO CHANGE THE WORLD AND BRING OTHERS TO HIM!! THAT'S WHAT'S IT'S ALL ABOUT, BRINGING OTHERS TO HIM!!

GOD'S DESIRE IS NOT FOR ONE TO PERISH, BUT THAT ALL SHOULD COME TO REPENTANCE AND THE SAVING KNOWLEDGE OF JESUS CHRIST, 2 PETER 3:9. HIS RETURN IS EVER SO NEAR, JOHN 14:3, 1 THESSALONIANS 4:13-18, AND WE CAN WASTE NO MORE TIME, FOR WE KNOW NOT THE DAY, NOR DO WE KNOW THE HOUR, THAT THE SON OF MAN COMETH, MATTHEW 24:36-44. WE ARE HIS HANDS, HIS FEET, AND HIS VOICE AND MUST TELL OTHERS ABOUT WHAT HE HAS DONE FOR US, MATTHEW 28:19, 20. I PRAY THIS BOOK SERVES TO HELP RESTORE YOU AND HELP YOU TO BECOME ALL GOD HAS PLANNED AND PURPOSED FOR YOUR LIFE!!

PERSONAL EXPERIENCE

I, MYSELF, WAS A VICTIM OF ABUSE IN SOME WAY, ALL MY LIFE BUT IT WASN'T UNTIL 2009, THAT I WAS ABLE TO ACTUALLY BREAK FREE, AND GOD IS HEALING AND RESTORING MY LIFE WITH EACH PASSING DAY, AND I KNOW I HAVE A LONG WAY TO GO YET. HE IS TAKING ME OUT FROM UNDER A SPIRIT OF OPPRESSION, TO A LIFE OF RESTORATION; HE IS TAKING ME OUT OF THE MIRY CLAY I WAS SINKING IN, AND SETTING MY FEET UPON THE ROCK TO STAY, AND IS ESTABLISHING MY GOINGS. GLORY TO GOD!!

PSALMS 40:2, 3 SAYS THAT HE HAS PUT A NEW SONG IN MY MOUTH. GOD BEGAN SHOWING ME THE DESTINY HE HAD LAID OUT FOR ME. IN JEREMIAH 29:11, GOD SAYS HE KNOWS THE THOUGHTS AND PLANS HE HAS FOR US, THOUGHTS OF PEACE AND NOT OF EVIL, TO GIVE US AN EXPECTED END. NOW ALTHOUGH I DON'T KNOW ALL HE HAS PLANNED, I TAKE EACH DAY AS IT COMES, AND WHAT A JOURNEY IT IS. I'M LEARNING THAT EACH STAGE OF MY LIFE SERVED AS A STEPPING STONE, TO GET ME TO WHERE I AM TODAY, THE PLACE HE WANTS ME TO BE. IT HAS IN NO WAY BEEN EASY, MANY TIMES, I'VE WANTED TO GIVE UP, TO LEAVE THIS WORLD AND THE PAIN BEHIND, BUT THAT WOULD HAVE BEEN A COP OUT. EACH THING WE FACE, SERVES TO MAKE US STRONGER, AND CAN BE USED TO BRING OTHERS JOY AND A SENSE OF HOPE.

AS I SAID EARLIER IN THE FIRST PART OF THIS BOOK, NO AMOUNT OF SCHOOLING CAN EVER COMPARE TO LIFE EXPERIENCES. UNLESS YOU'VE BEEN THROUGH TOUGH TIMES, THERE'S NO WAY YOU CAN EFFECTIVELY MINISTER TO SOMEONE ELSE. I USED AN EXAMPLE OF SOMEONE HAVING CHILDREN WITH ADHD, AND ODD, ALONG WITH OTHER DISORDERS, THERE ARE MANY OTHER SITUATIONS. I MEAN, CAN ONE TRULY UNDERSTAND HOW TO MINISTER TO A MOM OF A CHILD WITH LEARNING DISABILITIES, AND YOU HAVE A CHILD THAT IS NOTHING LESS THAN A GENIUS? WE ALL HAVE SOMETHING IN OUR LIFE IN SOME WAY OR ANOTHER THAT WE'VE GONE THROUGH, THAT WE CAN USE TO HELP COMFORT AND SUPPORT SOMEONE ELSE. LET'S TURN OUR TRIALS INTO TESTIMONY'S INSTEAD OF ALLOWING OUR CIRCUMSTANCES TO HOLD US BOUND.

I'D LIKE TO SHARE MY STORY. IT WILL TAKE YOU FROM INFANCY, INTO ADULTHOOD TO THE POINT WHERE I AM AT THIS VERY MOMENT. MUCH TIME, THOUGHT AND PRAYER WENT INTO WRITING THIS BOOK AND I PRAY YOUR LIFE WILL BE CHALLENGED AND CHANGED BY THE MIGHTY HAND OF GOD AS YOU READ. MOST NAMES HAVE BEEN LEFT OUT FOR A REASON, I PRAY YOU'LL BE ABLE TO FOLLOW ALONG AND MAKE SENSE OUT OF WHAT IS BEING WRITTEN. THANK YOU

THE DAY I ENTERED THE WORLD

I WAS BORN ON SEPT.28TH 1963, THE FIRST BORN OF 3 AND THE ONLY GIRL. MY MOM CARRIED ME FULL TERM, AND HAD A FAIRLY EASY PREGNANCY AND DELIVERY. AS I GOT OLDER, MY MOM HAD SHARED STORIES WITH ME, AS WELL AS PICTURES, THAT FROM THE TIME I WAS BORN, SHE BELIEVED SOMETHING HAD BEEN INSTILLED IN ME, THEY WEREN'T AWARE OF WHAT IT WAS AT FIRST, BUT NOTICED AROUND THE TIME I WAS A TODDLER, I SEEMED TO HAVE A LOVE FOR MUSIC. YOU SEE, MY DAD PLAYED DRUMS FOR A BAND HE WAS IN. HE HAD HIS OWN DRUM SET AT HOME AND WOULD PRACTICE DURING THE WEEK, FOR HIS WEEKEND PERFORMANCES AT THE LOCAL LODGE. MY PARENTS TOLD ME STORIES ABOUT THOSE TIMES WHEN MY DAD WOULD BE PRACTICING AT HOME AND I'D STAND UP IN MY CRIB AND DANCE, GIGGLING THE WHOLE TIME, THEN JUST FALL RIGHT OFF TO SLEEP AS IF NOT BOTHERED BY THE CONSTANT BEATING OF THE STICKS AGAINST THE DRUM HEAD OR THE FOOT PEDAL THAT MADE A DEEP BONG SOUND AS IT HIT AGAINST THE BASE DRUM.

MOM TOLD ME ABOUT SOME SLEEPING ISSUES I WAS HAVING AT THE TIME, AND IT SEEMED AS IF NOTHING WOULD SOOTHE ME. THEY WERE AT THEIR WITS END TRYING TO FIGURE OUT WHAT THE PROBLEM WAS. ONE NIGHT, BEING SO TIRED, AN IDEA STRUCK MY MOM, SHE TOLD MY DAD TO GET ON THE DRUMS AND START PLAYING. MY DAD THOUGHT IT WAS AN

ODD REQUEST AND WAS RELUCTANT UNTIL MY MOM TOLD HIM ABOUT THE OTHER TIMES HE HAD PLAYED AND AFTER DANCING IN MY CRIB, WOULD SOON FALL ASLEEP. MOM TOLD DAD THAT AS SILLY AS IT SOUNDED WHAT COULD THEY LOSE? THEY HAD TRIED OTHER THINGS, AND UNLESS THEY WANTED TO SPEND ANOTHER NIGHT WITH VERY LITTLE SLEEP, JUST TO HUMOR HER.

MY DAD, WENT AND PUT ON A RECORD, SHAKING HIS HEAD IN UNBELIEF, HE GOT ON THE DRUMS AND STARTED PLAYING. MOM CHECKED ON ME TO FIND ME STANDING IN MY CRIB, DANCING AWAY, JUST HAVING A BLAST. SHE WENT BACK TO TELL MY DAD, I THINK IT'S WORKING AND WHEN SHE RETURNED, I WAS FAST ASLEEP. I CAN ONLY IMAGINE AFTER HEARING HER SHARE THAT, THE LOOK THEY HAD ON THEIR FACE. IT WOULD BE PRICELESS AS THEY STOOD THERE AMAZED AT THE STRANGE WAY FOR SOMEONE TO FALL ASLEEP, AND AFTER TALKING ABOUT IT FURTHER, THEY CONCLUDED THAT THE SLEEP ISSUES STARTED WHEN DAD HADN'T BEEN PRACTICING THE DRUMS MUCH. THE GIGS THEY WERE GETTING HAD SLOWED DOWN, THEREFORE THERE WASN'T MUCH NEED TO PRACTICE AND SOON THE BAND BROKE UP. ALTHOUGH MY DAD SURELY COULDN'T PLAY THE DRUMS EVERY NIGHT TO GET ME TO GO TO SLEEP, ESPECIALLY DURING THE WEE HOURS OF THE MORNING, THEY BEGAN TO PONDER WHAT THEY COULD DO, AND AFTER SOME THOUGHT AND DISCUSSION, THEY DECIDED TO PURCHASE A CLOCK RADIO. THIS SERVED TO BE QUITE USEFUL AND A VERY SMART INVESTMENT. THE PROBLEM WAS NOW SOLVED AND THEY WERE RELIEVED TO FINALLY BE GETTING SOME SLEEP.

AS I GREW OLDER AND WENT OUT ON MY OWN, I'D HAVE TROUBLE TRYING TO FALL ASLEEP IN TOTAL SILENCE. I FIND THE NEED TO HAVE A CD PLAYING, OR A FAN RUNNING IN ORDER TO DRIFT OFF. EVEN NOW, OVER 40 PLUS YEARS LATER, I'LL PUT A CD ON; SET THE BOOM BOX ON SLEEP TIMER, SO AS NOT TO BURN ELECTRIC ALL NIGHT LONG. EVEN AT THAT I FIND MYSELF WAKING UP ONCE OR TWICE, SOME NIGHTS MORE OFTEN, AND IF I HAVE TROUBLE DRIFTING OFF, THEN ON GOES THE CD PLAYER, AND I'M CERTAIN THIS CAME ABOUT BECAUSE OF THE WAY I GREW UP.

MY CHILDHOOD WAS DIFFICULT AND LONELY, I DON'T REMEMBER A LOT OF IT, MAYBE IT WAS DUE TO BLOCKING SOME OF IT OUT, I'M NOT SURE. MY FATHER NEVER MUCH INTERACTED WITH US KIDS, AS WE GREW OLDER AND WAS STARTING SCHOOL. HE WOULD OFTEN STAY UP LATE, WHILE WE SLEPT, THEN SLEEPING MOST OF THE DAY. HE WORKED OFF AND ON, BUT HAD TROUBLE INTERACTING WITH PEOPLE HIMSELF, SO HE WAS OFTEN IN AND OUT OF JOBS. HE TRIED SOME ODD JOBS THINKING BY WORKING FOR HIMSELF, IT MAY HELP WITH WHATEVER HE WAS DEALING WITH OR CAUSING HIM TO HAVE TROUBLE WORKING FOR SOME ONE ELSE, BUT THESE DIDN'T PAN OUT, FORCING MY MOM TO WORK IN A FACTORY JUST TO MEET THE MORTGAGE AND PUT FOOD ON THE TABLE ALONG WITH OTHER HOUSEHOLD BILLS.

MY DAD HAD EXPERIENCED AN ABUSIVE CHILDHOOD, FROM LITTLE TID-BITS I HAD GATHERED, MAINLY FROM PHOTOS I HAD SEEN IN OUR PHOTO ALBUMS. NO ONE, HOWEVER, REALLY WENT INTO

DETAIL WHAT MY DAD HAD ENDURED HIMSELF, AND I DIDN'T LEARN FOR QUITE A FEW YEARS, WHAT HE HAD INDEED ENDURED. IT WAS NOT PRETTY FROM WHAT I HAD HEARD AND I WAS BEGINNING TO UNDERSTAND, ALTHOUGH NOT COMPLETELY, AS I WAS STILL A YOUNGSTER. I DO BELIEVE THIS CAUSED MY DAD TO SUFFER FROM DEPRESSION, WHICH LED TO MANY HEALTH ISSUES FOR HIM.

SOMETIMES IT WAS HARD TO TALK TO MY DAD, AS WE WERE NEVER SURE WHEN HE WAS IN THE MOOD TO TALK WITH US. THERE WERE TIMES WHEN HE DIDN'T WANT TO BE BOTHERED WITH STUFF, SO HE'D SEND US TO OUR MOM. MOM WORKING, SOMETIMES 10 OR 12 HOUR DAYS, WAS OFTEN WORE OUT AND IF SHE CAME HOME AND FOUND THE HOUSE IN DISARRAY, THEN SHE WOULD GET UPSET AND GRUMBLE THEN THAT WAS IT, THERE WAS NO USE TRYING TO TALK ABOUT THINGS WITH HER. SOMETIMES IT WAS LIKE WALKING ON EGGSHELLS, OR EVEN A TICKING TIME BOMB, NOT SURE WHERE TO STEP FOR FEAR IT WOULD BLOW UP.

EVENTUALLY MOM TRIED TO ENCOURAGE MY DAD TO VISIT THE DOCTOR AND GET SOME HELP SO HE COULD GET A JOB, AND TAKE SOME WORKLOAD OFF HER, IT WAS GETTING VERY HARD FOR HER TO WORK ALL THOSE HOURS, THEN COME HOME AND HAVE TO CARE FOR THE HOUSE, KIDS, AND WHATEVER ELSE WAS EXPECTED OR DEMANDED OF HER. AT TIMES HE AGREED TO GO TO THE DOCTOR, SO THE APPOINTMENT WOULD BE SET, BUT THEN HE'D FEEL SOMEWHAT BETTER, SO HE WOULD CANCEL THE APPOINTMENT AT THE LAST MINUTE AND THIS ONLY

PUT A STRAIN NOT JUST ON THEIR RELATIONSHIP, BUT ON EVERYONE'S RELATIONSHIP, IF THEY WERE FUSSING, THEN WE WOULD BE AT THE BLUNT END.

I DON'T REMEMBER STARTING KINDERGARDEN, I THINK I WENT RIGHT INTO FIRST GRADE, I KNOW I WAS A SHY ONE, AND SEEMED TO HAVE TROUBLE CONCENTRATING. THE TEACHER WOULD OFTEN ASK QUESTIONS PERTAINING TO A STORY SHE HAD JUST READ. I WOULD HAVE THE ANSWER AND THEN WHEN SHE CALLED ON ME, I SHRANK BACK. MAYBE IT WAS FROM ALL THE OTHER CLASSMATES EYES BEING ON ME, I'M NOT SURE, BUT I WAS FROZEN SOLID AS AN ICE CUBE. SHE'D EVENTUALLY MOVE ON, BUT BY THE END OF THE YEAR WHEN SCHOOL HAD LET OUT FOR THE SUMMER, THE TEACHER INFORMED MY PARENTS, I'D BE SPENDING ANOTHER YEAR IN THE FIRST GRADE, AS I COULDN'T READ AND MY COMPREHENSION WAS OFF. I FLUNKED? HOW IN THE WORLD DOES ONE FLUNK THE FIRST GRADE? I WAS SAD. I THINK IF I WOULD HAVE UNDERSTOOD THE WORD HUMILIATION AT THE AGE OF 6, I WOULD BE VERY HUMILIATED TO FAIL 1ST GRADE, AND I'M SURE MY PARENTS WERE A LITTLE UPSET TO. I MEAN MY MOM GRADUATED AND NEVER FLUNKED, OR AT LEAST NEVER TOLD ME SHE HAD, THAT I REMEMBER ANYWAY. MY FATHER DROPPED OUT OF SCHOOL IN THE 10TH GRADE TO GO TO WORK FOR THE FAMILY. MY MOM OFTEN SHARED ABOUT HER CHILDHOOD AND HOW STRICT IT WAS, BUT WAS THANKFUL HER PARENTS TOOK THE TIME WITH HER AND MY UNCLE. SHE ALSO TOLD ME THE IMPORTANCE OF GETTING AN EDUCATION AND IT TOOK WORK IN ORDER TO GET GOOD GRADES.

MY MOM WAS THE YOUNGER OF THE 2 KIDS, HAVING AN OLDER BROTHER. HER UPBRINGING WAS HARD AND THERE WASN'T A LOT OF MONEY. MANY TIMES FOR BIRTHDAY'S AND AT CHRISTMAS THEY ONLY RECEIVED ONE GIFT, BUT THEY TREASURED THOSE GIFTS, AND THE FAMILY TIMES THEY SHARED. AS YOUNG AS I CAN REMEMBER, I OFTEN SPENT TIMES AT MY GRANDPARENTS. I BELIEVE I WAS THE FIRST GRANDCHILD FOR THEM AND I HELD A WARM PLACE IN THEIR HEART. MY GRANDFATHER USED TO BE A JANITOR AT OUR SCHOOL, I OFTEN ENJOYED SEEING HIM THERE, AND GETTING THOSE DAILY HUGS, BUT SADLY, WITH HIM BEING DIABETIC, HE HAD STARTED LOSING HIS EYESIGHT, AND HAD TO GIVE UP HIS JOB. EVENTUALLY BLOOD VESSELS HAD BURST IN HIS EYES, WHICH CAUSED HIM TO BE PERMANENTLY BLIND WHEN HE WAS 35 YEARS OLD. I'M SURE THIS WAS TRAGIC FOR HIM. HAVING TO DEPEND ON OTHER PEOPLE TO DO THINGS FOR HIM, LEARN WHERE EVERYTHING WAS AND NOT BEING ABLE TO SEE HIS FAMILY AND WATCH HIS GRANDCHILDREN GROW UP, NOT TO MENTION THE GREATER RESPONSIBILITY THAT FELL ON MY GRANDMOTHER. SHE NEVER LEARNED TO DRIVE, SO THINGS LIKE TRIPS TO THE GROCERY, BECAME DIFFICULT AND SHE OFTEN WALKED 6 BLOCKS EVERY DAY TO THE STORE, THEN AGAIN BACK HOME FOR THEIR GROCERIES AS MY GRANDFATHER DIDN'T LIKE FROZEN MEAT, IT HAD TO BE FRESH DAILY.

I'M SURE MY GRANDFATHER FELT BADLY ABOUT THIS, AND HIS WHOLE DEMEANOR CHANGED AFTER THAT. HE WAS GROUCHY AND YOU DIDN'T KNOW HOW TO TALK TO HIM SOMETIMES, I FELT BADLY FOR HIM AND COULDN'T IMAGINE WHAT HE WAS GOING

THROUGH. MY UNCLE LIVED THERE AND WORKED, AND AT LEAST MADE THE HOUSE PAYMENT, BUT HE WAS A DRINKER AND OFTEN BLEW HIS CHECK THE SAME DAY HE WAS PAID, LEAVING MORE FINANCIAL RESPONSIBILITY ON MY GRANDPARENTS TO PAY WHICH ONLY ADDED TO THEIR FRUSTRATION. I LIKED GOING DOWN THERE TO HELP, AND IT OFTEN WORE ME OUT, I MEAN I WAS A YOUNGSTER, SO I OFTEN TOOK NAPS YET. I REMEMBER ONE DAY FALLING ASLEEP IN THEIR BED, I DIDN'T REALIZE THEY SLEPT IN SEPARATE BEDS, BUT IT MADE SENSE THAT WITH MY GRANDFATHER BEING BLIND, HE WOULD NEED SPECIAL THINGS TO HELP HIM ADAPT TO THIS NEW LIFESTYLE HE HAD. I REMEMBER WAKING UP TO HIM MESSING WITH MY PRIVATE AREA, AND WONDERED HOW HE GOT IN THE BED WITH ME, THEN IT HIT ME, I WAS IN HIS BED, WHY DIDN'T ANYONE MOVE ME? WELL MAYBE IT WASN'T A BIG DEAL TO THEM, I WAS JUST A YOUNG CHILD, BUT STILL I DIDN'T DARE TELL ANYONE, AND I'M NOT SURE IF IT EVER HAPPENED AGAIN AFTER THAT TIME, I KNOW I WAS SCARED. I MEAN LITTLE THINGS I WOULD SAY, LIKE ABOUT MY UNCLE EATING TO MUCH WOULD UPSET THEM AND THEY WOULD HAVE ME PRAY AND SAY SORRY, SO WHAT WOULD THEY SAY OR EVEN DO IF I TOLD THEM THIS. AT SUCH A YOUNG AGE HOW COULD I EVEN KNOW IT WAS WRONG? COULD IT JUST HAVE BEEN INSTINCT? I THINK IT WAS AFTER THIS THAT I LEARNED MASTURBATION, MY MOM WAS HORRIFIED, BUT I NEVER TOLD HER WHAT HAPPENED WITH MY GRANDFATHER, NOR DID SHE ASK WHERE I HAD PICKED THAT UP, SHE JUST ASSUMED I STARTED DOING IT AND CORRECTED ME FOR IT. BUT I FOUND I ENJOYED IT, SO IT BECAME A REGULAR HABIT.

WHEN I WAS ABOUT 9 MY DAD DECIDED TO TEACH ME TO COOK AND HELP WITH CHORES AS MY MOM WENT ON NIGHTS AND WOULDN'T FEEL MUCH LIKE DOING ANYTHING WHEN SHE GOT OFF WORK. THIS WAS NOT SUCH A BAD THING I SUPPOSE, HAVING A FEW CHORES, SUCH AS KEEPING ROOM CLEAN, PICKING UP AFTER YOUR SELF, SETTING THE TABLE OR EVEN FEEDING THE FAMILY PET. FOR US, WE HAD A DOG. BUT YOU WOULDN'T THINK A 9 YEAR OLD WOULD NEED TO LEARN TO COOK? MY DAD HAD CAME FROM A FAMILY OF 5 KIDS, HAVING 2 OLDER SISTERS, THEN HIM AND 2 YOUNGER SIBLINGS, ONE BROTHER AND A SISTER WHO CAME MUCH LATER IN LIFE. FOR HIM, BEING THE FIRST BOY, HE HAD TO QUIT SCHOOL AND GO TO WORK. IT WAS JUST HIS WAY OF LIFE, SO MY THINKING IS, IF IT WAS GOOD ENOUGH FOR HIM, THEN WHY SHOULD US KID'S BE TAUGHT ANY DIFFERENT.

I REMEMBER ONE PARTICULIAR DAY, IT MUST HAVE BEEN THE WEEKEND BECAUSE MOM WAS AT HOME, AND WE HAD A POT OF FOOD COOKING ON THE STOVE. I WAS BUSY WIPING UP A MESS I HAD MADE ON THE STOVE FROM STIRRING THE FOOD AND I GOT THE DISH CLOTH TO CLOSE TO THE BURNER AND CAUGHT IT ON FIRE. I PANICKED!! I MEAN I WAS 8 OR 9, WHAT WAS I TO KNOW RIGHT? THEREFORE, I THREW THE BURNING CLOTH IN THE LAUNDRY ROOM, CATCHING THE LAUNDRY ON FIRE. BOY, DID WE HAVE A MESS!! I DON'T REMEMBER WHAT HAPPENED AT THAT POINT, BUT EVEN AT THAT, I WANTED TO BE DONE WITH THIS COOKING STUFF.

I FOUND THAT MOST OF THE TIME, IT WAS ME CLEANING AS MY BROTHERS WERE IN SCOUTS, AND

INVOLVED IN SPORTS AND NOT AROUND VERY MUCH, AND WHEN THEY DIDN'T HAVE A GAME, THEN IT WAS SPENDING TIME WITH FRIENDS. WITH MY MOM WORKING SO MUCH, MOST DAYS IT WAS JUST ME AND MY DAD, SO I FELT I TOOK THE BLUNT OF HIS MOOD SWINGS. I GUESS I SHOULDN'T HAVE COMPLAINED ABOUT MY BROTHERS NOT PITCHING IN, AS IT MADE MY DAD UPSET AND DOING THE CHORES DID HELP PASS THE TIME AND I WAS ALWAYS LOOKING TO HAVE SOMETHING TO OCCUPY MY MIND, SO I DIDN'T THINK ABOUT THE PROBLEMS MY FAMILY WAS HAVING OR WHAT HAD BEEN DONE TO ME BY MY GRANDFATHER. I DISCOVERED THAT AS LONG AS MY DAD AND MY BROTHERS DIDN'T HAVE TO DO MUCH, THAT WAS JUST PEACHY FOR THEM, THEY'D KNEW I HAD TO IF WE WANTED PEACE WHEN MOM CAME HOME.

THEN CAME THE TIME WHERE IT WAS AS IF MY CLEANING WASN'T GOOD ENOUGH, THERE ALWAYS SEEMED TO BE SOMETHING THAT WAS WRONG, I MEAN I'M JUST A YOUNGSTER STARTING OUT, HOW GOOD CAN ONE BE WITH NO EXPERIENCE? I'M SURE IT WAS ALL THE PRESSURE MY PARENTS WERE UNDER, MY MOM THE ONLY ONE WORKING, MY DAD DEPRESSED AND SITTING AROUND,NOT ABLE TO KEEP A JOB, SMOKING LIKE A CHIMNEY AND DRINKING, HARDLY A LIFE THEY ENVISIONED FOR THEMSELVES, BUT TRYING TO MUTTER THROUGH AND MAKE THE BEST OF THE SITUATION THAT THEY COULD.

MY DAD WAS ONE THAT HE DIDN'T LIKE FOR US TO CREATE ANY CONFUSION AT THE DINNER TABLE. I WAS BEGINNING TO BELIEVE THAT HE HAD THE MOTTO CHILDREN ARE TO BE SEEN, AND NOT HEARD. IF MY

DAD FELT THERE WAS TOO MUCH TALKING BEING DONE AT THE DINNER TABLE, IT WOULD MAKE HIM UNCOMFORTABLE AND HE WOULD SIMPLY GET UP AND REFUSE TO EAT UNTIL WE WERE ALL FINISHED, EVEN IF IT MEANT HE DIDN'T EAT TILL WE WERE IN BED. IT WAS AS IF THE SIGHT OF US MADE HIM LOSE HIS APPETITE.

WHEN MY DAD WAS HAVING A GOOD DAY AND FEELING UP TO IT, WE'D HAVE MY GRANDMA AND UNCLE OVER AND PLAY CARDS. OH HOW I ALWAYS ENJOYED THOSE TIMES, I'D STAY UP LATE AND PLAY CARDS WITH THEM. WHEN IT WAS BEDTIME, I DIDN'T WANT TO GO, I LOVED MY DAD AND WANTED TO SPEND TIME WITH HIM. I REMEMBER TIMES WHEN AFTER GOING TO BED, I'D BE LAYING THERE THINKING ABOUT MY DAD AND WHY HE WAS SO DARN DIFFICULT TO GET ALONG WITH AT TIMES. I WONDERED WHAT MUST HAVE WENT ON IN HIS LIFE, THAT MADE HIM SO BITTER, TO THE POINT THAT HE DIDN'T WANT TO LEAVE THE HOUSE. I WAS JUST STARTING TO DOZE OFF WHEN I HEARD MY BEDROOM DOOR OPEN, WHEN I LOOKED TO SEE WHO WAS COMING INTO MY ROOM, AS THIS WAS VERY STRANGE. NO ONE EVER CAME TO MY ROOM UNLESS THEY WANTED ME TO DO SOMETHING FOR THEM OR TO GRIPE. NOT TO TALK, SEE HOW I WAS, NOTHING!!

I SEEN THAT IT WAS MY UNCLE AND WONDERED WHAT HE WANTED. OUR FAMILY NEVER SHOWED MUCH AFFECTION, HARDLY ANY HUGS, I LOVE YOU'S, NOTHING, NOT EVEN OUR OTHER FAMILY MEMBERS. HE CAME OVER, SAT DOWN ON THE EDGE OF MY BED AND KISSED MY FOREHEAD, YUCK!! IT WAS WET AND NASTY. I FELT KIND OF UNCOMFORTABLE, BUT DIDN'T WANT TO

MAKE WAVES, WE HAD ENOUGH FAMILY ISSUES GOING ON AS IT WAS, AND MOST CERTAINLY MY DAD WOULD BLAME ME, SO I PUSHED IT ASIDE AND I DIDN'T GIVE IT ANY MORE THOUGHT, UNTIL IT HAPPENED AGAIN AND AGAIN. IT HAD GOTTEN TO BE A REGULAR OCCURRENCE AND I DIDN'T LIKE IT. HAVING SOMEONE COME IN AND INVADE MY ROOM? NO WAY!!! HOWEVER, I WAS STILL AFRAID TO SAY ANYTHING TO MY PARENTS. WHEN I THOUGHT ABOUT TELLING THEM, I'D GET A MENTAL PICTURE OF MY DAD. SEEING MY DAD LAUGH AND APPEAR TO BE HAVING A GOOD TIME WHEN MY GRANDMA AND UNCLE CAME OVER, ALWAYS BROUGHT JOY TO ME, YET IN THE BACK OF MY MIND WONDERED HOW LONG IT WOULD LAST AND SADNESS WOULD YET SET IN, SO I THOUGHT NO, I CAN'T TELL, IT MAY ONLY INCREASE MY DAD'S MOOD SWINGS, AND I WAS AFRAID HE MAY BECOME VIOLENT.

EVENTUALLY HOWEVER, MY GRANDMA AND UNCLE STOPPED COMING OVER FOR A WHILE, I'M NOT EXACTLY SURE WHY, MAYBE WHILE I WAS IN BED ONE NIGHT, THEY HAD A FALLING OUT, OR SOMETHING MAY HAVE BEEN SAID THAT MADE MY DAD UNCOMFORTABLE. I ALSO HAD THOUGHT MAYBE THEY CAUGHT MY UNCLE TRYING TO COME INTO MY ROOM, AND CONFRONTED HIM. THE BATHROOM WAS RIGHT ACROSS THE HALL FROM MY ROOM AND I HAD BEGUN TO THINK THAT HE WAS TELLING THEM HE WAS MAKING A BATHROOM TRIP, OR SO MY PARENTS THOUGHT, AND INSTEAD WAS SNEAKING INTO MY ROOM. WHO KNOWS WHAT HE MAY HAVE TRIED NEXT, I SHUDDERED TO THINK, I DIDN'T CARE, IT DIDN'T MATTER ANYMORE, HE NEVER GOT THAT FAR AND AT LEAST HE STOPPED COMING IN BEFORE IT DID.

AFTER THAT MY DAD'S MOOD CHANGED FOR THE WORSE, AND IT SEEMED HE'D FIND SOMETHING TO UPSET HIM, THEN IT WAS HARD TO LIVE WITH HIM AND ONLY IN OUR LITTLE MINDS, DID IT CONFIRM THE IDEA THAT THE VERY SIGHT OF US SICKENED HIM. I'M SURE HE LOVED US VERY MUCH, OR DID HE?? HE CERTAINLY NEVER SHOWED IT MUCH, I SUPPOSE WITH HIM HAVING A DIFFICULT CHILDHOOD HIMSELF, ALTHOUGH I DIDN'T KNOW THE FULL STORY AT THIS TIME, IT WEIGHED HEAVILY ON HIM. MAYBE THE WAY HE WAS INTERACTING WITH THE FAMILY WAS ALL HE KNEW TO DO. HE PROBABLY FELT HE WAS DOING WHAT WAS ONLY NATURAL FOR HIM. I ALSO LEARNED THAT THIS WAS PROBABLY WHY MY BROTHERS WAS GONE MOST OF THE TIME, THEY DIDN'T WANT TO BE AROUND ALL THAT, AND WITH ME, BEING SO BACKWARD AND SHY, WAS LEFT TO DEAL WITH IT ALL, NOT HAVING MANY FRIENDS AT ALL. MAYBE IT WAS DUE TO THE FACT I TREATED THEM, THE SAME WAY I WAS BEING TREATED, AND THEY KNEW IT WASN'T RIGHT AS THEY CAME FROM A LOVING HOME.

ONE SUMMER DAY, MY DAD WAS HAVING A REALLY GOOD DAY, AND MY MOM WAS ON VACATION, THEY DECIDED TO HAVE SOME FRIENDS OVER FOR A COOKOUT. WE WERE ALL HAVING A GOOD TIME, PLAYING BADMINTON UNTIL IT GOT TOO DARK TO PLAY, EVEN WITH THE PATIO LIGHTS BEING ON SO WE ALL WENT IN THE HOUSE. AS WE ALL SAT IN THE LIVING ROOM, I REMEMBER CRAWLING UP ON MY DAD'S FRIENDS LAP. HIS FRIEND, AND WIFE WERE REALLY NICE PEOPLE AND I FELT COMFORTABLE WITH THEM, SORT OF DRAWN TO THEM. YOU COULD SENSE THEY

WERE VERY LOVING AND AFFECTIONATE PEOPLE. I REMEMBER THE GUY PUT ME UP ON HIS LAP, AND WAS TICKLING ME, AND I ENJOYED THE ATTENTION, AS WE NEVER GOT MUCH ATTENTION LIKE THAT. I DIDN'T KNOW IT ANGERED MY DAD, BUT IT MUST HAVE TICKED HIM OFF, BECAUSE AFTER THEY LEFT, I GOT THE BELT. WHEN MY DAD WENT TO SWING IT, HE LET GO OF ONE END AND THE BUCKLE CAME AROUND AND CAUGHT ME IN THE EYE. I ENDED UP WITH A BLACK EYE, AND IT HAD SWOLLEN SHUT. THAT WAS THE FIRST TIME MY DAD EVER LAID A HAND ON ME. I WAS REALLY SCARED. I DIDN'T UNDERSTAND WHAT I HAD DONE WRONG FOR HIM TO GET SO ANGRY. DID HE THINK I ENCOURAGED THIS COUPLE AND DEMANDED ATTENTION? DID HE THINK I WAS SHOWING OFF? AFTER THAT, WHILE MY EYE WAS HEALING, WHENEVER WE'D COME IN CONTACT WITH PEOPLE AFTER THAT AND THEY ASKED WHAT HAPPENED TO MY EYE, I'D TRY AND EXPLAIN, AND WOULD BE CUT OFF BY MY MOM. SHE'D SAID I TRIPPED, OR WAS PUSHED BY ONE OF MY BROTHERS. IT WOULD MAKE MY DAD ANGRY WHEN I SPOKE THE TRUTH AND I WOULD BE PUNISHED, SO I'D LEARN TO LIE.

THEN MY GRANDFATHER WHICH WAS MY DAD'S DAD, BECAME ILL WITH CANCER AND PASSED AWAY. I'M NOT SURE IF MY DAD WAS SAD OR RELIEVED, BUT THIS WAS THE FIRST TIME MY DAD OPENED UP ABOUT HIS FATHER BEING AN ABUSIVE MAN. IT WAS LIKE A RELEASE FOR MY DAD, AS IF, WHILE MY GRANDFATHER WAS STILL ALIVE, MY DAD WAS LIVING UNDER HIS SHADOW, ALTHOUGH MY DAD WAS ON HIS OWN WITH HIS OWN FAMILY. WHAT A HAUNTING FEELING IT MUST HAVE BEEN, OF COURSE I WOULDN'T COME TO

UNDERSTAND THAT FEELING TILL I WAS MUCH OLDER AND SOMEHOW I HAD THE IDEA, NOT ALL THE STORY WAS TOLD AT THAT PARTICULIAR TIME. I HAD WITNESSED TIMES HOWEVER, WHEN MY DAD WOULD GET CALLS THAT MY GRANDFATHER HAD BEAT UP MY GRANDMA ONCE AGAIN, WE'D GET IN THE CAR AND GO DOWN THERE AND SHE'D BE A MESS, SOMETIMES YOU COULDN'T STICK A TOOTHPICK IN BETWEEN THE BRUISES ON HER FACE AND I WONDERED IF THIS WAS WHY WE HADN'T SEEN MY UNCLE OR MY GRANDMA FOR A WHILE. NOT THAT I WANTED HER TO BE BEAT UP, BUT I DIDN'T CARE THAT THEY WERE AWAY FOR A WHILE, AT LEAST MY UNCLE WASN'T COMING INTO MY ROOM ANYMORE. MY GRANDFATHER, I NOTICED, WAS AN ALCOHOLIC AND WHEN HE WASN'T DRINKING, HE HAD NOTHING TO DO WITH US KIDS, OR MY PARENTS. I DIDN'T UNDERSTAND WHY, I MEAN WHAT DID WE DO?? WHEN HE WAS DRUNK, WE WERE HIS LIFE!! HIS BEAUTIFUL GRANDCHILDREN!! TILL HE SEEN MY DAD, THEN HE GOT ANGRY, OR MAYBE WHEN HE SEEN MY GRANDMA, HE HAD FLASHBACKS, WHO KNOWS, ALL I REMEMBER IS THAT AFTER THE WAR WHEN MY GRANDPA RETIRED FROM THE SERVICE, THE BEATINGS TO MY GRANDMA HAD BECOME A REGULAR OCCURRENCE. MAYBE IT WAS ALL THE VIOLENCE OF THE WAR THAT CHANGED HIM. I HAD HEARD MANY STORIES OF PEOPLE BEING IN THE SERVICE AND GOING TO WAR CAN HAVE A NEGATIVE AFFECT ON THEM.

I DIDN'T COME TO REALIZE TILL I WAS OLDER THAT THE ABUSE HAD BEEN GOING ON EVER SINCE MY GRANDMA BECAME PREGNANT WITH MY FATHER. MY GRANDPA HAD COME HOME ON LEAVE FROM THE

SERVICE, AND ALTHOUGH I DON'T KNOW HOW LONG HE WAS HOME, WHEN HIS LEAVE WAS OVER AND HE RETURNED TO BASE, MY GRANDMA DISCOVERED A FEW WEEKS AFTER, THAT SHE WAS PREGNANT. MY GRANDPA DIDN'T BELIEVE SHE GOT PREGNANT THAT QUICK AND ASSUMED SHE HAD AN AFFAIR ON HIM. HE WENT TO HIS GRAVE STILL BELIEVING MY DAD WASN'T HIS KID,THEREFORE HE HAD A HATRED FOR MY DAD AND WAS ABUSIVE, AND WHEN MY DAD LEFT HOME, MY GRANDPA TURNED HIS ANGER OUT ON MY GRANDMA.

I SUPPOSE IT WAS HARD FOR MY DAD TO SEE THIS, ESPECIALLY IF HE WAS A VICTIM OF ABUSE HIMSELF ALL OF HIS LIFE. I'M SURE THERE WAS MANY TIMES WHERE HE WANTED TO LET GO OF HIS PAST, BUT IT KEPT CREEPING UP TO HAUNT HIM. I THOUGHT IF I COULD WORK HARD TO PLEASE HIM, IT WOULD SHIFT HIS FOCUS ON TO THE HERE AND NOW, WHICH WAS HIS WIFE AND KID'S WHO LOVED HIM. BUT HE SEEMED TO BE SINKING FURTHER AND FURTHER INTO WHATEVER WAS TROUBLING HIM, AND HE JUST NEVER WANTED TO TALK ABOUT IT ANYMORE AFTER THAT DAY HE RECEIVED THE NEWS HIS DAD PASSED AWAY. NO MATTER WHAT WE DID, IT WASN'T GOOD ENOUGH OR DIDN'T HELP AT ALL, ONLY MADE HIM ANGRY. YOU'D THINK IT WOULD BE SOMEONE'S RELEASING POINT AND HE'D NO LONGER HAVE TO FEAR HIS FATHER, BUT IN HIS MIND, MAYBE HE THOUGHT IF HE JUST CLOSED THAT CHAPTER IN HIS LIFE, AND NOT TALK OR EVEN THINK ABOUT IT, IT WOULD GO AWAY. BUT THEN AGAIN, I WAS A YOUNG WHIPPERSNAPPER, SO I CAN ONLY SPECULATE, AS I'M NOT A MIND READER, BUT I DO BELIEVE ACTIONS CAN SPEAK LOUDER THAN ANY WORDS SPOKEN!!! I'M ALSO SURE HE FELT WE WERE

TOO YOUNG TO UNDERSTAND, BUT WHAT HE DIDN'T NOTICE WAS IT WAS CAUSING US TO WITHDRAW AND WE STARTED HAVING DIFFICULTY FORMING RELATIONSHIPS WITH OTHERS OURSELF.

AS I MENTIONED JUST BRIEFLY BEFORE, I ALWAYS SEEMED TO HAVE TROUBLE MAKING FRIENDS, AND KEEPING THEM, I WAS ALWAYS AFRAID IF THEY APPEARED DISTANT THAT IT WAS SOMEHOW MY FAULT, NOT UNDERSTANDING THAT THEY MAY HAVE BEEN HURT BY SOMEONE, OR LOST A LOVED ONE, OR BEEN PUNISHED FOR A WRONGDOING THEY MAY HAVE DONE BY GETTING GROUNDED OR SOMETHING OF THAT NATURE. I WOULD HAVE TO RIDE A BUS TO AND FROM SCHOOL WHEN I WAS IN 5TH AND 6TH GRADE AND THERE WAS A LOT OF OLDER KIDS ON THE BUS TOO. I ALWAYS APPEARED TO BE A TARGET FOR THESE OLDER KIDS AS IF WEARING SOME SORT OF SIGN THAT SAID, THIS GIRL IS EASY TO BEAT UP, AND A SCAREDY CAT. AFTER SCHOOL LET OUT FOR THE DAY, AND WE REACHED THE BUS STOP, SOMEONE WOULD KNOCK MY BOOKS OUT OF MY HAND AND WHEN I BENT DOWN TO GET THEM, BE PUNCHED OR KICKED.

I DIDN'T UNDERSTAND AND ALWAYS WONDERED WHY, MANY TIMES I'D WALK HOME, LIMPING AND CRYING, WONDERING WHY I WAS EVEN AROUND WHEN NO ONE SEEMED TO LIKE ME. MAYBE THEY WERE JUST BULLIES WHO GOT KICKS OUT OF PICKING ON OTHERS TO MAKE THEMSELVES FEEL GOOD AND LOOK GOOD. MAYBE THEY TOO WERE HAVING A TOUGH TIME AT HOME AND WERE LASHING OUT TO RELEASE ANGER THEY WERE FEELING. IT WAS NEVERENDING, EACH AND EVERY DAY AFTER SCHOOL THE SAME THING,

WHY NOT BEFORE SCHOOL? MY IDEA WAS THAT THEY WOULD GET IN TROUBLE BY SCHOOL PERSONEL AND THROW THEIR DAY OFF. I KNOW AFTER SCHOOL, PERSONEL WAS RELIEVED OF THEIR DUTIES OF PROTECTING THE STUDENTS AND WE AGAIN BECAME THE RESPONSIBILITY OF THE PARENT.

I BEGAN TO HATE SCHOOL AND PRAYED FOR THE DAY I DIDN'T HAVE TO GO ANYMORE. THERE WOULD BE TIMES I HAD TO RUN ERRANDS FOR MY DAD, SO I'D GET ON MY BIKE, NOT WANTING TO GO, BUT WANTING TO PLEASE MY DAD AND BE OBEDIENT. THE BULLIES WOULD SEE ME RIDE PAST AND BEGIN TO CHASE ME, SOMETIMES KNOCKING ME OFF MY BIKE, AND THEY WOULD LAUGH, I THINK JUST TO SEE ME CRY. I WAS USUALLY A LONER AND NEVER HURT ANYONE, WHY WAS OTHER PEOPLE TREATING ME THIS WAY? I WENT OUT OF MY WAY TO AVOID GOING PAST THEIR HOUSE, SOMETIMES TAKING THE LONG WAY AND PRAY FOR MY PROTECTION AND THAT I WOULDN'T RUN INTO ANYONE. IT WAS A SHAME TO HAVE TO LIVE IN FEAR LIKE THIS, AND AT AGE 11 NOT WANTING TO LEAVE YOUR OWN HOUSE, BUT THAT WAS EVEN GETTING HARD TO BE AT HOME. WHERE WAS I TO GO? WHEN I TRIED TALKING TO MY PARENTS, AT LEAST MY MOM TRIED TO BE REASSURING, BUT MY DAD WOULD JUST SAY IGNORE THEM, WELL SOMETIMES THAT WAS HARD TO DO, WHEN YOU'RE BEING CHASED OR WAITED ON AS SOON AS YOU GET OFF THE BUS, YOU KNOW?

I CAME TO THE POINT OF EVEN REGRETTING HAVING TO RIDE THE BUS, I ALREADY HAD A HATRED FOR SCHOOL, AND WAS NOW COMTEMPLATING WHETHER MY LIFE ON THIS PLANET HAD ANY WORTH

OR PURPOSE OTHER THAN BEING USED FOR SOMEONE ELSES PUNCHING BAG, OR AS A SPONGE TO SOAK IN PEOPLE'S HARSH WORDS WHEN THEY WERE IN A BAD MOOD. HAVE YOU EVER JUST NOT WANTED TO DO SOMETHING, AND YOU HAD YOURSELF SO WORKED UP INSIDE TO THE POINT OF MAKING YOU SICK, KNOWING THAT YOU HAD TO DO IT ANYWAY? IT JUST BUILT UP ALL KINDS OF ANXIETY WITHIN ME, AND I THOUGHT I'D HAVE A NERVOUS BREAKDOWN. I EVEN TRIED JOINING THE CROWD AND GET IN TROUBLE IN SCHOOL, JUST TO FIT IN. I REMEMBER BEING IN 6TH GRADE, THE TEACHER LEFT THE ROOM FOR A FEW MINUTES AND SOMEONE DARED ME TO DO SOMETHING I KNEW WASN'T ALLOWED, BUT I DID IT TO FIT IN AND JUST AS I DID IT, THE TEACHER CAME BACK IN, THAT WAS THE TIME SPANKINGS WAS ALLOWED IN SCHOOL AND I GOT SENT TO THE HALL FOR A WHACK.

THEN THE NIGHTMARES BEGAN, SOMEONE WOULD BE CHASING ME WITH AN AXE, THEN I WOULD GET THIS SINKING FEELING OF FALLING OFF A CLIFF, WAKE UP AND MY HEART WOULD BE RACING, AS IF IT WAS GOING TO COME RIGHT OUT OF MY CHEST. IT REMINDED ME OF THIS RIDE I RODE ONE TIME AT KING'S ISLAND, THE GRAVITRON I THINK IT WAS CALLED. IT SPUN AROUND SO FAST, THEN THE FLOOR GAVE OUT, AND AS GRAVITY CLUNG YOU TO THE WALLS, IT FELT AS IF YOU WERE BEING PULLED DOWN THROUGH A NEVER ENDING HOLE. I'D HAVE SWEATS AND FEAR WOULD GRIP ME. I TRIED TALKING ABOUT IT, BUT I ALWAYS GOT THE FEELING I WAS BOTHERING MY PARENTS, WHEN ALL I WANTED WAS TO BE REASSURED THAT THEY LOVED ME AND WOULD PROTECT ME AT ALL COSTS AND THINGS WERE OK.

WHEN I WAS 12 I GOT A PAPER ROUTE, IT WAS A COMPANY CALLED GRIT, YOU WENT AROUND SELLING NEWSPAPERS FOR 25 CENTS, IF NO ONE BOUGHT ANY THEN YOU SIMPLY RETURNED THEM, I MADE A FEW DOLLARS, AND HAD A FEW STEADY CUSTOMERS WHO ACTUALLY LIKED THE PAPER. IT WAS THE HIGHLIGHT OF MY LIFE, GETTING OUT, MEETING NEW PEOPLE, OTHER THAN AT SCHOOL. THE GRIT WASN'T A HUGE PAPER. BUT IT HAD SOME GOOD STORIES, RECIPES TO TRY AND GAMES TO DO. THE REAL MONEY CAME AT CHRISTMAS WITH TIPS, ALTHOUGH IT WAS HARD TO TRUDGE THROUGH SNOW ON YOUR BIKE. I ALWAYS LOVED CHRISTMAS TIME, I THINK BECAUSE IT WAS MY FAVORITE TIME OF YEAR, WELL I KNOW IT WAS, BECAUSE IT STILL IS TODAY.

AT CHRISTMAS TIME, WE GATHERED WITH OTHER FAMILY MEMBERS, GOING TO MY MOM'S PARENTS ON CHRISTMAS EVE, COME HOME AND OPEN ONE OR TWO GIFTS, THEN GET UP ON CHRISTMAS DAY AND OPEN THE REST, THEN GOING TO MY FATHER'S SIDE OF THE FAMILY IN THE AFTERNOON ON CHRISTMAS DAY. WE PLAYED GAMES AND HAD A GREAT TIME EXCHANGING GIFTS AND SHARING STORIES, AND THE FOOD, OH, LOTS OF GREAT FOOD. WHEN I WOULD GET TIPS, I WOULD USE THEM TO SHOP FOR MY FAMILY, AS I LOVED GIVING AND SEEING SMILES ON PEOPLES FACES. IT GAVE ME GREAT JOY AND TO SEE SOMEONE TOUCHED BY MY GENEROSITY, ALWAYS BROUGHT TEARS TO MY EYES AND MADE ME HAPPY. THAT'S WHAT I LONGED FOR, TO BE LOVED AND HAPPY.

I THINK THIS WAS ONE TIME OF THE YEAR WHERE MY DAD WAS REALLY JOYFUL. MAYBE GROWING UP THE HOLIDAYS WAS A TIME HIS FATHER WAS MOST JOYFUL AND IT GAVE MY DAD A LONGING FOR THIS FEELING YEAR ROUND, I ONLY PRAYED HE WOULD STAY THIS WAY AND FIND SOME PEACE AND HAPPINESS HIMSELF. THIS WAS A TIME I LONGED FOR, THAT EVERYDAY WOULD BE LIKE THIS DAY. HOWEVER, AFTER ALL OF US KID'S AND OUR COUSINS BECAME TEENAGERS, THE FAMILY SORT OF DRIFTED APART. THE FAMILY QUIT GETTING TOGETHER AND IT GAVE ME SUCH AN EMPTY FEELING INSIDE, TO ME THERE'S NOTHING LIKE TOGETHERNESS FOR THE HOLIDAYS, SPREADING CHRISTMAS CHEER.

THE TEENAGE YEARS

WHEN I BECAME A TEENAGER, WOO-HOO, I WAS EXCITED. I WAS NOW 13, PLUS I KNEW JUST A FEW MORE YEARS AND I COULD BE OUT OF THE HOUSE AND ON MY OWN. NO MORE SCHOOL, AND AWAY FROM BULLIES. IT WAS THE YEAR I STARTED MY MENSTRUAL CYCLE AND I REMEBER LAUGHING. WHY WOULD ONE LAUGH? IT WAS ALSO AT THIS AGE, THAT I CAME TO KNOW JESUS AS MY SAVIOR. WHAT A PEACE THAT WAS FILLING MY HEART, AND I ACTUALLY LOOKED FORWARD TO THE DAYS THAT CHURCH TIME ROLLED AROUND, ESPECIALLY WEDNESDAY NIGHTS. I WOULD COME IN FROM SCHOOL, HURRY TO GET DONE WITH CHORES AND WHATEVER ELSE I WAS TO DO, BECAUSE IF EVERYTHING WASN'T FINISHED BY THE TIME MY RIDE CAME FOR CHURCH THEN I DIDN'T GET TO GO AND THIS WAS HEARTBREAKING FOR ME.

DURING THE OTHER TIMES OF THE WEEK, I WOULD COME HOME AS SOON AS SCHOOL WAS OUT, GO TO MY ROOM TO START HOMEWORK AND TURN ON THE RECORD PLAYER. AT THAT TIME THERE WAS STILL THE KIND OF STEREO'S THAT PLAYED 45'S AND ALSO ALBUMS. I'D SING AND WORSHIP GOD WHILE DOING HOMEWORK, AND THIS SEEMED TO HELP ME FOCUS. THIS BEGAN MY ROUTINE OF HOW MY DAY WENT. I'D GET UP, PREPARE FOR SCHOOL, GO TO SCHOOL, COME HOME, TO MY ROOM FOR HOMEWORK AND MUSIC, AND THEN IT WAS TIME FOR SUPPER AND CHORES, THEN BED. I ALWAYS SEEMED TO BE TIRED

AND WOULD COUNT THE HOURS OF SLEEP I'D GET BEFORE STARTING ANOTHER DAY. WHEN A FEW WEEKS WENT BY AND I WASN'T FEELING MUCH BETTER, MY MOM FINALLY TOOK ME TO THE DOCTOR. ON THE WAY I STARTED FEELING HOT, I THOUGHT IT WAS DUE TO THE WEATHER OUTSIDE, AS IT WAS AN UNUSUALLY HOT DAY FOR SPRING TIME. THE DOCTOR TOLD US THAT MY TONSILS WERE INFLAMED, I HAD MONO, AND IF MY FEVER GOES MUCH HIGHER, I'D HAVE RHEUMATIC FEVER. I WAS ONE SICK GIRLY. NO WONDER I WAS FEELING SO TIRED. HE TOLD HER THAT INSTEAD OF MY TONSILS FIGHTING OFF INFECTIONS, IT WAS CREATING INFECTIONS, AND SHE MAY WANT TO CONSIDER ME EVENTUALLY HAVING MY TONSILS TAKEN OUT.

IT HAD TAKEN ME A WHILE TO GET BETTER, I THINK I MISSED THE REST OF THE SCHOOL YEAR, BUT THERE WASN'T MANY DAYS LEFT ANYWAY BEFORE SUMMER BREAK, AND I STILL PASSED, SO THAT WAS A RELIEF. BUT I DIDN'T MUCH LIKE THE FACT THAT I MISSED GOING TO CHURCH. WHAT I FOUND DIFFICULT WAS THE FACT THAT I ATTENDED A BAPTIST CHURCH AT THE TIME, BUT WAS GOING TO A CATHOLIC SCHOOL. I WAS IN PUBLIC SCHOOL, AND THEN WHEN I ENTERED 7TH GRADE, MY PARENTS BECAME CONCERNED ABOUT DRUGS IN THE PUBLIC SCHOOL SO THEY PUT ME IN A CATHOLIC SCHOOL FOR MY JUNIOR HIGH YEARS. THIS PUZZLED ME, THERE WAS CONCERN ABOUT GETTING INVOLVED WITH DRUGS, BUT WHEN I WAS BEING BEAT UP AT THE BUS STOP AND WAS HAVING NIGHTMARES, THAT WAS OK?

THE BAPTIST CHURCH I ATTENDED, DIDN'T BELIEVE IN WOMEN WEARING PANTS, BUT FOR THE CATHOLIC CHURCH THEY DID, SO IN THE WINTER TIME I'D WEAR A DRESS WHILE OUT AT RECESS AND OFTEN THE OTHER GIRLS WOULD WHERE PANTS AND ASK WHY I NEVER WORE PANTS. I'D EXPLAIN MY FAITH AND WAS OFTEN LAUGHED AT. ALTHOUGH ADDING TO THE LONELINESS OF FEELING ABANDONED ALREADY BY MY PARENTS AND THEN MY FRIENDS, THERE WAS STILL THIS DRIVE IN ME, THAT IF I SUCCUMB TO THE WAYS OF THE WORLD I WOULD BE DISHONORING GOD. I'M SURE I HAD LOTS TO LEARN YET AS I WAS A YOUNG TEEN AND CHRISTIANITY WAS STILL NEW TO ME AND I DIDN'T UNDERSTAND A LOT YET, BUT I HAD THIS EXCITEMENT INSIDE AND PEACE THAT THINGS WOULD TURN OUT OK, DESPITE ALL THE RIDICULE I WAS GETTING.

I DIDN'T LIKE ATTENDING A CATHOLIC SCHOOL, ESPECIALLY WHEN IT CAME AROUND TO MAY THEY HAD WHAT THEY CALLED MAY CROWNING, DON'T ASK ME WHAT IT WAS BUT IT WAS ALWAYS HELD DURING THE MONTH OF MAY. WE WERE ALL REQUIRED TO PARTICIPATE IN EVENTS THAT WENT ON, AND I DIDN'T BELIEVE IN THE CATHOLIC WAYS ANY MORE, SO IT WAS HARD FOR ME TO GET THROUGH THIS. HOWEVER, IT WAS PART OF YOUR GRADE SO I SUFFERED THROUGH IT. ONCE AGAIN, I HAD THIS GNAWING FEELING INSIDE AND REGRETTED HAVING TO GO TO SCHOOL. THERE WERE DAYS WHEN MY MOM, BEING SWITCHED TO DAY SHIFT, WOULD LEAVE BY 6:30 AM, SO IF I DIDN'T FEEL UP TO GOING TO SCHOOL, THEN I STAYED HOME. I'M NOT QUITE SURE HOW I PASSED THE 7TH GRADE, BUT I DID, I WAS HAPPY WHEN SCHOOL LET OUT FOR THE SUMMER, AND I WAS RELIEVED AT BEING OUT OF THE

CATHOLIC SCHOOL, AT LEAST FOR A COUPLE OF MONTHS, THEN I'D HAVE ONE MORE YEAR THERE, AS THE SCHOOL ONLY WENT TO 8TH GRADE. I WAS PRAYING WHEN IT WAS TIME FOR HIGH SCHOOL THAT MY PARENTS WOULDN'T SEND ME TO LEHMAN, WHICH WAS A CATHOLIC HIGH SCHOOL IN SIDNEY. BUT THAT TIME HADN'T COME YET, SO WHY WORRY ABOUT IT NOW?

DURING THE SUMMER I HOOKED UP WITH A COLORED GUY I HAD KNEW, WE STARTED DATING AND I WAS EXCITED AT HAVING A BOYFRIEND, I WENT HOME AND TOLD MY DAD ABOUT HIM AND THAT HIS BROTHER WAS A BASKETBALL STAR, OF COURSE MY DAD KNEW IMMEDIATELY THAT HE WAS COLORED, AS WAS THE CASE WITH MOST GUYS WHO PLAYED BASKETBALL AND MY DAD HAD A FIT AND GROUNDED ME FOR A MONTH. A MONTH FOR DATING A COLORED GUY!!! UGH!!! ARE THEY SERIOUS? I'M NOT DISPUTING THAT EVERY CHILD NEEDS CORRECTION FROM TIME TO TIME, AND IT MAY NOT SEEM A BIG DEAL TO SOME, BUT I THOUGHT IT WAS A LITTLE EXTREME. A TALKING TO WOULD HAVE BEEN SUFFICIENT IN MY OPINION, BUT I WAS A TEENAGER, SO WHAT DID I KNOW??

AFTER MY GROUNDING WAS UP, THERE WAS SOME CHURCH ACTIVITIES, AND I WAS EAGER TO GO AND HAVE SOME FUN, AS SUMMER WAS PASSING FAST. I MEAN I HAD WASTED A MONTH ALREADY BY GETTING MYSELF GROUNDED. I WAS ESTATIC WHEN MY DAD SAID I COULD GO AND SURPRISED, BUT I DIDN'T QUESTION IT, I ACTUALLY LOOKED FORWARD TO LEAVING HOME FOR A COUPLE DAYS.

AFTER THAT WEEKEND, THE REST OF THE SUMMER PASSED WITH LITTLE GOING ON, AND SOON SCHOOL HAD ONCE AGAIN STARTED. I REGRETTED GOING BACK TO THE CATHOLIC SCHOOL, BUT SOON CALMED MYSELF, KNOWING THIS WAS MY LAST YEAR THERE, AND THAT THE ONES WHO HAD POKED FUN WHEN I WAS IN 7TH GRADE HAD NOW MOVED ON TO ANOTHER SCHOOL. THE THOUGHT OF NOW BEING AN 8TH GRADER AND BEING THE TOP CLASS OF THE SCHOOL, WOULD MAKE THIS SCHOOL YEAR EASIER TO GET THROUGH FOR SURE.

A MONTH INTO THIS SCHOOL YEAR, I TURNED 14, IT WAS 1977, AND MY DAD TOLD ME IT WAS TIME TO GET A JOB. MY MOM HAD WORKED FOR A ROOT BEER STAND AND THEY DIDN'T HAVE A PROBLEM HIRING AT 14. I WASN'T TOO SURE ABOUT GOING TO WORK SO YOUNG, BUT THE JOB SEEMED EASY ENOUGH, AND ALTHOUGH THE PAY WAS SMALL, YOU HAD THE OPPORTUNITY TO EARN TIPS AND I LIKED THAT, THE HOURS WEREN'T VERY LONG EITHER. THEY WERE ONLY OPEN IN THE AFTERNOON'S, WHEN KID'S GOT OUT OF SCHOOL. IT WAS MAINLY SCHOOL KIDS THAT WORKED THERE, AND THEY CLOSED AROUND 10 P.M. THEN THEY OPENED ALL DAY SATURDAY AND WERE CLOSED ON SUNDAY. I LIKED HAVING SUNDAY OFF FOR CHURCH, BUT WOULD MORE THAN LIKELY MISS WEDNESDAY NIGHTS, WHICH I DIDN'T MUCH LIKE,BUT WHAT CHOICE DID I HAVE?

SINCE MY MOM KNEW THE OWNERS AND HAD A GOOD RELATIONSHIP WITH THEM, THEY WERE DELIGHTED TO GIVE ME A JOB, AND SO AFTER GETTING THE NECESSARY PAPER WORK IN ORDER, I BEGAN MY

WORK CAREER. I WOULD GET OUT OF SCHOOL AT AROUND 3 AND NEED TO BE AT WORK BY 3:30 AND ONLY WORKED ABOUT 3 DAYS A WEEK TO START. IT WAS SEASONAL WORK, WHICH MEANT THEY OPENED FOR THE SEASON IN MARCH AND CLOSED IN OCTOBER SOMETIME, BEING CLOSED FOR THE WINTER SEASON. I LIKED THE IDEA OF HAVING A JOB, FOR IT GAVE ME SOME RESPONSIBILITY AND A SENSE OF WORTH. I SOON LEARNED THAT IF I NEEDED THINGS, LIKE PERSONAL PRODUCTS OR SPECIAL THINGS THEN I HAD TO PAY FOR IT MYSELF OUT OF MY EARNINGS. I SAID WHAT? I GRUMBLED AND DIDN'T UNDERSTAND WHY, THINKING IT WAS MY PARENTS RESPONSIBILITY TO PROVIDE FOR ME, BUT I CAN SEE NOW IT WAS TO TEACH ME HOW TO BUDGET AND MANAGE MONEY AND TO BE RESPONSIBLE. NOW THAT I WAS GROWING UP, MY DAD SEEMED TO PAY ATTENTION TO WHAT I DID AND SHOW CONCERN, I SHOULDN'T ACT AS IF I'M UNAPPRECIATIVE, I WAS GRATEFUL FOR THE ATTENTION, FINALLY!!! BUT WHERE HAVE YOU BEEN ALL MY LIFE?

FINALLY!! I HAD MADE IT THROUGH MY 8TH GRADE YEAR. I THINK WHAT HELPED WAS THE FACT I HAD A JOB TO FOCUS ON, AS WELL AS CHURCH. NOW IT WAS SUMMER AND THE OWNERS DECIDED TO TAKE THE CREW TO THE STATE FAIR, I WAS SO EXCITED, NEVER BEFORE HAD I BEEN TO THE STATE FAIR AND IT WAS A CHANCE TO GET AWAY FROM MY HOMETOWN AND ACTUALLY BE FREE AND PUT OUT OF MY MIND ALL THAT WAS GOING ON AT HOME. LUCKILY I DIDN'T HAVE TO ENDURE A LOT DURING TIMES OF WORK AND SCHOOL, ONLY BEARING THROUGH ON MY DAYS OFF. I HAD BEEN PRAYING AS MY 8TH GRADE YEAR WAS

DRAWING TO A CLOSE, FOR A VERY FULL SUMMER TO KEEP ME BUSY. LATELY MY DAD WAS SINKING FURTHER INTO DEPRESSION, AGAIN, AND DIDN'T SEEM TO MIND US BEING AWAY FROM HOME, THE LESS HE HAD TO DEAL WITH, I GUESS THE BETTER. SOMETIMES I THOUGHT HE'D MUCH RATHER BE ALONE, SITTING IN HIS ROCKER, DRINKING BEER AND SMOKING AS HE WATCHED TV. SOMETIMES WE'D COME IN TO SEE HIM AT THE TABLE, HAVING A BEER WHILE HE BURIED HIMSELF IN A NEWSPAPER,NOT EVEN PEERING AT US FROM AROUND THE PAPER, AND BARELY MUTTERING A HELLO. WE JUST LEARNED TO SHRUG IT OFF AND GO ON, I MEAN, IT WASN'T A SURPRISE TO US, WE'D BECOME ACCUSTOMED TO THIS LIFE STYLE.

THE DAY OF THE FAIR FINALLY ARRIVED, I THOUGHT IT WOULD NEVER GET HERE, AND I HAD ACTUALLY WON A BIG STUFFED BEAR ON A RING TOSS GAME. I WAS SO PROUD OF MYSELF. I DON'T REMEMBER EVER WINNING ANYTHING. I EITHER RECEIVED THINGS AS GIFTS JUST FOR BIRTHDAYS OR CHRISTMAS, OR WORKED FOR EVERYTHING ELSE I HAD. I DON'T REMEMBER MUCH ELSE ABOUT THE TRIP, BUT I HAD ACTUALLY MADE SOME FRIENDS. I WAS ESTACTIC THAT I WAS FINALLY ABLE TO HAVE SOME SORT OF A SOCIAL LIFE. LOOK OUT WORLD, HERE I COME, I, TERESA ENGLAND WAS GROWING UP AND LEARNING SOME INDEPENDENCE!!

ONE NIGHT WHILE STAYING OVERNIGHT AT A FRIENDS HOUSE, YEAH!! I ACTUALLY GOT TO SPEND THE NIGHT AT A FRIENDS HOUSE. I WANTED TO SHOW MY APPRECIATION FOR THIS NEW FOUND FRIENDSHIP, WE HAD JUST CLICKED AND WERE BECOMING VERY

GOOD FRIENDS, SO I ENDED UP GIVING HER THE BEAR I HAD SO PROUDLY WON AT THE FAIR. I'M NOT SURE WHY, I JUST HAD A GIVING SPIRIT, AND THOUGHT PEOPLE WOULD LIKE ME MORE. MAYBE IT WAS GOD DOING A WORK IN ME, SHAPING MY LIFE. IT FELT REALLY GOOD TO BE MAKING FRIENDS, AND GETTING OUT. I UNDERSTAND NOW, THIS IS NOT THE TRUE MEANING OF FRIENDSHIP, IT'S NOT SOMETHING THAT CAN BE BOUGHT BY EITHER MONEY OR GIFTS, BUT BY BEING YOURSELF. IT WAS A LEARNING CURVE FOR ME. AND MY DAD DIDN'T SEEM TO CARE I WAS GONE. AS LONG AS MY CHORES AND EVERYTHING WAS DONE BEFORE MY MOM CAME HOME, IT WAS OK WITH HIM. EVEN IF IT WAS ONLY A COUPLE OF HOURS, IT WAS OUT OF THE HOUSE FOR ME!! WOO-HOO!! FREEDOM!! I THINK MY DAD WAS ACTUALLY GETTING QUITE ACCUSTOMED TO US KIDS BEING GONE. I REMEMBER ONE NIGHT I HAD NOTHING TO DO, I WAS OFF WORK THAT NIGHT, NO CHURCH, AND MY FRIENDS HAD OTHER PLANS, HE LIKED TO CHASE ME OUT OF THE HOUSE AND SAID GO FIND SOMETHING TO DO, GET OUT OF MY HAIR. I LEARNED THAT GETTING OUT OF MY HAIR DIDN'T MEAN I WAS IN HIS HAIR LITERALLY, IT MEANT HE DIDN'T WANT TO BE BOTHERED BY THE SIGHT OF ME AT THAT PARTICULIAR TIME.

SUMMER WAS ALMOST OVER AND YET ANOTHER SCHOOL YEAR WAS GETTING READY TO START, WHERE DID THE TIME GO? MY HOURS I KNEW, WOULD SOON DWINDLE DOWN AT WORK, AS THEY WOULD GO BACK TO OPENING AT 3:30, IN PREPARATION NOT JUST FOR SCHOOL BEING BACK IN SESSION BUT ALSO CLOSING FOR THE SEASON. WHEN SCHOOL HAD LET OUT FOR SUMMER, THEY HAD STARTED OPENING AT 11 AM, SO I

HAD AN INCREASE IN HOURS WHICH WAS NICE. IT WAS HARD TO BELIEVE I HAD BEEN THERE ALMOST A YEAR ALREADY AND HAD REALLY ENJOYED WORKING THERE. THE OWNERS WERE JUST AMAZING, AND I MET SOME NEW FRIENDS AND EVEN DEVELOPED MORE SOCIAL SKILLS I THINK.

I WAS ENTERING MY FRESHMAN YEAR IN HIGH SCHOOL, AND I WAS SUPER EXCITED TO BE IN HIGH SCHOOL, NOT TO MENTION, WELL I SUPPOSE I AM MENTIONING IT, THAT MY PRAYERS WERE ANSWERED. MY PARENTS DIDN'T HAVE THE TUITION TO SEND ME TO LEHMAN IN SIDNEY, AS IT WAS QUITE EXPENSIVE, AND THEY STILL DIDN'T WANT ME IN PUBLIC SCHOOL. SO, THEY FOUND A CHRISTIAN SCHOOL INSIDE A LOCAL CHURCH, NOT FAR FROM WHERE WE LIVED. IT WAS QUITE REASONABLE ON TUITION, AND I WAS EXCITED, ALTHOUGH I DIDN'T KNOW WHAT THE CHURCHES DENOMINATION WAS, THEY BELIEVED IN GOD, SO THAT'S ALL THAT MATTERED AND I WAS SO LOOKING FORWARD TO BEING WITH OTHER CHRISTIANS. I LEARNED WE WERE REQUIRED TO WEAR A UNIFORM, SO A LADY FROM THE CHURCH GRACIOUSLY MADE ME TWO OF THEM AND DIDN'T CHARGE ME OTHER THAN FOR THE MATERIAL NEEDED. WE HAD TO HAVE A SPECIFIC COLOR FOR MY SHIRT, EITHER WHITE OR RED AND THE SKIRT AND VEST A NAVY BLUE. I THOUGHT THAT WAS SO KIND OF HER TO DO THIS FOR US, NOT KNOWING US VERY WELL, AND MY PARENTS I'M SURE WAS PLEASED.

ONE SATURDAY, I WENT TO WORK AND I SEEN WHERE THEY HAD JUST HIRED A GUY TO WORK BEHIND THE COUNTER, IT DIDN'T MAKE SENSE SINCE THEY'D

BE CLOSING FOR THE SEASON IN ANOTHER WEEK OR SO, I MEAN WHY NOT THE OWNER JUST FILL IN TILL THEY OPENED NEXT SEASON, THEN HIRE SOMEONE. BUT I WASN'T THE OWNER, SO I SHRUGGED IT OFF. ANYWAY I LEARNED HIS NAME WAS KEVIN AND I WAS IMMEDIATELY SMITTEN WITH HIM, SO WHY SHOULD I HAVE EVEN GIVEN THOUGHT AS TO WHY THEY HIRED HIM? BUT I GAVE UP ON THE THOUGHT THAT HE'D EVEN BE INTERESTED IN SOMEONE LIKE ME. I MEAN I WASN'T EVEN SURE WHO I WAS YET, IT WAS AS IF I WAS JUST STARTING OUT IN LIFE AND I HAD JUST TURNED 15. MY MIND KEPT GOING BACK TO THE THOUGHTS OF US TOGETHER, GOING PLACES, EVEN WHAT OUR FIRST KISS WOULD BE LIKE, BUT I BRUSHED OFF THE IDEA KNOWING WE'D HARDLY HAVE TIME TO GET TO KNOW ONE ANOTHER, THEN THE ROOT BEER STAND WOULD BE CLOSED AND NOT REOPEN TILL MARCH, SO I WOULD NOT EVEN SEE HIM TILL THEN, UNLESS…UNLESS HE DIDN'T COME BACK!! WHAT WAS I TO DO? I REALLY LIKED HIM, ESPECIALLY WHEN HE'D RIDE TO WORK ON HIS MOPED!! I WANTED SO MUCH TO TALK TO HIM, GET TO KNOW HIM BETTER, BUT I JUST SHRUNK BACK INTO MY SHELL I'D BEEN SLOWLY POKING MY HEAD OUT OF AND TOLD MYSELF TO LET IT GO, I WAS WAY OUT OF HIS LEAGUE.

I WAS ENJOYING MY FRESHMAN YEAR, I SAT NEXT TO A GUY WHO WAS A SOPHMORE AND ALTHOUGH WE HAD DIVIDER'S ON OUR DESKS TO PREVENT US FROM CHEATING AND GOOFING OFF, HE FOUND A WAY TO SLIP NOTES UNDER THE DIVIDER. HE WAS ONE OF THE POPULAR GUYS WHO DATED ONE OF THE POPULAR GIRLS, HARDLY SOMEONE WHO WOULD GIVE A SECOND LOOK TO ME, BUT BEING A CHRISTIAN

CHURCH, HE WAS KIND ENOUGH TO HELP ME ADAPT TO HIGH SCHOOL, AND THE WAY CHRISTIAN SCHOOL WAS RUN. I HAD MADE A FEW FRIENDS AND I THOUGHT TO MYSELF HOW THINGS HAVE CHANGED OVER THE YEARS. WOW!! HIGH SCHOOL, I FINALLY MADE IT!! AND I WAS COUNTING THE YEARS TILL I WAS ON MY OWN. I TECHNICALLY HAD 3 YEARS OF SCHOOL LEFT AFTER THIS SINCE I WAS HELD BACK A YEAR. I'D BE OVER 18, CLOSE TO 19 AT GRADUATION, BUT NEVERTHELESS IT WAS GETTING CLOSER.

IT WAS DIFFERENT BEING IN A CHRISTIAN SCHOOL VERSUS HAVING GONE TO A CATHOLIC SCHOOL AND I WAS ADJUSTING QUITE WELL. YOU BASICALLY WORKED AT YOUR OWN PACE, SETTING GOALS FOR HOW MUCH WORK YOU WANTED TO DO IN EACH SUBJECT. YOU HAD TO BE CAREFUL NOT TO SET THE GOALS TOO HIGH, CAUSE IF YOU DIDN'T COMPLETE THOSE GOALS BY THE END OF THE DAY WHEN YOU TURNED IN YOUR SHEET, THEN YOU HAD TO TAKE IT HOME FOR HOMEWORK. THE NICE THING WAS, YOU COULD STILL TAKE THEM HOME, EVEN IF YOU DIDN'T HAVE HOMEWORK, AND DO ALL THE PAGES, TAKE IT BACK AND TURN IT IN FOR THE TEST, JUST MAKE SURE YOU STUDY WELL FIRST.

THE SCHOOL YEAR WAS FLYING BY, WE HAD JUST GOTTEN THROUGH THE HOLIDAYS AND THE NEW YEAR WAS UPON US. I OFTEN THOUGHT OF KEVIN, THROUGH THOSE WINTER MONTHS WHEN THE ROOT BEER STAND WAS CLOSED AND I WAS COUNTING DOWN THE DAYS TILL THE STAND WOULD OPEN AND PRAYED KEVIN WOULD BE RETURNING. IT WAS AGONY HAVING TO WAIT, AND I ACTUALLY BELIEVE I WAS

BECOMING SOMEWHAT BOY CRAZY. I HAD MET SOME BOYS AT CHURCH WHO SEEMED INTERESTED IN ME, BUT I THINK THEY WERE JUST AFTER ONE THING. SEX!!! I WAS A LITTLE AFRAID OF THIS, SO I FILLED MY TIME WITH SCHOOL WORK, CHORES, AND FRIENDS CLOSER TO HOME.

FINALLY THE STAND WAS DUE TO OPEN IN ANOTHER WEEK, I WAS CALLED TO COME GET MY SCHEDULE AND I WAS THRILLED. THAT NEXT WEEK WAS LIKE A LIFETIME WAITING, AND I THINK I CHEWED MY NAILS CLEAR PAST THE QUICK, I WAS SO NERVOUS. WHY WAS I GETTING THESE BUTTERFLY FEELINGS IN MY BELLY, I HADN'T FELT LIKE THIS, WAS IT LOVE I WONDERED? THE WEEK CAME FOR THE STAND TO OPEN AND TIME FOR ME TO REPORT TO WORK THAT NIGHT. I WENT TO SCHOOL AND KEPT WATCHING THE CLOCK. I WONDERED IF THE BATTERY WAS GOING DEAD, IT SEEMED TO TICK AND TICK, YET THE HANDS WERE MOVING EVER SO SLOWLY. I PUT MY MIND INTO MY SCHOOL WORK AND WAS ALERTED WHEN THE END OF THE DAY BELL RANG, YIPPEE!! TO WORK I WENT, PRAYING KEVIN WOULD BE THERE. TO MY DELIGHT, WHEN I ARRIVED, HE WAS THERE. MY HEART BEGAN TO POUND, MY BLOOD RACING IN MY BODY, I WAS GETTING NERVOUS. I QUICKLY CHANGED OUT OF MY UNIFORM INTO JEANS AND WAS READY TO GET STARTED. WHEN I GOT MY APRON ON AND WAITED ON MY FIRST CUSTOMER, I CAUGHT KEVIN'S EYE AND HE SMILED THE BIGGEST, MOST BEAUTIFUL SMILE I'D EVER SEEN. MY HEART WAS MELTING. I THINK IF I WOULD BE ICE CREAM, I'D BE A PUDDLE IN THE MIDDLE OF THE PARKING LOT RIGHT ABOUT THEN.

THE SCHOOL YEAR WENT BY QUICKLY, I THINK THIS WAS THE BEST YEAR I EVER EXPERIENCED AND I HAD LEARNED A LOT, EVEN MADE SOME WONDERFUL FRIENDS, SOME OF WHOM WANTED TO MAKE PLANS FOR GET TOGETHERS OVER THE SUMMER. I WAS SURPRISED TO LEARN THAT ONE GIRL LIVED RIGHT ACROSS THE STREET FROM ME AND HAD LIVED THERE A FEW YEARS. THEY TRAVELED A LOT AS HER FAMILY WERE SINGERS AND OFTEN WENT TO DIFFERENT CHURCHES AND SOCIAL FUNCTIONS TO PERFORM, THIS DIDN'T GIVE THEM MUCH ROOM FOR SOCIALIZING WITH FRIENDS, BUT THIS YEAR THEY WERE SLOWING DOWN A BIT, SO WE MADE PLANS TO GET TOGETHER. I WAS CERTAINLY LOOKING FORWARD TO IT, AS LONG AS I DIDN'T HAVE TO BE AT HOME ANY LONGER THAN NECESSARY, AND WORKING EVENTS AROUND MY WORK SCHEDULE TOO, AS THE STAND WOULD SOON OPEN AT 11 EVERYDAY WITH SCHOOL BEING OUT.

THE SUMMER WAS STARTING OFF TO BE QUITE A HOT ONE. ONE DAY WHILE AT WORK, KEVIN WAS OFF THAT DAY, BUT HAD SHOWN UP TO GET HIS SCHEDULE FOR THE NEXT WEEK. HE CAME RIDING IN ON HIS MOPED,WHICH WAS LIKE A MINI MOTORCYCLE,AND MY HEART WENT PITTER PATTER. NEVER BEFORE HAD SOMEONE HAD SUCH AN AFFECT ON ME, LIKE THIS GUY. I TOLD MYSELF TO PULL IT TOGETHER BEFORE SOMEONE CAUGHT ON, BUT I WAS TOO LATE. ONE OF THE OTHER GIRLS HAD CAUGHT ON AND SAID SO TO ME. I TOLD HER TO KEEP IT QUIET, I DIDN'T WANT HIM TO KNOW, ALTHOUGH I DID, BUT THOUGHT HE WOULDN'T GIVE ME THE TIME OF DAY OUTSIDE OF THE WORK PLACE. WHILE WAITING ON A CUSTOMER AT CURBSIDE, SHE MUST HAVE SAID SOMETHING TO HIM

THAT I WASN'T AWARE OF. WHEN I COME BACK IN, SHE WAS OUT WAITING ON A CUSTOMER AND IT WAS JUST HIM AND ME. HE SPOKE UP AND ASKED IF I WANTED TO GO FOR A RIDE ON HIS MOPED AFTER WORK. MY MOUTH DROPPED OPEN!! I DON'T KNOW HOW LONG I STOOD THERE BUT MUTTERED A YES BEFORE QUICKLY PAYING FOR THE CUSTOMERS ORDER THEN DELIVERING IT, KNEES KNOCKING AND ALL. THE REST OF THE EVENING WAS A BLUR, I KNOW I PONDERED OVER AND OVER THE EVENTS THAT TOOK PLACE, I'M NOT EVEN SURE IF I ASKED THE OTHER GIRL WORKING WITH ME IF SHE SAID ANYTHING TO HIM, I DIDN'T CARE IF SHE DID, THE POINT WAS I WAS GOING OUT WITH KEVIN AFTER WORK, EVEN IF IT WAS ONLY A RIDE ON HIS MOPED!!

AFTER WORK, HE INDEED SHOWED UP, I HAD WONDERED IF HE WOULD, OR IF IT WAS SOME SORT OF A TRICK OR SICK JOKE THAT WAS BEING PLAYED ON ME. BUT NOPE, THERE HE WAS IN THE FLESH. OH HE WAS SO HAND SOME, I COULDN'T BELIEVE I WAS ACTUALLY GOING TO BE SEEN WITH HIM. I HAD GOTTEN OFF A LITTLE EARLY AS IT WAS SLOW, AND IT WAS STILL DAYLIGHT. I WONDERED HOW HE KNEW I WAS OFF EARLY, USUALLY WHEN WE ARE SCHEDULED IT'S FOR THE WHOLE SHIFT, EITHER 11-4 OR 4-10. MAYBE HE WAS LINGERING SOMEWHERE AND I DIDN'T KNOW IT, BUT I DIDN'T CARE, I WAS OFF, HE WAS HERE, AND AWAY WE WENT. I WRAPPED MY ARMS TIGHTLY AROUND HIS WAIST, AND TOOK IN THE SMELL OF HIS COLOGNE. I WAS DEFINITELY IN HEAVEN!!! I DIDN'T LIVE VERY FAR FROM WORK, BUT TO NOT HAVE TO WALK WAS CERTAINLY RELIEVING. MY MOM SOMETIMES OFFERS TO PICK ME UP IF I WORK TILL 4. WHEN SHE IS

ON THE DAY SHIFT SHE GETS OFF AT 3 AND ONCE IN A WHILE THEY GET FOOD FROM MY WORK PLACE AND THEN PICKS ME UP. BUT THIS I CALLED AND TOLD HER I HAD A RIDE. I KNEW THEY WOULD BE SOME WHAT CURIOUS AS THIS WASN'T AN OCCURRANCE FOR ME TO HAVE PEOPLE DROPPING ME OFF.

THE RIDE WASN'T LONG ENOUGH THOUGH AND SOON HE DROPPED ME OFF AT HOME, AND JUST AS I SUSPECTED MY PARENTS WERE OUT FRONT WAITING, WONDERING WHO WAS BRINGING THIER DAUGHTER HOME AND IT HAD TO BE A GUY. HOW DO THEY KNOW THESE THINGS? THEY MET AND SHOOK HANDS, AND APPARENTLY KEVIN WAS A HIT, BECAUSE MY DAD, RATHER THAN IMPOSE, WENT ON IN THE HOUSE TELLING ME NOT TO BE TOO LONG. I WAS SHOCKED. WAS THAT EVEN MY DAD JUST NOW? I NEVER SAID THAT OUT LOUD AS I DIDN'T WANT TO INSINUATE TO KEVIN THAT OUR FAMILY LIFE WASN'T THE GREATEST.

IN THE WEEKS THAT FOLLOWED, KEVIN AND I SAW A LOT OF EACH OTHER, AND I WAS THRILLED AT A GUY HAVING AN INTEREST IN ME. HE WOULD COME BY THE HOUSE OFTEN TO SEE IF I COULD GO FOR A RIDE AROUND THE BLOCK OR SOMETHING. MY DAD TO MY SURPRISE ALLOWED ME TO GO, AND MY PARENTS SEEMED TO LIKE KEVIN A LOT. KEVIN EVEN LET MY MOM TRY TO DRIVE HIS MOPED ONE NIGHT, THAT DID NOT GO WELL AS SHE HAD TROUBLE KEEPING IT UP, AND SOON GAVE UP TRYING.

OUR BOSSES AT WORK TOOK OUR CREW TO KING'S ISLAND THAT SUMMER. IT WAS ON A SUNDAY

AND THE STAND WAS CLOSED, AND KEVIN AND I WENT AS A COUPLE, HOWEVER WHEN WE ARRIVED I WAS REALLY CLINGY. I'M NOT SURE IF I WAS AFRAID OF GETTING OUT OF HIS SIGHT OR HIM OUT OF MINE. BUT WE SAT AT THE POND MOST OF THE TIME, I REMEMBER HIM KISSING ME AND IT WAS SO TENDER AND SWEET. I WANTED TO LOSE MYSELF IN HIM, AS I NEVER EXPERIENCED THIS TENDERNESS BEFORE. I THINK IT WAS A DRAG FOR HIM, CAUSE AFTER THAT KEVIN AND I WAS KIND OF ON AND OFF. I KEPT WRITING NOTES AND ASKING IF HE WAS MAD AT ME, AND HE SAID NO, BUT SOMETHING INSIDE WAS GNAWING AT ME THAT SOMETHING WAS TERRIBLY WRONG.

SOON WE STOPPED SEEING EACH OTHER ALL TOGETHER AND I WAS BROKEN. I KEPT GOING OVER AND OVER IN MY MIND WHAT WENT WRONG. HAD I DONE SOMETHING, WAS IT MY PARENTS, BUT GOT NO ANSWER. IT HAD TO BE THE WAY I HAD ACTED AT KINGS ISLAND, BEING SO CLINGY. ALL I WANTED WAS TO STAY IN HIS ARMS AT THE POND AND FOR IT NOT TO END THAT I DIDN'T ALLOW HIM TO HAVE ANY FUN. OH HOW I HATED MYSELF. ESPECIALLY SINCE I HAD GOTTEN AWAY FROM CHURCH FOR A WHILE AND KIND OF GIVEN UP SOME THINGS SUBCUMBING TO THE WAYS OF THE WORLD. CHALK IT UP YO TEENAGE YEARS I GUESS.

ONE NIGHT, SOMEONE HAD CAME BY MY HOUSE AND INVITED ME TO COME TO A CHURCH FUNCTION AT THE BAPTIST CHURCH I HAD ATTENDED FOR THAT NEXT WEEKEND. AFTER STAYING AND CHATTING FOR A FEW MINUTES, I DECIDED TO GO. A LOT OF WHAT WAS SHARED WITH ME MADE SENSE AND BY THE

WEEKEND REALIZED THAT ALTHOUGH THINGS SEEMED TO BE LOOKING UP AS FAR AS HAVING A SOCIAL LIFE AND STUFF, REALLY IT WAS GOING NO WHERE FAST AND HAD ALL STARTED WHEN I HAD GOTTEN AWAY FROM CHURCH. I HAD FELT SOME CONVICTION OVER THE TYPE OF MUSIC I HAD BEGUN LISTENING TO AS WELL, SO I GATHERED ALL OF THE RECORDS UP AND WHEN THE TIME CAME TO ATTEND THE YOUTH FUNCTION, I TOOK THEM WITH ME TO THE MEETING, I WASN'T SURE WHY, I MEAN, WHY NOT THROW THEM AWAY, MAYBE IT WAS TO BE A TESTIMONY IN FRONT OF OTHER YOUTH THAT I WAS ON THE WRONG PATH, AND TURNING MY LIFE AROUND, IN HOPES OF ENCOURAGING OTHERS TO FOLLOW AFTER GOD AND GET THEIR LIVES RIGHT WITH HIM.

ONCE THE MEETING HAD STARTED AND THEY GAVE THE WORD, THEY HAD AN ALTAR CALL, I WENT FORWARD AND BROKE EVERY RECORD I BROUGHT AND THREW IT IN THE TRASH CAN THAT WAS PROVIDED, AFTERWARD, I NOTICED A GUY STARING AT ME, HE SEEMED TO TAKE AN INTEREST IN ME. WE WERE STARTING WEEKLY YOUTH MEETINGS AND HE WAS GOING TO BE HELPING OUT AND I ONCE AGAIN THOUGHT HOW NICE IT WOULD BE TO HOOK UP WITH A CHRISTIAN GUY TO HELP KEEP MY LIFE ON TRACK. NEVERMIND THE FACT I HAD BEEN THROUGH ANOTHER RELATIONSHIP.

WE HAD WENT OUT A FEW TIMES, AND THEN ONE NIGHT WHILE AT THE DRIVE-IN, HE HAD HIS WAY WITH ME, BEFORE I KNEW IT, IT WAS OVER AND AFTER TAKING ME HOME, THAT WAS IT. I ONLY HEARD FROM HIM WHEN HE WANTED TO GET LUCKY. HE WAS A

PLAYER FOR SURE. I FELT DIRTY AND HUMILIATED. IT DIDN'T APPEAR TO TAKE TO LONG TO GET OVER IT THOUGH. I GUESS WITH ALL I HAD ENDURED TO THIS POINT, ANOTHER REJECTION WAS JUST ANOTHER NOTCH IN THE BELT SO TO SPEAK. I FELT LIKE AN OLD USED RAG DOLL. BUT AT 15, AND HORMONES OUT OF WHACK ANYWAY, I SUPPOSE I SUPPRESSED IT ALL, JUST COVERED IT UP AND GOT MY FOCUS ON OTHER THINGS, NOT REALIZING THAT BY NOT DEALING WITH THINGS AS THEY AROSE WOULD ONE DAY HURT ME MORE.

ABOUT 2 WEEKS AFTER THAT RELATIONSHIP ENDED, ANOTHER GUY CAME ALONG, GO FIGURE. I SUPPOSE I FELT EMPTY INSIDE SINCE MY RELATIONSHIP WITH KEVIN ENDED. I WAS SEARCHING FOR SOMETHING AND JUST COULDN'T PUT MY FINGER ON IT, BUT ALL IT ENDED UP DOING WAS GIVING ME A BAD REP. ALTHOUGH I WASN'T SLEEPING AROUND, PEOPLE STILL HAD THE IDEA I WAS A HOE. AFTER KEVIN, IT WAS LIKE A DIFFERENT GUY I WOULD GO OUT WITH EVERY OTHER DAY OR SO. HOW DO I CHANGE THIS? I MEAN IT WASN'T BAD ENOUGH TO TRY AND FIGURE OUT HOW TO HAVE SOME SORT OF DECENT LIFE, BUT NOW I FELT I HAD TO CONVINCE PEOPLE I WASN'T A HOE TO BOOT, BUT TURNING TO GUYS AT THE DROP OF A HAT CERTAINLY WASN'T DOING ANYTHING FOR MY REP. WELL THEN, I JUST TOLD MYSELF THIS GUY WOULD BE IT, I WAS GOING TO REALLY WORK AT IT AND MAKE THIS LAST. DO THEY EVER REALLY LAST THOUGH? I ASKED MYSELF THAT QUESTION A LOT THROUGHOUT MY LIFE!! BUT THIS GUY SEEMED DIFFERENT FOR SURE. HE WAS INVOLVED WITH THE YOUTH AT CHURCH, HAD A JOB

AND A CAR. HE SEEMED LIKE A RESPECTABLE, MATURE GUY. THE NEXT WEEK AFTER THE YOUTH MEETING, THIS GUY DAVE HAD COME OVER AND WAS HELPING ME TO FINISH THE CLEAN-UP. AS WE LOADED THINGS IN HIS CAR, WE TALKED ABOUT THE EVENING'S MEETING, HE SEEMED REAL NICE AND I LIKED THE FACT HE HAD A JOB AND A CAR.

AFTER WE FINISHED CLEANING UP, WE EXCHANGED NUMBERS AND I LEFT WITH A NEW EXCITEMENT THAT WAS DIFFERENT FROM ALL THE OTHER GUYS I HAD BEEN ASSOCIATED WITH. MAYBE THIS WAS THE ONE I THOUGHT AS I GOT ON THE BUS FOR THE 30 MINUTE DRIVE HOME. MY MIND KEPT GOING OVER AND OVER THE CONVERSATION WE HAD, AND THEN I REMEMBERED ALL THE OTHER GUYS WHO HAD TAKEN OFF OR I HAD DESTROYED OUR RELATIONSHIP BY INSECURITIES. WHAT IF I WAS TO RUIN THIS ONE TOO?? WHAT IF HE JUST TOOK OFF AFTER LEARNING MY FAMILY LIFE WASN'T THE GREATEST. I FINALLY ARRIVED HOME, AND AS USUAL MY DAD WAS BURIED IN A NEWSPAPER, ONLY LOOKING OVER THE TOP A BRIEF SECOND TO SEE WHO WAS COMING THROUGH THE DOOR, THEN PEERED BACK IN, NOT MUTTERING A WORD, I JUST WENT STRAIGHT TO MY ROOM AND WENT TO BED NOT WANTING TO DEAL WITH HIS MOOD SWINGS HE WAS ONCE AGAIN HAVING.

THE NEXT WEEK WAS BUSY, AS I WAS GETTING THINGS PREPARED FOR SCHOOL, WORKING, AND TRYING TO KEEP PEACE AT HOME. I USUALLY STAYED IN MY ROOM A LOT AFTER HAVING CHORES AND EVERYTHING FINISHED, IT WAS BETTER THAT WAY. OUT OF SIGHT, OUT OF MIND! AS THE WEEKEND GREW

CLOSER, IT WAS ALMOST TIME FOR THE NEXT YOUTH MEETING AND DAVE HAD CALLED TO ASK IF HE COULD PICK ME UP, WHICH SEEMED OK WITH MY PARENTS, MAINLY MY DAD AS WITH MY MOM WORKING A LOT, MY DAD WAS ALWAYS WATCHING US, IT WAS CHURCH SO WHAT KIND OF TROUBLE COULD I GET INTO RIGHT? I WAS ACTUALLY EXCITED TO HAVE A GUY PICK ME UP IN A REAL CAR, TOTALLY DIFFERENT FROM RIDING ON A MOPED. I THOUGHT I WAS IN THE BIG LEAGUE NOW.

HE LIVED IN SIDNEY AND WITH HIM HAVING A JOB, FOR THE TIME BEING WE ONLY SEEN EACH OTHER AT CHURCH OR THE YOUTH MEETINGS AND WHEN HE COULD ATTEND CHURCH FUNCTIONS. HE WOULD PICK ME UP AT HOME AND THEN DROP ME BACK OFF WHEN OVER. I WAS ON CLOUD NINE, AND WONDERED FOR A SECOND HOW I COULD GET OVER KEVIN SO QUICKLY, AFTER BEING SO SMITTEN WITH HIM, AND THEN MOVE ON TO THE NEXT, AND NOW DAVE, I STARTED TO FEEL GUILTY AND WONDERED IF WHAT PEOPLE THOUGHT WAS ACTUALLY TRUE, BUT I SOON SHRUGGED IT OFF, AS DAVE PULLED UP, THERE WAS NO SENSE DWELLING ON IT. THERE WAS ANOTHER GUY IN THE PICTURE NOW AND I WAS GOING TO FOCUS ON HIM AND TRY TO MAKE THIS WORK. OH HOW IF I HAD COME TO REALIZE THEN WHAT I HAVE NOW LEARNED AFTER 2 FAILED MARRIAGES, THE AFFECT THAT HAD ON ME, JUMPING FROM RELATIONSHIP TO RELATIONSHIP, ON THE REBOUND,THINGS WOULD HAVE BEEN DONE DIFFERENTLY. MIND YOU, I DIDN'T SEE MYSELF AS SOMEONE WHO SLEPT AROUND, IT WAS MAINLY JUST HANGING OUT, NOT ALWAYS WAS IT SEXUAL IN NATURE, THEN IT ENDING, AND JUMPING RIGHT INTO ANOTHER RELATIONSHIP.

IT WAS NOW THE END OF AUGUST 1979. I HAD JUST RECEIVED MY LEARNER'S PERMIT TO DRIVE AND WAS GOING THROUGH DRIVER'S TRAINING CLASSES. WOW!!! SOON I WOULD HAVE MY LICENSE AND BE ABLE TO DRIVE MYSELF AROUND INSTEAD OF WALKING, OR RIDING MY BIKE. SO DAVE ON HIS DAYS OFF FROM WORK GRACIOUSLY TOOK ME AROUND AND HELPED ME PRACTICE. HE EVEN OFFERED TO LET ME USE HIS CAR FOR MY DRIVER'S TEST AFTER I TURNED 16, I WAS EXCITED!! ANOTHER SCHOOL YEAR HAD NOW BEGUN AND I REALLY LIKED THE FACT OF GOING TO A CHRISTIAN SCHOOL. IT HELPED ME KEEP MY FOCUS. I WAS ENJOYING WORKING AT MY OWN PACE. BASICALLY, WE SET OUR OWN GOALS FOR EACH SUBJECT WE WANTED TO COMPLETE FOR THAT DAY AND HAD TO ADJUST OUR TIME TO GET IT DONE, THERE WERE ELECTIVE CLASSES WE TOOK AS WELL AND I ENJOYED TAKING OLD AND NEW TESTAMENT AND LEARNING ABOUT GOD'S WORD. I HAD LEARNED THE CHURCH WAS AN APOSTOLIC DENOMINATION, WHICH BELIEVED IN JESUS NAME ONLY, AND I WASN'T UNDERSTANDING THE CONCEPT OF THAT AFTER ATTENDING THE BAPTIST CHURCH FOR SO LONG, BUT DECIDED TO ATTEND A SERVICE SINCE IT WAS IN MY HOMETOWN ANYWAY. IT WAS DIFFERENT AND TOOK SOME GETTING USED TO, BUT I ENJOYED THE SERVICE, IT WAS SO ALIVE AND FREE. I WASN'T SURE IF I'D GO BACK, I HAD MY CHURCH AND DAVE, BUT I COULDN'T HELP BUT FEEL A TWINGE AND TINGLE WHEN I THOUGHT OF RETURNING, IT WAS LIKE I WAS BEING DRAWN.

FINALLY SEPT 28TH 1979 HAD ARRIVED, MY 16TH BIRTHDAY!! THAT NEXT WEEK AS PROMISED DAVE CAME TO PICK ME UP TO GO TAKE MY DRIVER'S TEST AND I BREEZED RIGHT THROUGH AND PASSED!! WOO-HOO!! NOW I WAS A LICENSED DRIVER!! A WHOLE NEW WORLD OF POSSIBILITIES JUST OPENED UP FOR ME AND OF COURSE MORE RESPONSIBILITY TOO. WHEN OCTOBER CAME AND THE ROOT BEER STAND CLOSED FOR THE WINTER, I APPLIED FOR A JOB AT A RESTAURANT, EMPIRE WAS THE NAME, AND GOT IT. I WOULD START OUT AS A DISHWASHER, THEN MOVE TO HOSTESSING ONE OR TWO DAYS A WEEK. I LIKED IT REAL WELL AND THE THOUGHT OF SAVING EXTRA MONEY FELT REALLY GOOD, AS I MADE A LITTLE MORE IN WAGES THERE COMPARED TO THE ROOT BEER STAND AND THE FACT THEY WERE OPEN YEAR ROUND AND THE ROOT BEER STAND WAS SEASONAL WORK.

CHRISTMAS WAS SOON UPON US AND I RECEIVED MY FIRST CAR, IT WAS A DODGE AND THAT'S ALL I CAN REMEMBER, BUT MY PARENTS GOT IT FOR 250.00. WOW CAN YOU IMAGINE THAT THESE DAYS? MY PARENTS HAD TO PUT ME ON THEIR INSURANCE OF COURSE, AS I WAS TOO YOUNG FOR MY OWN POLICY, BUT I WOULD HAVE TO HELP PAY IT. I WAS EXCITED THOUGH!! MY FIRST CAR, WOW!! WAS LIFE STARTING TO TURN AROUND? OH HOW I PRAYED IT WAS. I WAS NOW 16, HAD MY LICENSE, A BOYFRIEND, SCHOOL WAS GOING GOOD AND IN LESS THAN 2 YEARS, I'D BE ABLE TO MOVE ON MY OWN, YEAH LIFE WAS LOOKING UP, OR SO I HOPED.

THAT SPRING 1980 I DECIDED NOT TO RETURN TO THE ROOTBEER STAND, I WAS ENJOYING MY JOB AT

THE RESTAURANT AND IT WAS PAYING WELL AND WITH GAS AND CAR INSURANCE NOW, I NEEDED THE BETTER PAYING JOB. HOWEVER A MONTH LATER, EMPIRE HIRED SOME NEW GIRLS IN AS WAITRESSES AND WE DIDN'T HIT IT OFF AT ALL, ACCUSATIONS WOULD OFTEN FLY THAT ON THE DAYS I WOULD HOSTESS, THEY FELT LIKE THEIR TIPS WASN'T GOOD, AND ACCUSED ME OF STEALING THEM. I MAY HAVE DONE OR BEEN A LOT OF THINGS BUT A THIEF WAS NOT ONE OF THEM! NO SIREE!! IT JUST GOT TO BE TOO MUCH SO I STARTED LOOKING FOR ANOTHER JOB FOR I WASN'T GOING TO WORK SOMEWHERE AND TAKE THAT, NOT AFTER ALL I WAS GOING THROUGH ALREADY.

I ENDED UP LANDING A JOB AT ANOTHER RESTAURANT, BUT THIS WAS A FAST FOOD PLACE WITH A DRIVE THRU CALLED BURGER CHEF. IT WAS FAST PACED WHICH WAS RIGHT UP MY ALLEY. I LOVED TO KEEP BUSY AS IT HELPS TAKE YOUR MIND OF THINGS FOR A BIT. THIS JOB THOUGH WAS THE BEGINNING OF YET ANOTHER BACKSLIDDEN STATE. I MET SOME GIRLS AND WE STARTED TO HANG OUT AFTER WORK ON WEEKENDS, HOOKED UP WITH GUYS, WENT CRUISING AROUND THE SQUARE WHICH WAS REALLY HOPPIN ON FRIDAY AND SATURDAY NIGHTS. OH YEAH I THOUGHT, THIS WAS THE LIFE. YET THE SAD THING WAS, I HURT THE ONE PERSON, WHO TRULY CARED FOR ME. HE HELPED ME GET MY LICENSE, WAS THERE FOR ME, AND AFTER THINKING HE WAS FINALLY THE ONE FOR ME, I CHOSE SOMETHING ELSE, GAVE INTO FLESHLY DESIRES AND DUMPED HIM. HE WAS CRUSHED. I WILL NEVER FORGET AFTER SENDING ME FLOWERS, TELLING ME HOW HE MISSED ME HE SHOWED UP ONE DAY AND AS I BROKE IT OFF WITH

HIM, HE WALKED AWAY IN TEARS AND SOBBING. I DON'T KNOW HOW LONG HE SAT IN HIS CAR BEFORE HE WAS ABLE TO DRIVE, I GUESS AT THAT POINT IN TIME, I COULD HAVE CARED LESS, BUT NOW AFTER ALL THESE YEARS I REGRET THE WAY I TREATED HIM. YET HERE WE WENT AGAIN, ANOTHER RELATIONSHIP DOWN THE DRAIN AND YET MORE GUYS IN THE PICTURE.

SHORTLY AFTER TURNING 17 I HAD STARTED SMOKING, ONE OF MY BESTIES I WORKED WITH HAD GOT ME STARTED AND SUPPLIED MY CIGARETTES FOR A WHILE, THEN I GOT MY OWN. THE MANAGER THERE AT BURGER CHEF WAS A REAL PARTIER AND OFTEN GOT OUR CIGARETTES FOR US. THIS WAS THE SAME TIME I TRIED SPEED, WHOA, WHAT A TRIP, WE HAD THE FASTEST CLOSING AT THE RESTAURANT WE EVER EXPERIENCED, JUST SO WE COULD GO AND PARTY SOME MORE, THIS IS THE TIME I BECAME PROMISCUOUS. I REMEMBER GOING TO A PARTY ONCE AND SOMEONE SLIPPED SOMETHING INTO MY DRINK AND I WAS OUT OF IT, WOKE UP TO FIND MYSELF IN SOME GUYS BED, DON'T KNOW HOW I GOT THERE, WAS ALMOST SURE I WAS RAPED, AFRAID I'D BE PREGNANT, DIDN'T KNOW WHERE MY CAR WAS, NOTHING!! I REALIZED AT THAT POINT THAT MY MANAGER AT BURGER CHEF WAS A LESBIAN, WHO LIVED WITH 2 GUYS WHO HAD THEIR WALLS IN THEIR APARTMENT DECORATED WITH PICTURES OF NAKED WOMEN. THEY WERE ALL AT THIS PARTY AND KNEW SOMEONE HAD LACED MY DRINK, IT WENT BAD AS THEY DIDN'T EXPECT ME TO REACT THE WAY I DID, SO THEY TOOK ME BACK TO THEIR PLACE IN HOPES I WOULD SNAP

OUT OF IT AND YET NOT GET THEIR FRIENDS BUSTED FOR DRUGS.

WELL OUT OF THE BLUE, MY DAD SHOWS UP, NOT EXACTLY SURE HOW HE FINDS THE PLACE, BUT OH BOY, HE TOOK ONE LOOK AT THE WALLS AND HIS EYES ABOUT POPPED OUT OF HIS HEAD. BOY DID I GET GROUNDED AND I WOULD HAVE TO SAY, I DID DESERVE IT. I WANTED SO DESPERATELY TO HAVE A NORMAL LIFE, I WISH MY DAD HAD ALWAYS BEEN THERE LIKE HE WAS THAT DAY, BUT HE WASN'T THERE. HE WAS SO HIDDEN WITHIN HIMSELF AND BATTLING HIS OWN STRUGGLES, THAT HE HARDLY GAVE US THE TIME OF DAY, AND WHEN HE DID IT WAS CRITICISM. MAYBE HE COULDN'T HELP IT, MAYBE HE DIDN'T KNOW HOW. BUT IS THAT AN EXCUSE?? AT THE TIME, I WAS SO YOUNG, BEEN MOLESTED, RAPED, BEAT UP BY BULLIES AND I THOUGHT IT WAS THE WAY LIFE WAS TO BE. I DON'T UNDERSTAND WHY HE TOOK HIS FRUSTRATIONS OUT ON US KIDS, INSTEAD OF SEEKING HELP, MAINLY ME AS I WAS AROUND HOME SO MUCH MORE THAN MY BROTHER'S AS IT WAS HARD AT FIRST TO MAKE FRIENDS AND SOCIALIZE. MY BROTHERS DIDN'T SEEM TO HAVE TROUBLE MAKING FRIENDS. IT WAS AS IF EVERYTHING I DID, HE DIDN'T LIKE, SO IT WAS YOU'RE GROUNDED!! NO CAR!! IT WAS AS IF I WAS IN PRISON OR SOMETHING AND PUT IN LOCK DOWN FOR EVERY LITTLE THING. WE COULDN'T EVEN VOICE OUR OPINION, I MEAN THEY ASKED YOU A QUESTION, AND IF YOU GAVE AN ANSWER YOU WERE TOLD TO SHUT UP, AND IF YOU DIDN'T SAY ANYTHING, WELL, YOU WERE GROUNDED. THAT MAY SEEM LIKE I'M BEING EXTREME BUT BEING A TEENAGER THAT'S WHAT IT FELT LIKE, A PRISON. ALL I HAD COME TO KNOW, FROM MY DAD, TO

MY UNCLE, TO ALL THESE GUYS IN AND OUT OF MY LIFE, I WAS DEFINITELY SPINNING OUT OF CONTROL, AS IF ON SOME ROLLER COASTER RIDE OR MERRY-GO-ROUND THAT SEEMED TO GO ON FOREVER WITH NO STOPPING POINT OR WAY TO GET OFF. MY EMOTIONS WERE RUNNING WILD, I DIDN'T KNOW HOW TO ACT, WASN'T SURE OF MYSELF, AND WANTED FRIENDS SO DESPERATELY TO FILL THIS VOID I HAD THAT I GOT TALKED INTO DOING THINGS, I DON'T THINK I WOULD EVER HAD DREAMED OF DOING HAD I HAD ANOTHER CHANCE AT IT. I FELT TRAPPED!

I THINK FOR MY DAD, SUFFERING FROM DEPRESSION, LIVING A LIFE STYLE OF ABUSE HIMSELF, LIVING WITH AN ALCOHOLIC FATHER, I'M SURE IT MADE IT HARD FOR HIM TO COPE WITH HAVING HIS OWN KIDS. MAYBE IT JUST OVERWHELMED HIM TO THE POINT, HE DIDN'T KNOW WHAT TO DO ANYMORE OR DIDN'T KNOW HOW TO. IT WAS GROWING HARDER AND HARDER AS TIME WENT ON FOR HIM TO GET A JOB. HE TRIED MANY WORK AT HOME JOBS, BUT ONE UPSET CUSTOMER OR ONE BAD SALE, HE'D THROW HIS HANDS UP, QUIT AND SIT AND WALLOW IN SELF PITY. HE JUST COULD NOT HANDLE IT. I'M SURE THE ADDED STRESS FROM MY MOM DIDN'T HELP MATTERS ANY, BUT SHE HERSELF WAS CRYING OUT FOR HELP. SHE HAD TO WORK IN A FACTORY, SOMETIMES 10-12 HOUR DAYS, COME HOME AND HELP TAKE CARE OF 3 KIDS, A HOUSE, SUPPORTING THE HOUSEHOLD ON LITTLE WAGES SHE EARNED, HER FEET ACHING TO THE POINT, SHE DEVELOPED CORNS AND ENDED UP HAVING FOOT SURGERY THAT GOT SCREWED UP, BUT HAD TO CONTINUE WORKING AND OFTEN TIMES SHE LASHED OUT TOO. I'M SURE THERE WERE MANY DAYS SHE

CRIED OUT IN PAIN WHILE ON THE JOB, WANTED TO QUIT, BUT SOMEHOW FOUND THE STRENGTH, NO DOUBT IN GOD TO CONTINUE ON.

FOR 27 YEARS SHE STRUGGLED WITH THE JOB UNTIL SHE DEVELOPED A WORK RELATED INJURY AND HAD TO GO ON DISABILITY, EVENTUALLY LOSING HER JOB. MY DAD JUST SANK FURTHER BY HER NAGGING, AND THE FACT SHE COULDN'T WORK NOW, HE STARTED SMOKING MORE, SAT AROUND ALL THE TIME IN HIS PJ'S, RARELY GETTING DRESSED, HE DIDN'T EVEN HAVE MUCH OF A DESIRE TO DRIVE OR LEAVE THE HOUSE, HE JUST PLAIN DIDN'T WANT TO BE BOTHERED WITH THINGS. HE EVEN TOLD MY MOM TO HANDLE THE DISCIPLINE AFTER HITTING THE WALL AND BREAKING A FINGER TRYING TO GET TO MY YOUNGER BROTHER WHO WAS 13 AT THE TIME, FOR DOING SOMETHING WRONG. MY DAD WENT TO HIT HIM AND MY BROTHER DUCKED AND MY DAD HIT THE WALL PUTTING A HOLE IN IT. HE REFUSED TO CORRECT US KIDS AFTER THAT. MANY TIMES AS I LAY IN BED, I'D HEAR DISHES BREAKING AS MY PARENTS WOULD BE INTO AN ARGUMENT. SOMETIMES THEY WOULD COME BARRELING INTO OUR ROOMS YELLING AT US BECAUSE WE DIDN'T GET THIS DONE OR THAT DONE, OR WE MISBEHAVED.
THERE WOULD BE TIMES IF MY MOM WORKED THE NIGHT SHIFT, WE'D ALREADY BE ASLEEP AND THEY'D START IN, BURSTING IN OUR ROOMS AND WAKING US UP SCARING US TO THE POINT IT WAS HARD TO GO BACK TO SLEEP. OFTEN TIMES WE WERE AFRAID TO GO TO BED, WONDERING IF WE HAD DONE SOMETHING WRONG AND THEY WOULD COME AND WAKE US UP. WE LIVED IN FEAR.

I REMEMBER MY DAD HATING NOISE WHEN HE WAS TRYING TO SLEEP, GOT WOKE UP ONE DAY WHEN WE CAME IN FROM SCHOOL. THAT NIGHT AFTER WE WENT TO BED AND FELL ASLEEP, HE CAME IN WITH ICE CUBES AND PUT THEM DOWN OUR BACKS, SAYING THAT'S FOR WAKING ME UP, HOW DO YOU LIKE IT? IT WAS GETTING TO BE MORE THAN I COULD HANDLE, I MADE EXCUSES AT TIMES OF HAVING TO WORK, JUST SO I COULD GET OUT OF THE HOUSE. I'D GO TO A GIRLFRIENDS AND HANG, HOWEVER, EVEN THAT ENDED IN A DISASTER, AS ONE DAY I WAS DESPERATE FOR MONEY, MY CAR HAD CAUGHT ON FIRE AND BURNED UP, I ENDED UP GETTING ANOTHER, BUT MY PARENTS COULDN'T PAY FOR IT, SO THEY TOOK OUT A LOAN WHICH I HAD TO PAY, AND WITH NOW HAVING TO GET FULL COVERAGE INSURANCE IT TOOK MOST OF MY CHECK. I ENDED UP SEEING HER MOM'S CHECKBOOK OUT ONE DAY AND SO I STOLE SOME CHECKS AND FORGED HER NAME. I WAS EVENTUALLY CAUGHT, I HAD TO MAKE RESTITUTION, BUT IT ENDED MY FRIENDSHIP I DEVELOPED OVER THE LAST YEAR AND MY MOM'S FRIENDSHIP WITH HER MOM TOO AS SHE HAD WORKED WITH THE LADY. I DIDN'T GET ANY TIME OR ANYTHING, I WAS GRATEFUL, BUT THE HUMILIATION OF WHAT I HAD DONE, REALLY STUCK WITH ME AND TOOK ME A LONG WHILE TO GET OVER, ESPECIALLY BETRAYING A FRIENDS TRUST LIKE THAT. NOW I WAS A THIEF TO BOOT!! I PRAYED IT DID NOT GET AROUND.

SOON I GAVE UP MY JOB AT BURGER CHEF WHERE WE WORKED TOGETHER AND LANDED A JOB AT WOOLWORTH, THE GUY I WAS DATING AT THE TIME

WAS MY CRUISING BUDDY WHO HAD A RED JEEP. WE WENT CRUISING ON THE WEEKENDS AND OFTEN WENT TO THE LOCKINGTON DAM TO DRINK, THOSE WERE SOME FUN CRUISING DAYS. HE EVEN TAUGHT ME HOW TO DRIVE HIS JEEP WHICH WAS A STICK SHIFT, I THOUGHT IT WAS SO COOL AND OFTEN DROVE IT, BUT ONLY IN THE COUNTRY, I WASN'T READY FOR CITY DRIVING.

AS CHRISTMAS CAME AND WENT AND SCHOOL WAS BACK IN SESSION AFTER THE HOLIDAY BREAK, I LEARNED THAT I WOULD HAVE ENOUGH CREDITS BY THE END OF THE SCHOOL YEAR TO GRADUATE. I WAS ESTACTIC. YOU SEE TECHNICALLY I WAS TO GRADUATE IN 1981, BUT WITH FAILING ONE YEAR IT MOVED IT TO 1982. BUT NOW I LEARNED BY CRAMMING 2 YEARS INTO ONE, I WOULD GRADUATE ON TIME WHEN I WAS SUPPOSE TOO, WHAT AN ACCOMPLISHMENT, SOMETHING DEFINITELY TO BE PROUD OF. THOSE HOPES THOUGH WERE ALMOST SHATTERED WHEN A MONTH BEFORE GRADUATION, I HAD TO HAVE MY TONSILS REMOVED. I WAS TO MISS THE REST OF THE SCHOOL YEAR. I THOUGHT NOOOOOOOOO, I'M SO CLOSE, BUT LUCKILY I WAS ALLOWED TO MAKE UP MY WORK, WHICH ENDED UP LOWERING MY GRADE AS I MISSED THE FINAL EXAMS, BUT I STILL HAD ENOUGH CREDITS AND I GRADUATED. OH HAPPY DAY!! I WAS NOW OFFICIALLY OUT OF SCHOOL, WE HAD A PARTY AND I RECEIVED LOTS OF CASH, BUT I STILL WAS ONLY 17 AND NOT OFFICIALLY AN ADULT, SO I COULDN'T MOVE OUT. I WAS PRAYING THE SUMMER WENT BY QUICK AND SEPTEMBER WOULD SOON BE HERE!!

MY ADULT YEARS

FINALLY IT WAS MY 18TH BIRTHDAY, WOO-HOO OFFICIALLY AN ADULT!! TIME TO MOVE OUT!! ON MY 18TH BIRTHDAY WHILE WORKING AT WOOLWORTH, MY BOYFRIEND, THE ONE WITH THE JEEP, DECORATED MY CAR ALL UP FOR MY BIRTHDAY, IT WAS AWESOME, BUT SOON AFTER THAT DAY MY BOYFRIEND WAS GOING THROUGH SOME STRUGGLES AT HOME AND DIDN'T WANT TO BRING ME INTO IT, OF COURSE I DIDN'T KNOW THAT AT THE TIME. HE HAD ALL OF A SUDDEN QUIT CALLING ME, QUIT COMING AROUND, WHEN I CALLED I WAS TOLD HE WASN'T THERE, YET I WOULD DRIVE BY THE HOUSE AND HE'D BE THERE, I COULDN'T UNDERSTAND WHAT I DID WRONG, AND YES I BLAMED MYSELF. EVENTUALLY WE BROKE UP AND ALL MY FRIENDS SEEMED TO HAVE SCATTERED, I WAS SADDENED, MAYBE WORD HAD GOTTEN OUT FROM LISA WHO'S FAMILY I HAD DONE WRONG AND I WASN'T TRUSTED. I BEGAN TO SINK WITHIN MYSELF AND MY SELF ESTEEM WAS SO LOW, I FELT LIKE DYING, UNTIL YET ANOTHER GUY CAME ALONG.

I MET GEORGE AT WOOLWORTH WHERE I WORKED IN THE COFFEE SHOP AND HE WAS THE SPORTING GOODS MANAGER. IT WAS APPROACHING CHRISTMAS 1981 AND HE WAS THROWING A BIG PARTY AT HIS PLACE, I THOUGHT HE WAS GOING WITH SOMEONE SO I ACCEPTED A DATE TO ANOTHER PARTY BY HIS FRIEND TIM. TIM AND I ENDED UP AT GEORGE'S HOUSE ANYWAY, ALTHOUGH I DIDN'T KNOW IT WAS

GEORGE'S PLACE AND AFTER MAKING OUT IN THE CAR WITH TIM WITH THE OTHER'S WATCHING OUT THE WINDOW, WE WENT INSIDE. WE DRANK AND PARTIED A WHILE AND HAD A GREAT TIME. I HAD LOST SIGHT OF TIM THOUGH AND WENT THRU THE ROOMS LOOKING FOR HIM WHEN SOMEONE SAID TIM WAS GONE. I SAID WELL THAT'S NICE, WONDER WHY HE LEFT. NO ONE HAD AN ANSWER, JUST WENT ABOUT THEIR BUSINESS.

I WENT TO THE RESTROOM ONLY TO BE DRAGGED INTO THE BEDROOM BY GEORGE AND WELL, THERE YOU HAVE IT. I THINK I WAS SET UP BIG TIME. YOU THINK? FROM THAT POINT ON GEORGE AND I STARTED DATING, ABOUT 3 MONTHS AFTER THAT NIGHT, I DISCOVERED I WAS PREGNANT WITH OUR FIRST CHILD. I HAD QUIT WOOLWORTH AT THAT TIME AND WAS WORKING IN A FACTORY WHEN I HAD BECOME ILL, AT FIRST I THOUGHT IT WAS DUE TO THE PLASTIC IN THE FACTORY, BUT SOON DISCOVERED THE TRUTH, I WAS ABOUT 6 TO 8 WEEKS PREGNANT.

GEORGE SEEMED OK, BUT OH BOY, MY DAD WAS NOT SO ENTHUSIASTIC, I SOON MOVED OUT OF MY PARENTS AND IN WITH GEORGE, WE GOT A NICE PLACE IN THE COUNTRY FROM A LADY MY MOM KNEW AND THUS WE STARTED OUR LIFE TOGETHER. NO MORE PARTIES, NO MORE CHANGING GUYS. IT WAS TIME TO GET MYSELF TOGETHER AND CONCENTRATE ON THE NEW RESPONSIBILITY OF HAVING A BABY. AFTER ALL I WAS 18 NOW AND HAD LOOKED FORWARD TO GETTING OUT ON MY OWN RIGHT? WELL MY FAMILY SOON GOT USED TO THE IDEA OF ME HAVING A BABY, THEIR FIRST GRANDCHILD, I WAS THANKFUL FOR THEIR SUPPORT, BUT WHAT A WAY TO MEET GEORGE, UP TO THIS POINT

MY PARENTS HADN'T MET HIM, IT DIDN'T TAKE MY DAD LONG TO START NAGGING ABOUT NUTRITION, AND GETTING REST. I'M SURE IT WAS JUST BEING CONCERNED FOR HIS FIRST GRANDCHILD, BUT I ACTUALLY SENSED EXCITEMENT AND MAYBE SAW A TWINKLE IN HIS EYE I HADN'T SEEN BEFORE. COULD THIS CHILD ACTUALLY TURN MY DAD AROUND? GIVE HIM HOPE AND BRING HIM OUT OF A DEPRESSIVE STATE. I ONLY PRAYED IT WOULD.

I SOON QUIT WORK, AS IT GOT TO BE TOO MUCH WITH BEING PREGNANT, THE MORNING SICKNESS WAS CRAZY, BUT OTHER THAN THAT WAS DOING PRETTY GOOD. THE BABY WAS GROWING ON SCHEDULE AND I LEARNED I WAS DUE AROUND THE 6TH OF DECEMBER 1982. IT WAS IN MY 7TH MONTH AND I REALLY STARTED SHOWING, THOSE HOT SUMMER MONTHS MADE IT ESPECIALLY MISERABLE. MY HORMONES WAS OUT OF BALANCE, I WAS HAVING MOOD SWINGS, REALLY GREW SENSITIVE AND CRIED OUT OF THE BLUE. I DIDN'T UNDERSTAND WHAT WAS HAPPENING TOO ME AND DIDN'T HAVE MY MOM TO EXPLAIN TO ME WHAT WAS GOING ON WITH ALL THE CHANGES I WAS EXPERIENCING. I JUST HAD INSTINCT I SUPPOSE AND WORKED THROUGH IT. GEORGE, BEING MARRIED BEFORE KNEW SOME THINGS, SO I RELIED A LOT ON THAT AND CALLS TO THE DOCTOR, BUT STILL FELT LIKE AN EMOTIONAL WRECK.

I WAS NOW 19 AND AS THE TIME GREW CLOSER TO MY EXPECTED DELIVERY DATE, WE WENT TO STAY AT MY PARENTS. WITH GEORGE WORKING A LOT AND ME BEING IN THE COUNTRY WITH WINTER COMING A LITTLE EARLY THAT YEAR, HE DIDN'T WANT TO TAKE

ANY CHANCES OF ME GOING INTO LABOR. I BECAME EVEN MORE MOODY AND UNCOMFORTABLE.

DEC.6TH CAME AND WENT WITH NO BABY, I WAS GETTING FRUSTRATED. I WAS AT THE POINT I WANTED THIS BABY OUT. WE DIDN'T KNOW WHAT WE WERE HAVING AS THE ULTRASOUND DIDN'T SHOW US ANYTHING. SO I JUST CALLED IT BABY. AT MY NEXT OB APPOINTMENT AROUND THE 13TH OF DEC. THEY TOLD ME THEY'D GIVE ME ANOTHER WEEK AND IF I DIDN'T HAVE THE BABY BY THEN, THEY WOULD INDUCE, THEY DIDN'T LIKE FOR YOU TO GO TO FAR OVER YOUR DUE DATE AND I WOULD BE ALMOST 2 WEEKS.THE WEEK SEEMED TO DRAG BY, I WAS GETTING SO UNCOMFORTABLE BUT YET EXCITED. I WENT TO THE ROOM I HAD PREPARED AND GOING THRU ALL THE LAST MINUTE THINGS MAKING SURE I HAD ENOUGH THINGS FOR OUR BABY.

FINALLY ON SUNDAY DEC 19TH 1982 AT 4:30 AM I WENT INTO LABOR. LITTLE DID I KNOW THAT FOR THE NEXT 14 HOURS I WOULD LAY AT MY PARENTS IN SO MUCH PAIN. ALTHOUGH MY CONTRACTIONS WERE NOT VERY CONSISTENT, I WAS GROWING MORE AND MORE UNCOMFORTABLE AS EACH MINUTE WENT BY UNTIL FINALLY, AROUND 6 PM THAT EVENING THE CONTRACTIONS REACHED 20 MINUTES APART, AND FOR US IT WAS CONSISTENT ENOUGH TO HEAD FOR THE HOSPITAL. MY BAG WAS ALREADY PACKED SO OFF WE WENT. WE GOT ALL CHECKED IN AND GOT SETTLED IN BED AND WE WAITED. WE WAITED AND WE WAITED AND NOTHING. I THOUGHT NOOOOOOO, WHATEVER YOU DO, DON'T SEND ME HOME. I WAS REASSURED THAT I WAS ALREADY OVERDUE SO I WAS

HAVING THIS BABY. IT WAS NOW WELL AFTER MIDNIGHT ON MONDAY DEC 20TH 1982, THE CONTRACTIONS WAS GETTING CLOSER TOGETHER AND I WAS GETTING SICK, AND I WAS DEMANDING GEORGE TO MAKE THE DOC TAKE THE BABY CESARIAN AS I COULDN'T STAND THE PAIN ANY LONGER, IT HAD BEEN ALMOST 21 HOURS OF LABOR ALREADY, I WAS DONE!!

WHEN 7 AM CAME AND MY WATER HAD NOT BROKEN, THEY WHEELED ME DOWN TO EX-RAY TO SEE WHAT WAS GOING ON, AS SOON AS I GOT IN THE ELEVATOR, MY WATER BROKE. EVERYTHING WAS OK BY THE XRAY, JUST ONE STUBBORN BABY. THEY PREDICTED BY THE HEART BEAT THAT I WOULD HAVE A GIRL, BUT WE STILL WEREN'T SURE. FINALLY AT 8:30 I WAS FULLY DIALATED. BECAUSE OF THE FACT THAT GEORGE AND I WASN'T MARRIED, THEY WOULDN'T ALLOW HIM IN THE DELIVERY ROOM SO FROM THIS POINT, I WAS ON MY OWN AND I WAS SCARED. THEY MOVED ME TO ANOTHER TABLE, GOT ME ALL PREPPED AND BY THIS TIME I WAS READY TO PUSH, THEY DIDN'T WANT ME TO PUSH YET AND LOST THE BABY'S HEARTBEAT, I THOUGHT MY GOODNESS I KILLED MY BABY. I STARTED CRYING, I CAN'T DO THIS. AT THE POINT OF DELIVERY THEY HAD TO DO AN EPISIOTOMY. IT'S WHERE THEY CUT YOU TO MAKE IT EASIER FOR THE BABY TO BE DELIVERED SO NO TISSUES GET RUPTURED. AFTER DOING THAT AND PUSHING, MY BABY WAS FINALLY BORN. AT 8:58 AM ON MONDAY DEC.20TH 1982, I GAVE BIRTH TO A GIRL AFTER 29 AND ½ HOURS OF LABOR WEIGHING 8 LBS 2 OZ. I WAS SO GLAD IT WAS OVER. THEY GOT ME ALL CLEANED UP, 24 STITCHES IT TOOK TO SEW ME AS SHE TORE ME

DURING BIRTH, THEN I WAS WHEELED TO MY ROOM WITH OUR NEW BUNDLE OF JOY, ANGELA JOLENE.

IT WAS STRANGE BEING A NEW MOM, I WAS 19 WHEN ANGELA WAS BORN AND KNEW THERE MUCH RESPONSIBILITY THAT LAY AHEAD. I WAS RELEASED FROM THE HOSPITAL ON CHRISTMAS EVE, SO WE DECIDED TO STAY AT MY PARENTS FOR A COUPLE OF DAYS TO GET THROUGH THE HOLIDAYS. WE DIDN'T HAVE A CRIB OR ANYTHING THERE, SO MY DAD TOOK A DEEP DRESSER DRAWER THAT THEY HAD AND MADE IT UP INTO A NICE LITTLE BED. IT WAS GOOD TO SEE MY DAD INVOLVED AND HE SEEMED HAPPY, BUT I COULDN'T HELP WONDERING IN THE BACK OF MY MIND, HOW LONG WOULD IT LAST? I KNOW IT WAS NEGATIVE THINKING, AND I ALWAYS PRAYED MY DAD WOULD SNAP OUT OF THIS TRANCE HE WAS IN, BUT I COULDN'T SHAKE THE FEELING. THINGS WERE ALWAYS UP, DOWN, UP, DOWN IN OUR HOUSE, AND WHAT I WANTED MORE THAN ANYTHING WAS SOME STABILITY, AND I PRAYED HAVING ANGELA WOULD BRING JUST THAT.

ANGELA QUICKLY BECAME THE APPLE OF MY DAD'S EYE AND HE SEEMED PLEASED TO FINALLY BE A GRANDFATHER, ANGIE BEING THEIR FIRST. ANGIE WAS EARLY IN LEARNING THINGS AND IT WAS FUN TO SEE MY DAD SHARE IN THE JOY OF WATCHING HER GROW AND LEARN. WHAT WAS SUPPOSE TO BE A COUPLE OF DAYS STAYING AT MY PARENTS, TURNED INTO A COUPLE OF WEEKS AND SO MY DAD GOT PRETTY ATTACHED TO HER. I WOULD BE A LITTLE SAD TO GO AND PRAYED MY DAD WOULD BE OK, BUT I WAS EAGER TO GET BACK TO OUR HOUSE. FINALLY THE DAY CAME AND WE WENT BACK HOME, WHICH WAS ON THE

OTHER SIDE OF FLETCHER, ABOUT A 20 MINUTE DRIVE. IT WAS GOOD TO BE HOME AND DIDN'T TAKE US LONG TO GET SETTLED INTO OUR ROUTINE. WE HAD A VISIT FROM GEORGE'S MOM, WHO RESIDED IN A NURSING HOME. THIS WAS THE FIRST I HAD MET HER AND SHE WASN'T DOING WELL AT ALL. I BELIEVE SHE HAD DEMENTIA, SO WHEN HOLDING ANGIE SHE WAS A LITTLE CARELESS AND I GOT NERVOUS. SHE ENDED UP SPENDING THE NIGHT WITH US AND ABOUT 5:00 AM I WOKE WITH A START TO THE SOUND OF ANGIE CRYING. IT WAS STRANGE BECAUSE SHE WAS PRETTY GOOD ABOUT SLEEPING THROUGH THE NIGHT AND WAKING ABOUT 7:00 AM. WHEN I DIDN'T FIND HER IN HER BED, I WENT OUT TO THE LIVING ROOM AND FOUND GEORGE'S MOM WITH ANGIE. HOW DID SHE GET HER I WONDERED, ANGIE'S CRIB WAS IN OUR BEDROOM. BUT I SHOVED THE THOUGHT OUT AND QUICKLY GOT HER AS I WAS AFRAID SHE WOULD FORGET SHE HAD HER AND DROP HER.

GEORGE'S PARENTS DIVORCED WHEN GEORGE WAS YOUNG AND HIS FATHER WENT TO LIVE IN ARIZONA. HE SUFFERED FROM EMPHYSEMA AND THE WEATHER WAS DRYER THERE AND EASIER ON HIM TO BREATHE. GEORGE MAINLY GREW UP WITHOUT A DAD AND HAD TO WORK EARLY TO HELP SUPPORT THEIR MOM ALL THE WHILE GEORGE GOING THROUGH SCHOOL. SO FOR GEORGE IT WAS THE HIGHLIGHT OF HIS LIFE WHEN HIS DAD CALLED US AFTER HEARING THE NEWS OF ANGELA BEING BORN TO CATCH UP ON LIFE AND ENDED UP GETTING OUR ADDRESS SO HE COULD SEND US 20.00 TO HELP WITH SOME EXPENSES. WE WERE GRATEFUL, AS WITH GEORGE THE ONLY ONE WORKING AND RENT AND ALL THOSE OTHER BILLS,

NOT TO MENTION HOW EXPENSIVE A NEW BABY WAS, IT SURE CAME IN REAL HANDY.

LATER THAT DAY GEORGE TOOK HIS MOM BACK TO THE NURSING HOME, DROPPED ME OFF AT MY PARENTS HOUSE AND THEN WENT OFF TO HIS JOB AT WOOLWORTH'S. THAT DAY WAS THE FIRST SINCE ANGIE WAS BORN THE MONTH BEFORE THAT MY DAD WAS DOWN IN THE DUMPS. I THOUGHT OH BOY, WHAT HAD I WALKED INTO TODAY? THE WHOLE TIME I WAS THERE, HE WAS DRILLING ME ON HOW THINGS WERE WITH ANGIE, ARE YOU DOING THIS, FEEDING HER ENOUGH, BURPING HER RIGHT, I THOUGHT FOR PETE'S SAKE, I KNOW I'M A NEW MOM BUT GIVE ME SOME CREDIT. I'M SURE HE WAS BEING A LITTLE OVER PROTECTIVE AND WAS JUST A NATURAL RESPONSE, BUT AFTER THAT BEGAN THE PHONE CALLS. ALL SEEMED TO BE LATE AT NIGHT AS WE WERE ABOUT TO GO TO BED. HE'D BE UP DRINKING AS HE ALWAYS HAD DONE, HAD A LITTLE TOO MUCH AND THEN THOUGHTS OVER TOOK HIM, AND HE WAS ON THE PHONE, RANTING.

IN FEBRUARY OF 1983, ANGIE WAS ABOUT 2 MONTHS OLD GEORGE HAD GOTTEN A DIFFERENT JOB IN GREENVILLE, AFTER LOSING HIS JOB AT WOOLWORTH'S. THINGS WERE TIGHT, BUT WE FOUND A NICE PLACE AND GEORGE HAD MORE FAMILY MEMBERS THERE AND LOT OF WILLINGNESS TO HELP US OUT IF NEEDED. I MYSELF HAD BOUTS OF TIREDNESS, AND FOUND IT HARD SOMETIMES TO CARE FOR ANGIE, ESPECIALLY DURING THE WEE HOURS OF THE MORNING. I WAS NOT A MORNING PERSON AND STILL TO THIS DAY NOT MUCH OF A MORNING PERSON

ALTHOUGH I HAD TO LEARN TO BE. GEORGE HELPED WHEN HE COULD, BUT HE NEEDED TO WORK, SO HE WAS LIMITED, SO I WAS GRATEFUL FOR FRIENDS TO HELP. THIS LADY, WHO HAD GROWN UP WITH GEORGE, COULDN'T BEAR CHILDREN OF HER OWN, SO SHE WAS ONLY TOO GLAD TO HELP ME CARE FOR ANGELA.

WE WERE GETTING SETTLED IN OUR NEW HOME, BUT THE WEARINESS WAS GROWING MORE INTENSE, SOMETIMES TO THE POINT IT WAS HARD TO KEEP MY EYES OPEN. ANGIE WAS SUCH A SMART BABY AND LEARNING THINGS SO EARLY AND I FELT I WAS BEING CHEATED IN EXPERIENCING THINGS WITH HER. ALL I COULD DO SOMETIMES WAS TURN ON CARTOONS, PUT HER IN HER PLAYPEN WITH SOME TOYS, MAKE SURE SHE WAS CHANGED AND HAD A BOTTLE, AND I'D FALL ON THE COUCH FOR A NAP. I HAD BEEN TO THE DOCTOR FOR A CHECK-UP AND THEY SUGGESTED IRON PILLS AND CHANGE IN DIET WHICH SEEMED TO HELP SOME, BUT I STILL FOUND MYSELF, IN THE SAME ROUTINE, PUT ANGIE IN THE PLAYPEN, MAKE SURE SHE'S FED AND CHANGED THEN OFF TO SLEEPYTOWN FOR ME.

IT AMAZED ME AT HOW SMART ANGIE HAD BECOME OVER THE NEXT COUPLE OF MONTHS, SHE WAS ABOUT 4 ½ MONTHS OLD AT THIS TIME AND COULD SAY A FEW WORDS, HAD HER FIRST TOOTH AND WAS TRYING TO SIT UP. I SAT AND WONDERED WHERE THE TIME HAD WENT, AS SHE WAS GROWING SO FAST. IT BECAME EVIDENT, HOWEVER, THAT HER FORMULA WAS NO LONGER SATISFYING HER SO WE STARTED HER ON BABY FOOD. THE DOCTOR'S DON'T LIKE WHEN YOU DO THIS, BUT IF THEY'RE HUNGRY AND WE'RE THE

71

ONES DEALING WITH THEM, WHAT DO YOU DO?? THEY MADE THESE INFANT FEEDERS THAT YOU PUT BABY FOOD IN AND THEY CAN SUCK THEIR FOOD RATHER THAN BEING SPOONFED, I WAS EVER SO GRATEFUL FOR THESE, ESPECIALLY WHEN THE DAYS CONTINUED OF HAVING NO ENERGY TO DEAL WITH SPOON FEEDING. THERE WERE TIMES I COULDN'T EVEN FUNCTION IT SEEMED AND I KNEW SOMETHING HAD TO BE WRONG BUT COULDN'T PUT MY FINGER ON IT. IT WAS LIKE I WAS ON DRUGS OR SOMETHING, BUT I KNEW I WASN'T. THE DOCS ALWAYS SAID INCREASE FLUIDS, EXERCISE, MAYBE GET SOMEONE TO CARE FOR THE BABY OVERNIGHT SO YOU CAN GET A GOOD NIGHTS SLEEP. ALL SEEMED LIKE GOOD ADVICE, BUT IT WASN'T HELPING ME.

GEORGE TRIED TO HELP, BUT THINGS WERE GETTING TIGHT AND HE HAD TO LAND A SECOND JOB, THIS TIME AT A PIZZA PLACE IN PIQUA, SO WHEN HE WORKED THERE, I OFTEN WENT AND SPENT TIME AT MY PARENTS, BUT OF COURSE ONCE THERE, IT WASN'T LONG BEFORE MY DAD STARTED NAGGING ABOUT WHAT I WAS DOING WITH ANGIE, I WAS LIKE PLEASE LAY OFF WOULD YA? I'VE BEEN EXTREMELY TIRED. I WONDERED IF THERE WOULD EVER BE AN END.

WHEN ANGIE WAS ABOUT 6 OR 7 MONTHS OLD, I SUSPECTED I WAS PREGNANT AGAIN, I WAS FEELING EVEN MORE OVERWHELMED AND AT TIMES FELT LIKE CRAWLING IN A HOLE SOMEWHERE. IT WASN'T THE FACT OF NOT WANTING ANOTHER BABY, BUT THE TIMING WAS WAY OFF. OUR FINANCES, MY DAD, ME NOT BEING MARRIED. I KNEW WE WERE WRONG FOR LIVING TOGETHER, FOR WE WERE COMMITTING

ADULTERY, BUT GEORGE HAD BEEN MARRIED BEFORE AND HAD A CHILD AND THEIR DIVORCE WASN'T FINALIZED, SO WE WERE KIND OF STUCK, WE HAD NO MONEY TO PAY FOR A DIVORCE AND I WASN'T EVEN SURE AT THE TIME I WANTED TO BE MARRIED, EVEN IF HE WAS DIVORCED. IT SEEMED EASIER TO LIVE TOGETHER, IF THINGS DIDN'T GO RIGHT, JUST PICK UP AND LEAVE, NO STRINGS ATTACHED, JUST LIKE I HAD LEARNED GROWING UP. WITH ALREADY HAVING ONE CHILD OUT OF WEDLOCK, IT SEEMED A SHAME TO HAVE ANOTHER AND GOD ONLY KNEW WHAT MY DAD WOULD SAY, I'D NEVER HEAR THE END OF IT. HE ALWAYS THOUGHT AT SOME POINT GEORGE AND I WOULD BE MARRIED ONCE HE GOT DIVORCED, AND HE ACCEPTED THE FACT OF ME HAVING ONE CHILD, BUT ANOTHER? AND SO SOON? I WAS KIND OF EXCITED THOUGH AT THE THOUGHT OF ANOTHER CHILD, BUT AT THE SAME TIME, HAD A SINKING FEELING IN THE PIT OF MY STOMACH OF HOW WOULD WE MANAGE, I MEAN WE WERE MAKING IT WITH HAVING ONE CHILD BUT TWO?? I WASN'T EVEN 20 YET, AND HOW IN THE WORLD WAS I GOING TO TELL MY PARENTS, MY DAD WOULD HIT THE ROOF, I JUST KNEW IT.

LATER THAT WEEK WAS MY BIRTHDAY, I'D BE 20 AND MY PARENTS INVITED US OVER FOR DINNER, IT WAS A NICE EVENING AND I THOUGHT IT WOULD BE APPROPRIATE SINCE MY DAD SEEMED TO BE IN A GOOD MOOD TO BREAK THE NEWS OF HAVING ANOTHER CHILD ON THE WAY. AFTER WE FINISHED EATING AND CLEANED UP, I DECIDED TO BREAK THE NEWS TO MY PARENTS THAT I THOUGHT I WAS PREGNANT. IT WAS SILENT FOR THE LONGEST TIME. I MEAN SO QUIET, YOU COULD ABSOLUTELY HEAR A PIN

DROP. I THOUGHT, SOMEBODY SPEAK, SAY SOMETHING. WHEN I LOOKED AT MY DAD, I COULD TELL HE WAS BOILING; HIS FACE WAS GETTING RED, LIKE IT HAD JUST SUNK IN WHAT I SAID. HE HIT THE ROOF ALRIGHT, TO THE POINT I THOUGHT IT WOULD FLY RIGHT OFF THE HOUSE, HE YELLED SO LOUD. ANGIE WOKE UP AND WAS CRYING, IT WAS TOTAL CHAOS.

HE LOOKED AT BOTH GEORGE AND ME AND SAID WE WAS TO GET MARRIED, ONE CHILD OUT OF WEDLOCK WAS ENOUGH TO HANDLE, BUT NOT TWO, AND IF WE DIDN'T GET MARRIED HE WOULD TAKE A SHOT GUN AFTER GEORGE AND MAKE US GET MARRIED. HE INFORMED US HE WOULD HAVE NOTHING TO DO WITH THIS BASTARD CHILD AND TO NOT BRING IT AROUND, THAT IT WAS NOT HIS GRANDCHILD AND WANTED NO PART OF THE BABY'S LIFE. I WAS SO CRUSHED. I KNEW IT WASN'T RIGHT LIVING THE LIFESTYLE I WAS, BUT I HAD INTENTIONS OF MAKING IT RIGHT, EVEN THOUGH I WAS STILL UNSURE OF MARRIAGE. I FELT LIKE A PUPPET, ALWAYS BEING PULLED HERE AND THERE BY STRINGS, AND YET AGAIN WANTING TO BE LIKED AND AT PEACE, NEVER KNOWING WHAT TO DO TO MAKE PEOPLE HAPPY, ALL I HAD EVER KNOWN FROM MEN WAS SEX AND ABUSE OF SOME SORT AND YET THOUGHT THERE HAD TO BE BETTER THINGS, BUT YET, BETTER THINGS SEEM TO ELUDE ME, SO I SUBMITTED TO ALL KINDS OF THINGS JUST TO FIT IN AND BE LIKED OR PUT AN END TO THE ENDLESS, NEGATIVE THINGS INSTEAD OF LOOKING OUT FOR ME, I THREW MYSELF INTO BEING A PEOPLE PLEASER AND I WAS DRAINED. THE PRESSURE WAS ON NOW, I NEVER FELT SO OVERWHELMED. I WANTED TO JUST DIE, AS MY NERVES WERE SHOT.

I'M NOT SURE HOW WE GOT THROUGH THE WEEKEND I WAS STILL NUMB FROM MY DAD'S OUTBURST, WHAT A BIRTHDAY THAT WAS. I WAS PRAYING THAT WHEN I WENT TO THE DOCTOR'S THE NEXT MORNING SHE WOULD TELL ME SHE WAS WRONG, THAT I WASN'T PREGNANT, NOT THAT I DIDN'T WANT THE BABY, BUT I WAS AFRAID MY DAD WOULD LIVE UP TO WHAT HE SAID AND I DIDN'T WANT THAT FOR THIS BABY. ANGIE WOULD BE GETTING THINGS AND THE OTHER ONE BEING TREATED LIKE AN OUTCAST, WHAT KIND OF LIFE IS THAT FOR A CHILD? BY GOLLY I WOULDN'T ALLOW IT, IT WAS ENOUGH TO GET THROUGH THE WAY I WAS RAISED AND TREATED, I SWORE FROM THAT DAY FORWARD I WOULD DO DIFFERENTLY WITH MY KIDS!!

I DON'T THINK I SLEPT WELL THAT NIGHT CAUSE WHEN I WOKE THE NEXT MORNING, I COULD BARELY GET OUT OF BED. IT FELT AS IF ALL MY MUSCLES WERE TIED AND I ACHED. I NOTICED I HAD STARTED BLEEDING AFTER NOT HAVING A PERIOD FOR THE LAST 2 MONTHS, AND I HAD WONDERED IF THE THOUGHT OF BEING PREGNANT HAD BEEN A DREAM, AND I UPSET MY PARENTS FOR NOTHING BY OPENING MY MOUTH. I HAD MY APPOINTMENT LATER THAT DAY WITH THE GYNECOLOGIST, SO I WOULD DEFINITELY GET SOME MUCH NEEDED ANSWERS. ENOUGH WAS ENOUGH WITH ME BEING SO TIRED AND ACHY ALL THE TIME. I WAS GLAD GEORGE WAS OFF THAT DAY SO HE COULD GO WITH ME, MY APPOINTMENT WAS OUT OF TOWN AND I WAS IN NO SHAPE TO DRIVE, NOT TO MENTION THAT I RECEIVED A CALL FROM OUR FRIEND WHO HAD AN IDEA I WAS PREGNANT AND WAS UPSET TOO. I'M

NOT SURE WHY, UNLESS JEALOUSLY WAS CREEPING IN BECAUSE SHE COULDN'T BEAR CHILDREN, AND I HAD ONE WITH POSSIBLY ANOTHER ON THE WAY.

WE FINALLY GOT TO MY APPOINTMENT, AND IT WAS CONFIRMED I WAS PREGNANT. SHE WANTED TO DO SOME TESTS AND DO A PELVIC EXAM AS WELL, BECAUSE OF THE FACT I WAS BLEEDING. AS I UNDRESSED, I BEGAN TO CRY, LORD WHAT'S GOING ON? WHAT IS HAPPENING TO ME? THE DOCTOR CAME IN AND SEEN ME CRYING AND ASKED ME, AREN'T YOU EXCITED? DON'T YOU WANT TO BE PREGNANT? I CHOKED BACK THE TEARS AND LIED BY SAYING OH NO, NOTHING LIKE THAT, WE'RE VERY EXCITED, JUST SURPRISED US, AND MY PARENTS WON'T BE VERY PLEASED. THE DOCTOR DECIDED TO DO AN ULTRASOUND TO SEE WHAT WAS GOING ON. AFTER THE EXAM AND EVERYTHING WAS FINISHED, SHE ASKED ME QUESTIONS ABOUT HOW I'D BEEN FEELING, TOOK NOTES AND TOLD ME TO GO AHEAD AND GET DRESSED AND SHE'D BE BACK IN TO TALK WITH ME. AFTER ABOUT 10 MINUTES THE DOCTOR CAME IN TO TELL ME THAT I WAS ALMOST 3 MONTHS ALONG. I WAS SURPRISED, HOW COULD I BE THAT FAR ALONG AND NOT EVEN KNOW IT OR EVEN BEGIN TO SHOW AT ALL?

THEN I REMEMBERED I DIDN'T EVEN SHOW WITH ANGIE TILL I WAS ALMOST 7 MONTHS ALONG.I WAS EXPERIENCING SUCH TIREDNESS FOR SO LONG, THAT I ASSOCIATED ALL THE THINGS YOU USUALLY EXPERIENCE WITH PREGNANCY AS BEING A PART OF WHAT I HAD BEEN DEALING WITH SINCE ANGIE WAS BORN, NOT TO MENTION THAT SINCE SHE TORE ME AND I HAD SOME ISSUES WITH PAIN AFTER CHILD

BIRTH, IT MADE HAVING SEX VERY DIFFICULT, ESPECIALLY HAVING BEEN RAPED. THIS DEFINITELY PUT A STRAIN ON GEORGE'S AND MY RELATIONSHIP, SO ALTHOUGH I SUSPECTED I WAS PREGNANT, HOW COULD I BE IF I HAD A HARD TIME HAVING SEX AND HAD TO QUIT DURING, BECAUSE IT HURT SO BAD. I ASKED MYSELF WHY I HAD THE NEED TO EVEN TELL MY PARENTS WHAT I SUSPECTED. WHERE WAS MY HEAD? I WAS BROUGHT BACK BY THE DOCTOR'S VOICE, STARTING TO EXPLAIN WHAT WAS GOING ON. THERE IS A POSSIBILITY YOU ARE HAVING A MISCARRIAGE, THE BABY IS BIG AND THE HEAD A LITTLE OVERSIZED FOR BEING ONLY 3 MONTHS ALONG. THAT COULD EXPLAIN THE BLEEDING BUT IT'S A LITTLE EARLY TO TELL. I WANT YOU ON BED REST AND TAKE IT EASY AND IF THERE'S ANY PAIN OR ANYTHING OUT OF THE ORDINARY GET TO THE HOSPITAL, OTHERWISE I WANT TO SEE YOU NEXT WEEK. WELL AFTER HEARING ALL THAT, I REFUSED TO CONFIRM WITH ANYONE THAT I WAS INDEED PREGNANT. I THINK I CRIED ALL THE WAY BACK TO GREENVILLE. OH HOW MY LIFE HAD TAKEN A TURN AND I WAS ONLY 20.

TWO DAYS LATER AND NOTHING CHANGED, I WAS STARTING TO HURT AND STILL BLEEDING, RATHER THAN GO TO THE HOSPITAL I DECIDED TO GET A SECOND OPINION AND FOUND A DOCTOR AT A WOMEN'S CLINIC IN DAYTON, WHO WAS A SPECIALIST IN HIGH RISK PREGNANCIES. THEY CONFIRMED WHAT MY OTHER DOCTOR HAD SAID, BUT I HAD LOST THE BABY, I HAD SO MUCH SWELLING AND WASN'T OPEN FAR ENOUGH FOR ALL THE HEAD TO GET THROUGH, WHICH IS WHY I WAS IN SO MUCH PAIN. THEY HAD TO GO IN AND REMOVE THE BABY AND CLEAN ME OUT. I

WAS TORN, MY BABY WAS GONE, AND I DON'T REMEMBER MUCH AFTER THAT. I BLAMED MY DAD, I WAS SO ANGRY, FELT SO ASHAMED AND SEEM TO SINK INTO A DEPRESSIVE STATE. ANGELA BY THIS TIME WAS 9 MONTHS OLD, SHE WAS REALLY GETTING AROUND AND HAD STARTED PULLING HERSELF UP AND WALKING AROUND FURNITURE, EVERY ONCE IN A WHILE LETTING GO AND TAKING A STEP OR TWO. I GAVE A BRIEF SMILE AT HOW MUCH SHE'D GROWN, BUT FELT SAD THAT I WAS SO FOCUSED ON OTHER THINGS GOING ON, I HAD MISSED SOME IMPORTANT THINGS WITH HER. I SO NEEDED TO MAKE UP FOR LOST TIME.

AT 9 MONTHS SHE WAS ALREADY DRINKING FROM A CUP, WITH ONLY A BOTTLE AT NIGHT, SO WE DECIDED TO BREAK HER FROM THE BOTTLE. IT WAS A LOT EASIER THAN WHAT WE THOUGHT AND AT 9 MONTHS SHE WAS COMPLETELY BROKE FROM THE BOTTLE. HOWEVER, WHEN SHE WENT TO STAY AT MY PARENTS THAT NEXT WEEKEND, I TOLD THEM, AND MY DAD ONCE AGAIN FLEW OFF THE HANDLE. JUST WENT ON AND ON ABOUT HOW SHE WAS GOING TO SUFFER FROM MALNUTRITION. SHE WAS GETTING MILK AND VITAMINS, IN HER CUP AND FOOD FOR CRYING OUT LOUD. JUST NOT GETTING A BOTTLE, WHAT WAS THE DEAL? WE LEFT TO GO HOME, I WAS COMPLETELY DRAINED, I WAS BLEEDING SO MUCH I WORE TOWELS TO HELP SOAK IT UP AND THANKFUL THAT ANGIE WAS STAYING WITH THEM FOR A COUPLE DAYS AND FOR THE TIME TO MYSELF TO REST UP. HOWEVER ALL WEEKEND WAS INTERRUPTED BY MY DAD WHEN ALL HE DID WAS CALL UP AFTER A NIGHT OF DRINKING AND COMPLAIN ABOUT HOW I WASN'T CARING FOR ANGIE

PROPERLY. ON AN ON HE WENT, I JUST SAID YES DAD, WHATEVER YOU SAY DAD, JUST TO GET OFF THE PHONE. OH WHAT WAS I IN FOR? I WAS GROWING WEAKER AND I DEFINITELY DIDN'T WANT TO DEAL WITH HIM HOUNDING ME, AS IF HE HAD ROOM TO TALK ABOUT PARENTING SKILLS. WHERE WAS MY MOM? WHY WASN'T SHE COMING TO MY DEFENSE? OR WASN'T SHE AWARE OF WHAT HE WAS DOING?

GEORGE HAPPENED TO GET CALLED IN AT THE PIZZA PLACE THAT SUNDAY NIGHT, SO I DECIDED TO GO TO MY PARENTS HOUSE AND PICK UP ANGIE AND STAY TILL GEORGE GOT OFF. I'M NOT SURE WHY I DID IT, BUT I PULLED OPEN A DRAWER IN THE KITCHEN AND IN THERE LAY A BOTTLE. I HADN'T BROUGHT ONE AS SHE WAS BOTTLE BROKE. I ASKED WHAT IT WAS AND I LEARNED THEY WENT OUT AND BOUGHT IT AND PUT HER BACK ON THE BOTTLE. I WAS SO FURIOUS WITH HIM THAT I THOUGHT I WAS GOING TO EXPLODE. WHAT RIGHT DID THEY HAVE ANY WAY. MY WHOLE LIFE WAS LIKE THIS, BEING CRITICIZED AND BEAT DOWN. I HAD ENOUGH!! I MEAN I WAS THE ONE RAISING MY DAUGHTER AND I THOUGHT I WAS DOING A DARN GOOD JOB.

I DON'T EVEN THINK WE GOT TOGETHER FOR THANKSGIVING THAT YEAR, THINGS WERE IN A WHIRLWIND, MY MIND IN A FOG, I WAS FORGETTING A LOT OF THINGS, PLUS TRYING TO RECOVER FROM LOSING MY BABY. I STILL BLAMED HIM. BUT I SOON HAD MY FOCUS ON OTHER THINGS WHEN WE GOT THE NEWS THAT GEORGE'S DIVORCE WAS NOW FINAL. HE MADE PLANS ALREADY FOR US TO GET MARRIED BY THE END OF THE YEAR, THIS WAY HE'D GET A TAX

CREDIT OFF OF HIS INCOME TAX WHEN HE FILED. WHAT A WAY TO WANT TO MARRY SOMEONE.

DECEMBER WAS HERE, SOON IT WOULD BE CHRISTMAS, AND OUR DAUGHTER WOULD BE A YEAR OLD ON THE 20TH. GEORGE MADE ARRANGEMENTS TO BE MARRIED ON DECEMBER 29TH IN THE HOME OF A RETIRED JUDGE. I WAS GLAD THINGS WERE GETTING SITUATED IN MY LIFE. THE NEXT HURDLE TO GET OVER WAS DEALING WITH MY PARENTS. ANGIES BIRTHDAY WAS HERE, HER FIRST. WE HAD A PARTY AT MY PARENTS, MY GOODNESS WHEN WE PUT THAT CAKE IN FRONT OF HER SHE DOVE RIGHT IN. CAKE ALL OVER HERSELF. MY DAD SEEMED TO BE IN A GOOD MOOD THAT DAY AND FOR ONCE NOTHING NEGATIVE CAME OUT OF IT. I WAS THANKFUL AND BREATHEDD A GREAT SIGH OF RELIEF. CHRISTMAS CAME AND WENT AND IT WAS WEDDING DAY. IT WAS CERTAINLY AMAZING WITH THE HELP FROM OUR FRIENDS IN GREENVILLE HOW QUICKLY WE PUT EVERYTHING TOGETHER, WITH ANGIES BIRTHDAY AND CHRISTMAS AS WELL, BUT WE MANAGED. I FOUND A DRESS AT A GARAGE SALE FOR 20.00, AND MY FRIEND HAD A CAKE CUTTER AND GLASSES. AND SHE GOT THE CAKE FOR US. WE JUST WANTED A SMALL SIMPLE CEREMONY ANYWAY. THE SHOCKER WAS MY DAD ACTUALLY SHOWED UP TO GIVE ME AWAY, OH HAD IT NOT BEEN FOR CREATING A SCENE, I WOULD HAVE DEMANDED HE LEAVE, BUT I TRIED TO BE SOCIAL, ALWAYS BELIEVING PEOPLE HAD THE POTENTIAL TO CHANGE.

THE NEW YEAR WAS GETTING OFF TO A FINE START. I WAS MARRIED NOW AND FINALLY TRYING TO GET MY LIFE IN ORDER, AT LEAST IN THE EYES OF GOD.

ANGIE WAS WALKING, HAD BEEN FOR A FEW WEEKS, SO CHASING HER WAS A JOB IN ITSELF, ESPECIALLY SINCE I STILL HAD BOUTS OF TIREDNESS. I KNEW HAVING A CHILD COULD TAKE A LOT OUT OF YOU, BUT THIS WAS SOMETHING ELSE. ONE WEEKEND WHEN ANGIE HAD WENT TO MY PARENTS, IT WAS UNUSUALLY COLD OUT FOR BEING SPRINGTIME, AND SO I TURNED UP THE HEAT BEFORE GOING TO BED. IT DIDN'T TAKE LONG TO FALL ASLEEP AND I BARELY REMEMBER GEORGE GETTING UP FOR WORK. THE NEXT THING I KNEW I WAS AWAKENED BY A HEAVY BANGING ON THE DOOR, I WAS GROGGY AND COULD HARDLY MAKE IT TO THE DOOR, BUT WHEN I DID THE PERSON INFORMED ME AS THEY WERE WALKING BY THEY SMELLED GAS. WE HAD GAS HEAT WHICH HAD SPRUNG A LEAK SOMETIME DURING THE NIGHT.

WHEN I LOOKED AT THE CLOCK WONDERING WHAT TIME IT WAS, IT READ 4:00 IN THE AFTERNOON, I HAD SLEPT ALL DAY!! THANK GOD THIS PERSON CAME BY AND ALMOST BEAT THE DOOR DOWN, I COULD HAVE DIED. I KNOW GOD SENT AN ANGEL THAT DAY!! I IMMEDIATELY CALLED THE LANDLORD AND REPORTED IT, THEY CAME OUT AND CHECKED AND SURE ENOUGH THERE WAS A CRACK IN THE FURNACE, BUT THEY DIDN'T WANT TO DO ANYTHING ABOUT IT. IN FACT, HE SAID IF WE DIDN'T LIKE IT, WE COULD MOVE. SO CAME THE HUNTING FOR ANOTHER HOUSE. I MEAN OUR LIVES WERE AT STAKE, WAS THIS GUY SERIOUS? THANK GOD ANGIE WASN'T HOME. WHEN I TOLD GEORGE THE NEWS, HE WAS OUTRAGED, AND IT CERTAINLY EXPLAINED ALL MY TIREDNESS OFF AND ON THE LAST YEAR. SO THE SEARCH BEGAN FOR ANOTHER PLACE, THANK GOODNESS IT WAS ALMOST

SPRING TIME AND THE WEATHER WOULD BE GETTING NICER. UNTIL THEN WE'D JUST HAVE TO BUNDLE UP, BUT THE HEAT WASN'T COMING BACK ON!!

THE NEXT DAY WAS SUNDAY AND GEORGE HAD TO WORK AT THE PIZZA PLACE IN PIQUA, SO I DECIDED TO TAG ALONG AND VISIT MY PARENTS AND JUST PICK ANGIE UP FROM THEM, OUR PHONE HADN'T BEEN WORKING RIGHT, SO THERE WAS NO CHANCE TO CALL THEM TO LET THEM KNOW AND BESIDES, I WAS ACTUALLY GETTING SOME PEACE FROM PHONE CALLS FROM MY DAD. THE WHOLE TRIP OVER I KEPT WONDERING IF I WAS GOING TO GET THE THIRD DEGREE ABOUT ANYTHING. WHEN I GOT THERE, IT WAS JUST IN THE NICK OF TIME, MY MOM WAS JUST GETTING READY TO BRING HER HOME. I ACTUALLY THOUGHT THEY WOULD BE GLAD TO SEE ME, BUT ALL I GOT WAS IRRITATION. MY MOM HAPPENED TO BE OUTSIDE AND SAID DAD WAS IN ONE OF HIS MOODS AGAIN AND SHE WAS GETTING FED UP. DO THIS AND WHY DON'T I DO THAT, REALLY?? I NEVER FELT MORE WORTHLESS AS A PERSON IN MY LIFE. WHY WAS I EVEN BORN?

I REMEMBER ASKING MY MOM TO WATCH ANGIE FOR ME, JUST A WHILE LONGER. I WANTED TO TAKE A DRIVE, CLEAR MY HEAD, MAYBE SEE SOME FRIENDS AND GET AWAY FROM DAD'S NAGGING. SHE REFUSED AS SHE DIDN'T WANT TO HEAR GRIPING FROM MY DAD, SO I PUT ANGIE IN THE CAR AND TOOK HER WITH ME. I DROVE DOWNTOWN, SEEING WHO ALL WAS OUT, USUALLY TOWN WASN'T HOPPING MUCH ON SUNDAY EVENING'S, PEOPLE STAYING AT HOME GETTING READY FOR THE START OF ANOTHER WORK WEEK. AS I

WAS DRIVING AROUND, I SEEN MY OLD BOYFRIEND BOB CRUISING AROUND. WE STOPPED ON THE SQUARE AND CHATTED A WHILE AND SOMEONE WHO MUST HAVE KNEW GEORGE, SEEN US AND WENT AND CALLED HIM AND TOLD HIM WHAT THEY HAD SEEN. WHEN IT WAS TIME TO PICK GEORGE UP FROM WORK, I WENT IN TO SEE HOW CLOSE HE WAS TO BEING FINISHED, WHEN HE GRABBED ME AND HE THREW ME AGAINST THE WALL, AND A VEIN POPPED IN MY CHEST. HE ASKED IF I WAS MESSING AROUND, I TOLD HIM NO, BUT HE WOULDN'T LISTEN, SO I CALLED OUR FRIEND FROM GREENVILLE AND HAD HER COME PICK ANGIE AND ME UP AND I STAYED THE NIGHT WITH HER. GEORGE CAME OVER THERE WHEN HE GOT TO TOWN TO TALK BUT I WANTED NO PART OF IT, SO THE NEXT DAY I PACKED UP SOME THINGS AND WENT BACK TO PIQUA AND GOT AN APARTMENT OF MY OWN.

THE APARTMENT I GOT WAS OFF OF A HOUSE. THE OWNERS OF THE HOUSE TURNED A SMALL PORTION INTO A 1 BEDROOM APARTMENT. THE RENT WAS CHEAP WHICH I THINK INCLUDED THE UTILITIES AND THE PLACE CLEAN, A NICE LITTLE PLACE TO GET STARTED. I WASN'T SURE WHAT WAS GOING TO HAPPEN NOW, WHETHER I WOULD BE DIVORCING GEORGE, BUT MY PARENTS MADE IT CLEAR, THEY WANTED OUT OF IT, SO I WAS ALL ALONE TO RAISE MY DAUGHTER. I APPLIED FOR WELFARE AND RECEIVED ENOUGH TO COVER MY RENT AND RECEIVED SOME FOOD STAMPS, I ALSO RECEIVED WIC FOR ANGIE, AND I WAS SO THANKFUL. SINCE I NOW HAD SOME FREEDOM I STARTED CRUISING AGAIN ON FRIDAY AND SATURDAY NIGHTS, ONCE IN A WHILE MY PARENTS WOULD WATCH ANGIE BUT WHEN MY PARENTS REFUSED TO WATCH

ANGELA ON FRIDAY AND SATURDAY NIGHTS, I TOOK HER WITH ME. IT WAS OK AT FIRST, HARDLY A PLACE YOU WANT TO TAKE A TODDLER, BUT SHE'D STARE AT THE LIGHTS AND SOON FALL ASLEEP, BUT EVEN MY SO CALLED FRIENDS WOULD CRITICIZE HAVING MY DAUGHTER WITH ME. I WAS BEGINNING TO WONDER AS I'D DONE BEFORE, WHAT MY LIFE ON THIS EARTH WAS FOR. SOMEONE'S WHIPPING POST? I UNDERSTAND PEOPLE GO THROUGH THINGS, THAT'S A PART OF LIFE RIGHT? I'M SURE IT'S NOT ALL A BED OF ROSES, BUT COME ON, HOW MUCH CAN ONE PERSON TAKE? I FELT LIKE I WAS A WALKING TARGET WITH A HIDDEN SIGN ON HER BACK SAYING WALK ALL OVER ME!!

I WAS ONLY IN MY PLACE A FEW MONTHS WHEN I DECIDED TO GO BACK TO GEORGE. MY FRIENDS WEREN'T REALLY MY FRIENDS, MOST SAW ME AS AN EASY LAY, WHICH I REFUSED TO BE AND BESIDES, GEORGE HAD APOLOGIZED AND HAD PROMISED TO TREAT ME BETTER. OF COURSE MY PARENTS HAD BEEN ON ME TO OWN UP TO MY RESPONSIBILITIES AND THAT WAS TO HAVE ANGIE'S FATHER IN HER LIFE AND GIVE HER STABILITY. MAYBE BY LISTENING TO THEM, I WOULD GET SOME PEACE, THAT'S ALL I LONGED FOR. JUST LET ME LIVE MY LIFE AND RAISE MY DAUGHTER, AND ALLOW ME TO MAKE MISTAKES. THE CONSEQUENCES OF MY CHOICES WOULD FALL ON ME NOT THEM, BUT THEY NEVER SEEN IT THAT WAY. THEY ALWAYS TOLD US THAT HOW WE TURNED OUT, AND WHAT WE DID WITH OUR LIFE WAS A REFLECTION ON THEM. WELL IF THAT WAS THE CASE THEN, I THINK THEY WERE ASHAMED MAYBE THAT THE TRUTH WOULD COME OUT AND MAKE THEM LOOK BAD.

GEORGE WAS STILL LIVING IN OUR HOUSE WE HAD IN GREENVILLE, THE ONE WITH THE BROKEN FURNACE, HE HAD MANAGED TO SAVE A LITTLE MONEY, SO WE STARTED LOOKING FOR ANOTHER HOUSE AND IT WASN'T EASY. WE DECIDED TO LOOK BACK IN PIQUA SINCE GEORGE WAS WORKING THERE ANYWAY, AND I FIGURED MY PARENTS WOULD BE HAPPY HAVING US CLOSER. MY DAD DIDN'T LIKE LEAVING THE HOUSE AND IT WAS HARD ON MY MOM TO MAKE THE DRIVE ALONE AT TIMES. ANGIE BY THIS TIME WAS 18 MONTHS OLD, AND WE HAD STARTED POTTY TRAINING HER, SHE WAS DOING QUITE WELL AND IT ONLY TOOK ABOUT TWO WEEKS AND SHE WAS COMPLETELY BROKE. WHAT AN ACCOMPLISHMENT AND A SAVINGS ON DIAPERS.

THAT WEEKEND MY PARENTS ASKED TO HAVE HER, I AGREED AS IT WOULD GIVE GEORGE AND I TIME TO FIND A PLACE. AFTER THEY PICKED HER UP, GEORGE CALLED DOWN HIS FRIEND TO LOOK AT OUR TV AS IT WASN'T WORKING RIGHT. I HAD FALLEN ASLEEP ON THE COUCH AND DIDN'T REALIZE HE CAME OVER, WHEN I WOKE UP, MY BLOUSE WAS UNDONE SOME AND HE WAS GONE. I THOUGHT WHAT THE HECK HAPPENED? GEORGE SAID HE HAD NO IDEA, THAT IT MUST HAVE COME UNDONE WHILE I WAS A SLEEP, BUT I DIDN'T BUY IT FOR A MINUTE. I DIDN'T WANT TO MAKE WAVES BUT THAT WAS WRONG. I KNOW GEORGE WAS UPSET ABOUT OUR SEX LIFE, BUT I WAS HAVING PAIN DURING INTERCOURSE AND THE DOCTOR'S HAD RUN TESTS AND COULDN'T UNDERSTAND WHAT WAS WRONG. THEY GAVE SUGGESTIONS, BUT THEY DIDN'T ALWAYS HELP. THIS AT TIMES PUT A STRAIN ON OUR RELATIONSHIP. HE OFTEN TOLD ME I WAS

WITHHOLDING AND REFUSING TO PUT OUT, BUT THAT WASN'T THE CASE. SOMETHING DEFINITELY HAPPENED AFTER I HAD ANGIE, AND I WONDER IF IT WAS DUE TO BEING CUT TO ALLOW ROOM FOR DELIVERY, OR IF IT WAS WHEN SHE TORE ME ALONG WITH THE AFFECTS OF BEING RAPED SO MUCH OF MY CHILDHOOD WAS A BLUR THAT I OFTEN WONDERED IF SOMETHING BAD HAPPENED TO ME THAT I BLOCKED OUT. I KNOW GEORGE LIKED TO USE THINGS ON ME TOO AND NOT SURE IF THAT DID DAMAGE, BUT WHO WANTS TO TALK TO THE DOCTOR ABOUT THAT?? I HAD TESTS RUN, ESPECIALLY AFTER BEING RAPED, BUT EVERYTHING CAME BACK CLEAN. I FELT BAD, BUT I COULDN'T HELP IT, AND I DEFINITELY DIDN'T NEED ANY ADDED STRESS. I PRAYED LORD, HEAL ME OR LET HIM LEAVE ME ALONE ABOUT IT.

THE WEEKEND WAS OVER AND THIS TIME MY MOM BROUGHT ANGIE HOME. I NOTICED HOWEVER THAT ANGIE HAD AN ACCIDENT IN HER PANTS. I THOUGHT IT WAS ODD AS SHE WAS DOING SO WELL USING THE POTTY. I CLEANED HER UP AND PUT HER TO BED, ONLY FOR HER TO WAKE UP AND HAD WET THE BED. THE NEXT DAY I CALLED FOR A DOCTOR APPOINTMENT TO SEE IF THERE WAS AN INFECTION OR SOMETHING GOING ON TO CAUSE HER TO ALL OF A SUDDEN HAVE ACCIDENTS. I WAS ABLE TO GET HER IN RIGHT AWAY, AND AFTER RUNNING TESTS, SAID SHE WAS FINE. JUST AS YOU WOULD HAVE IT, MY DAD CALLED THAT NIGHT. OF COURSE HE HAD BEEN DRINKING AND WAS GOING ON ABOUT ANGIE AND HOW SHE WAS TOO YOUNG TO BE POTTY BROKE AND I WAS RUSHING HER INTO GROWING UP. HE INFORMED ME THEY PUT HER BACK IN DIAPERS. ARE YOU FREAKING

KIDDING ME? KNOW WONDER SHE HAD ACCIDENTS WHEN SHE CAME HOME, THE POOR GIRL WAS CONFUSED. I HAD TO LITERALLY START OVER AGAIN AND IT WAS TAKING WHAT SEEMED LIKE FOREVER TO GET HER BROKE. SHE WANTED NO PART OF IT AND I WAS ANGRY. WHY COULDN'T MY DAD JUST BUTT OUT OF MY LIFE? HE DIDN'T SEEM TO WANT TO BE THERE WHEN I WAS HOME AND NEEDED HIM, SO WHY NOW? WAS IT TO MAKE MY LIFE A LIVING HELL? WHY? WHAT DID I EVER DO TO HIM? I JUST COULDN'T BELIEVE IT, AND I JUST TOOK IT, SO MAYBE IT WAS MY OWN FAULT.

THAT NEXT MONTH, JULY TO BE EXACT, WE FOUND A ONE BEDROOM APARTMENT IN PIQUA, IT WAS IN AN APARTMENT BUILDING THAT HAD 2 OTHER APARTMENTS BUT YOU COULD ACCESS EACH ONE FROM THE OUTSIDE. GEORGE AND I HAD THE BACK APARTMENT WHICH THE ENTRANCE WAS IN AN ALLEY. IT WAS SMALL, BUT JUST ENOUGH ROOM FOR THE 3 OF US TILL SOMETHING BIGGER OPENED UP. GEORGE HAD RECEIVED A PROMOTION WITH GODFATHER'S PIZZA WHERE HE'D BEEN WORKING AND NOW WAS MANAGING THE SIDNEY STORE. THERE HE MET MIKE AND DIANA, WHO LATER BECAME GOOD FRIENDS OF OURS. WE HAD MANY GET TOGETHERS AND IT WAS GOOD TO BE ABLE TO SOCIALIZE SOME AND FOCUS ON OTHER THINGS OTHER THAN OUR PROBLEMS. EITHER THEY WOULD BE AT OUR PLACE OR WE WENT TO THEIR PLACE, HAD DINNER, PLAYED CARDS, DRANK. ONE NIGHT WHEN THEY WERE AT OUR PLACE, WE HAD JUST FINISHED HAVING SUPPER, AND DIANE WANTED TO GO FOR A WALK, JUST ME AND HER. THE GUYS STAYED BACK AND PLAYED VIDEO GAMES. AS WE WERE WALKING SHE BEGAN SHARING HOW SHE WAS INTO

OUIJA BOARDS AND ASTROLOGY, AND THE AMAZING THINGS THAT SHE WAS TAPPING INTO, SHE ASKED ME IF I EVER THOUGHT OF HAVING SEX WITH A COLORED GUY. I TOLD HER I HAD THAT I HAD DATED ONE BRIEFLY IN THE 6TH GRADE, THEN BROKE IT OFF WHEN I GOT GROUNDED FOR A MONTH, BUT I WAS MARRIED NOW.

SHE TOLD ME SHE WAS HAVING AN AFFAIR ON HER HUSBAND WITH A BLACK GUY AND IT WAS AWESOME, SHE DECLARED THAT AFTER FANTASIZING OVER A COLORED GUY, SHE WOULD GO TO HER HUSBAND AND IT WOULD BE THE BEST EXPERIENCE. WHY WAS SHE TELLING ME THIS? AFTER RETURNING FROM OUR WALK, THEY WERE GETTING READY TO LEAVE AND WE MADE PLANS TO GO TO THEIR HOUSE THE FOLLOWING WEEK, WHEN THAT WEEK CAME, THE GUYS HAD TO END UP WORKING, SO HER AND I HUNG OUT TILL THEY GOT OFF WORK. WHILE THERE SHE SHOWED ME THE OUIJA BOARD AND WAS ATTEMPTING TO HAVE A SÉANCE. IT WAS WILD TO SAY THE LEAST, THE LITTLE CURISOR WAS ACTUALLY MOVING, BUT I COULDN'T HELP FEELING APPREHENSIVE ABOUT IT. SOON AFTER THAT, SHE STARTED HAVING THIS COLORED GUY COME AROUND SAYING I WAS AVAILABLE BUT TO SHY TO ASK, I SOON ENDED MY FRIENDSHIP WITH HER. I MEAN IT WASN'T RIGHT WHAT SHE WAS DOING, I DIDN'T LIKE IT.

YET EVEN AFTER ENDING THE FRIENDSHIP, THE GUY KEPT COMING AROUND, WHEN I TOLD HIM NOT TO COME AROUND, HE ENDED UP BREAKING INTO MY CAR AND STEALING A NICE STEREO SET WE HAD JUST INSTALLED A FEW DAYS BEFORE. WE NEEDED OUT OF THAT NEIGHBORHOOD BUT FAST, ESPECIALLY WITH

GEORGE WORKING SO MUCH AND WITH HIM OUT OF TOWN AND FEAR THAT SHE SPREAD IT AROUND THAT I WAS ALONE, PEOPLE MAY GET THE IDEA I WAS SELLING MYSELF OUT AND HAD MONEY. THIS DEFINITELY ADDED TO THE STRESS, I WAS IN SOME VICIOUS CIRCLE WITH NO WAY OUT, ROUND AND ROUND IT WENT, SEARCHING FOR ONE BROKEN PART THAT I COULD BREAK FREE FROM THIS MADNESS AROUND ME.

WE HADN'T BEEN AT THE APARTMENT 3 MONTHS WHEN A HOUSE OPENED UP, SAME STREET BUT DOWN AT THE OTHER END. IT SEEMED TO BE A VERY NICE NEIGHBORHOOD AND THE HOUSE WAS HUGE. NICE SIZE LIVING ROOM, DINING ROOM, KITCHEN, UTILITY ROOM WITH A HALF BATH, ONE BEDROOM DOWN, NICE PORCH OUT FRONT, A DECK OUT BACK, THEN IT HAD A BASEMENT, THE UPSTAIRS HAD 2 BEDROOMS WITH A FULL BATH AND WALK IN CLOSETS. IT WAS BEAUTIFUL. WE WERE SO EXCITED. WE WERE ABLE TO GET MOVED IN AND SETTLED JUST IN TIME FOR THE HOLIDAY SEASON AND HAD EVERYONE OVER TO OUR HOUSE THIS YEAR FOR THANKSGIVING RATHER THAN TRAVELING TO MY PARENTS HOUSE.

SOON IT WAS ANGIE'S 2ND BIRTHDAY, AND THEN CHRISTMAS, IT WAS ESPECIALLY MEMORABLE THIS YEAR HAVING A BIG PLACE TO DECORATE. CHRISTMAS WAS ALWAYS MY FAVORITE TIME OF YEAR. IT WAS GREAT TO SEE ANGIE OPEN HER PRESENTS AND THE EXCITEMENT ON HER FACE, WHAT A JOY, SUCH JOY THAT I NEVER WANTED IT TO END. I HAD WISHED IT WAS SOMETHING WE COULD BOTTLE UP AND STORE FOR THOSE DAYS THAT WASN'T SO PLEASANT, PICK UP

THE BOTTLE AND POPPED THE CORK AND PRESTO, A JOYFUL DAY. BUT IT JUST DIDN'T WORK THAT WAY, THAT WAS FANTASY LAND AND THIS WAS REALITY.

GEORGE AND I HAD JUST CELEBRATED OUR ONE YEAR ANNIVERSARY. WE HAD GOTTEN MARRIED WHEN ANGELA WAS A YEAR OLD. WE HAD BEEN POTTY TRAINING HER AGAIN AND WITH SUCCESS SHE WAS NOW POTTY BROKE, WE WERE SO HAPPY, AND SHE WAS A BIG KID NOW, SHE HAD BRAGGED TO MY PARENTS. SOON IT WAS NEW YEARS EVE AND WE DECIDED TO HAVE A PARTY, GEORGE INVITED OUR FRIENDS OVER FROM GREENVILLE AND THEY HAD BROUGHT DRINKS AND DIRTY MOVIES WITH THEM. I HATED WHEN THIS HAPPENED, I DIDN'T LIKE WATCHING THEM, IT WAS EMBARASSING, BUT I DIDN'T WANT TO BE A PARTY POOPER AND A DRAG, SO I SHUT UP AND WATCHED. WHAT DO PEOPLE GET OUT OF THAT?

THEN THE TOPIC OF DISCUSSION CAME UP WHEN A SCENE THAT HAD JUST PLAYED SHOWED 2 WOMEN WITH ONE GUY. I WAS BUZZING FROM TOO MUCH DRINK AND ASKED WHAT IT WOULD BE LIKE, TWO ON ONE? I WASN'T SERIOUS, BUT I THINK IT WAS SOMETHING THAT STUCK IN GEORGE'S MIND. I THINK GEORGE FIGURED THAT BY GETTING ME BUZZED AND WATCHING THOSE DIRTY FLICKS, I WOULD BE TURNED ON BY THEM AND HAVE A DESIRE FOR SEX, SINCE OUR SEX LIFE WAS HINDERED BY PAIN. BUT IT WAS TO NO AVAIL, AND AN ARGUMENT INSUED, HE JUST COULDN'T UNDERSTAND AND I FELT LIKE I WAS LESS THAN A WOMAN BECAUSE I COULDN'T SATISFY MY MAN.

IT WASN'T THAT I WAS PUNISHING HIM BY WITHHOLDING, OR MAKING IT UP. I HAD EXPERIENCED SOME ABUSE AND WHO KNOWS WHAT ALL HAPPENED, THEN I HAD A BABY, THAT NOT ONLY DID I HAVE TO BE SURGICALLY CUT TO ALLOW ROOM, BUT SHE WAS BORN SO FAST SHE TORE ME. HE HAD MENTIONED SEVERAL TIMES THAT HE THOUGHT I WAS HAVING AN AFFAIR, THIS REALLY HIT HARD AND HURT MORE THAN I COULD EVER HAVE IMAGINED. I COULDN'T EVEN BE WITH MY HUSBAND, I WAS DEVOTED TO HIM, EVEN AFTER EVERYTHING, AND HE STILL MADE ACCUSATIONS.

GEORGE HAD BEEN IN THE MILITARY, THE ARMY NATIONAL GUARDS, HE HAD DRILLS ONCE A MONTH AND THAT WEEKEND WAS THEIR DRILL, IT WAS NOW 2 WEEKS INTO THE NEW YEAR, AND VERY COLD THAT WINTER. AT THE END OF THE WEEKEND, GEORGE BROUGHT HOME ONE OF THE GUYS WHO HE WORKED WITH AT THE ARMORY. HE HAD BEEN KICKED OUT OF WHERE HE LIVED AND HE NEEDED A PLACE TO STAY FOR A COUPLE OF DAYS, I WAS OK WITH IT, BUT THAT NIGHT AS I WAS PREPARING FOR BED, GEORGE HAD ME COME DOWN STAIRS AND WATCH A MOVIE WITH THEM. I DIDN'T WANT TO AS I WAS SO TIRED, I SAID HE'S YOUR FRIEND, GO AHEAD AND VISIT, BUT GEORGE PERSISTED. HE DIDN'T LIKE THE FACT OF ME GOING TO BED BEFORE HIM AS HE WAS AFRAID THAT IF HE WANTED SEX, HE WOULDN'T GET IT. I CAME DOWNSTAIRS, AND SAT TO WATCH A MOVIE, PRAYING IT WAS NOT AN X-RATED MOVIE. I MEAN I DIDN'T KNOW THIS GUY AND IT WOULD BE EMBARRASSING TO SIT AND WATCH ONE WITH A STRANGER. THE MOVIE GOT STARTED AND I THOUGHT COOL, NO SEX SCENES, BUT

I HAD SPOKE TOO SOON, A DIRTY MOVIE WITH A PLOT. OH MAN, I GOT UP AND LEFT THE ROOM. GEORGE CAME AFTER ME AND SAID NOT TO EMBARRASS HIM, SO I BROUGHT IN SNACKS AS IF TO MAKE THEM THINK I WAS HUNGRY AND OFFERED SOME TO HIS FRIEND.

I STRETCHED OUT ON THE LIVING ROOM FLOOR AND MUST OF DOZED OFF BECAUSE I DON'T REMEMBER THE MOVIE ENDING. WHAT I WOKE UP TO WAS GEORGE MAKING MOVES ON ME, BUT IT WASN'T JUST GEORGE, THERE WERE MORE THAN 2 HANDS. HE WAS ALLOWING HIS FRIEND TO HAVE HIS WAY WITH ME!! THOSE TIMES OF WATCHING THOSE DISGUSTING FLICKS WITH HIS OTHER FRIENDS HAD PUT IDEAS IN HIS HEAD. I WAS SHOCKED, WHAT HAD JUST HAPPENED? I WAS AFRAID TO MAKE A DEAL OF IT, I ALREADY HAD BEEN THROUGH SO MUCH EVEN TO THE POINT OF ALMOST DYING ONCE, AS MY MIND REFLECTED ON THE HOUSE IN GREENVILLE WITH THE GAS LEAK. MY SELF ESTEEM WAS SO LOW AND I FELT CHEAP AND DIRTY AND REMEMBERED TAKING A SHOWER TRYING TO SCRUB OFF THE DIRTINESS. I CLIMBED INTO BED, TRYING TO SHOVE OUT THE THOUGHTS THAT CAME FLOODING IN AT WHAT GEORGE HAD ALLOWED TO HAPPEN AND I PRAYED IT WOULDN'T HAPPEN AGAIN.

I MEAN ALL THOSE ACCUSATIONS OF AFFAIRS, WAS IT HIM THAT WAS HAVING ONE? WAS HE THINKING THIS WOULD FIX OUR SEX LIFE SO HE COULD GET SATISFIED BY MAKING HIS WIFE HAVE SEX IN FRONT OF HIM SO HE COULD JOIN IN? HE TOTALLY PLAYED ON THE FACT THAT I WAS SO GULLIBLE AND REFUSED TO STAND UP FOR MY SELF, REFUSED TO OPEN MY

MOUTH. I WAS OUT AND OUT A TRAMP, DISGUSTING PIECE OF GARBAGE TO JUST LET THIS STUFF GO ON. I MEAN I WAS A GROWN WOMAN. WASN'T I THE WEAKER VESSEL THOUGH? WASN'T I SUPPOSED TO BE SUBMISSIVE? I DON'T THINK TO THE POINT OF LOWERING YOURSELF TO SUCH NONSENSE AND ALLOW YOUR SELF TO BE USED LIKE THAT.

GEORGE DIDN'T BRING IT UP AFTER THAT NIGHT, AND I TRIED TO PUSH IT ASIDE, I THOUGHT MAYBE I DESERVED IT, OR MAYBE IT WAS JUST A PART OF LIFE, I HAD ALWAYS LONGED TO BE LOVED AND ACCEPTED AND TO BE HELPFUL SO PEOPLE WOULD APPRECIATE ME, BUT TIME AND TIME AGAIN, ALL I FELT WAS USED, AND REJECTED. I WAS ONE THAT HATED MAKING MISTAKES, I KNEW YOU COULDN'T BE PERFECT, FOR ONLY JESUS WAS PERFECT, BUT IT WAS BY MAKING MISTAKES AND THE CORRECTION I COULDN'T HANDLE, I BELIEVED I WAS BEING REJECTED AND HATED. MANY TIMES IN TRYING TO DO GOOD, I WOULD GO OVERBOARD, THEN WORRY ABOUT WHAT PEOPLE THOUGHT, BE OVERBEARING AND RUIN WHAT FRIENDSHIPS I DID HAVE. I NEVER FELT GOOD ENOUGH.

ABOUT A MONTH LATER, GEORGE CAME TO TELL ME HE WAS ALLOWING THIS GUY HE WENT TO DRILL WITH TO MOVE IN MORE LONG TERM, THE PLACE HE FOUND TO STAY WASN'T WORKING OUT. I TOLD HIM IT WASN'T A GOOD IDEA, BUT HE SAID IT WOULD HELP US WITH THE BILLS. THE PIZZA PLACE WASN'T DOING WELL AND THEY HAD BEEN TALKING ABOUT CLOSING SOME STORES AND GEORGE'S MIGHT BE ONE OF THEM. HE WAS IN THE PROCESS OF LOOKING FOR ANOTHER JOB

AGAIN. I WAS BESDIE MY SELF WITH ANGER AND GRIEF!! THIS GUY MOVED INTO THE ROOM UPSTAIRS, AND I PRAYED WE NEVER HAVE TIME ALONE, I WAS AFRAID OF WHAT WOULD HAPPEN. ONE NIGHT WHEN GEORGE WAS WORKING LATE COVERING A SHIFT FOR ANOTHER, I CAME HOME FROM A DAY OF SHOPPING, WENT UPSTAIRS TO FIND THIS GUY IN MY BED WITH NOTHING ON BUT A PAIR OF PANTYHOSE. I TOLD HIM TO GET OUT, THAT I WASN'T THAT KIND OF WOMAN, BUT HE HAD A GUN, I DON'T KNOW IF IT WAS LOADED OR NOT, HE POINTED IT RIGHT AT ME AND TOLD ME TO GET NAKED. I STARTED CRYING, BEGGING HIM NOT TO DO THIS, BUT HE WOULDN'T LISTEN, HE TRIED TO GET ME TO GO TO THE STORE WITH NO UNDIES ON, I TOLD HIM I WOULDN'T DO THAT, I HAD JUST COME BACK FROM THERE.

INSTEAD, HE HAD ME LAY DOWN AND HE HAD HIS WAY WITH ME, USING TOYS AND CLOTHES PINS WHICH HE PINNED TO MY BREASTS. IT WAS THE MOST HORRIFYING EXPERIENCE I EVER WENT THROUGH AND I HAVE BEEN THROUGH SOME STUFF. I WAS AFRAID TO TELL GEORGE FOR FEAR HE WOULD LEAVE ME, THINKING I WAS HAVING AN AFFAIR WHEN REALLY I WAS RAPED. AGAIN!! THIS GUY HAD A GUN AND IF HE WAS THERE BEFORE WHEN GEORGE WAS GONE, HE WOULD BE AGAIN, FROM WHAT I UNDERSTAND WHEN GEORGE LET HIM STAY, HE DIDN'T TRUST THE GUY WITH ME, SO HE HAD TOLD HIM NOT TO COME AROUND WHEN GEORGE WASN'T HOME, BUT GEORGE HAD TO WORK LATE THAT NIGHT AND FORGOT ABOUT INFORMING THIS GUY. THIS GUY USED IT TO HIS ADVANTAGE, I DON'T EVEN KNOW HOW HE GOT IN, AND CERTAINLY DON'T REMEMBER HIM HAVING A KEY. WELL

THAT WASN'T THE LAST TIME, IT GOT TO BE A REGULAR OCCURANCE, AND I WAS TOO STUPID TO SAY ANYTHING.

THEN ONE DAY I NOTICED SOME PAINFUL URINATION, AFTER GOING TO THE DOCTOR AND BEING TESTED, I HAD DEVELOPED A YEAST INFECTION. THIS GUY APPARENTLY HAD BEEN SLEEPING WITH ANOTHER LADY, THEN COMING TO HAVE HIS WAY WITH ME AND GAVE ME AN INFECTION. HE HAD STOPPED HELPING WITH THE BILLS AND SO I TOLD GEORGE HE HAD TO GO AND EXPLAINED WHAT WAS GOING ON AND ABOUT THE GUN, GEORGE TOOK IT BETTER THAN I THOUGHT AND AGREED. I WAS SO GRATEFUL.

HOWEVER, DEBT WAS MOUNTING UP, I WASN'T SURE WHAT WAS GOING TO HAPPEN, WE GOT BEHIND IN THE RENT AND I FEARED WE'D LOSE THE HOUSE IF THINGS DIDN'T SOON CHANGE. ON TOP OF THAT MY FATHER WHO IN A NIGHT OF DRINKING AGAIN, CALLED TO COMPLAIN ABOUT SOMETHING WE WERE DOING WITH ANGIE. I WAS SO IRRITATED THAT I BLEW UP AT MY DAD. I SAID, LISTEN DAD, I'M ALMOST 22 YEARS OLD. I'M DOING THE BEST I CAN IN RAISING ANGELA AND I DO NOT ANY LONGER NEED TO LIVE UNDER YOUR SHADOW OR ANY ONE ELSES FOR THAT MATTER. I KNOW WHAT I'M DOING AND SHE IS GROWING JUST FINE, I DON'T NEED THIS RIGHT NOW. AFTER THAT, THINGS WITH MY DAD STARTED CALMING DOWN, HE SEEMED TO RELAX AND APPEARED CONTENT WITH HOW WE WERE RAISING HER. IT WAS JUST THAT ANGELA WAS THE QUEEN BEE TO THEM AND THEY WANTED THE BEST FOR HER. WHAT? WAS I HEARING RIGHT? THE DAD WHO GAVE ME SUCH A HARD TIME

GROWING UP, CRITICIZING WHAT EVER I DID, NOW CONCERNED WITH SOMEONE'S UPBRINGING, WELL IF THAT WASN'T THE POT CALLING THE KETTLE BLACK.

A FEW WEEKS LATER, I THINK IT WAS AROUND APRIL 1985 MY BROTHER DOUG DECIDED TO MOVE IN WITH GEORGE AND I, WHICH WOULD HELP US TREMENDOUSLY IN GETTING THINGS CAUGHT UP, WE WERE STRUGGLING WITH GEORGE'S HOURS BEING CUT AND I HADN'T WENT BACK TO WORK SINCE BECOMING PREGNANT WITH ANGELA. MY BROTHER WAS STILL IN SCHOOL AND DUE TO GRADUATE THE FOLLOWING MONTH FROM HIGH SCHOOL ALSO BEING HELD BACK, BUT NOT OF HIS OWN DOING. HE WENT TO THE SAME CHRISTIAN SCHOOL I HAD ATTENDED, BUT HE DIDN'T LIKE IT THERE. HE STUCK IT OUT ONE SCHOOL YEAR, BUT WHEN THE NEXT SCHOOL YEAR STARTED HE WENT BACK TO PUBLIC SCHOOL. HOWEVER, THEY DIDN'T RECOGNIZE THE CHRISTIAN SCHOOLS CREDITS, SO HE HAD TO START HIGH SCHOOL OVER. WE ALLOWED HIM TO HAVE A GRADUATION PARTY AT THE HOUSE AND SO PREPARATIONS WERE MADE FOR THAT AND HE WAS THRILLED.

ONE EVENING AT THE END OF JUNE OR SO AS WE WERE FINISHING DINNER, MY PARENTS HAPPENED TO STOP BY, I THOUGHT SOMETHING WAS WRONG BECAUSE MY DAD HARDLY WENT ANYWHERE UNLESS IT WAS THE HOLIDAYS. ISN'T IT KIND OF IRONIC, THAT WHENEVER YOU SEE A FRIEND OR FAMILY MEMBER, YOU AUTOMATICALLY PUT UP DEFENSES AND THINK THERE'S SOMETHING WRONG? ANYWAY, THEY HAD COME TO TALK TO US ABOUT A BUSINESS PROPOSEL

THEY CAME UP WITH. MY DAD WAS ABLE TO GET A JOB DELIVERING PIZZA'S AND HAD BEEN THERE A COUPLE OF MONTHS WHEN THE OWNER RAN THIS IDEA BY HIM TO BUY INTO PART OF THE BUSINESS LIKE A PARTNERSHIP AND RUN THE PIZZA PLACE IN PIQUA FOR HIM SO HE COULD GO BACK TO TROY WHERE HE LIVED AND OPEN ANOTHER. MY DAD LAID ALL THE PLANS OUT, TALKED OF TAKING OUT A LOAN TO GET STARTED AND WANTED GEORGE AND ME TO HELP THEM OUT WITH IT. WE THOUGHT IT WAS A GOOD IDEA, ANGIE WAS 2 ½ AND WE COULD TAKE HER WITH US AND LET HER PLAY IN A ROOM THERE WITH TOYS. SO MY PARENTS SIGNED THE AGREEMENT, TOOK A LOAN ON THEIR HOUSE FOR 2000.00 AND WE WERE SET. MY DAD WOULD DO THE DELIVERING, MY MOM THE CLEAN UP, AND GEORGE AND I WOULD HANDLE THE PHONES, MAKE THE ORDERS, AND DO THE BOOKS.

THINGS WERE GOING REAL WELL, MY DAD SEEMED REAL HAPPY AT FINDING SOMETHING HE LIKED TO DO, AND WE ALL STARTED TO RELAX, BUSINESS WAS PICKING UP, JUST THE WAY I LIKED IT, KEEPING BUSY BECAUSE IT TOOK YOUR MIND OFF OTHER THINGS AND KEPT YOU FROM WORRYING. WE MADE IT THROUGH THANKSGIVING AND WAS INTO THE CHRISTMAS SEASON, ANGIE'S BIRTHDAY WAS A COUPLE WEEKS AWAY YET AND SHE WOULD TURN 3, SHE WAS GETTING SO BIG, AND VERY SMART FOR HER AGE. IT HAD BEEN SNOWING THE LAST COUPLE OF DAYS AND WAS REALLY SLICK OUTSIDE, REALLY MAKES FOR TREACHEROUS DELIVERIES. WE WERE PARTICULARLY BUSY THAT NIGHT AND MY DAD WAS TRYING TO KEEP UP WITH THE DELIVERIES, AS HE CAME AROUND THE CORNER, HE MUST HAVE HIT A

SLICK SPOT, BECAUSE NEXT THING WE KNEW, HE FELL UP THE STAIRS AND RAMMED HIS SHOULDER INTO THE DOOR JAM. WE MANAGE TO GET HIM INSIDE AND SAT HIM DOWN. WE CALLED THE AMBULANCE AS WE WEREN'T SURE IF HE HIT HIS HEAD OR WHAT, IT WAS A PRETTY HARD HIT FROM THE SOUND OF IT. SUDDENLY HE FAINTED AND WE HAD TO STICK A SPOON IN HIS MOUTH TO KEEP HIM FROM SWALLOWING HIS TONGUE. HE MUST HAVE BEEN HAVING A SEIZURE, BECAUSE I ONLY THOUGHT THEY DID THAT TO PEOPLE WHO SUFFERED FROM THEM. HE GOT TO THE HOSPITAL AND THEY DID TESTING, AND DISCOVERED HE FRACTURED HIS COLLAR BONE; HE WOULD BE OFF FOR AT LEAST 6 TO 8 WEEKS. HE HAD PRETTY MUCH DECIDED HE WASN'T WORKING AFTER THAT, SO IT WAS LEFT UP TO US TO RUN THE BUSINESS FOR THEM, MOM WOULD HAVE TO STAY HOME AND HELP MY DAD.

WE RAN THE BUSINESS FOR A WHILE AND WE NOTICED IT WAS SLOWING DOWN SOME, BILLS WERE COMING IN AND THE AMOUNTS WERE REALLY HIGH, WE COULDN'T UNDERSTAND HOW IT COULD BE SO HIGH, GEORGE WAS MANAGING THE BOOKS AND ASSURED US THINGS WERE BEING PAID ON TIME. BY THIS TIME SUMMER WAS ONCE AGAIN UPON US, GEORGE WHO WAS STILL IN THE NATIONAL GUARD WAS PREPARING TO LEAVE FOR SUMMER CAMP AND WAS TO BE GONE FOR TWO WEEKS. WE HAD CALLED OUR FRIEND FROM GREENVILLE TO COME AND HELP US WHILE GEORGE WAS GONE, AS MY MOM REALLY DIDN'T KNOW MUCH ABOUT THE BUSINESS. MY DAD DID COME BACK SINCE IT WAS NICER OUT NOW AND DO THE DELIVERING UNTIL GEORGE GOT HOME FROM THE GUARDS AND COULD TAKE OVER FOR HIM, SO THAT HELPED GET

THINGS SITUATED. THE FIRST FEW DAYS AFTER GEORGE LEFT FOR CAMP WAS AWKWARD, BUT SOON WE GOT INTO A ROUTINE, THEN WE GOT THE NEWS THAT ONE OF THE SUPPLIERS WAS CUTTING US OFF FOR LACK OF PAYMENT.

WHAT? THIS COULDN'T BE TRUE, GEORGE WAS MAKING THOSE PAYMENTS. WE GOT TO SEARCHING THE OFFICE AND SURE ENOUGH, STUCK IN A DRAWER WAS UNPAID BILLS, WE JUST COULDN'T BELIEVE IT. WELL AS YOU CAN IMAGINE, MY DAD HIT THE ROOF, BEGAN YELLING AT ME ABOUT HOW MY HUSBAND WAS GOING TO COST THEM THEIR HOME AND THE BUSINESS. THAT I WAS WORTHLESS. WHAT HAPPENED TO ALL THE MONEY THAT CAME IN, WE MUST HAVE BEEN STEALING. I NEVER SEEN THE MONEY, THE ONLY MONEY I SEEN WAS OUR PAY FOR WORKING. THIS NEWS WAS ALSO DEVASTATING TO THE OTHER OWNER OF THE BUSINESS; MY PARENTS WERE ONLY IN PARTNERSHIP, NOT FULL OWNERS YET. SO THE BUSINESS HE HAD BUILT FROM THE GROUND UP WAS SINKING FAST.

NEEDLESS TO SAY MY DAD PULLED OUT OF THE BUSINESS, CUT THEIR LOSSES AND MY DAD DIDN'T HAVE MUCH TO DO WITH GEORGE AFTER THAT. GEORGE CAME BACK AND MY DAD YELLED AT HIM AND FROM THAT DAY ON, ANYTIME WE CAME UP TO THE HOUSE WITH ANGIE, HE LEFT THE ROOM AND REFUSED TO TALK TO US. MOM WOULD TAKE ANGIE OUT TO WHERE HE WAS SO HE COULD SEE HER. WHAT A WAY TO HAVE TO LIVE. IT WASN'T MY FAULT, BUT BECAUSE I WAS MARRIED TO GEORGE, I WAS TREATED AS AN OUTCAST. WITH THE DOWNFALL OF THE BUSINESS, WE

STARTED GETTING BEHIND IN OUR BILLS AGAIN, AND DEFAULTED ON THE RENT, WE HAD TO MOVE SO WE FOUND ANOTHER HOUSE AND SCRAPED ENOUGH MONEY TO PAY THE RENT, THEY ALLOWED US TO SLIDE ON THE DEPOSIT AS WE CLEANED THE PROPERTY FOR THEM. IT ALWAYS SEEMED BETTER TO MAKE THE MOVES, THINKING IT WOULD BE CHEAPER ON SOMETHING, WHETHER THE RENT, UTILITIES, WHAT HAVE YOU.

GEORGE EVENTUALLY GOT A JOB AT A CONVENIENCE STORE, AND WAS HELPING AT THE PIZZA PLACE, OUR FRIEND FROM GREENVILLE CAME DOWN TO HELP US THERE AND I HAD GOTTEN A PART TIME JOB AT SEARS. MY MOM HELPED WATCH ANGELA FOR US WHILE WE WORKED, AND WOULD TAKE HER TO THE PIZZA PLACE SOMETIMES HELPING OUR FRIEND. BUT OUR SCHEDULES WERE DIFFERENT SO THERE WERE NOT THAT MANY TIMES WE REALLY NEEDED A SITTER, MOSTLY WHEN GEORGE WORKED AT THE CONVENIENCE STORE AS IT WAS THIRD SHIFT, SO HE WAS STILL ABLE TO MAKE PIZZA DELIVERIES, BUT IT WAS REALLY SLOWING DOWN. WHEN I WASN'T AT SEAR'S, I WAS AT THE PIZZA PLACE, MOSTLY WE WORKED FOR NOTHING TO TRY AND GET THE BUSINESS UP AND RUNNING AGAIN. THEN IN SEPTEMBER 1986 I FOUND OUT I WAS PREGNANT.

I WAS STRUGGLING WITH THIS PREGNACY THEREFORE ENDED UP QUITTING MY JOB AT SEARS AND JUST WORKING AT THE PIZZA PLACE. BUSINESS WAS REALLY DROPPING AND EVENTUALLY OUR FRIEND HAD TO QUIT WORKING THERE AS WE COULDN'T AFFORD TO PAY HER. WE MANAGED TO GET THROUGH

THE HOLIDAYS, AND SHORTLY AFTER MY BROTHER, WHO HAD BEEN LIVING WITH US, NOW HAD A GIRLFRIEND SO HE MOVED OUT AND MOVED IN WITH HER SO WE LOST THAT PORTION OF HOUSEHOLD INCOME. WE GOT BEHIND ON THE RENT, THE BUSINESS FINALLY SHUT DOWN, AND I WAS OUT OF A JOB. WHILE GEORGE WAS STILL WORKING AT THE CONVENIENCE STORE, BUT BARELY MAKING ANYTHING. WE WERE GETTING WORRIED, HERE I WAS PREGNANT, ALREADY HAD A CHILD WHO WAS NOW 4 AND VERY SOON WOULD BE ON THE STREETS IN THE MIDDLE OF WINTER IF THINGS DIDN'T TURN AROUND. AND FAST.

ONE DAY WHILE GEORGE WAS AT WORK, HE GOT A CALL FROM OUR FRIENDS IN GREENVILLE. THEY HAD AN EXTRA ROOM AND OFFERED FOR US TO COME THERE, PAY A SMALL FEE TO HELP WITH COST OF ELECTRICITY AND WATER, UNTIL WE GOT OUT OF DEBT AND COULD LIVE ON OUR OWN AGAIN, WE WERE REALLY DEEP IN DEBT AS WE HAD ALL THE BUSINESS EXPENSES TOO THAT MY PARENTS BAILED ON, SO WE AGREED, AND WE MOVED IN WITH THEM IN JANUARY 1987. IT WAS TOUGH AT FIRST, BUT WE ALL MANAGED. I WAS THANKFUL FOR THE HELP AND BEING AWAY FROM MY PARENTS AND THE HUMILATION THAT WE LEFT BEHIND. HOPEFULLY THIS WOULD BE THE START OF A BETTER LIFE. GEORGE WAS ONLY PAID EVERY 2 WEEKS, HIS PAY WAS DECENT, BUT WE HAD SO MUCH DEBT, THAT IT TOOK ME SO LONG WHEN IT CAME TO DOING BILLS, WHO DO I PAY FIRST AND HOW MUCH? AS IT GOT CLOSER TO THE TIME FOR OUR CHILD TO BE BORN, WHICH WAS IN JUNE, WE WERE MAKING GOOD PROGRESS ON OUR DEBTS. I HAD A FEW OF THEM PAID OFF, GEORGE HAD PLAYED THE LOTTERY AND WON

500.00 SO THAT WAS A HUGE PLUS FOR US, THEN A FEW WEEKS LATER HE WON AGAIN, 500.00, HE WAS REALLY GETTING LUCKY. THAT WAS TWICE IN A LITTLE OVER A MONTH.

THE TIME HAD FINALLY ARRIVED TO GIVE BIRTH, I HAD GONE INTO LABOR AND THE CONTRACTIONS WERE COMING CLOSER TOGETHER. I WAS SO GLAD AS I HAD GONE A WEEK OVERDUE AND WAS REALLY HUGE AND UNCOMFORTABLE. LABOR WAS QUICK, ONLY FOUR HOURS LONG COMPARED TO ANGELA, BUT ONCE I WAS FULLY DIALATED, IT TOOK A WHILE FOR THE BIRTH. THIS WAS THE PERFECT OPPORTUNITY AS BEING SUGGESTED BY MY DOCTOR TO DETERMINE IF THERE WAS ANYTHING OUT OF THE ORDINARY THAT WAS HINDERING ME FROM HAVING A PLEASURABLE SEX LIFE. WITH BEING STRETCHED LIKE I WAS, AWAITING THE BABY'S BIRTH, THE DOCTOR WAS ABLE TO EXAMINE AND DIDN'T SEE ANYTHING WRONG WITH ME. I WAS REALLY UPSET, SO WHAT WAS WRONG WITH ME THEN? GEORGE TOLD ME IT MUST BE PSYCHOLOGICAL. I SAID NO, IT'S NOT IN MY HEAD, I KNOW MY BODY AND IF IT HURTS THEN IT HURTS. DELIVERY WAS STILL SLOW, HE WAS WAITING TO SEE IF I COULD PUSH THE BABY OUT, BUT IT WAS LIKE THE BABY WAS STUCK, THE HEAD HAD CROWNED. BUT IT WAS BIG AND THEY NEVER CUT ME LIKE THEY HAD DONE WITH ANGIE, I WONDERED WHY.

THEY THOUGHT IT WAS EASIER ON THE WOMAN AND CHEAPER BY NOT HAVING TO PERFORM SURGERY. THE DOCTOR ENDED UP USING FORCEPS TO HELP EASE THE BABY OUT AND EVENTUALLY WE HAD BIRTH. BORN ON JUNE 16TH AT 6:11 AM, WEIGHING

IN AT 8LBS 15 OZ. WAS A SON, ERIC LEE. WE WERE ESTATIC TO HAVE A SON, ESPECIALLY GEORGE, HE WAS HEARTBROKEN AFTER HIS FIRST MARRIAGE BROKE UP AND WASN'T ABLE TO HAVE HIS SON. HE COULDN'T PAY HER CHILD SUPPORT, SO ONE DAY SHE SENT CERTIFIED PAPERS IN THE MAIL AND IT STATED THAT EITHER HE PAY THE BACK SUPPORT IN FULL OR SIGN OVER THE RIGHTS OF HIS SON TO HER NEW HUSBAND SO THAT HE COULD BE ADOPTED. WITH THE FINANCIAL STATE WE WAS IN AND ALREADY HAVING ANGELA AT THE TIME, HE OPTED TO SIGN OVER HIS RIGHTS AND GAVE UP HIS SON. NOW THIS WAS THE CHANCE TO SHARE IN ANOTHER BOY'S LIFE.

AFTER 3 DAYS I WAS RELEASED FROM THE HOSPITAL AND WAS GETTING SETTLED BACK AT OUR FRIENDS. WE WERE STILL LIVING THERE FOR THE TIME BEING BUT WE WERE MAKING SOME HEADWAY INTO BEING ABLE TO ONCE AGAIN LIVE ON OUR OWN. AFTER ABOUT 2 WEEKS OF BEING HOME, I HAD STARTING SUFFERING FROM DEPRESSION, NO DOUBT BROUGHT ON FROM THE BIRTH OF ERIC. ANGIE WAS HAVING A DIFFICULT TIME ADJUSTING TO HAVING A NEW BABY AROUND. SHE WAS 4 AND ½ AND THE QUEEN BEE FOR SO LONG, THAT THE THOUGHT OF SOMEONE REIGNING ON HER PARADE WAS UNHEARD OF. WHEN WE WERE NOT LOOKING, SHE'D PICK ERIC UP AND DROP HIM AND WAS REALLY REBELLIOUS. WE EVENTUALLY SOUGHT COUNSELING TO TRY AND HELP HER COPE AND HOPEFULLY SNAP ME OUT OF THE DEPRESSION. I THOUGHT I WAS GOING TO GO CRAZY, I HAD BOUTS OF CRYING FOR NO REASON, THOUGHT NO ONE CARED FOR ME, BUT I KNEW THAT OUR FRIENDS DID AS SHE OFTEN HELP TAKE CARE OF ERIC. SHE ALWAYS ASKED

TO BUY THINGS FOR HIM; SHE HAD GROWN SO ATTACHED, ESPECIALLY SINCE SHE COULDN'T HAVE KIDS OF HER OWN.

WHEN ERIC WAS ABOUT 3 MONTHS OLD, GEORGE CAME HOME WITH MORE WINNINGS FROM THE LOTTERY, ANOTHER 500.00, ONLY THIS TIME, HE HAD LOST HIS JOB TOO. APPARENTLY HE HAD BEEN UNDER INVESTIGATION FOR STEALING LOTTERY TICKETS. HE WOULD SCAN THEM AND WHATEVER ONES WERE BIG WINNERS, HE WOULD BUY THEM AND THEN CASH THEM IN. I WAS SO FURIOUS! WE WERE WELL ON OUR WAY OF GETTING SOME BILLS PAID OFF AND POSSIBLY GETTING OUR OWN PLACE AND HE BLOWS IT BY LOSING HIS JOB.

I SNAPPED AND TOLD HIM OFF, AND I MEAN I LET IT ALL OUT. I WENT CLEAR BACK TO WHEN HE ALLOWED HIS FRIEND TO HAVE HIS WAY WITH ME, AND SAID IT WAS SICK, HOW COULD HE DO THAT THEN ACCUSE ME OF HAVING AN AFFAIR, WHEN HE ALLOWED IT. THEN I TOLD HIM ABOUT OPENING THE DOOR TO MORE OF IT AND WHAT I HAD ENDURED, AND HOW I COULDN'T TELL BECAUSE HE HAD A GUN IN THE HOUSE. HE HUMILIATED ME AND IT ONLY BROUGHT DEEPER HURTS, ESPECIALLY WHAT I ENDURED SEXUALLY. ALTHOUGH THERE WERE MANY TRIPS TO THE DOCTOR AND EXPENSES WITH THAT, NOTHING COULD EVER BE FOUND, MAYBE IT WAS TRAUMA, WHO KNEW, BUT I BLAMED HIM RIGHT ALONG WITH MY FATHER. THEN I TOLD HIM ABOUT THE PIZZA PLACE AND WHAT HE DID THERE, I DIDN'T MEAN TO BEAT HIM DOWN BUT I HAD IT UP TO MY EARS WITH MEN AND THEIR STUPIDITY. WHY THEY FEEL THE NEED TO BE IN

CONTROL AND RUN ALL OVER WOMEN. YET I WAS JUST AS BAD IN A SENSE FOR PUTTING UP WITH IT ALL OVER THE YEARS. I SHOULD HAVE TAKEN A STAND MUCH SOONER AND SAVED MYSELF A LOT OF HEARTACHE. I GOT SO TIRED OF TRYING TO KEEP THE PEACE, TAKING THE BLUNT OF EVERYONE'S ANGER JUST SO OTHERS COULD BE HAPPY,MAKING EXCUSES FOR PEOPLE TO TRY AND CREATE AN ATMOSPHERE OF PEACE, WALKING AROUND ON EGG SHELLS HAVING TO BE CAREFUL WHAT I DO OR SAY FOR FEAR SOMEONE WILL LASH OUT AT ME. IT WAS RIDICULOUS TO SAY THE LEAST AND I WAS TIRED OF IT.

I WANTED OUT OF THIS HOLE THAT HAD BEEN CREATED BEFORE SOMEONE CAME ALONG AND STARTED KICKING DIRT AND BURY ME ALIVE. THERE HAD TO BE A WAY OF ESCAPE FROM ALL THIS CAVING IN AROUND ME. THIS HAD PUT A STRAIN ON MY FRIENDSHIPS AS I FELT EVERYONE WAS AGAINST ME. I BECAME ANGRY AND GRUMPY, AND A VERY MOODY PERSON, SO IT WAS NO WONDER, I SUPPOSE, THAT NO ONE WANTED TO BE AROUND. I SO NEEDED TO GO TO COUNSELING, BUT MY MEDICAID HAD STOPPED AFTER ERIC WAS BORN BECAUSE GEORGE MADE TO MUCH MONEY, BUT NOW SINCE HE WASN'T WORKING, I COULD REAPPLY, BUT IT'S STILL A PROCESS TO GO THROUGH. I JUST HAD TO HOPE AND PRAY THINGS WOULD CHANGE.

2 WEEKS LATER, GEORGE DID GET ANOTHER JOB, THIS TIME WORKING FOR A FRIEND OF THE FAMILY IN HIS CHICKEN PLACE, I WAS RELIEVED, THINGS WERE DIFFERENT FOR US, I KNEW OUR MARRIAGE WAS STRAINED, BUT WE MANAGED TO BEAR

THROUGH IT, HOPEFULLY SOON BEING ABLE TO GET OUT ON OUR OWN WOULD HELP GET THINGS SETTLED. WE FOUND A HALF DOUBLE THAT WAS WITHIN OUR BUDGET, WE HAD REALLY TIGHTENED OUR BELTS AND COMMITTED TO FOLLOWING IT IF WE WERE GOING TO STAY ON OUR OWN AND MAKE IT. OUR FRIEND'S COUSIN HAD STARTED VISITING AND WAS A BIG HELP WITH THE KID'S, ANGIE WAS NOW 5 AND ERIC WAS 6 MONTHS OLD. WE WERE SETTLING IN QUITE NICELY, AND LOVING OUR NEW HOME. WE HAD SOME NICE PLACES, BUT THIS ONE SEEMED EXTRA SPECIAL AS IT TOOK SOME DOING TO BE ABLE TO GET IT. WE HAD TO PAY OFF SOME DEBTS AND LEARN HOW TO HAVE A BUDGET. I WAS ACTUALLY STARTING TO RELAX AND START HAVING SOME FUN.

ONE NIGHT WHILE WATCHING A MOVIE, I NOTICED THAT OUR FRIEND'S COUSIN WAS MASSAGING GEORGE'S FEET, I WAS TAKEN ABACK BUT THOUGHT WELL OK, SHE'S JUST BEING NICE. I WENT ON UP TO BED AND WAS NO SOONER ASLEEP WHEN THE PHONE RANG. OF COURSE IT WAS MY DAD. HE HAD BEEN DRINKING AND WAS RANTING ABOUT HOW ANGIE'S TANTRUMS WAS GETTING RIDICULOUS AND WHAT WERE WE DOING ABOUT IT? I ASSURED HIM WE HAD IT UNDER CONTROL; WE HAD HER IN COUNSELING FOR IT. I JUST PRETENDED TO HEAR THE REST OF THE CONVERSATION, I SO WANTED TO HANG UP ON HIM, BUT HE WOULD ONLY CALL BACK, SO I MUTTERED YES DAD, WE'LL TAKE CARE OF IT DAD, AND THEN WE'D HANG UP. WHEN I WENT TO GET UP TO GO TO THE BATHROOM, I NOTICED THAT MY FRIENDS COUSIN WAS IN BED WITH ME. I WOKE THEM UP AND ASKED WHAT THE HECK WAS GOING ON. APPARENTLY SHE HAD A

BAD BACK AND COULDN'T SLEEP DOWNSTAIRS ON THE COUCH, SO GEORGE LET HER LAY IN THE BED. IT WOULD HAVE BEEN NICE TO LET ME KNOW, BUT I COULDN'T HELP BUT THINK HE WAS IN THE BED TOO AND WHEN THE PHONE RANG, WAS AFRAID OF BEING CAUGHT SO HE SCURRIED OUT BEFORE I COULD ANSWER.

THE NEXT DAY I WAS DOING SOME CLEANING AND REFLECTING ON MY PHONE CONVERSATION WITH MY DAD THE NIGHT BEFORE, I SO PRAYED THIS WASN'T GOING TO START UP AGAIN. WE WERE FINALLY MAKING SOME HEAD WAY. I WAS BROUGHT BACK TO REALITY WHEN I HEARD MOVING AROUND UPSTAIRS. WHAT IN THE WORLD? THE ONLY ONES HERE WAS ANGELA AND ERIC AND I. WHEN I WENT UP THE STAIRS THE NOISE I HAD HEARD WAS COMING FROM ANGIE'S ROOM, I WENT TO GO IN AND THE DOOR WOULDN'T OPEN. I THOUGHT WHAT IN THE WORLD? SHE COULDN'T HAVE LOCKED IT AS THERE WAS NO LOCK ON THE DOOR. I KEPT ASKING HER TO OPEN THE DOOR BUT SHE DIDN'T DO IT. FINALLY I WAS ABLE TO GET IN THE ROOM. SHE HAD BARRICADED HERSELF IN THERE. I TRIED TALKING TO HER BUT SHE WOULDN'T ANSWER, WOULDN'T TELL ME WHY SHE WAS HIDING AND DIDN'T WANT ANYONE TO COME IN. I GREW CONCERNED AND WOULD DEFINITELY TALK TO THE COUNSELOR ABOUT IT, BUT FOR NOW I HAD TO ATTEND TO ERIC WHO HAD WOKEN UP FROM HIS NAP.

WHEN GEORGE CAME IN FROM WORK I WAS TELLING HIM ABOUT WHAT ANGELA HAD DONE, HE JUST BRUSHED IT OFF AS HER GETTING ADJUSTED TO A NEW BROTHER, AND A NEW HOUSE. I SHRUGGED

KNOWING HE WAS PROBABLY RIGHT, BEING AN ONLY CHILD AND GETTING ALL THE ATTENTION FOR 4 ½ YEARS AND THEN IT HAS TO BE SHARED, JUST DIDN'T SET RIGHT WITH HER. GEORGE GOT A QUICK BITE AND RAN OUT, MUTTERING THAT HE MET A GUY WHO HAS A BASEBALL CARD SHOP AND HE WAS GOING TO HELP HIM OUT. GEORGE WAS A SPORTS FANATIC, OFTEN TIMES WHEN HIM AND MY PARENTS WERE ON GOOD TERMS, THEY'D HAVE SOME CONVERSATIONS ABOUT THE DIFFERENT TEAMS. GEORGE STARTED DOING WORK ON THE SIDE FOR HIS NEW FOUND FRIEND, SORTING CARDS AND HELPING TO MAKE SETS. HE OFTEN BROUGHT THE WORK HOME AND PAID US NICELY SO I HELPED GEORGE ALONG WITH OUR FRIEND'S COUSIN. WE ENJOYED MANY HOURS TOGETHER SORTING CARDS AND SHOOTING THE BREEZE.

THE FOLLOWING DAY, GEORGE CAME HOME FROM WORK AND HAD BROUGHT A FRIEND HE WORKED WITH. HE WAS HAVING TROUBLE IN HIS RELATIONSHIP SO GEORGE HAD HIM COME OVER FOR SUPPER AND TO WATCH A MOVIE WITH US THAT GEORGE HAD JUST RENTED, A NEW RELEASE WE WERE ANXIOUS TO WATCH, JUST WAITING FOR IT TO COME OUT ON VHS AS WE HAD STRICTLY CUT OUT GOING TO THE THEATER'S AND TO RESTAURANTS FROM OUR BUDGET TILL WE COULD AFFORD TOO. THE MOVIE WAS FINAL INSTINCT WITH MICHAEL DOUGLAS WHO WAS ONE OF OUR FAVORITE ACTORS. ABOUT 15 MINUTES INTO THE MOVIE, GEORGE WAS TELLING US PARTS THAT WAS GOING TO HAPPEN NEXT, WHEN IT ACTUALLY HAPPENED ON THE MOVIE, I ASKED HIM HOW HE KNEW THAT AND HE SAID, I DON'T KNOW,

INSTINCT I GUESS. WHEN HE DID IT AGAIN, I ASKED GEORGE, HAVE YOU SEEN THIS MOVIE? HE ASSURED ME HE DIDN'T, BUT HE MUST HAVE, THE MOVIE HAD JUST CAME OUT ON VHS, SO WHEN AND WHERE WOULD HE HAVE SEEN IT? I WAS STUMPED AND HE WASN'T GIVING ME ANSWERS, SO I LET IT GO. IT CAME OUT LATER THOUGH FROM HIS FRIEND THAT THEY HAD TAKEN A COUPLE OF GIRLS TO THE DRIVE IN TO SEE IT. GEORGE HAD AN AFFAIR, TELLING ME HE HAD TO WORK LATE AND YET TOOK A GIRL TO THE DRIVE IN, I WAS DEVASTATED.

WHEN I CONFRONTED HIM, HE SAID IT WAS A REWARD THING FROM MANAGEMENT FOR HAVING GREAT SALES THE MONTH BEFORE. I DIDN'T BELIEVE IT BUT WHAT PROOF DID I HAVE? THEN ONE NIGHT WHILE PREPARING DINNER AT OUR FRIENDS HOUSE WE HAD LIVED WITH FOR A WHILE, WE NOTICED WE WERE MISSING SOME THINGS FOR THE DINNER. I SENT GEORGE TO OUR HOUSE TO GET IT AND OUR FRIEND'S COUSIN ASKED TO RIDE ALONG AS SHE WANTED TO GO TO THE STORE FOR CIGARETTES. GEORGE SAID OK, AND THEY LEFT. 2 HOURS LATER THEY CAME BACK, WHEN I ASKED WHAT TOOK THEM SO LONG, HE SAID THEY WERE CAUGHT IN TRAFFIC, THERE WAS A CAR ACCIDENT AND HAD TO DETOUR, THEN THE STORE WAS BUSY. I COULDN'T UNDERSTAND THAT. I WAS SHOCKED WHEN I LEARNED HE AGAIN HAD LIED, IT FINALLY CAME OUT THAT THEY WENT BACK TO OUR PLACE AND HAD SEX IN OUR BED! SO BEING FURIOUS, I DID A TURN ON HIM AND SLEPT WITH HIS FRIEND, I KNOW TWO WRONGS DON'T MAKE A RIGHT, BUT I WANTED REVENGE.

I ENDED UP LEAVING GEORGE, WITH NO WHERE ELSE TO GO, I WENT, WITH TAIL BETWEEN MY LEGS TO MY PARENTS HOUSE AND ASKED TO STAY THERE. I EXPLAINED WHAT HAPPENED AND BECAUSE OF HAVING THE KID'S THEY LET ME STAY BUT THERE WOULD ONLY BE ROOM FOR ONE CHILD. I HATED TO SEPARATE THEM BUT FELT BETTER HAVING ANGIE SINCE SHE WAS 5 ½, AND ERIC WAS 13 MOS. I FIGURED IT WOULD BE BETTER FOR MY PARENTS NOT HEARING A BABY CRY, UNDER WHAT WAS ALREADY A DIFFICULT SITUATION, SO I KEPT ANGIE AND GEORGE KEPT ERIC, UNTIL OTHER ARRANGEMENTS COULD BE MADE. YOU JUST NEVER KNOW UNDER SUCH CIRCUMSTANCES HOW LONG A SEPARATION COULD BE OR EVEN IF DIVORCE WAS NECESSARY. I NEEDED TIME!!

THE NEXT DAY I BEGAN TO LOOK FOR WORK, BUT JOBS WAS A LITTLE SCARCE, AS I DIDN'T HAVE A LOT OF SKILLS. I NEEDED TO GET A PLACE FAST, AS I HAD TO GET ANGIE WHO WAS IN KINDERGARDEN, TRANSFERRED FROM GREENVILLE TO PIQUA SCHOOLS AND I KNEW IT WOULD BE HARD BEING AT MY PARENTS WITH MY DAD AND I NOT HAVING THE BEST RELATIONSHIP. I SPENT MANY NIGHTS CRYING MYSELF TO SLEEP WONDERING WHAT I WAS GOING TO DO. I FELT IT WAS NO USE TALKING TO MY PARENTS ABOUT ANYTHING, MY MOM WOULD BE ON PINS AND NEEDLES ALREADY DEALING WITH MY FATHER NOW THAT I WAS BACK HOME. I JUST COULDN'T BELIEVE THAT RIGHT UNDER MY NOSE, GEORGE WAS HAVING AN AFFAIR. I SUPPOSE I SHOULD HAVE SUSPECTED SOMETHING WAS UP THE FIRST TIME I SEEN HER IN OUR BED. THE EXCUSE GIVEN WAS SHE HAD A BAD BACK AND

COULDN'T SLEEP ON THE COUCH OR THE FLOOR. I WAS SO GULLIBLE THAT I BELIEVED ANYTHING.

I STILL BLAMED MYSELF, IF I DIDN'T HURT DURING SEX, I'D BE ABLE TO SATISFY MY HUSBAND AND HE'D HAVE NO REASON TO LOOK ELSEWHERE, AND I WOULDN'T BE ON MY OWN NOW, WITH 2 KID'S TO THINK ABOUT EVEN THOUGH I HAD ONE AND GEORGE HAD THE OTHER. IT WAS STILL A LOT TO DEAL WITH AND I FELT AS IF I WAS ON A MERRY-GO-ROUND AND COULDN'T GET OFF, THINGS SPINNING AROUND ME SO UNSURE OF WHAT TO DO. GEORGE KEPT CALLING TRYING TO GET ME TO COME BACK, USING THINGS LIKE, ERIC NEEDS ME, HE'LL TAKE HIM AWAY AND ERIC WON'T KNOW ME. HE EVEN TRIED TO GET ME TO TALK TO A PASTOR FRIEND OF HIS FAMILY AS A LAST DASH EFFORT TO GET ME TO COME HOME.

ONE NIGHT ANGIE AND I WAS OUT BACK PLAYING WHEN THE PHONE RANG. WHEN I ANSWERED IT, THE GUY ON THE OTHER END ASKED FOR ME, I SAID SPEAKING, AND HE INTRODUCED HIMSELF AS GEORGE'S OLD PASTOR. OH, I WAS FURIOUS, I MEAN THE NERVE OF GEORGE TO PRESSURE ME LIKE THAT. I TOLD HIS PASTOR OF GEORGE'S AFFAIR AND ALL THAT HAD HAPPENED AND HE SAID HE UNDERSTOOD, BUT THERE COULD BE FORGIVENESS AND RESTORATION. I DIDN'T WANT TO HEAR THAT. I THOUGHT HEAR WE GO AGAIN, SOMEONE TRYING TO CONTROL ME INSTEAD OF UNDERSTANDING THAT I WAS A VICTIM. WELL I WOULDN'T BE PRESSURED, EVEN THOUGH I TOO WAS IN THE WRONG FOR RETALIATING AGAINST HIM BY HAVING AN AFFAIR MYSELF, I HAD THE CONCEPT THAT

GEORGE HAD LEFT FOR SUMMER CAMP WITH THE NATIONAL GUARDS AND WOULD BE GONE TWO WEEKS. DURING THIS TWO WEEK PERIOD, I WAS SEEING HIS FRIEND WHOM WAS THE ONE WHO TOLD ME OF HIS AFFAIR AT THE DRIVE-IN. I WAS STILL MAKING EXCUSES AND JUSTIFYING WHY I FELT I WAS RIGHT IN DOING THIS. THIS GUY WAS A WORK MATE OF GEORGE'S WHICH WOULD MAKE FOR A DIFFICULT SITUATION, BUT GEORGE BEING GONE FOR TWO WEEKS MADE IT SOME WHAT EASIER AT THE TIME. I'M NOT SURE IF THIS GUY HAD ULTERIOR MOTIVES ABOUT ME IN THE BEGINNING AND HAD WANTED ME ALL ALONG AND THAT'S WHY HE OPENED UP IN THE FIRST PLACE, BUT OUR FLING DIDN'T LAST LONG. ONE NIGHT I HAD TREATED HIM BADLY AFTER A NIGHT OF DRINKING. I'M NOT A DRINKER, BUT SOMEHOW FELT THAT I COULD SOLVE MY PROBLEMS BY DRINKING. I WAS TOLD I REALLY MADE A SPECTACLE OF MYSELF AND I WAS SO ASHAMED. I WONDERED WHY I THOUGHT I COULD FIND WHAT I NEEDED IN ALCOHOL, OR IN ANOTHER MAN FOR THAT   MATTER.

I SOON FOUND A JOB AT HILLS DEPARTMENT STORE, IT WAS A NEW PLACE AT THE PIQUA MALL AND I WAS HELPING TO OPEN THE STORE, I WAS EXCITED. AFTER A COUPLE MONTHS THERE, I WAS ABLE TO FIND A 2 BEDROOM APARTMENT WHICH WAS PERFECT FOR JUST ANGIE AND ME AND HER ROOM WOULD BE JUST BIG ENOUGH FOR A CRIB FOR THE TIMES I WOULD GET ERIC. IT WAS HARD BEING AWAY FROM MY SON, ALTHOUGH HE WAS NOW 15 MOS, I COULDN'T HELP BUT WORRY WHETHER HE WOULD FORGET WHO I WAS.

MY PARENTS WERE RELIEVED I WOULD BE MOVING OUT SOON, ESPECIALLY MY MOM AS NOW SHE WOULDN'T HEAR MY DAD'S COMPLAINING ON HOW THINGS WERE GOING ALL WRONG EVER SINCE I SHOWED BACK UP. MY BROTHER WHO HAD BEEN OUT ON HIS OWN HAD NOW CAME BACK HOME AND THIS ADDED TO MY DAD'S AGGRAVATION AND OF COURSE I GOT BLAMED. I REMEMBER MY DAD POINTING HIS FINGER AT ME AND SAYING WE WERE ALL DOING FINE TILL YOU CAME BACK, TOLD ME I WOULD NEVER AMOUNT TO ANYTHING. I WAS CRUSHED, THAT STUNG ME SO BAD AS IF BEING SLAPPED IN THE FACE AFTER COMING IN FROM A COLD WINTER'S DAY. I WAS ONLY TOO GLAD TO BE LEAVING THEIR HOUSE!!

I JUST COULDN'T UNDERSTAND WHY MY DAD WAS LIKE THIS, AFTER ALL I WAS HIS CHILD, HIS FIRST BORN. IT WAS HARD TO IMAGINE THIS WAS THE SAME MAN WHO USED TO PLAY DRUMS TO HELP ME GO TO SLEEP AS A BABY, YET NOW HE COULDN'T STAND THE SIGHT OF ME. I HAD HEARD REPORTS ABOUT MY DAD HAVING A ROUGH CHILDHOOD BUT WAS NEVER TOLD THE FULL STORY OF THINGS HE'D BEEN THRU. I WOULD OFTEN SEE MY DAD JUST SITTING AT THE TABLE OR IN HIS RECLINER STARING INTO SPACE AS IF LOST AND TRYING TO FIND HIS WAY, DRINKING HIS BEER AND SMOKING AS IF THERE WAS NO TOMORROW, ONE RIGHT AFTER THE OTHER, NOT WANTING TO BE BOTHERED BY ANYTHING. TO AVOID DEALING WITH FAMILY, HE OFTEN STAYED UP ALL NIGHT AND SLEPT ALL DAY. GEORGE ONLY ADDED TO MY GRIEF WHEN HE BEGAN USING ERIC AS A PAWN IN A GAME OF CHESS. HIS GAME WAS THAT UNLESS I DROVE TO GREENVILLE, THEN I WOULDN'T GET TO SEE ERIC, CAUSE HE WASN'T

DRIVING TO PIQUA TO BRING HIM. WHEN I WENT THERE HE WOULDN'T ALLOW ME TO BRING ERIC BACK TO PIQUA BECAUSE GEORGE HAD THE IDEA HE WOULDN'T GET HIM BACK AND HE WOULDN'T HAVE THAT. HE'D LOST ONE SON, HE WASN'T ABOUT TO LOSE ANOTHER.

ONE DAY ON THE JOB I STARTED FEELING SICK, I LEFT EARLY THAT DAY, THINKING IT WAS JUST AN UPSET STOMACH FROM SOMETHING I ATE AT LUNCH, BUT THEN I HAD BOUTS OF SICKNESS IN THE MORNING. I THOUGHT OH NO, I CAN'T BE PREGNANT, I PUT IT OUT OF MY MIND AS MY BROTHER WAS GETTING MARRIED THE NEXT MONTH AND I WAS IN THE WEDDING. WE WERE BUSY WITH GETTING OUR DRESSES AND MAKING ALL THE PREPARATIONS. I HAD TRIED MY DRESS ON AND IT WAS FINE, JUST A MINOR ALTERATION WAS NEEDED. BUT WHEN WE WENT BACK FOR THE FINAL FITTING TO MAKE SURE ALTERATIONS WERE CORRECT, THE DRESS WAS TIGHT. I WAS ASKED IF I GAINED WEIGHT AND I SAID NOT THAT I'M AWARE OF, ARE YOU PREGNANT SOMEONE ASKED, I THOUGHT NO, I CAN'T BE, BUT IT WAS SURE FUNNY HOW MY DRESS GOT TIGHT JUST IN A COUPLE OF WEEKS. SURE ENOUGH I WENT TO THE CLINIC THE NEXT DAY FOR A TEST AND I WAS PREGNANT, FROM CALCULATIONS THEY BELIEVED I WAS 4 MONTHS ALONG, I COULDN'T BELIEVE IT, JUST WHAT I NEEDED. I TOLD GEORGE ABOUT IT AND OF COURSE THE PRESSURE WAS ON TO BE REUNITED.

WHILE TALKING ABOUT HOW FAR ALONG I WAS, I DISCOVERED THAT I HAD GOTTEN PREGNANT A WEEK BEFORE FINDING OUT THAT GEORGE HAD AN AFFAIR, THIS WAS ALSO THE TIME I HAD AN AFFAIR WITH HIS FRIEND AS PAY-BACK. I WAS AFRAID THIS GUY WAS

THE FATHER AND NOT GEORGE, WHAT A PRICE TO PAY FOR REVENGE HUH? I SAT DOWN WITH THIS GUY AND TOLD HIM I WAS PREGNANT AND THERE COULD BE A POSSIBILITY IT WAS HIS. HE ASSURED ME THERE WAS NO NEED TO WORRY ABOUT SAYING ANYTHING TO GEORGE OR WORRY ABOUT A PATERNITY TEST ONCE THE BABY WAS BORN BECAUSE HE WAS CERTAIN HE COULD NOT HAVE CHILDREN, GEORGE WAS THE FATHER. I WAS RELIEVED, I KNEW IN THE BACK OF MY MIND THAT GEORGE WAS THE FATHER, BUT I HAD TO BE DOUBLY SURE AND NOW THAT I WAS PREGNANT, IT WOULD ONLY KEEP GEORGE AFTER ME TO WORK THINGS OUT IN OUR MARRIAGE. I WAS STILL HURT AND CONFUSED, I HAD ALLOWED PEOPLE TO CONTROL ME ALL MY LIFE. I ALWAYS WORRIED ABOUT WHAT PEOPLE THOUGHT OF ME AND IT MADE IT VERY HARD TO MAKE FRIENDS AND KEEP THEM AS FRIENDS. I'M NOT EXACTLY SURE WHERE IT STEMMED FROM, WHETHER FROM MY DAD, THINGS I WENT THRU IN CHILDHOOD, THE FACT MY MOM WORKED ALL THE TIME AND MY DAD DIDN'T, BUT I HAD LOST CONTROL OF MY LIFE, OR SO I BELIEVED I DID. ONE THING I DID KNOW FOR SURE, I HAD LEFT GOD OUT OF THE EQUATION.

AFTER MY BROTHER GOT MARRIED IN OCT 1988. I LEARNED THAT GEORGE LOST HIS JOB AND APPARENTLY HAD NO WHERE TO GO. MY JOB WAS GOING WELL AND DIDN'T WANT TO GIVE IT UP SO I DECIDED TO RECONCILE WITH GEORGE AND ALLOWED HIM TO MOVE IN WITH ME. I DIDN'T KNOW IF THIS WAS A RIGHT DECISION, I FELT TRAPPED INTO MAKING IT, BUT DIDN'T WANT TO SEE HIM ON THE STREET WITH OUR SON ERIC. I MADE UP MY MIND FOR THE KIDS SAKE TO MAKE THE BEST OF THINGS, ESPECIALLY NOW THAT I

AFTER ABOUT 2 WEEKS GEORGE FOUND A JOB AS A MANAGER OF A CONVENIENCE STORE IN SIDNEY, OHIO. HE SEEM EXCITED AND WILLING TO WORK THINGS OUT, I SEEN SOME CHANGES FOR THE BETTER AND PRAYED IT WOULD LAST. I HAD STARTED EXPERIENCING SOME DIZZINESS SOMETIMES TO THE POINT OF PASSING OUT SO IN JANUARY 1989 I HAD TO TAKE AN EARLY MATERNITY LEAVE FROM MY JOB DUE TO MISSING LOTS OF WORK BECAUSE OF DIFFICULTIES IN MY PREGNANCY. I WASN'T DUE TILL APRIL 7TH AND WONDERED IF I WOULD MAKE IT TILL THEN OR HAVE THE BABY EARLY. MANY THOUGHTS RAN THRU MY MIND OF HAVING A PREMATURE BABY, I HADN'T GIVEN IT MUCH THOUGHT BEFORE AS BOTH MY OTHER CHILDREN WERE OVERDUE. NOW I WAS EVEN MORE CONCERNED.

APRIL 7TH CAME AND WENT AND NO BABY. THE NEXT MORNING I GET A CALL FROM GEORGE ASKING IF EVERYTHING WAS OK, I SAID YES, WHY? HE MENTIONED AS HE WAS GETTING READY FOR WORK EARLIER THAT MORNING, I HAD LOST MY PLUG. I THOUGHT IT ODD AS I WASN'T HAVING ANY TYPE OF CONTRACTIONS. I HAD ANOTHER CALL COMING IN AND TOLD HIM I NEEDED TO GO, I SWITCHED OVER AND IT WAS MY LANDLADY. SHE HAD ALWAYS PICKED UP THE RENT AND WAS RUNNING BEHIND IN HER ROUNDS THIS MONTH AND WANTED TO KNOW A GOOD TIME TO STOP BY, I LOOKED AT THE CLOCK AND IT WAS 10 AM. AS I WAS SITTING THERE ABOUT TO GIVE HER A TIME, I SUDDENLY FELT SOMETHING EXTREMELY WET AND VERY WARM. AT FIRST I THOUGHT I SPILLED MY DRINK

THAT HAD BEEN SITTING NEXT TO THE PHONE, BUT SOON REALIZED IT WAS MY WATER THAT BROKE. I TOLD HER, WELL, I'M NOT SURE NOW, I BELIEVE MY WATER JUST BROKE, SHE TOLD ME TO BE CALM,TO CALL MY HUSBAND AND SHE WOULD COME OVER RIGHT AWAY AND SIT WITH ME TILL HE GOT THERE TO TAKE ME TO HOSPITAL, I WAS SO GRATEFUL AS GEORGE WAS ABOUT 20 MINUTES AWAY. YOU NEVER KNOW WHAT CAN HAPPEN. GEORGE FINALLY ARRIVED AND WE WERE ON OUR WAY TO THE HOSPITAL, A FRIEND IN GREENVILLE HAVING ERIC AND MY PARENTS HAVING ANGELA. I WAS THANKFUL ARRANGEMENTS HAD ALREADY BEEN MADE FOR THEM.

WE ARRIVED AT THE HOSPITAL AND STILL NO CONTRACTIONS, AFTER EXAMINING ME, I WAS 2 CM DIALATED SO THEY DECIDED TO INDUCE LABOR SO AS NOT TO RISK INFECTION TO THE BABY. I IMMEDIATELY WENT INTO HARD LABOR, TALK ABOUT NO WARNING!! GOODNESS. I THOUGHT LABOR GRADUALLY BUILT UP BUT THIS WAS HARD LABOR FROM THE START. FINALLY AFTER ABOUT 2 HOURS OF LABOR OUR SON JASON ALLEN WAS BORN. WHEN THEY BROUGHT HIM TO ME HE WAS GRAY AND I WAS CONCERNED SOMETHING WAS WRONG WITH HIM, BUT THEY ASSURED ME HE WAS FINE. I WAS HAPPY TO HAVE IT OVER WITH, IT WENT SO FAST AND HE WAS DEFINITELY MY EASIEST OF THE 3.

A FEW WEEKS LATER, I DECIDED TO GET MYSELF FIXED, I HAD ISSUES FOR A WHILE HAVING SEX AS IT WAS ALWAYS SO PAINFUL. THE DOCTOR'S COULDN'T PINPOINT THE PROBLEM AS ALL TESTS THEY DID CAME BACK NORMAL. THEY COULD ONLY SPECULATE, THAT I

WAS BORN THAT WAY, ABUSED SEXUALLY AND BLOCKED IT OUT, OR WHEN I WAS PREGANT BEFORE AND HAD STITCHES, THAT ONE WAS STUCK SOMEWHERE, THEY EVEN WENT AS FAR AS SAYING IT WAS OF A PSYCHOLOGICAL NATURE AS HAVING A FEAR OF BEING PREGNANT BECAUSE SO MUCH PAIN IS INVOLVED IN GIVING BIRTH. WHATEVER THE REASON, I WAS COVERING ALL BASES IN ORDER TO BE A WHOLE WOMAN AGAIN. I WASN'T GOING TO JUST HAVE MY TUBES TIED, THAT CAN BE REVERSED, I WAS HAVING THEM BURNT! I WANTED TO PLEASE MY HUSBAND AND I DIDN'T WANT TO RISK HAVING MORE CHILDREN AND CAUSE THEM OR ME TO ANY PROBLEMS.

WHILE IN SURGERY, THEY TOLD GEORGE I NEEDED A D&C TO CLEAN ME OUT, THIS APPARENTLY WOULD HELP FIX ANY ISSUES I WAS HAVING. WHEN THEY DID THE D&C THERE WAS AN INFECTION IN MY UTERUS AND I STARTED HEMORRAGING, I ALMOST DIED ON THE OPERATING TABLE. THEY GOT ME STABILIZED AND MOVED ME TO RECOVERY. WHEN I WOKE UP IN RECOVERY, I HAD MANY IV'S IN AND A CATHETAR AS WELL. WHEN THEY MOVED ME TO MY ROOM, I LEARNED I HAD LOST A LOT OF BLOOD AND I WOULD NEED A BLOOD TRANSFUSION OF ABOUT 1 ½ PINTS. WHAT NEXT? I HAD ALREADY BEEN THRU SO MUCH, BUT I THANKED GOD I WAS ALIVE! THIS HOWEVER WAS SCARY, I MEAN THEY WERE JUST LEARNING THINGS ABOUT AIDS WHICH IS A VERY DEADLY DISEASE. PEOPLE CAN CONTRACT THE HIV VIRUS WHICH CAUSES AIDS A FEW DIFFERENT WAYS BUT ONE IS THRU BLOOD TRANFUSIONS AND THERE IS NO CURE. TO RECEIVE A BLOOD TRANSFUSION, EVEN THOUGH THEY WERE STARTING TO SCREEN THE

BLOOD, THERE WAS ALWAYS THE CHANCE THEY STILL HAD BAD BLOOD FLOATING AROUND. IT WAS A DIFFICULT DECISION, BUT IF IT WAS NECESSARY, I HAD TO GO THRU WITH IT.

AFTER RECEIVING THE BLOOD, I HAD MY FIRST CIGARETTE SINCE SURGERY, I BECAME SO DIZZY, THAT THE ROOM WAS SPINNING. I THINK THAT WOULD HAVE BEEN A GOOD TIME TO JUST QUIT SMOKING, BUT I DIDN'T. ALTHOUGH I WAS GRATEFUL FOR BEING ALIVE, I STILL PUT GOD FAR FROM ME. I WOULD NEVER THINK TO DO THIS ON PURPOSE, BUT I THINK MY FOCUS WAS ON WHAT YOU COULD SEE RATHER THAN THOSE THINGS I COULDN'T SEE. ALTHOUGH I EXPECTED SOME WEAKNESS FROM THE ORDEAL I JUST WENT THRU, I STARTED DEVELOPING SOME HEALTH ISSUES. TIREDNESS, WEAKNESS, DIZZY SPELLS UPON RISING, AND IT BECAME WORSE WHEN LEAVING THE HOUSE, SO I GOT SO I WAS AFRAID TO GO ANYWHERE. MY MOM HELPED WHEN SHE COULD WHILE GEORGE WORKED AND A FRIEND FROM GREENVILLE CAME A STAYED A FEW DAYS TO HELP WITH KIDS SO I COULD SLEEP, BUT SYMPTOMS REMAINED.

EVENTUALLY I HAD TO QUIT MY JOB, OUR FRIEND HAD TO RETURN HOME SO SHE TOOK THE 2 BOYS TO HER HOUSE IN GREENVILLE AND MY MOM TOOK ANGELA TILL WE FIGURED OUT WHAT WAS GOING ON. I'D SLEEP AND FEEL FINE, BUT AS SOON AS I HAD TO LEAVE THE HOUSE, PANIC AND FEAR GRIPPED ME AND SYMPTOMS RETURNED. THE FEELING I WOULD FAINT, BREAKING OUT IN A SWEAT AND KNEES FEELING LIKE THEY WOULD BUCKLE UNDER ME. I FELT LIKE A PRISONER IN MY OWN HOME. INSTEAD OF CALLING ON

GOD, I RAN FROM DOCTOR TO DOCTOR IN SEARCH OF EXPLANATIONS WHEN FINALLY ONE TOLD ME I WAS HAVING PANIC ATTACKS WHICH ARE SOMETIMES CAUSED BY A CHEMICAL IMBALANCE. I WAS GIVEN DIFFERENT MEDICATIONS IN WHICH ONLY MADE ME FEEL WORSE, LIKE MY BLOOD WAS RUNNING SOME SORT OF RACE YET I WAS STANDING STILL. I FELT AS IF I WAS GOING INSANE. WHENEVER WE WOULD GO OUT WITH FRIENDS, I ENDED UP FEELING LIKE A PARTY POOPER WHEN I WOULD BE HIT WITH AN ATTACK AND HAVE TO LEAVE, NOT SOMETHING SOME PEOPLE COME TO UNDERSTAND. I TRIED COUNSELING FOR A WHILE AND IT HELPED BUT THEN I LOST MY INSURANCE AND HAD TO QUIT GOING.

AFTER ABOUT A YEAR AND A HALF TO TWO YEARS, WE FINALLY MADE SOME PROGRESS IN UNDERSTANDING WHAT MAY HAVE BEEN THE FACTOR IN WHAT I WAS EXPERIENCING AND IT DIDN'T COME FROM THE DOCTOR. I BELIEVE IT WAS THE HOLY SPIRIT! WE WERE BROUGHT BACK TO WHEN I WAS PREGNANT WITH JASON. IT WAS CHRISTMAS TIME AND WE WENT TO AN EMPLOYEE CHRISTMAS PARTY FROM GEORGE'S WORK THAT WAS HELD IN SIDNEY. DURING THE PARTY SOMEONE BROUGHT IN WHAT GEORGE AND I THOUGHT WAS MARIJUANA JOINTS. GEORGE WAS TAKING HITS AND ALTHOUGH BEING PREGNANT AND NOT WANTING TO DO IT, I FELT PRESSURED FROM HIM TO TAKE A HIT IN WHICH I DID. I WANTED TO FIT IN FOR ONCE. A COMBINATION OF THAT AND THE FUMES, I WAS THROWN FOR A LOOP, I STARTED GETTING REAL DIZZY, AND FELT AS IF I WOULD PASS OUT. I'M NOT SURE IF IT WAS LACED WITH SOMETHING, BUT I HAD NEVER BEFORE HAD AN EXPERIENCE SUCH AS THAT

120

FROM SMOKING JUST PLAIN MARIJUANA. I'M NOT SURE HOW WE MADE IT TO THE CAR, I VAGUELY REMEMBER THE TRIP HOME. I DO KNOW GEORGE WAS HAVING TROUBLE DRIVING AND I REMEMBER GOING IN AND PUT OF CONCIOUSNESS CRYING OUT TO GOD TO PLEASE HELP US!! WE DIDN'T DARE CALL ANYONE FOR HELP ALL WE HAD WAS EACH OTHER AND GOD!

THE NEXT DAY WHEN WE WOKE UP, I WAS BETTER AND GEORGE WAS ABLE TO MAKE IT TO WORK. I THANKED GOD FOR PROTECTING US AND HELPING US THRU. WHEN GEORGE GOT HOME FROM WORK HE TOLD ME THAT SOMEONE LACED THE MARIJUANA WITH ACID, OH HOW LUCKY WE WERE TO BE OK AND TO HAVE MADE IT HOME. I REFLECTED ON THE PREVIOUS NIGHT AND JUST THANKED GOD. IT COULD HAVE BEEN DISASTROUS FROM ALL ASPECTS NOT TO MENTION IF WE WOULD HAVE BEEN IN AN ACCIDENT AND TOOK SOMEONE'S LIFE. GOD WAS DEFINITELY WITH US! THEN GOD SHOWED ME THAT THIS INCIDENT IN COMBINATION WITH THE BLOOD TRANSFUSION COMBINED WITH MY BLOOD MAY BE A CONTRIBUTING FACTOR FOR THESE PANIC ATTACKS I WAS NOW EXPERIENCING. I WAS SO GRATEFUL,FINALLY, I WAS GETTING SOME REVELATION, SOME MUCH NEEDED ANSWERS. I WAS SO THANKFUL FOR FRIENDS WHO ALTHOUGH THEY DIDN'T UNDERSTAND, STOOD BY US THRU A TOUGH TIME IN OUR LIFE.

GEORGE ENDED UP LOSING HIS JOB WITH THIS COMPANY AND FOUND A JOB IN GREENVILLE, SO BACK WE WENT. OUR FRIEND'S GRANDMA HAD A HOUSE SHE OWNED,THAT CAME OPEN FOR RENT AND IT WAS CHEAP. IT WAS FALL TIME AND CHILLY OUT. I HATE

MOVING IN THE COLD, ESPECIALLY WITH 3 KIDS AGES 8, 3 ½ AND 8 MOS, BUT IT WAS CLOSER TO HIS FAMILY, FRIENDS, AND JOB WHICH WOULD SAVE GAS SO WE MADE THE MOVE. I DIDN'T WANT HIM HAVING TO DRIVE SO FAR WITH WINTER APPROACHING. SO WE MADE THE MOVE, GOT SETTLED IN AND SOON HAD A ROUTINE SET UP. ANGELA WAS SETTLING IN TO HER NEW SCHOOL AND MAKING FRIENDS AND I STAYED HOME WITH THE BOYS WHILE GEORGE WORKED 2 JOBS TO MAKE ENDS MEET AND HOPEFULLY START A SAVINGS. THINGS WERE STARTING TO REALLY LOOK UP FOR US. I WAS STARTING TO RELAX SOME. ALTHOUGH I WAS STILL HAVING PANIC ATTACKS, THEY WERE NOT AS BAD   AS   BEFORE.

IN THE SPRING OF 1990, JUST AFTER JASON'S 1ST BIRTHDAY, I RECEIVED A CALL FROM MY MOM THAT MY DAD HAD BEEN ILL AND HAD SOME ODD OCCURRANCES. HE WOULD HAVE HER LEAVE LIGHTS OFF AFTER DARK, EXCEPT FOR A FEW NIGHTLIGHTS OR CANDLES SITTING AROUND. HE HAD HER PURCHASE ROOM DARKENING BLINDS AND INSTALL THEM CAUSE HE WAS AFRAID PEOPLE WERE WATCHING THE HOUSE AND LOOKING IN. SHE SAID OFF AND ON SHE WOULD CATCH HIM PEERING OUT THE BLINDS AS IF TO BE WATCHING SOMETHING. IT EVEN GOT AS ODD THAT WHEN SHE WOULD GO SOMEWHERE AT NIGHT, HE WOULD ASK HER TO SHUT OFF HER HEADLIGHTS A BLOCK FROM THE HOUSE SO THE NEIGHBORS WOULDN'T SEE HER PULL IN THE DRIVEWAY. WE DIDN'T REALIZE WHAT WAS GOING ON TILL MUCH LATER WHEN, THRU TESTING THEY FOUND POLYPS ON MY DAD'S RECTUM. THEY SCHEDULED SURGERY AND WHEN IT HAD BEEN COMPLETED THEY

FOUND 6 POLYPS. THEY REMOVED 5 WITH THE 6TH ONE BEING ATTACHED TO HIS APPENDIX, THEY DIDN'T WANT TO REMOVE HIS APPENDIX AT HIS AGE SO THEY DECIDED TO SEND THE 5 IN FOR A BIOPSY, AND IF THEY CAME BACK BENIGN, THEN THE CHANCES OF THE ONE ATTACHED TO HIS APPENDIX BEING CANCEROUS WAS SLIM.

I CAN'T IMAGINE WHAT WAS GOING THRU HIS MIND, BUT HE WAS NOT ONE TO GO TO THE DOCTOR, MANY APPOINTMENTS WOULD BE SCHEDULED WHEN HE DIDN'T FEEL WELL BUT ALWAYS CANCELED THEM, SO FOR HIM TO FOLLOW THRU, HE MUST HAVE BEEN PRETTY CONCERNED. HIS WHOLE DEMEANOR HAD CHANGED. HE BECAME SOLEMN AND WITHDRAWN. I KNOW HIS THOUGHTS DRIFTED BACK TO HIS FATHER WHO HAD PASSED OF COLON CANCER AT THE YOUNG AGE OF 52. WE TRIED TO RAISE MY DAD'S SPIRITS BY TELLING HIM HE WAS ONLY 46 AND HAD A LOT OF YEARS AHEAD OF HIM YET. IT BROUGHT EVEN MORE HOPE WHEN THE RESULTS CAME BACK AND THE 5 POLYPS THEY REMOVED WAS BENIGN, NO SIGN OF CANCER, SO THEY WAS LEAVING THE LAST ONE ALONE AND DECIDED NOT TO PUT HIM THRU ANOTHER SURGERY TO REMOVE HIS APPENDIX.

THIS TIME HAD REALLY BEEN HARD ON THEM, ESPECIALLY MY MOM. SHE HAD BEEN OFF WORK A WHILE DUE TO A WORK INJURY. SHE HAD DEVELOPED CARPAL TUNNEL AND HAD SURGERY THAT MESSED UP HER HAND. SHE DREW WORKMAN'S COMP FOR A WHILE BUT THAT RAN OUT. SHE THEN TRIED TO GET DISABILITY FROM SOCIAL SECURITY AND HAD BEEN TURNED DOWN. FOR THREE MONTHS THEY REALLY

PINCHED WHAT SAVINGS THEY HAD. MY DAD DIDN'T WORK AND ALTHOUGH US 3 KIDS HAD LONG MOVED OUT, AND IT WAS JUST THE 2 OF THEM,IT WAS STILL HARD TO MAKE ENDS MEET.

FINALLY, AFTER THE 5TH TRY, MY MOM'S SOCIAL SECURITY DISABILITY WENT THRU, AND SHE WAS ESTATIC. IT TOOK A LOAD OF HER MIND FOR SURE AND I KNOW SHE THANKED GOD FOR HEARING AND ANSWERING HER PRAYERS! ALTHOUGH THEY HAD INSURANCE, IT DIDN'T COVER A WHOLE LOT AND THE BILLS WERE MOUNTING UP. SHE HAD TOLD ME MANY TIMES IF IT WASN'T FOR GOD AND HER FAMILY AND FRIENDS, SHE WOULDN'T HAVE KNOWN WHAT TO DO. ALTHOUGH SHE LOVED GOING TO CHURCH, IT BECAME HARD TO GO WITH HAVING TO CARE FOR MY DAD, BUT HER FAITH WAS STRONG.

2 MONTHS HAD PASSED AND IT WAS SOON THANKSGIVING, WE CERTAINLY HAD A LOT TO BE THANKFUL FOR. I LIVED IN GREENVILLE AT THE TIME AND MY PARENTS WAS COMING TO OUR PLACE FOR THANKSGIVING DINNER THIS YEAR, AS WE THOUGHT THE CHANGE WOULD DO THEM GOOD. WE PLANNED FOR THEM TO COME UP THE NIGHT BEFORE THAT WAY THEY COULD STILL HELP WITH PREPARATIONS. I WAS EXCITED THEY WERE COMING CAUSE MY DAD DOESN'T USUALLY LIKE TO LEAVE THE HOUSE. HE WAS PRETTY MUCH A HERMIT SO TO SPEAK, JUST SITTING AROUND THE HOUSE WATCHING TV OR PLAYING WITH THE FAMILY DOG.

WHEN MY PARENTS ARRIVED, THE KIDS WERE SO EXCITED. I TRIED TO CONTAIN THEM AS I DIDN'T WANT

124

MY DAD BEING OVERWHELMED, BUT ANGIE WAS 8 ½, ERIC WAS 4 AND JASON WAS 2 SO TO TRY AND CONTAIN THEM WAS A DEFINITE CHORE. MY DAD SEEMED IN GOOD SPIRITS, WE REALLY STRUGGLED TO HAVE A RELATIONSHIP WHEN I WAS GROWING UP. HE WAS SO HARD ON ME AND SO VERBALLY ABUSIVE, BUT AS I LOOKED AT HIM, NOTICING HOW HE HAD AGED, I COULDN'T HELP BUT WELL UP WITH TEARS AND PRAY THAT GOD WOULD HEAL HIM AND THAT HE WOULD COME TO KNOW CHRIST AS SAVIOR.

ONCE THE KIDS WERE SETTLED, WE STARTED WORKING ON THE PREPARATIONS FOR DINNER, AS WE SAT TALKING ABOUT DIFFERENT THINGS, MY DAD GOT A SAD LOOK ON HIS FACE, AND BEGAN TO SHARE THINGS ABOUT HIS LIFE THAT APPARENTLY HAD BEEN BOTTLED UP FOR A LOT YEARS AND MY HEART SANK. MY DAD HAD NEVER DONE THAT BEFORE. HE WAS ONE TO KEEP THINGS TO HIMSELF AND I COULDN'T HELP BUT THINK THERE WAS SOMETHING HE WASN'T TELLING ME AS HE SHARED THINGS FROM HIS CHILDHOOD, SPEAKING OF THE MANY PHOTO'S I HAD SEEN IN THE ALBUMS BUT NEVER REALLY KNOWING THE FULL STORY BEHIND THEM, ONLY WHAT HE CHOSE TO SHARE AT THE TIME, WHICH WAS VAGUE. I LEARNED THAT HE HAD BEEN A VICTIM OF CHILD ABUSE, BEYOND ANYTHING I COULD HAVE IMAGINED.

ONE INCIDENT IN PARTICULIAR WAS WHEN HIS FATHER WAS IN THE SERVICE. HE CAME HOME ON A SHORT LEAVE. AFTER A FEW WEEKS, HIS FATHER RETURNED TO THE SERVICE AND MY GRANDMOTHER SOME TIME AFTER THAT LEARNED SHE WAS PREGNANT. SHE HADN'T HAD ANY SYMPTOMS AND

125

WAS SHOCKED WHEN SHE WENT FOR A ROUTINE DOCTOR VISIT AND WAS GIVEN THE NEWS. WHEN SHE TOLD MY GRANDFATHER, HE COULDN'T BELIEVE IT AND THOUGHT MY GRANDMA HAD AN AFFAIR. AFTER MY DAD WAS BORN AND THROUGH OUT HIS CHILDHOOD MY GRANDFATHER HAD BEAT HIM, SET HIM ON FIRE, HAD HIM PUT IN JAIL, SELLING ALL HE HAD WHILE MY DAD WAS INCARCERATED. I COULDN'T BELIEVE WHAT I WAS HEARING AND MY EYES WERE OPENED TO A LOT OF THINGS. I CAME TO UNDERSTAND THE EXTENT OF DEPRESSION MY DAD WAS SUFFERING, WHY IT WAS HARD FOR HIM TO HOLD A JOB. WHENEVER HE WOULD BE REPRIMANDED ON THE JOB, HE COULDN'T HANDLE IT AND WOULD QUIT. I THOUGHT OF HIS HARSHNESS TOWARD ME AND WONDERED IF HE COULD HELP IT. COULD IT BE HE KNEW NO OTHER WAY, THAN HOW HE WAS TREATED BY HIS FATHER?

I REMEMBER ONE TIME WHEN MY PARENTS HAD COMPANY OVER, THE COUPLE WAS SO SMITTEN WITH US KIDS. THEY DIDN'T HAVE CHILDREN, AND NOT SURE IF THEY COULD HAVE ANY. I REMEMBER SITTING ON THEIR LAPS AND JUST LOVING THE ATTENTION AS I NEVER RECEIVED MUCH FROM MY PARENTS. MY MOM WORKED ALL THE TIME AND MY DAD JUST KEPT TO HIMSELF, SLEEPING ALL DAY AND UP ALL NIGHT. MY DAD ONE NIGHT BECAME SO ANGRY AT MY CLINGINESS AND HE WHIPPED ME WITH A BELT, THE BUCKLE LET LOOSE AND CAUGHT ME IN THE EYE GIVING ME A BLACK EYE. IN SOME WAYS I THINK BY OPENING UP, HE WAS TRYING TO MAKE IT RIGHT, I DON'T REMEMBER HIM APOLOGIZING, BUT MAYBE IN HIS OWN WAY BY SHARING HIS HEARTACHES, IT WAS HIS WAY OF APOLOGIZING AND TRYING TO GET ME TO

UNDERSTAND WHY HE REACTED THE WAY HE DID. I THINK FROM THAT MOMENT MAY HAVE BEEN THE BEGINNING STAGES OF THE HEALING PROCESS BETWEEN MY FATHER AND I. ONE I HAD ALWAYS LONGED FOR.

IT HAD GOTTEN VERY LATE, SO WE PREPARED FOR BED, I HAD BUNKED THE BOYS WITH THEIR SISTER FOR THE NIGHT AND PUT MY PARENTS IN THE BOYS ROOM. AS I LAID DOWN FOR THE NIGHT, MY MIND PLAYED OVER AND OVER AGAIN THE WORDS MY DAD HAD SHARED. I FELT JOY AND SADNESS AT THE SAME TIME, IF THAT MAKES SENSE. JOY WITH HAVING SPENT SOME TIME WITH MY DAD ACTUALLY TALKING INSTEAD OF BEING DOWNGRADED, SADNESS AT HOW MUCH HE ENDURED WHICH EXPLAINED WHY HE PREFERRED TO HANG OUT AT HOME AND HIS INABILITY TO HAVE RELATIONSHIPS.

I THINK WHAT IMPACTED ME THE MOST WAS WHEN MY DAD HAD SHARED ABOUT THE TIME HE HAD LEARNED TO DRIVE. HE HAD WENT AWAY AND WHEN HE CAME HOME AND PARKED THE CAR IN FRONT OF THE HOUSE, HE HAD RUN OVER A ROCK IN SUCH A WAY THAT IT FLIPPED UP AND HIT THE NEIGHBORS CAR PUTTING A DING IN THEIR BUMPER. HE DIDN'T REALIZE AT THE TIME IT HAD HAPPENED AND JUST WENT ON IN THE HOUSE, BUT THE NEIGHBOR HAD HEARD A NOISE AND WENT TO INVESTIGATE AND SEEN THE SLIGHT DENT. THEY HAD CALLED THE POLICE AND MY GRANDPA HAD MY DAD PUT IN JAIL FOR HIT AND RUN. HE HAD SPENT 3 DAYS IN JAIL AND WHEN HE GOT OUT FOUND THAT MY GRANDPA HAD SOLD HIS BED AND ALL HIS BELONGINGS. I BEGAN TO WEEP. I'M NOT SURE

WHEN I DRIFTED OFF TO SLEEP AND I MUST HAVE TOSSED AND TURNED ALL NIGHT BECAUSE WHEN I WOKE THE NEXT MORNING, I FELT AS THOSE I HADN'T SLEPT A WINK, BUT HAD TO GET STARTED PREPARING THANKSGIVING MEAL. AS I WALKED INTO THE KITCHEN MY DAD WAS ALREADY PREPARING THE TURKEY, I'M SO USED TO HIM SLEEPING ALL DAY WHILE THE OTHERS MADE THE DINNER, SO THIS WAS A NEW SITE FOR ME TO SEE, ALTHOUGH LOOKING A BIT WORN,HE SEEM TO HAVE A DIFFERENT OUTLOOK ON THINGS.

MY MOM WAS MAKING HER FAMOUS DRESSING AS SHE HAD DONE EVERY YEAR. AS I WATCHED THEM WORKING AROUND, MY THOUGHTS OF LAST NIGHTS CONVERSATION CAME TO MIND AND I WONDERED HOW HE MUST HAVE WRESTLED WITH HIMSELF ALL THESE YEARS, WASTING PRECIOUS MOMENTS WITH FAMILY, BEING SO LOST IN HIMSELF, BUT I QUICKLY SHOOK IT OFF NOT WANTING TO PUT A DAMPER ON THE DAY AND WENT IN TO WATCH THE THANKSGIVING DAY PARADE. PRETTY SOON MY DAD CAME INTO THE LIVING ROOM, SAT DOWN IN THE CHAIR, SAID HE WASN'T FEELING WELL AND PASSED OUT. WE IMMEDIATELY CALLED 911 AND AN AMBULANCE SOON ARRIVED AND OFF TO THE HOSPITAL THEY WENT. MOM HAD WENT WITH THEM AND GEORGE AND I STAYED BACK TO FINISH THE DINNER. A FEW HOURS LATER, MY MOM CAME BACK TO SAY WHEN THEY TOOK A CHEST X-RAY THEY FOUND A SPOT ON MY DAD'S LUNGS. THEY WERE GOING TO ADMIT HIM FOR FURTHER TESTING, BUT WAS THINKING HE MAY HAVE PNEUMONIA. WE WENT AHEAD AND ATE DINNER, THE EVENING BEING SORT OF A HAZE, IT JUST WASN'T THE SAME NOT HAVING MY DAD THERE, AT

LEAST HE ALWAYS TRIED TO BE SOCIAL AND PLEASANT AROUND THE HOLIDAYS.

AFTER DINNER WE WENT TO VISIT HIM AND HE SEEMED TO BE IN GOOD SPIRITS CONSIDERING HE WAS IN THE HOSPITAL OVER THANKSGIVING INSTEAD OF WITH FAMILY. I CAN'T IMAGINE WHAT HE WAS FEELING BUT IT WAS IF HE KNEW IT WAS SERIOUS. I SURE IT CROSSED HIS MIND A TIME OR TOO THAT HE MAY DIE YOUNG LIKE HIS FATHER. IN FACT HE MADE MENTION OF IT AND WE WERE QUICK TO SHOOT THAT IDEA DOWN AND TOLD HIM TO QUIT TALKING NONSENSE. IT NEVER MADE SENSE TO ME, HOW PEOPLE WOULD WANT THEIR LIFE TO END AND NOT FIGHT TO LIVE, BUT IT'S NOT FOR US TO JUDGE. WE DON'T KNOW TO WHAT EXTENT A PERSON GOES THRU AND NOT EVERYONE IS AS STRONG AS ANOTHER.

I, HOWEVER, EXPERIENCED MUCH HARDSHIP, MADE MILLIONS OF MISTAKES AND CAME TO FEEL WHAT MY FATHER MUST HAVE FELT MANY A TIME. THAT THERE HAD TO BE SOMETHING BETTER THAN WHAT WE DEALT WITH NOW. BUT I ALSO BELIEVE THAT PEOPLE ARE IN CHARGE OF THEIR OWN DESTINIES AND CAN MAKE WHAT THEY WANT OUT OF THEIR LIVES. SADLY, HOWEVER FOR MY DAD THE ABUSE HE ENDURED WAS MORE THAN HE COULD HANDLE AND ALTHOUGH HE HAD SOME HAPPY TIMES, HE WAS HAUNTED, I THINK CONTINUOUSLY BY MEMORIES OF HIS FATHER. I CAME TO UNDERSTAND WHY HE SLEPT ALL DAY AND STAYED AWAKE AT NIGHT, WHY HE DIDN'T WANT TO SPANK US KIDS AND USED HARSH WORDS, WHICH I BELIEVE IS WORSE, BUT JUST MY OPINION. I FINALLY UNDERSTOOD WHY HE COULDN'T HOLD A JOB.

I'M NOT EVEN SURE IF HE TOLD MY MOM EVERYTHING, ONLY WHAT MY MOM SEEN WHEN THEY WOULD GET A CALL FROM MY GRANDMA SAYING MY GRANDPA WAS BEATING HER AGAIN. WE WOULD GO DOWN AND SHE WOULD BE SO BLACK AND BLUE THAT YOU COULDN'T STICK A TOOTHPICK IN BETWEEN THE BRUISES. MY DAD NEVER SHARED DREAMS, GOALS, THINGS HE WANTED FROM LIFE, ONLY SAID WHAT HE HAD TO AND KEPT QUIET AND TO HIMSELF AS IF TRAPPED IN HIS OWN LITTLE WORLD TRYING TO FIND A WAY OF ESCAPE AND THINKING THAT SOMEHOW THE WAY OUT WAS THRU LASHING OUT FROM WITHIN A CAGED AREA AND EVENTUALLY JUST GAVE UP THE FIGHT.

THE NEXT DAY WE LEARNED THAT THRU FURTHER TESTING, MY DAD HAD EMPHYSEMA, 3 BRAIN TUMORS AND CANCER. WE LEARNED THAT APPARENTLY THE 6TH POLYP ATTACHED TO MY DAD'S APPENDIX, THE OTHER DOCTOR DIDN'T REMOVE WAS INDEED CANCEROUS AND HAD SPLIT OFF SPREADING TO HIS LUNGS AND BRAIN. THEY WERE GOING TO START RADIATION, WHICH THEY WERE CONFIDENT ENOUGH WOULD GET RID OF 2 BRAIN TUMORS, BUT THE OTHER WAS QUITE LARGE, AND INOPERABLE AND ALTHOUGH MAY SHRINK DOWN, DIDN'T HAVE MUCH HOPE OF IT GOING AWAY. WE WERE JUST FLOORED AND WONDERED WHY THE DOCTOR DIDN'T JUST REMOVE THE OTHER POLYP. BUT SINCE THE 5 WAS BENIGN IT SEEMED POINTLESS TO PUT MY DAD THRU ANOTHER SURGERY TO REMOVE A HEALTHY APPENDIX.

WHEN MY DAD WAS RELEASED, THEY TRAVELED BACK HOME. WHEN MY DAD HAS HIS FOLLOW UP VISIT

WITH HIS FAMILY DOCTOR, HE GAVE MY PARENTS THE DREADED NEWS. MY DAD WAS TERMINAL AND GIVEN 6 TO 8 MONTHS TO LIVE. WE WERE ALL JUST DEVASTATED AT THE NEWS, BUT I'M SURE IT REALLY HIT MY MOM HARD AND I FELT FOR HER, THAT UNLESS GOD HEALED MY DAD SHE WOULD LOSE SOMEONE SHE LOVED AND SPENT 28 YEARS WITH. WE KNEW THAT CHRISTMAS THAT YEAR WAS GOING TO BE TOUGH, WE HAD MY PARENTS COME OVER, DESPITE THE FACT OF HIM BEING ILL. I THINK MY DAD KNOWING THAT COULD BE HIS VERY LAST CHRISTMAS GAVE HIM THE STRENGTH TO ENDURE THE TRIP OVER. HE WAS STILL UNDERGOING RADIATION SO THEY HADN'T STARTED WITH THE CHEMO AS OF YET, AND IT WOULD BE ANOTHER COUPLE WEEKS BEFORE DOING SO. WE DIDN'T KNOW WHAT TO EXPECT WHEN HE DID START CHEMO SO WE WANTED TO SQUEEZE THINGS IN WHILE WE HAD THE OPPORTUNITY TO DO SO. YOU HEAR ALL KINDS OF STORIES ABOUT THOSE WITH TERMINAL ILLNESSES, BUT UNLESS YOU ACTUALLY WALK THRU IT OR EXPERIENCE SOMEONE CLOSE TO YOU WHO DOES YOU CAN NEVER FULLY UNDERSTAND THEIR PAIN. IT'S A VERY HEARTWRENCHING THING TO WATCH THEM GO THRU, WATCHING THEIR VERY LIFE BEING SUCKED AWAY AND NOTHING YOU CAN DO FOR THEM BUT MAKE THEM AS COMFORTABLE AS POSSIBLE AND OF COURSE PRAY!!

NORMALLY AT CHRISTMAS WE HAD THE KIDS OPEN GIFTS ON CHRISTMAS MORNING, THEN WE WENT TO THE FAMILIES IN THE AFTERNOON. THIS YEAR, THINKING IT WOULD BE MY DAD'S LAST ONE, WE WANTED IT TO BE EXTRA SPECIAL FOR HIM, SO WE MADE THE KIDS WAIT. IT WASN'T OFTEN THAT MY

BROTHERS AND THEIR WIVES GOT TOGETHER, THE FAMILY KIND OF WENT THEIR OWN WAYS AS SOME DIVORCED, OTHERS MARRIED AND HAD THEIR SPOUSES FAMILY GATHERINGS TO SCHEDULE AROUND NOW, BUT THIS YEAR MY BROTHERS AND THEIR WIVES MADE PLANS TO JOIN US SINCE THIS COULD BE OUR DAD'S LAST, WHICH WAS GREAT TO HAVE US ALL TOGETHER ALTHOUGH WISHING IT WAS UNDER BETTER CIRCUMSTANCES. MY DAD SEEMED TO ENJOY HIMSELF, BU I COULD TELL HE WAS WIPED OUT. OTHERS MENTIONED IT WAS TOO MUCH TO CRAM IN FOR HIM. I WANTED TO MAKE IT SPECIAL FOR HIM AND DIDN'T STOP TO ASK WHAT THEY WANTED TO DO. THEY DECIDED TO LEAVE EARLY SINCE THEY HAD A LONG DRIVE HOME AND I FELT SO GUILTY PUTTING HIM THRU SUCH A LONG DAY. HE NEVER COMPLAINED, BUT I SHOULD HAVE BEEN MORE CONSIDERATE.

SOON THE NEW YEAR WAS UPON US, AND DAD WOULD SOON START CHEMO. HE WAS SCARED WHICH WAS TOTALLY UNDERSTANDABLE. MOM TOLD ME THEY HAD STARTED HAVING A COUPLE COME OVER. IT WAS A LADY SHE WORKED WITH AND THEY BECAME GOOD FRIENDS. THEY WERE A PART OF A CHURCH AND MY MOM THOUGHT IT MAY BE GOOD TO TALK TO MY DAD ABOUT THE LORD. THEY HAD MANY BIBLE STUDIES AND TIMES OF PRAYER WHEN MY DAD FELT UP TO IT THAT IS. ONE DAY MY MOM SAID MY DAD HAD STUMBLED ACROSS A GIANT PRINT BIBLE OF MINE AND HAD BEEN READING SOME. I HAD FORGOTTEN ALL ABOUT HAVING IT WHEN I MOVED OUT AND WAS GLAD IT WAS FOUND. SHE SAID MY DAD MARVELED AT SOME OF THE SCRIPTURES THAT I HAD HIGHLIGHTED IN THERE AND EVEN SAID TO MY MOM HOW MUCH OF AN EXAMPLE I

HAD BEEN GROWING UP AND DOTED ON MY KNOWLEDGE OF THE BIBLE. I WAS FLOORED.

IT WASN'T LIKE MY DAD TO NOTICE ANYTHING POSITIVE WHEN IT CAME TO ME, HE WAS ALWAYS SO MEAN AND KEPT TO HIMSELF MOST OF THE TIME. THAT JUST MELTED MY HEART WHEN SHE TOLD ME THIS CAUSE I WENT MANY YEARS BELIEVING MY DAD NEVER TRULY LOVED ME. WHAT SHE TOLD ME NEXT, BROUGHT TEARS TO MY EYES. ONE NIGHT IN A BIBLE STUDY THEY WERE HAVING, MY DAD ACCEPTED THE LORD AS HIS SAVIOR!! I WAS ESTACTIC AND STARTED TO THINK ABOUT MY OWN SPIRITUAL LIFE. I MEAN I HAD ACCEPTED JESUS AS SAVIOR AT 13, BUT HAD ALLOWED OTHER THINGS TO CLOUD MY JUDGEMENT AND MADE THEM A PRIORITY IN MY LIFE. IT'S KIND OF HEART BREAKING AS I TYPE THIS TO THINK HOW MY LIFE WAS AS A TEEN, BEING SO EXCITED ABOUT GOD, AND GOD DOING SO MUCH IN MY LIFE, GETTING ME THRU SOME VERY HARD TIMES AND NOW I HAD TURNED MY BACK ON HIM. I DEFINITELY CHOKED BACK SOME TEARS.

MY DAD WAS NOW IN HIS SECOND MONTH OF CHEMO AND IN TALKING WITH MOM, SHE SHARED HOW SICK HE WAS FROM IT. I FELT TERRIBLE LIVING SO FAR FROM THEM AT A TIME THEY MAY NEED ME THE MOST, BUT IN DEALING WITH PANIC ATTACKS MYSELF, HAVING KIDS, GEORGE WORKING 2 JOBS WITH ONE CAR, IT MADE IT HARD TO PICK UP AND GO. ANGELA WAS HAVING SOME ISSUES AGAIN, TO THE POINT SHE HID ALL HER CLOTHES BEHIND THE LIVING ROOM COUCH WANTING TO RUN AWAY. I DIDN'T UNDERSTAND WHY, SHE WAS ONLY 9, WHAT COULD BE SO WRONG THAT SHE DIDN'T WANT TO BE AT HOME ANYMORE. THINGS

WAS GOING REAL WELL, OR SO I THOUGHT. SO I TOLD MOM SORRY, I HAD 2 BROTHERS THAT WOULD HAVE TO START HELPING OUT SOME, I HAD ALOT ON MY PLATE FOR THE TIME BEING, BUT WOULD BE OVER SOON. I THINK I WAS JUST AFRAID, AND I KNOW I WAS DEALING WITH ALOT OF UNFORGIVENESS TOWARDS MY DAD.

THE FOLLOWING WEEK MY MOM HAD CALLED TO SAY THEY DIDN'T HAVE MUCH FOOD, SO GEORGE AND I GATHERED SOME THINGS AND MADE THE DRIVE OVER TO PIQUA TO DROP IT OFF. MY DAD WAS HAVING A GOOD DAY AND BEGAN TO SHARE HIS DREAMS OF WANTING ME TO GO TO COLLEGE AND BETTER MY CAREER BY BEING AN EX-RAY TECHNICIAN. HOWEVER, IT JUST WASN'T MY PASSION. I OFTEN WONDERED IF I WASN'T JUST BEING SELFISH, AFTER-ALL, WE WERE JUST STARTING TO BUILD A RELATIONSHIP, ONE I SO LONGED TO HAVE ALL MY LIFE GROWING UP AND WANTED TO PLEASE HIM. I FELT LIKE SUCH A DISAPPOINTMENT TO HIM, SO I BEGAN GIVING SOME SERIOUS THOUGHT TO THE IDEA OF GOING TO SCHOOL. MAYBE I HAD HOPED IT WOULD HELP HIM FIGHT FOR HIS LIFE AND NOT LEAVE US. I DID WANT HIM TO BE ABLE TO ENJOY HIS GRANDKIDS AND WANTED HIS GRANDKIDS TO KNOW HIM. I NEVER FOLLOWED THRU WITH THE IDEA THOUGH, IT JUST WASN'T IN MY HEART TO DO. I HAD TRIED MOST OF MY LIFE TO BE A PEOPLE PLEASER, AND YET AGAIN I FELT MY DAD, THRU HIS ILLNESS WAS SOMEHOW ONCE AGAIN TRYING TO RUN MY LIFE. IT'S OK FOR PARENTS TO HAVE DREAMS FOR THEIR KIDS AND SHARE THEM, BUT I BELIEVE IT HAS TO ALSO BE IN THE HEART OF THE CHILD AS WELL. WHY LIVE SOMEONE ELSES DREAM THRU YOURSELF?

3 DAYS HAD WENT BY SINCE BEING OVER TO THEIR PLACE WHEN I GOT A CALL FROM MY MOM TELLING ME MY DAD HAD TAKEN A TURN FOR THE WORST. HE HAD STOPPED EATING. HE WAS ALSO HAVING TERRIBLE MIGRANE HEADACHES, SO BAD IT MADE HIM CRY. I HAVE NEVER SEEN MY DAD CRY, SO I KNEW IT MUST HAVE BEEN BAD FOR HIM. THEY HAD JUST BEEN TO THE DOCTOR AND GOT SOME MEDICINE TO HOPEFULLY GET HIM SOME RELIEF AND THEY TOLD HER TO MAKE SOME PROTEIN SHAKES TO GET SOME NOURISHMENT IN HIM. THE NEXT DAY HOWEVER HE STARTED HAVING HALLUCINATIONS AGAIN AND WASN'T SLEEPING WELL. I KNOW THIS WAS ALL PUTTING A STRAIN ON MY MOM, AS SHE WASN'T ABLE TO SLEEP HERSELF FOR FEAR MY DAD WOULD HURT HIMSELF OR NOT KNOW WHAT HE WAS DOING AND LEAVE THE HOUSE. HE NOW HAD TO BE WATCHED ROUND THE CLOCK, SO BETWEEN MY MOM AND US 3 KIDS, WE WOULD HAVE TO TAKE SHIFTS TO WATCH MY DAD SO MOM COULD GET SOME SLEEP AS WE COULDN'T TRUST MY DAD.

SINCE I WAS STILL HAVING BOUTS OF PANIC ATTACKS, GEORGE WOULD USUALLY GO IN MY PLACE AFTER HE GOT OFF WORK OR ON HIS DAY OFF, I BECAME NERVOUS AT THE THOUGHT OF SOMETHING HAPPENING, WHAT IF I FAINTED WHILE THERE? WOULD MY DAD KNOW WHAT TO DO? WOULD MY MOM, BEING AS TIRED AS SHE WAS BE ABLE TO WAKE UP AND HELP ME? WHAT IF MY DAD, HAVING A HALLUCINATION HURT ME? I FELT BAD PUTTING ALL THE BURDEN ON EVERYONE ELSE, MAYBE IN A SENSE MY MOM RESENTED ME FOR NOT HELPING, AS HER ATTITUDE

WAS REALLY CHANGING, BUT I REALLY COULDN'T HELP IT. ONE DAY THOUGH, GEORGE HAD TO WORK, AND MY BROTHERS HAD OTHER PLANS, SO IT WAS LEFT UP TO ME TO HELP. EVEN WITH THE OTHERS TAKING SHIFTS MY MOM STILL WASN'T SLEEPING ALL THAT WELL, GETTING MAYBE 4 HOURS OR SO AT THE MOST. I TOOK THE KIDS TO A FRIENDS HOUSE FOR THE NIGHT, DROPPED GEORGE OFF AT WORK AND MADE ARRANGEMENTS FOR HIM TO HAVE A RIDE HOME AND I MADE THE DRIVE TO PIQUA, KNEES KNOCKING ALL THE WAY. AFTER NOT HAVING MUCH OF A PRAYER LIFE ANYMORE, THAT NIGHT ON THE DRIVE OVER, I PRAYED!! I PRAYED FOR GOD TO BE WITH ME AND GIVE ME A SAFE TRIP AND TO ALSO HELP ME NOT TO HAVE ANY PANIC ATTACKS SO I COULD BE A HELP TO MY MOM, AND FOR MY DAD TOO NOT TO HAVE ANY INCIDENTS.

WHEN I ARRIVED, MY MOM FILLED ME IN ON THE PARTICULIARS, THEN WENT TO BED. I LAYED DOWN ON THE COUCH WITH THE TV ON, MY DAD WAS ASLEEP AND I THANKED GOD THINGS WERE QUIET. I MUST HAVE DOZED OFF MYSELF BECAUSE I WAS SOON AWAKENED WITH A START BY THE SOUND OF SOMETHING BEING KNOCKED OVER. WHEN I GOT MY WITS ABOUT MYSELF, I NOTICED IT WAS MY DAD FUMBLING AROUND AND THOUGHT OH NO, HERE WE GO! HE HAD WENT TO THE CLOSET AND GOTTEN HIS JACKET OUT AND AS HE WAS TRYING TO PUT IT ON KNOCKED OVER A VASE ON THE TABLE BESIDE THE CLOSET. I SAID DAD WHERE ARE YOU GOING? HE RAMBLED ON ABOUT SOMETHING I COULDN'T MAKE ANY SENSE OUT OF AND THEN SAID HE HAD A TAXI WAITING OUTSIDE. I GOT UP TO PEER OUT THE

WINDOW AND THERE WAS NO TAXI THERE, BUT HE SNEERED AT ME SWEARING HE HEARD THE HORN BLOWING ANNOUNCING IT'S ARRIVAL. MY HEART SANK AND WITH TEARS IN MY EYES I TOLD MY DAD HE COULDN'T GO ANYWHERE AND THAT THE TAXI WASN'T THERE. HE GOT SO UPSET I HAD TO GO WAKE MY MOM, I WASN'T SURE WHAT TO DO FOR HIM, AND I, AFTER THE PAST I HAD WITH HIM WASN'T TAKING THE CHANCE OF HIM BECOMING VIOLENT TOWARDS ME. SHE WAS FINALLY ABLE TO GET HIM TO CALM DOWN, AND WHEN HE DRIFTED OFF TO SLEEP, WE LAID DOWN OURSELVES PRAYING HE WOULD SLEEP LONG ENOUGH FOR US TO REST AS WELL.

AS THE WEEKS WENT BY, DAD STEADILY GREW WORSE AND THE DAY CAME WHERE HE WAS ADMITTED TO THE HOSPITAL. OUR HEARTS SANK NOT WANTING TO THINK HE MAY NOT MAKE IT OUT. BUT WE ALSO HAD TO ACCEPT THE FACT THAT HE COULD DIE AT ANY MOMENT. THE DAY AFTER DAD WAS ADMITTED TO THE HOSPITAL, HE WAS HAVING A GREAT DAY. WHEN I ARRIVED HE WAS SITTING ON THE SIDE OF THE BED EATING A POPSICLE. WE HAD A GOOD TALK THAT DAY AND I REMEMBER ASKING HIM IF THERE WAS ANYTHING I COULD DO FOR HIM. WELL, I WAS QUITE TAKEN ABACK BY HIS RESPONSE. HE ASKED ME FOR A NEW PAIR OF LUNGS. I CRIED, IF THERE WAS ANYTHING I COULD HAVE DONE FOR MY DAD AT THAT MOMENT, I WOULD HAVE DONE IT. I KNEW I HAD TO LEARN TO FORGIVE HIM FOR ALL THOSE WASTED YEARS AND FOR THE HARSHNESS HE SHOWED TOWARDS ME. MAYBE HE WAS SICK ALL ALONG, I KNOW DEPRESSION CAN BE A SICKNESS AND HE DEFINITELY HAD BOUTS OF THAT. I REFLECTED BACK ON THE LAST 5 MONTHS BEFORE HE

ENTERED THE HOSPITAL. BACK TO THE TIME HE ACCEPTED CHRIST AS SAVIOR. I CHERISHED THOSE TIMES WE HAD, AND I LONGED FOR HIM TO BE HEALED SO WE COULD REBUILD OUR LIVES AND ENJOY THE GRANDCHILDREN. HOWEVER, IT WASN'T MEANT TO BE. GOD HAD OTHER PLANS. THE VERY NEXT DAY, JUNE 8TH 1991, MY DAD DIED. WE DON'T ALWAYS UNDERSTAND GOD'S PLAN, BUT IN THE COMING MONTHS AFTER THE DEATH OF MY FATHER I WOULD COME TO KNOW WHAT PART OF THE PLAN WAS IN MY FATHER DYING. I'LL SHARE IN ANOTHER PART OF THIS BOOK.

IT WAS DIFFICULT LOSING MY DAD, BUT IN LIGHT OF EVERYONE CRYING, I FELT I NEEDED TO BE STRONG FOR MY MOM AND THE FAMILY. IT WAS LIKE SOMETHING WAS RISING UP FROM WITH ME, AND FROM HIS DEATH I WAS BEING SET FREE FROM THINGS. I EVEN FOUND THAT ALTHOUGH I STILL HAD PANCI ATTACKS, THEY WERE NOT AS FREQUENT AS THEY HAD PREVIOUSLY BEEN. THE NEXT WEEK WAS KIND OF A BLUR,TRYING TO BE THERE FOR MY MOM, GETTING THRU THE FUNERAL AND HELPING HER SORT THRU THINGS. WE MANAGED TO GET IT ALL DONE AND IT WAS FINALLY TIME I WAS ABLE TO GRIEVE. ALTHOUGH WE HAD BEGUN TO SETTLE BACK INTO OUR NORMAL ROUTINES, WE COULDN'T HELP BUT BE CONCERNED NOW ABOUT MOM BEING BY HERSELF. THE DEATH OF MY FATHER BROUGHT US CLOSER AND NOW SHE WAS REACHING OUT TO US, THANKING ME FOR BEING HER ROCK. IT WAS DIFFICULT LOSING A PARENT, ESPECIALLY THAT YOUNG, MANY TIMES PLAYING OVER AND OVER IN MY MIND THE RECENTS MONTHS BEFORE HIS DEATH. LITLLE DID I KNOW I WAS BEING DRAWED BACK TO THE LORD FROM A BACKSLIDDEN

STATE.ALTHOUGH I HAD STOP GOING TO CHURCH FOR A WHILE, THERE WOULD BE MANY NIGHTS I STILL PRAYED BEFORE FALLING OFF TO SLEEP AND I KNOW THAT'S WHAT HELPED GET US THRU THIS DIFFICULT TIME AND THRU THE PANIC ATTACKS AS WELL.

WE HAD FINALLY INQUIRED OF A PASTOR FRIEND OF GEORGE'S. HE COME OVER TO PRAY WITH ME AND I JUST HAPPENED TO ASK HIM WHAT HE THOUGHT OF THE UNICORNS I HAD AROUND THE HOUSE. I WAS AN AVID COLLECTOR WITH ALL KINDS OF WALL HANGINGS, STATUES, SHOELACES, A CLOCK AND A JACKET. TO ME THEY WERE SO BEAUTIFUL AND I FOUND THAT I WOULD GET REALLY UPSET WITH THE KIDS IF THEY MESSED WITH THEM OR ANY HAD GOTTEN BROKE. THE PASTOR SHARED HIS THOUGHTS WITH ME ON THE ORIGIN OF THE UNICORNS AND HOW THEY WERE APART OF GREEK MYTHOLOGY AND I WAS BLOWN AWAY. I KNEW FROM ATTENDING CHURCH AS A TEENAGER AND LEARNING THE TEN COMMANDMENTS THAT WE WERE NOT TO HAVE ANY OTHER GODS BEFORE THE ONE TRUE GOD, BUT WITH DABBLING IN ASTROLOGY AND COLLECTING UNICORNS I HAD ALLOWED MYSELF TO BECOME INVOLVED WITH IDOL WORSHIP! THAT CERTAINLY EXPLAINED ALOT OF WHAT I HAD BEEN GOING THRU THE LAST 5 YEARS. I HAD OPENED THE DOOR TO DEMONIC ATTACK.

AFTER THE PASTOR HAD LEFT, I REFLECTED ON WHAT I HAD HEARD AND WAS THANKFUL THAT GEORGE WAS THERE TO HEAR IT TOO, AS I THOUGHT I WAS HEARING THINGS AND MY MIND WAS PLAYING TRICKS ON ME. THE CHRISTMAS SEASON WAS UPON US AND I WAS GETTING READY FOR A DINNER WE HAD BEEN

INVITED TOO WHEN MY THOUGHTS WENT TO THE UNICORNS I HAD SITTING AROUND , AND I WONDERED HOW I WAS WORSHIPPING THEM. I NEVER BOWED DOWN TO THEM OR EVEN PRAYED TO THEM FOR THAT MATTER. I BRUSHED IT OFF AS I FINISHED GETTING READY FOR THE DINNER. IT WAS BEING HELD AT ONE OF THE LOCAL CHURCHES AND WE HAD BEEN RECEIVING A LITTLE GOVERNMENT ASSISTANCE AT THE TIME FOR FOOD AND MEDICAL AND SOMEONE HAD TURNED OUR NAME IN TO RECEIVE HELP WITH GIFTS FOR OUR CHILDREN. WE WERE SO APPRECIATIVE.

THE DINNER WAS GOOD AND THE KIDS EACH RECEIVED A GIFT AND A BAG OF GOODIES. WHEN WE FINALLY ARRIVED HOME, WE WERE WORN OUT. WE HAD A REALLY GOOD TIME BUT IT WAS BEDTIME. I GOT THEM ALL SETTLED IN BED AND THEN WENT DOWNSTAIRS AND OPENED THEIR BAG OF GOODIES. AS I DUMPED THE CONTENTS OF THE BAGS IN A BOWL THERE WAS A SLIP OF PAPER IN THERE. ON THE PAPER WAS A 24 HOUR MAINLINE PRAYER LINE AND A NUMBER. I SET IS ASIDE THINKING COOL, I MAY NEED IT SOMEDAY, AND WENT OFF TO BED AND SAID MY PRAYERS. THE NEXT DAY I WOKE UP WITH A MIGRAINE. IT WAS SO BAD IT MADE ME SICK TO MY STOMACH. GEORGE HAD CALLED OUR FRIEND WHO WAS ALWAYS A HUGE HELP WITH THE KIDS AND DROPPED THE BOYS OFF TO HER AFTER TAKING ANGELA TO SCHOOL, THEN WENT OFF TO WORK. ME? I WENT BACK TO BED TO HOPEFULLY SLEEP IT OFF.

BY THE TIME GEORGE ARRIVED HOME FROM WORK WITH THE KIDS MY HEADACHE WAS GONE AND WE SETTLED IN FOR AN ENJOYABLE EVENING. THE

NEXT DAY HOWEVER WAS THE SAME THING, WOKE UP WITH ANOTHER MIGRAINE ALONG WITH A PANIC ATTACK. IT WAS SUGGESTED THEN THAT I SEE A CHIROPRACTOR. I HADN'T THOUGHT MUCH ABOUT THEM, MY FRIENDS DAD WAS GOOD AT GIVING BEAR HUGS THAT SEEM TO POP EVERY BONE IN YOUR BACK BUT LEFT YOU FEELING BETTER SO HE HAD CRACKED MINE A FEW TIMES WHICH HIELP GIVE ME SOME RELIEF ALTHOUGH TEMPORARY. I SET UP AN APPOINTMENT FOR THE NEXT DAY AND LOOKED FORWARD TO IT. IF IT WOULD HELP WITH THESE MIGRAINES SO I COULD FUNCTION THEN I WAS WILLING TO TRY ALMOST ANYTHING. THIS WAS AN ALL NATURAL WAY OF DOING THINGS RATHER THAN BEING TREATING WITH MEDS BY DOCTORS THAT ONLY GAVE YOU UNWANTED SIDE EFFECTS ESPECIALLY CAUSING THE PANIC ATTACKS TO CAUSE MY BODY TO RUN A RACE WHILE I WAS STANDING STILL.

FINALLY THE NEXT DAY CAME AND I WENT TO THE APPOINTMENT, GIVEN X-RAYS AND THE DOCTOR EXPLAINED ALL THAT WAS GOING ON WITH MY BACK, WHICH WASN'T REAL BAD AND HE GAVE ME INFORMATION SHOWING ME THAT THRU NATURAL MANIPULATIONS ON MY BODY THAT IT WOULD KEEP BLOOD FLOWING AND HELP STRAIGHTEN THINGS OUT AND PROVIDE SOME MUCH NEEDED RELIEF. FOR A WHILE I WENT ONCE A WEEK, THEN EVENUALLY ONCE EVERY 2 WEEKS, THEN IT GOT DOWN TO ONCE A MONTH THEN WHENEVER NEEDED. I WAS AMAZED HOW MUCH IT HELPED AND THE MIGRAINES HAD LEFT.

THE FOLLOWING SUNDAY I DECIDED TO START GOING TO CHURCH. IT WAS A PENTECOSTAL CHURCH

WHO'S PASTOR WAS THE FRIEND OF GEORGE'S, WHO CAME AND PRAYED WITH ME OVER THE PANIC ATTACKS. IT WAS A NICE CHURCH, THE SERVICE WAS GOOD. I WAS FAMILIAR WITH THE DENOMINATION FROM ATTENDING THE SAME TYPE OF CHURCH AS A TEENAGER, SO I FELT PRETTY COMFORTABLE. I WAS ACTUALLY LOOKING FORWARD THE NEXT WEEKS SERVICE AND THOUGHT IT WOULD BE GREAT FOR GEORGE AND I TO COMMIT OUR LIVES TO GOD AND CHURCH. ALTHOUGH GEORGE BELIEVED IN GOD, HE RARELY HAD TIME FOR CHURCH, AS HE WORKED 2 JOBS AND EVEN WHEN HE WOULD GET A SUNDAY OFF, HE WOULD SLEEP RATHER THAN GO AND FALL ASLEEP IN CHURCH.

THINGS HAD STARTED LOOKING UP FOR US, FINANCES WERE GOOD, BILLS PAID, AND WE ACTUALLY GOT A PHONE HOOKED UP. WE WERE SUPER EXCITED OVER THAT, ESPECIALLY WITH MY FAMILY LIVING OUT OF TOWN. THE HEADACHES HAD COMPLETELY SUBSIDED NOW WITH REGULAR VISITS AT THE CHIROPRACTOR, AND ALTHOUGH I STILL HAD THE PANIC ATTACKS FROM TIME TO TIME THEY WERE AT LEAST LESS FREQUENT THAT THEY HAD BEEN AND I WAS SO THANKFUL. THAT WAS DEFINITELY A FRIGHTENING TIME TO GO THRU. ONE DAY AS I WAS DOING SOME CLEANING, I HAD WENT TO DUST OFF THE UNICORN STAND I HAD AND FOUND THAT ONE HAD GOTTEN BROKE, SUDDENLY I BECAME ANGRY. I WAS SO UPSET THAT I SPANKED MY KIDS FOR MESSING AROUND, I MEAN THEY KNEW BETTER THAN TO MESS WITH THINGS THAT WASN'T THEIRS TO BEGIN WITH. I WENT BACK TO DUSTING AND AFTER A LITTLE WHILE, I HAD CALMED DOWN. IT WAS THEN THAT THE

THOUGHTS OF WHAT I HAD DONE OVERTOOK ME AND I SUDDENLY FELT BAD FOR GETTING SO UPSET OVER SOMETHING THAT COULD BE REPLACED. IT WAS SILLY AND WHO KNOWS WHEN IT HAD BEEN BROKE, IT COULD HAVE BEEN A COUPLE DAYS BEFORE.

I NEVER DUSTED EVERYDAY AND I THOUGHT OF MY POOR KIDS AND THE CONFUSION THEY MUST FEEL NOT KNOWING WHY THEY GOT SPANKED. I STARTED CRYING THINKING HOW STUPID THAT WAS TO DO, AND I WAS SO ASHAMED. I HAD FINISHED MY DUSTING AND PUT ALL THE UNICORNS BACK ON THE STAND WHEN I CAME ACROSS A PIECE OF PAPER THAT HAD FALLEN BACK BEHIND THE STAND. AS I PICKED IT UP AND LOOKED AT IT I REALIZED IT WAS THE PRAYERLINE NUMBER WE HAD GOTTEN AT THE CHRISTMAS DINNER THE YEAR BEFORE. I SAT HOLDING IT AND WONDERED HOW I FOUND IT AFTER ALL THIS TIME. ONCE AGAIN THE HOLIDAY SEASON WAS UPON US, IT WAS A LITTLE OVER 3 WEEKS BEFORE CHRISTMAS AND I WAS A VERY CLEAN AND ORGANIZED PERSON. I PICKED UP AND DID DISHES AND TRASH EVERYDAY, AND I THOROUGHLY CLEANED AND DUSTED EVERY 2 OR 3 DAYS AND NEVER NOTICED IT THERE, HOW COULD I HAVE MISSED IT? I SAT WONDERING WHETHER I SHOULD CALL IT OR NOT, I MEAN THE VERY THOUGHT OF GETTING SO UPSET OVER SOMETHING SO TRIVIAL AND HURTING MY KIDS FEELINGS WASN'T SETTING RIGHT WITH ME AT ALL. KIDS NEED CORRECTION, YES, BUT THERE ARE BETTER WAYS TO HANDLE THINGS. AFTER MAYBE 10 MINUTES OR SO, PONDERING WHETHER TO CALL OR NOT, I SUDDENLY FELT THIS OVERWHELMING PEACE LIKE I NEVER FELT BEFORE, I SUPPOSE A SENSE THAT GOD WAS TRYING TO TELL ME SOMETHING, LIKE MAYBE I

NEEDED TO MAKE THAT CALL AND ASK FOR PRAYER. HOW IRONIC IT WAS THE THINGS THAT TOOK PLACE THAT ALLOWED US TO HAVE A PHONE, THE CHIROPRACTOR TO HELP WITH HEADACHES SO I COULD FUNCTION AND THINK STRAIGHT, IF THAT WASN'T GOD, THEN I WAS A LOONEY TOON. SO I DECIDED TO MAKE THE CALL.

THE LADY THAT ANSWERED THE PHONE I LEARNED WAS THE SECRETARY OF THE CHURCH, SHE WAS VERY NICE AND VERY ATTENTIVE AS I EXPLAINED THE PASSING OF MY DAD, THE PANIC ATTACKS, THE UNICORNS AND MY BEHAVIOR. AFTER PRAYING WITH ME SHE ASKED IF SHE COULD SEND ME A COPY OF A MESSAGE THAT THEIR PASTOR HAD PREACHED A FEW WEEKS AGO CONCERNING SOME OF THE THINGS I WAS GOING THRU AND SHE THOUGHT IT WOULD BE HELPFUL. I AGREED AND GAVE HER MY ADDRESS. DURING THIS TIME, I HAD BEEN A SMOKER FOR ABOUT 10 YEARS. WITH MY DAD HAVING CANCER AND WHAT HE WENT THRU BEING A HEAVY SMOKER, I DECIDED IT WAS TIME TO STOP SMOKING. I WAS ALWAYS SICK WITH SOMETHING AND IT WAS DEFINITELY GETTING OLD FAST. I CERTAINLY DIDN'T WANT TO END UP LIKE MY FATHER AND SUFFER THE WAY HE DID.

I WAS HEADED IN THE RIGHT DIRECTION AT LEAST WITH THE NEW CHANGES TAKING PLACE AND GOING BACK TO CHURCH AND I WANTED THIS TO BE THE BEST CHRISTMAS FOR MYSELF AND MY FAMILY. ALTHOUGH IT WOULD BE THE FIRST CHRISTMAS WITHOUT MY DAD, I WAS GRATEFUL FOR THE LESSON I LEARNED THRU HIS DEATH. LIFE IS PRECIOUS, ESPECIALLY FOR THOSE YOU LOVE. ALTHOUGH WE

NEVER HAD THE BEST RELATIONSHIP, WHAT MATTERED WAS HE TRIED TO BE THE BEST PERSON HE COULD BE DURING THE LAST 5 MONTHS OF HIS LIFE WHEN HE ACCEPTED JESUS AS SAVIOR. THRU IT ALL, HE WAS STILL MY DAD WHETHER I WANTED HIM TO BE AT TIMES OR NOT. I DID HAVE RESENTMENT IN MY HEART TOWARDS HIM, BUT ALSO LEARNED SOME VALUABLE THINGS TOO. WE ALL HAVE CHOICES TO MAKE AND WE WILL REAP THE CONSEQUENCES IN SOME WAY, SHAPE, OR FORM AS A RESULT OF OUR CHOICES AND FOR ME THRU HIS SUFFERING I CHOSE TO BE HEALTHY AND WHOLE.

I WAS ALWAYS AN INTELLIGENT, FULL OF LIFE PERSON, FROM AS YOUNG AS I CAN REMEMBER. ALWAYS A TALKER, LIVING UP WELL TO MY NICKNAME WINDY. I WAS ALWAYS BLOWING OFF. I WAS ALWAYS MISUNDERSTOOD AND FELT AS IF I COULD NEVER BE WHO I WAS, I FELT I HAD TO BE WHATEVER OTHERS WANTED ME TO BE TO BE LOVED AND ACCEPTED. I GOT SO CAUGHT UP WITH THE PAIN AND CONFUSION AND FEELING AS IF I HAD TO GROW UP FASTER THAN MAYBE WHAT I SHOULD HAVE THAT I WENT AS FAR AS TO REBEL AGAINST MY PARENTS. AS A TEEN I TRIED GOING TO CHURCH THINKING THAT WOULD HELP, THAT MY PARENTS WOULD LOVE ME BUT I WAS STILL LOST IN MYSELF. EVERYDAY THERE WAS STILL REMINDERS, WORDS SAID, CRITICISM, ALWAYS FEELING AS IF I NEVER DID RIGHT IN THE EYES OF OTHERS. SO I STARTED RUNNING WITH THE WRONG CROWD, TRYING TO BE COOL AND A HOOD, TILL ONE DAY, I ONCE AGAIN FELL IN THE TRAP OF BEING A PEOPLE PLEASER. THERE WAS NO BALANCE IN MY LIFE, NO EVEN KEEL. YOU NEED BALANCE IN LIFE AS TO NOT BE TAKEN

ADVANTAGE OF AND I BELIEVE NOW THAT I WAS ROBBED. MY INNOCENCE TAKEN, HAVING TO HAVE SO MUCH RESPONSIBILITY AS SUCH A YOUNG AGE THAT DID NOTHING BUT BUILD UP WALLS THAT I DIDN'T KNOW IF THEY COULD EVER BE TORN DOWN.

I BELIEVE HAD I RECEIVED THE NURTURING, TRAINING AND LOVE OF MY PARENTS, AND RELATIVES INSTEAD OF PAIN, AND ABUSE I COULD HAVE LIVED OUT MY DREAMS, AND SAVED ME YEARS OF THE STRUGGLES I ENDURED. YES, LIFE HAPPENS, WE ALL FACE TOUGH TIMES, BUT IT'S EASIER TO GET THRU, I THINK, WHEN YOU HAVE A GREAT SUPPORT TEAM BEHIND YOU AND ALL I SEEMED TO HAVE WAS THOSE WHO WAS GREAT TO YOUR FACE, BUT WHEN YOUR BACK WAS TURNED DIDN'T HESITATE TO DIG THE KNIFE IN! NOW 11 YEARS LATER AS I WALK INTO CHURCH, I HAD THE ASSURANCE I WAS ON MY WAY TO A NEW ME!

A FEW DAYS LATER I RECEIVED THE TAPE IN THE MAIL THE SECRETARY HAD PROMISED. THE CHURCH WAS AN ASSEMBLY OF GOD CHURCH WHICH BELIEVED THE SAME WAY OF THE CHURCHES I WAS AFFILIATED WITH BEFORE SO I KNEW THE CULTURE. THE NAME OF THE MESSAGE ON THE TAPE WAS CALLED POSSESSING YOUR POSSESSIONS, PURITY. I PUT THE TAPE IN AND AS I LISTENED TO IT, MY MOUTH FELL OPEN, MY HEART SANK. MY EYES AND EARS BEING OPENED TO THINGS THAT I FOUND SO HARD TO BELIEVE. I WAS IDOLIZING THE UNICORNS. IT WAS IDOL WORSHIP. AS I LISTENED WITH GREAT INTENSITY, GOD BEGAN TO SHOW ME THINGS. WHERE IT ORIGINATED, MEANING WHEN I HAD OPENED THE DOOR AND BEEN ALLOWED MYSELF TO ENTER. IT WAS LONG AGO FROM A LADY GEORGE

WORKED WITH AT THE PIZZA PLACE IN SIDNEY. I HAD GOTTEN INTO ASTROLOGY AND TAROT CARDS AND THEN EVENTUALLY COLLECTING UNICORNS. PEOPLE THAT ALLOW THEMSELVES TO GET CAUGHT UP IN THINGS, CAN ACTUALLY MAKE IDOLS OUT OF THEM AND TO THE POINT YOU COULD REALLY HURT SOMEONE. MY THOUGHTS WENT BACK TO THE DAY I SPANKED MY KIDS FOR BREAKING ONE OF THE UNICORNS AND I CRIED, HOW COULD I DO THAT. ALL I BEEN THRU IN MY LIFE, ALL THE YEARS OF ABUSE, WAS TURNING ME INTO AN ANGRY BITTER WOMAN AND I HATED MYSELF RIGHT THEN.

IT WAS 2 WEEKS BEFORE CHRISTMAS AND THAT SUNDAY I HAD DECIDED TO VISIT FIRST ASSEMBLY OF GOD. THE PEOPLE WERE REALLY NICE AND RECEIVED ME WELL. THE MESSAGE WAS GOOD AND I JUST FELL IN LOVE WITH THE CHURCH! SUDDENLY I HAD A NEW ZEAL FOR LIFE AND I LEFT THERE MY OLD BUBBLY SELF. FUNNY HOW GOD WILL CAUSE YOU TO SEE YOURSELF AS YOU ARE SO YOU CAN REACH OUT TO HIM FOR HELP. THE ONLY ONE THAT HAS THE POWER TO HEAL AND RESTORE!

THAT NEXT SUNDAY WHEN I WENT TO CHURCH I REDEDICATED MY LIFE TO GOD. I MADE THE DECISION TO GET RID OF THE UNICORNS AS THAT DEC. 1991 I FOUND NEW MEANING IF LIFE IN JESUS CHRIST, NOT IN ANYONE ELSE OT ANYTHING ELSE. IDOL WORSHIP WAS THE WORKS OF THE DEVIL! THE NEXT DAY I PUT AN AD IN THE PAPER FOR MY HUGE UNICORN COLLECTION. I HAD NO IDEA WHAT TO ASK, I JUST WANTED TO BE RID OF THEM. SOMEONE CALLED ME AND SET UP A TIME TO COME LOOK AT WHAT I HAD, WHEN THEY ARRIVED,

THEY LIKED WHAT I HAD AND OFFERED ME 80.00 FOR IT ALL. I WAS ONLY TO PLEASED TO BE RID OF THEM AND ACCEPTED THEIR OFFER. WHAT I SEEN NEXT, MADE A BELIEVER OUT OF ME TO THE FORCES OF DARKNESS AND HOW SATAN WORKS! YOU SEE, GOD HAS ANGELS THAT WATCH OUT AND PROTECT HIS PEOPLE, TO BRING JOY AND LIFE. SATAN HAS ANGELS THAT BRING MISERY AND STRIFE AND ATTACH THEMSELVES TO PEOPLE AND THINGS TO BRING DESTRUCTION AND EVEN IN SOME CASES DEATH. AS THE GENTLEMAN WAS CARRYING OUT THE PICTURES, THE FACES OF THE UNICORNS BECAME SLIGHTLY DISTORTED AND THE EYES BECAME FIRE ENGINE RED, AS IF ANGRY THEY WERE LOSING THEIR DWELLING PLACE. MY GOODNESS I NEVER SEEN SUCH A THING BEFORE AND IT REALLY FRIGHTENED ME. NOT SO MUCH OF THE LOOKS OF THEM BY WHAT I HAD ENDURED AS A RESULT OF HAIVNG THEM IN MY POSSESSION. THE DOOR I HAD OPENED TO THE SPIRIT REALM OF THE ENEMY. I SORT OF FELT BAD FOR THE FAMILY THAT WAS GETTING MY COLLECTION, BUT NOT EVERYONE MAY EXPERIENCE A NEGATIVE THING FROM BEING A COLLECTOR, SO I PRAYED FOR THE FAMILY RECEIVING AND THAT NO HARM OR EVIL WOULD COME TO THEM! FROM THAT POINT ON THE DOOR TO THE ENEMY AS BEST AS I KNEW HAD BEEN CLOSED. I WAS FREE FROM SATANIC OPPRESSION AND AS A RESULT, I WAS INSTANTLY HEALED FROM PANIC ATTACKS! WOO HOO! I HAD QUIT SMOKING AND ONLY TOOK 3 WEEKS TO BREAK FREE FROM A 10 YEAR HABIT. I WAS FEELING GOOD!

THE NEXT WEEK WAS CHRISTMAS WEEK. ANGELA BEING BORN ON DEC 2OTH HAD JUST CELEBRATED

HER 9TH BIRTHDAY. ERIC WAS 4 1/2, JASON WAS 2 1/2 AND THEY WERE GROWING SO FAST, THE THINGS I MISSED WITH THEM BUT VOWED TO MAKE IT RIGHT! CHRISTMAS CAME AND WENT. ALTHOUGH IT WAS MEMORABLE WITH ALL THE POSITIVE CHANGES WE MADE, WAS SAD WITHOUT MY DAD THERE. I TOLD MYSELF I WOULDN'T CRY, BUT I DID. IT WAS MORE SO FOR THE FACT OF WHY DID HE HAVE TO BE SO HARSH ALL THESE YEARS? WHY COULDN'T HE HAVE BEEN THE GUY HE WAS THE LAST 5 MONTHS OF HIS LIFE WHEN HE ACCEPTED CHRIST? WHY DO PEOPLE GIVE UP?. THE THOUGHT OF MY KIDS GROWING UP AND NOT KNOWING THEIR GRANDFATHER WAS HEARTBREAKING, NOT TO MENTION HIS GREAT GRANDKIDS. BUT IT WASN'T MEANT TO BE. I KNEW HE WAS WITH GOD AND NO LONGER SUFFERING IN ANY CAPACITY HE DID WHILE HERE ON EARTH! A FEW DAYS AFTER CHRISTMAS GEORGE AND I CELEBRATED 10 YEARS TOGETHER, 8 AS HUSBAND AND WIFE. WE HAD OUR UPS AND DOWNS AS ANY COUPLE DOES, THAT'S LIFE. BUT AT THE TIME WE HAD A SOLID MARRIAGE AND I WAS THANKFUL THAT GOD HAD WORKED IN OUR LIVES THE WAY HE DID.

THE NEW YEAR WAS FINALLY UPON US AND I WAS GETTING MORE INVOLVED IN CHURCH ACTIVITIES, WHICH I WAS THOROUGHLY ENJOYING. I WAS IN MY ELEMENT DOING WHAT I LOVED TO DO BUT DOING SO WITH A MORE POSITIVE, AND DIFFERENT OUTLOOK. GOD HAD REALLY DONE A WORK IN OUR LIVES IN JUST A FEW SHORT MONTHS, I'M SURE ALL ALONG HE WAS BUT WE JUST GOT THE REVELATION IN THAT SHORT AMOUNT OF TIME. HE EVEN BLESSED US WITH A NEW HOME FOR RENT IN THE COUNTRY. GEORGE BEING

RAISED IN THE COUNTRY, WAS ESTACTIC AND THE RENT WASN'T A WHOLE LOT MORE THAN WE'D BEEN PAYING ALREADY, BUT WITH HAVING WELL WATER MEANT NO WATER BILL SO IT WOULD BALANCE OUT IN THE EXTRA RENT. THE HOUSE HAD 3 BEDROOMS, ONE CAR GARAGE AND A HUGE YARD WHICH WAS GREAT FOR THE KIDS. IT WAS STILL A COUPLE WEEKS YET BEFORE WE COULD MAKE THE MOVE. WE IN A SENSE WERE KIND OF DREADING IT AS IT WAS WINTER TIME, WHO LIKES TO MOVE IN THE WINTER? BUT ANYTIME WE MADE A MOVE IT WAS WINTER AND MESSY. BUT THAT PARTICULIAR WINTER WAS COLDER THAN WE'D HAD IN A WHILE. THE HEAT BILLS WENT THRU THE ROOF SO WE KNEW THAT GOD HAD HIS HAND IN THIS SO WE WAS TRUSTING HIM.

WE HAD BEGUN TO NOTICE MORE BEHAVORAL ISSUES WITH ANGELA. I REMEMBER WHEN SHE WAS 4 1/2 AND ERIC WAS JUST BORN, SHE BECAME EXTREMELY JEALOUS. SHE WAS OUR FIRST CHILD TOGETHER AND MY PARENTS FIRST GRANDCHILD. FOR 4 1/2 YEARS SHE WAS QUEEN BEE TO THEM AND WAS SPOILED. NOW THAT ERIC WAS HERE AND ATTENTION WOULD BE SHARED, SHE BECAME RESENTFUL. ONE TIME SHE WENT TO THE POINT OF BARRICADING HERSELF IN HER ROOM AND TOOK US A WHILE TO GET IN THERE. OH HOW I PRAYED THIS WAS NOT HAPPENING AGAIN. ONE MORNING AFTER GETTING ANGELA OFF TO SCHOOL, I WAS AWAITING THE ARRIVAL OF MY MOM FROM PIQUA. SHE WAS COMING TO SPEND THE DAY AND HELP ME PACK FOR THE MOVE. I HAD A CORNER CABINET THAT I HAD SITTING BEHIND OUR COUCH FOR DECORATION. WHEN I LEANED OVER THE COUCH TO CLEAR OFF THE KNICK

150

KNACKS, I NOTICED A BUNCH OF CLOTHING BEHIND THE COUCH, SOME OF THEM IN BAGS. I COULDN'T UNDERSTAND WHY THEY WERE THERE BUT KNEW THEY WERE ANGELA'S CLOTHES. I THOUGHT MAYBE THEY WERE DRESS UP CLOTHES. SOMETIMES WHEN THE KIDS OUT GREW THINGS THEY STILL WORE THEM TO PLAY AROUND IN. BUT AS I LOOKED AT THEM FURTHER THEY WERE NOT PLAY CLOTHES, SOME WERE HER NEWER THINGS SHE JUST GOT FOR CHRISTMAS.

WHEN ANGIE ARRIVED HOME FROM SCHOOL AND SEEN HER CLOTHES HAD BEEN MOVED, SHE GOT REAL UPSET. I ASKED HER WHAT WAS WRONG AND WHY THE CLOTHES WAS BEHIND THE COUCH WITH SOME BEING PACKED IN PAPER SACKS. SHE TOLD ME SHE WAS RUNNING AWAY, BUT WOULDN'T TELL ME THE REASON WHY SHE WANTED TO LEAVE. MY HEART BROKE. I WASN'T SURE WHAT HAPPENED, BUT I WENT WITH ALL IDEAS I COULD THINK OF, ALL THE MOTHERLY INSTINCTS ONE HAS AND ASSURED HER THINGS WERE FINE. WE WERE SORRY BUT WE HAD TO MAKE THE MOVE. THAT WE LOVED HER AND WANTED THE BEST FOR HER AND THE BOYS. SHE WOULD SOON HAVE A NEW SCHOOL AND NEW FRIENDS AND THINGS WOULD BE GREAT. IT SEEMED TO CALM HER BUT I COULDN'T HELP HAVING THIS GNAWING FEELING INSIDE THAT I COULDN'T PUT MY FINGER ON. WHAT WAS TROUBLING THIS 9 YEAR OLD GIRL TO THE POINT SHE WANTED TO LEAVE WHO FOR THE MOST PART DIDN'T WANT FOR ANYTHING. WE HAD HER IN COUNSELING FOR SOME TIME BUT EVEN THEY COULDN'T SHED ANY LIGHT AS TO WHAT WAS BOTHERING HER BUT DID SAY THERE WAS SOME TROUBLES SHE WAS HAVING. WHATEVER IT

WAS SHE WAS SUPRESSING IT REAL WELL TO NOT EVEN OPEN UP TO COUNSELORS. ALL I COULD DO WAS PRAY THE MOVE WOULD SNAP HER OUT OF IT.

A WEEK LATER AND WE GOT MOVED. IT WAS JAN 1992 AND ALMOST UNPACKED AND SETTLED IN. WE WERE ENJOYING OUR NEW HOME. ERIC WOULD BE STARTING SCHOOL IN THE FALL AND WAS HARD TO BELIEVE HOW THE YEARS FLEW BY AND WE'D SOON HAVE 2 KIDS IN SCHOOL. GEORGE HAD GOTTEN A JOB AS THE MANAGER OF A BAKERY AT THE LOCAL GROCERY STORE AND HE SEEMED TO LIKE IT REAL WELL. THE CHURCH I WAS ATTENDING HAD A DAYCARE CENTER THERE AND WAS LOOKING FOR HELP. SINCE I HAD BEEN WORKING IN CHILDRENS CHURCH, THEN BEING PROMOTED TO TEACHER, THEY FELT I WOULD BE A GREAT ASSET IN THE DAYCARE AND OFFERED ME A POSITION. WOW, I WOULD BE IN THE WORK FORCE AGAIN. I HADN'T WORKED IN A WHILE DUE TO ILLNESS AND OTHER ISSUES AND GEORGE WORKED 2 JOBS TO GET US THRU WHILE I TOOK CARE OF THE KIDS. BUT EVEN AT THAT THE ECONOMY WAS GETTING ROUGH. IT ALMOST PAID FOR BOTH PARENTS TO WORK. I REALLY ENJOYED BEING A PART OF THE CHURCH AND WAS ONLY TO EAGER TO ACCEPT THEIR OFFER FOR A JOB, BEING IT WAS A CHRISTIAN ENVIRONMENT AS WELL. YES, LIFE WAS GOOD. GOD WAS GOOD!

SPRING WAS ALMOST HERE. WOW HOW THE MONTHS FLEW BY. I WAS DEFINITELY LOOKING FORWARD TO WARMER WEATHER THOUGH. WE WERE SETTLING IN NICELY TO A ROUTINE. JOBS WERE GOING WELL. I ONLY WORKED MAYBE 4 HOURS IN AFTERNOON. GEORGE WORKED 3RD SHIFT AT THE

BAKERY. SO HE'D COME IN AND HELP GET KIDS OFF TO SCHOOL AND THEN GO TO BED FOR A WHILE. I WENT TO WORK AT 2:30 SO HE'D BE UP TO GET KIDS OFF THE BUS AND PREPARE SUPPER AND THEN I GOT OFF AT 6:30, EAT, SPEND A LITTLE TIME TOGETHER, THEN OFF TO BED WE WENT. I FOUND AS I STUDIED THE WORD OF GOD MORE AND MORE AND PREPARING MY LESSONS FOR CHILDREN'S CHURCH ON SUNDAY MORNINGS, I HAD A LOVE FOR WRITING. I WONDERED WHERE THAT CAME FROM. BUT THE MORE I STUDIED AND TOOK NOTES, THE MORE I PUT INTO MY LESSONS THE MORE IT BEGAN TO TAKE ROOT IN MY HEART. ONE NIGHT AS I WAS READING THE PAPER, I NOTICED AN ARTICLE FOR A POETRY CONTEST. I THOUGHT OF HOW NICE IT WOULD BE TO WRITE A POEM AND SEE IT PUBLISHED, BUT THOUGHT NOT ME, MY MIND BEING FLOODED WITH THE WORDS OF MY DAD SAYING I WOULDN'T AMOUNT TO ANYTHING.

BUT YET SOMETHING BURNED INSIDE TO GIVE IT A TRY. I MEAN WHY NOT ME? SO I SAT AND WOORKED THE REST OF THE EVENING AND THE NEXT MORNING ON A POEM AND SUBMITTED IT IN THE CONTEST. I WONDERED HOW COOL IT WOULD BE TO WRITE MY OWN BOOK ONE DAY AND HAVE IT PUBLISHED AS OTHERS HAD DONE. NOT THAT I WANTED FAME AND FORTUNE, AND NOTHING WRONG WITH THOSE THAT HAVE IT. I JUST HAD A DESIRE MORE THAN BEING IN THE SPOTLIGHT OF BEING A BLESSING TO SOMEONE ELSE. TO ENCOURAGE AND UPLIFT OTHERS, ESPECIALLY THOSE WHO BEEN THRU ABUSE OR TRAGIC SITUATIONS. TO HELP THEM TO KNOW JESUS IN A REAL AND PERSONAL WAY. GOD DESIRES US TO LIVE A VICTORIOUS AND PROSPEROUS LIFE AND CAN

OPEN THE DOORS NECESSARY TO REACH THOSE GOALS.MY OTHER DESIRE WAS TO BE A SINGER. I LOVE MUSIC AND LOVE TO SING. I WOULD OFTEN DAY DREAM OF WRITING A SONG AND HAVING IT RECORDED, OR MAKING A VIDEO OF IT. BUT I JUST PUSHED IT OUT OF MY MIND AND CARRIED ON AS A WIFE, MOTHER AND WORKING WOMAN.

IT WAS NOW 1996, WE HAD BEEN IN OUR HOUSE 4 YEARS NOW. ANGIE AND ERIC WAS GETTING ALONG WELL IN SCHOOL AND HAD MADE SOME FRIENDS. THE BOTH OF THEM WAS MORE RAMBUCTIOUS AND OUTGOING SO IT WASN'T SURPRISING HOW EASY THEY MADE FRIENDS. JASON WAS NOW IN THE FIRST GRADE BUT FOUND IT HARD TO MAKE FRIENDS. HE WAS SO BACKWARD AND QUIET. HE WAS HAPPY JUST KEEPING TO HIMSELF TEARING APART TOYS AND RADIOS TO SEE WHAT MADE THEM TICK. THERE WAS A GIRL IN HIS CLASS THAT WAS KEEN ON HIM THOUGH AND I THINK HE WAS HAPPY TO HAVE A FRIEND AT LEAST, EVEN THOUGH IT WAS A GIRL. IT WAS NICE HAVING THEM ALL IN SCHOOL THOUGH, AS I WAS IN ANOTHER BATTLE WITH MY HEALTH AND SEEMED TO WANNA SLEEP ALOT. I HAD THOUGHT BY GIVING UP SMOKING, GETTING RID OF THE UNICORNS PUT IN ON THE RIGHT TRACK TO BETTER HEALTH. BUT IT GOT SO THAT I WAS ON ANTIBIOTIC FOR ONE THING, GET OFF AND A COUPLE WEEKS LATER BACK ON FOR SOMETHING ELSE. THIS WENT ON FOR QUITE A WHILE TILL ONE DAY IT HIT ME THAT BY WORKING IN A DAYCARE IT WAS EXPOSING ME TO MANY VIRUSES AND MY SYSTEM ALREADY WEAK FROM YEARS OF SMOKING, IT WOULD BE IN MY BEST INTEREST TO SEEK OTHER MEANS OF EMPLOYMENT.

I SOON LANDED A JOB AT THE BAKERY GEORGE WAS THE MANAGER OF. GEORGE HAD STARTED ATTENDING CHURCH, WHICH WAS AWESOME, AND GOD HAD LED US TO ANOTHER CHURCH, WHERE WE QUICKLY GOT INVOLVED IN CHILDRENS MINISTRY. I STARTED A GIRLS MISSIONETTE PROGRAM AND GEORGE LED THE ROYAL RANGERS FOR THE BOYS, WHICH WE HELD ON WED EVENING WHILE BIBLE STUDY WAS GOING ON FOR THE ADULTS. ANGELA WAS A TEENAGER NOW AND STARTING TO HAVE MOOD SWINGS AGAIN AND THERE WAS AN AWESOME YOUTH GROUP PROGRAM AT OUR NEW CHURCH, SO I WAS LOOKING FORWARD TO HER BEING A PART OF THE GROUP AND HANG WITH CHRISTIAN FRIENDS HER OWN AGE.

IT WAS NOW 1997, HOLIDAYS WAS GOOD. SEEMS LIKE THE KIDS MAKE OUT LIKE BANDITS EVERY YEAR AT CHRISTMAS. NO MATTER WHAT COMES OUR WAY THRU THE YEAR, GOD MAKES SURE WE HAVE PROVISIONS FOR THE KIDS BIRTHDAYS AND CHRISTMAS. WE ARE SO BLESSED. I LOVE CHRISTMAS, MY FAVORITE TIME OF YEAR AND I LOVE TO GIVE. I HAD THE OPPORTUNITY TO TAKE PIANO LESSONS AND WAS SO EXCITED ABOUT IT. I FOUND A LADY WHO CHARGED ME 4.00 A HALF HOUR WHICH I THOUGHT WAS HARD BUT I KNOW GOD WOULD PROVIDE. WHEN I GOT BREAKS AT CHURCH, I WOULD GO INTO THE SANCTUARY AND PRACTICE AND I SO LOVED IT. SOMEONE EVEN DONATED A PIANO TO ME, IT NEEDED TUNED BUT IT WAS FREE. THE THOUGHT OF ME HAVING MY OWN PIANO AND PLAYING CHRISTMAS SONGS THRILLED ME TO KNOW END. MAYBE I WOULD PLAY

ONE DAY AT CHURCH, WHO KNEW, ANYTHING WAS POSSIBLE.

AT CHURCH, WE WERE GEARING UP FOR OUR BIG EASTER PRODUCTION. IT WOULD BE A 3 DAY EVENT OPENING GOOD FRIDAY EVENING, A SHOW SAT AND THEN SUNDAY MORNING AND OPEN TO THE PUBLIC. I KNEW PRACTICES WOULD BE LONG AND OFTEN BUT I LOVED BEING A PART OF THINGS LIKE THIS, YOU NEVER KNOW IF SOMEONE THAT COMES TO SEE IT MAY BE A PRODUCER OR WORK FOR ONE AND YOU GET YOUR BIG BREAK. THEY GAVE OUT THE PARTS AND I CHOSE TO TRY OUT FOR ONE OF THE LEADS AND WAS HONORED TO BE CHOSEN FOR IT. SO STOKED. SOON THOUGH I HAD STARTED EXPERIENCING THE MIGRAINES ONCE AGAIN. THIS TIME THEY SEEMED FIERCE AND HAD ME CONCERNED THERE WAS SOMETHING SERIOUSLY WRONG WITH ME. I PRESSED THRU IT THOUGH, DETERMINED THAT NOTHING WAS GONNA HINDER THIS EASTER PROGRAM. WE MANAGED TO GET THRU IT WITH MANY LIVES COMING TO KNOW CHRIST AS SAVIOR, YET STILL NO RELIEF FROM THE MIGRAINES. THIS TIME THEY GOT SO BAD IT WAS HARD TO FUNCTION. I HAD TROUBLE SEEING AND HAD TO WEAR SUNGLASSES, COULDN'T WORK AND WAS ON SEVERAL DIFFERENT PAIN KILLERS WHICH UPSET ME CAUSE I HATE MEDICINE, YET NOTHING EASED THE PAIN. IT FELT JUST LIKE I EXPERIENCED WHEN I COLLECTED THE UNICORNS BUT COULDN'T FIGURE OUT WHY. I WASN'T DABBLING IN ANYTHING. DIDN'T HAVE ANY COLLECTIONS. FOCUSE ON GOD AND FAMILY.

IT WAS GOING ON THE 3RD WEEK OF BATTLING THE MIGRAINES, GEORGE HAD BEEN HAVING SOME HEALTH ISSUES AND WE DISCOVERED HE WAS A TYPE 2 DIABETIC. ALOT OF CHANGES WAS ONCE AGAIN IN STORE FOR US. DIET CHANGES, MEDICINE, I HAD TO GIVE UP THE PIANO LESSONS FOR A WHILE DUE TO THE MIGRAINES AS I COULDN'T DRIVE. I PRAYED AND ASKED GOD TO PLEASE TOUCH OUR FAMILY. SOON MOTHER'S DAY WAS HERE, IT WAS 1997. MY FAMILY TRIED TO MAKE IT A SPECIAL DAY FOR ME IN LIGHT OF HAVING A MIGRAINE. I WAS PROUD OF THEM FOR THEIR EFFORT. I HELPED GEORGE TUCK THE KIDS IN BED AS THEY HAD SCHOOL THE NEXT DAY AND THEN LAYED DOWN MYSELF TO WATCH A MOVIE. I FELT SO BAD BEING DOWN AND NOT BEING ABLE TO SPEND TIME WITH THEM. THEY MEANT THE WORLD TO ME. I HAD MISSED SO MUCH WITH THEM DEALING WITH HEALTH ISSUES. I SHOULD HAVE BEEN ABLE TO CHERISH THE GROWING PROCESS, THE THINGS THEY LEARNED, BUT MOST OF THE TIME WAS SPENT IN BED SUFFERING FROM ONE THING OR ANOTHER AND NOW GEORGE WITH DIABETES.

THE MOVIE CAME ON AND GEORGE HAD ALREADY FALLEN ASLEEP. AS I WATCHED I BECAME SADDENED BY IT. THE MOVIE WAS ABOUT A GIRL WHO WAS BEING ABUSED AND MOLESTED BY HER FATHER AND SHE COULDN'T TELL ANYONE FOR THE LONGEST TIME. WHEN SHE HAD FINALLY DECIDED SHE NEEDED TO TELL HER MOM, SHE WAS HEADING OUT OF THE ROOM WHEN HER FATHER CAME INTO THE ROOM. THE GIRL COULDN'T LEAVE AND THE DAD BEGAN MESSING WITH HER, WHAT HE DIDN'T EXPECT WAS THE MOM TO WALK IN ON THEM. NEEDLESS TO SAY THE MOM WAS

HEARTBROKEN. SHE THREW THE DAD OUT, BUT INSTEAD OF COMFORTING THE DAUGHTER, SHE BLAMED HER FOR SEDUCING HER FATHER, WHICH THE GIRL DENIED DOING. THE MOTHER ONLY BECAME ABUSIVE TOWARDS THE DAUGHTER WHICH SUNK THE DAUGHTER INTO A DEEP DEPRESSION. SUCH A SAD MOVIE YET SO REAL IN THIS WORLD AND I COULDN'T HELP BUT SHED SOME TEARS AND BEING THANKFUL THAT GEORGE WAS A DECENT MAN AND WOULDN'T BE THE TYPE TO EVER DO SOMETHING LIKE THAT. I DON'T KNOW WHAT I WOULD DO IF MY DAUGHTER WAS EVER HURT IN THAT CAPACITY.

AFTER SAYING MY PRAYERS AND SETTING THE ALARM FOR GEORGE, I DRIFTED OFF TO SLEEP, PRAYING WHEN I WOKE UP, THE MIGRAINE THAT HAD POUNDED MY HEAD THE LAST 3 WEEKS WOULD BE GONE. BUT THE NEXT MORNING AS I WOKE THE SAME POUNDING MIGRAINE WAS THERE. I WOKE THE KIDS TO GET THEM READY FOR SCHOOL AS GEORGE WASN'T HOME YET FROM WORK. I HAD TO TRY AND MAKE IT TO WORK MYSELF. I HAD MISSED SO MUCH ALREADY, YET THANKFUL I WORKED FOR MY HUSBAND WHO SOMETIMES STAYED OVER TO COVER MY SHIFT FOR ME.

I MANAGED TO MAKE IT THRU WORK THAT DAY GETTING OFF AT 3. I WAS ABLE TO BE THERE FOR THE KIDS TO GET OFF THE BUS WHICH WOULD HELP GEORGE AS HE WAS PLANNING ON MOWING THE YARD AND BORROWING THE NEIGHBOR'S RIDER, WHICH WOULD CUT HIS MOWING TIME IN HALF SO ME BEING HOME EARLY WOULD BE ONE LESS WORRY OFF HIM HAVING TO MOW AND WATCH KIDS. ANGELA BEING IN

JUNIOR HIGH NOW ARRIVED HOME ABOUT 45 MINUTES BEFORE THE BOYS DID. WHEN SHE CAME IN THAT DAY SHE WAS IN A STRANGE MOOD HEADING RIGHT TO HER ROOM, I JUST SHOOK IT OFF AS HER HAVING A ROUGH DAY AND BEING WRAPPED UP IN MYSELF HAVING A MIGRAINE, I WENT ABOUT THINKING WHAT WE WAS GONNA HAVE FOR SUPPER AND WAITING THE ARRIVAL OF THE BOYS. WITH HER I FOUND THAT WHEN SHE WAS READY TO TALK SHE'D COME TALK, NO SENSE PUSHING HER, AS SHE WAS STUBBORN. ABOUT 15 MINUTES PASSED AND I WENT TO CHECK ON HER, LIKE ANY TYPICAL TEENAGER SHE WAS ON THE PHONE, SO I STEPPED OUT AND WENT BACK TO FIXING SUPPER. BY THIS TIME THE BOYS GOT HOME AND HANDED ME A STACK OF PAPERS I NEEDED TO GO THRU.

GEORGE HAD JUST FINISHED THE FRONT YARD, CAME IN FOR A DRINK, AND TO REST A MINUTE AND THEN WENT OUT TO GET STARTED ON THE BACK YARD. IT SEEMED AS IF WE HAD FARM LAND RATHER THAN A BIG YARD BUT IT HAD GROWN FAST AND WAS SO TALL IT TOOK SOME TIME TO GET THRU. ANGELA AT THAT MOMENT CAME INTO THE KITCHEN CRYING HYSTERICALLY, I ASKED WHAT ON EARTH HAPPENED. WHAT SHE BLURTED OUT WAS EVERY WOMAN'S NIGHTMARE, SOMETHING YOU NEVER WANT TO HEAR COME FROM YOUR CHILD'S MOUTH. SHE TOLD ME SHE WAS BEING MOLESTED BY HER FATHER!! I WAS FLOORED, I GRABBED AHOLD OF THE CHAIR AND SAT DOWN BEFORE I FELL, I JUST COULDN'T BELIEVE MY EARS IN WHAT I JUST HEARD. I BEGAN TO ASK QUESTIONS, HOW LONG? SHE SAID ABOUT 5 YEARS. SHE WAS 14 SO APPARENTLY SINCE AGE 9. IT WAS ALL I COULD DO TO SIT THERE. I WANTED SO BAD TO GO

AND CONFRONT GEORGE AND TAKE A BALL BAT AND START BEATING HIM WITH IT, YET A PART OF ME JUST COULDN'T BELIEVE HE WOULD EVER DO SOMETHING LIKE THIS, SHE HAD TO BE LYING, I MEAN, GEORGE IS SO EASY GOING, HAS A GREAT SENSE OF HUMOR. ALTHOUGH HIM AND ANGELA HAD ISSUES GETTING ALONG, I DON'T BELIEVE IT WAS TOO THE POINT OF HURTING HER THIS WAY.

I MEAN MOLESTING HIS OWN DAUGHTER?? MY GOODNESS HOW SICK, BUT THE WAY SHE WAS CRYING HYSTERICALLY, TOLD ME DIFFERENTLY. I HAD ALWAYS HAD THE IDEA THAT IF ONE WAS BEING MOLESTED THEY WERE TREATED MORE SPECIAL. RIGHT? BUT AS I SAT THERE LISTENING TO HER TELL ME THINGS, IT SORT OF HIT ME LIKE A TON OF BRICKS, PIECES STARTED FITTING TOGETHER LIKE A JIGSAW PUZZLE AND MAKING SENSE. I REPLAYED THE EVENTS THAT TOOK PLACE THE LAST 5 YEARS, THE CLOTHES BEHIND THE COUCH, HER WANTING TO RUN AWAY, BARRICADING HERSELF IN HER ROOM. I ASKED HER IF IT WAS CONTINUING, AND SHE SAID NO, THE ABUSE HAD STOPPED 3 WEEKS AGO WHEN I STARTED SUFFERING WITH THE MIGRAINES. WOW!! IMAGINE THAT, WHEN THE MIGRAINES GOT SO BAD THAT I COULDN'T WORK, HE DIDN'T HAVE OPPORTUNITIES TO MESS WITH HER. AS SHE CONTINUED TO POUR OUT HER STORY, I SUDDENLY WAS DRAWN TO HOW I WAS FEELING, I NOTICED THE MIGRAINE WASN'T AS SEVERE, IT WAS EASING UP, LIKE I WAS RECEIVING INSTANT HEALING THE MOMENT I WAS TOLD.

ALL THOSE WEEKS I SUFFERED, HAVING TO MISS WORK, WEAR SUNGLASSES CAUSE THE LIGHT HURT

MY EYES SO BADLY, THE MEDS I HAD TO TAKE, ALL THE TIME I MISSED WITH MY KIDS. I STARTED TO FEEL RESENTMENT AND WONDERED WHY THIS WAS HAPPENING. GEORGE WAS ONLY HALF FINISHED WITH THE YARD, SEEMED HE WAS TAKING FOREVER TO GET IT DONE BUT I SUPPOSE A GOOD THING AS I HAD QUESTIONS THAT FLOODED MY MIND. I ASKED HER WHAT HAPPENED AND WHEN DID IT HAPPEN. IT WAS GOING ON WHEN SHE GOT IN FROM SCHOOL, WHILE I WAS AT WORK BEFORE THE BOYS GOT IN. HE WOULD LOCK THE BEDROOM DOOR AND SHOW HER MOVIES, WHICH SHE TOLD ME WHERE HE HAD THEM. I WENT TO WHERE SHE SAID AND SURE ENOUGH IT WAS THERE. ALTHOUGH SHE SAID HE NEVER PENETRATED HER, HE DID MESS WITH HER AND HAD HER DO THINGS TO HIM. I WAS SICK, I JUST COULDN'T BELIEVE WHAT I WAS HEARING, BUT HOW COULD A 14 YEAR OLD MAKE SOMETHING UP LIKE THIS? I WANTED TO HANDLE THIS RESPONSIBLY, I KNEW SHE HAD SOME ISSUES TO WORK THRU HERSELF. SHE ALWAYS THOUGHT HER FATHER WAS MEAN TOWARDS HER, TELLING ME STORIES OF WHERE HE WOULD BE ANGRY AT HER AND THROW SHOES AT HER OR BREAK PLASTIC PLATES OVER HER HEAD, ALL WHICH GEORGE WOULD DENY WHEN I CONFRONTED HIM WITH THOSE ACCUSATIONS SHE MADE.

GEORGE AND I AT THIS POINT BEEN TOGETHER 15 1/2 YEARS AND I JUST DIDN'T KNOW WHAT TO DO. IT NEEDED DEALT WITH FOR SURE BUT I WANTED TO BE LEVEL HEADED ABOUT IT SO I CALLED OUR PASTOR AND TOLD HIM WHAT WAS GOING ON AND ASKED TO COME IN AND TALK. I HAD NO REAL FACTS OTHER THAN HER KNOWING WHERE GEORGE'S MOVIES WERE AND I

DIDN'T WANT TO ACCUSE HIM MAKING THINGS WORSE FOR HER, AND I WANTED ANGELA TO KNOW I WAS THERE FOR HER TOO. IT MAY STRIKE AS ODD SOMEONE WOULD HANDLE SOMETHING LIKE THIS CALMLY BUT I TRIED TO GIVE THE BENEFIT OF THE DOUBT WHEN NO PROOF WAS SUBSTANTIATED. WE MET WITH OUR PASTOR AND OF COURSE IT DIDN'T GO WELL. GEORGE WAS QUITE UPSET. MAYBE I SHOULD HAVE SHOWN HIM RESPECT ENOUGH TO TELL HIM WHY WE WERE MEETING WITH PASTOR; I JUST SAID THERE WAS AN ISSUE WE NEEDED SOME GOOD GODLY COUNSEL WITH. I DEFINITELY FELT AS IF I WAS BETWEEN A ROCK AND A HARD PLACE. WITH THE NATURE OF THE SITUATION, PASTOR WAS OBLIGATED BY LAW TO MAKE A REPORT WITH CHILDREN SERVICES. GEORGE WOULD HAVE TO MOVE OUT WHILE AN INVESTIGATION WAS DONE.

THE NEXT COUPLE OF MONTHS WAS A NIGHTMARE TO SAY THE LEAST. I STILL WORKED AT THE BAKERY GEORGE WAS THE MANAGER OF AND IT WAS REAL DIFFICULT. I FIGURED IT WOULD BE BEST TO JUST FIND ANOTHER JOB, BUT WITH COUNSELING, MANAGING THE KIDS, DOCTOR VISITS, COURT HEARINGS, AND TRYING TO KEEP BILLS PAID AND HOUSE STRAIGHTENED UP BUT A LITTLE MUCH TO HANDLE. I WAS FEELING A BIT OVERWHELMED DO I PRESSED THRU THE BEST I COULD. THERE WERE DAYS WHEN THE KIDS WERE IN SCHOOL I WOULD LAY OVER THE COUCH CRYING OUT TO GOD FOR STRENGTH AND GUIDANCE, WISDOM AND STRENGTH TO ENDURE THIS. MANY NIGHTS AFTER THEY WENT TO BED I WOULD CRY MYSELF TO SLEEP. I KNEW GOD WAS WITH ME, I KNEW THERE WERE TIMES HE AND ONLY HE CARRIED ME

THRU CAUSE I DON'T KNOW HOW I REMAINED SO STRONG.

FINALLY AFTER THEIR INVESTIGATION WAS COMPLETE, GEORGE WAS INDICTED ON 40 COUNTS OF GROSS SEXUAL IMPOSITION, GOING ALL THE WAY BACK FROM THE AGE OF 9 TO AGE 12. FROM AGES 13, AND 14 TH THEY DIDN'T INDICT HIM ON BECAUSE STATISTICS SHOWED THAT MOST GIRLS 13 AND 14 AND STARTING TO GO THRU PUBERTY ARE KIND OF PROMISCUOUS ANYWAY. BUT THEY DID HAVE ENOUGH TO RENDER THE CASE GOING TO TRIAL. IF CONVICTED, GEORGE WOULD GET TIME IN PRISON AND BE RENDERED A SEX OFFENDER. I CAN ONLY IMAGINE WHAT HE WAS GOING THRU, FOR ME I WAS DEVASTATED. 16 YEARS WITH SOMEONE, YOU WOULD THINK YOU KNEW THEM AND IT WAS ALL SHATTERED IN A MATTER OF A COUPLE DAYS.

It WAS JUNE 1997, AND SCHOOL WAS NOW OUT, IT WAS GONNA BE TOUGH BUT I WAS THANKFUL FOR GOD AND FOR FRIENDS. WE HAD GOTTEN A TRIAL DATE WHICH WAS SET FOR APRIL 1998, I HAD BEGUN DIVORCE PROCEEDINGS THRU LEGAL AID WHICH BECAUSE OF THE NATURE OF THE DIVORCE WOULD BE PAID FOR AND I WAS ALSO AWARDED METROPOLITAN HOUSING WHICH WOULD HELP ME WITH MY RENT. I THANKED GOD FOR THIS BECAUSE THERE WAS NO WAY ON JUST MY INCOME AND WHATEVER SUPPORT I WOULD GET FROM GEORGE BE ABLE TO COVER THE RENT LET ALONE THE OTHER BILLS WE HAD. MY WORK SCHEDULED CHANGED, I WOULD GO IN LATER AND GEORGE WOULD ALREADY BE OFF WORK. IT WAS EXTREMELY HARD WORKING WITH EVERYONE, OF

163

WHICH MOST WERE FRIENDS OF HIS HE HAD WORKED WITH FOR YEARS BEFORE I STARTED WORKING THERE, BUT UNTIL SOMETHING ELSE OPENED UP I JUST HAD TO GRIN AND BEAR IT AND STAY PUT. CHURCH WAS EVEN MORE DIFFICULT AND AS I WORSHIPPED GOD TEARS FLOWED. OVER THE LAST COUPLE OF YEARS GEORGE HAD BEEN MORE REGULAR IN CHURCH ATTENDANCE AND IT WAS SO GREAT TO LEAD THIS LIFE TOGETHER, BUT IN REALITY FRIENDS BECAME DISTANT AND I FELT SO ALONE AND ABANDONED AND I DID NOTHING. I WAS JUST AS MUCH A VICTIM IN THIS SITUATION AS GEORGE AND ANGELA AND WHAT ABOUT THE BOYS, WERE THEY NOT INNOCENT VICTIMS THAT WERE ROBBED OF BOTH PARENTS BEING TOGETHER?

SUMMER WAS NOW OVER AND THE KIDS WENT BACK TO SCHOOL. IT WAS NOW SEPT. 1997. GEORGE AND I HAD NOW BEEN SEPARATED 4 MONTHS AND IT WAS STILL SO HARD TO WRAP MY MIND AROUND ALL THAT HAPPENED. WE STILL HAD TO GET THRU THE TRIAL, WHICH WASN'T UNTIL THAT NEXT APRIL. WITH THE KIDS IN SCHOOL I COME TO ENJOY SOME ALONE TIME WITH GOD TO HELP SORT OUT MY THOUGHTS. ANGELA WAS 15 1/2 NOW AND ABLE TO WATCH HER BROTHERS WHILE I WORKED, WHICH WAS GREAT SO I DIDN'T NEED TO PAY A SITTER. METROPOLITAN CAME THROUGH, WHICH PAID OUR RENT. SO ALL I HAD WAS UTILITIES AND FEW OTHER BILLS. I WAS AT WORK ONE DAY, AND THEY HAD JUST HIRED A GUY IN THE PRODUCE DEPARTMENT WHICH WAS NEXT TO THE BAKERY DEPARTMENT. HE WAS GOOD LOOKING AND SEEMED TO HAVE A SENSE OF HUMOR AND WE WOULD OFTEN JOKE AROUND. HE HAD PLACED AN ORDER FOR A BIRTHDAY CAKE FOR HIS DAUGHTERS BIRTHDAY

THAT WAS SEPT. 15TH AND CAME IN TO PICK IT UP. I WENT BACK TO GET IT AND WHEN I HANDED IT TO HIM HE ASKED ME FOR MY PHONE NUMBER. NOW MIND YOU, GEORGE AND I HAD BEEN SEPARATED FOR 4 MONTHS, TRIAL FOR GROSS SEXUAL IMPOSITION SET AND DIVORCE PAPERS ALREADY FILED WHEN I DECIDED TO GIVE THIS GUY WILLIE MY NUMBER!

I ACTUALLY THOUGHT HE WAS A GOD SEND, AS FRIENDS HAD DESERTED ME OVER THIS WHOLE FIASCO WE WERE GOING THRU. IT WAS A COUPLE DAYS BEFORE HE ACTUALLY CALLED ME AND ASKED IF WE COULD GET TOGETHER. I WAS EXCITED AND GAVE HIM MY ADDRESS. I KNOW, KIND OF CREEPY HUH WHEN I DIDN'T REALLY KNOW HIM WELL, ONLY FROM WORK. BUT I FELT A PEACE ABOUT IT SO I INVITED HIM OVER. HE MUST NOT HAVE BEEN ABLE TO DRIVE BECAUSE HE RODE HIS BICYCLE FROM TOWN ALL THE WAY TO MY HOUSE IN THE COUNTRY, THAT WAS OVER 3 MILES. I SUPPOSE I MUST HAVE BEEN PRETTY SPECIAL AND I SURE NEEDED A FRIEND RIGHT THEN. WE HIT IT OFF GREAT AND TALKED FOR HOURS, AND I LEARNED HE HAD LOST HIS LICENSE DRIVING UNDER THE INFLUENCE OF ALCOHOL. HE HAD BEEN THRU HIS 2ND MARRIAGE WINNING CUSTODY OF 2 GIRLS BOTH AGE 5. THE MOM HAD ONE GIRL AND THEN GOT PREGNANT RIGHT AWAY AND HAD THE OTHER GIRL A MONTH BEFORE THE FIRST TURNED 1, SO THERE WAS ONE MONTH THEY WERE THE SAME AGE. HE WAS GETTING HIS LIFE BACK ON TRACK, HIM AND HIS DAUGHTERS LIVING WITH HIS MOM, SISTER AND BROTHER IN LAW AND ANOTHER BROTHER. HE WAS WORKING AS AN ASSISTANT MANAGER FOR HIS OTHER BROTHER IN LAW BUT WORKING THE PRODUCE DEPARTMENT FOR

EXTRA MONEY TO GET HIS LICENSE BACK. I TOLD HIM SOME OF WHAT I WAS GOING THRU AND HE SEEMED REAL COMPASSIONATE TOWARDS ME AND HE EVEN KISSED ME BEFORE HE LEFT, HIS LIPS SOFT AND WARM, I WAS SMITTEN AND THANKED GOD FOR HIM.

THE NEXT DAY, IT WAS MY DAY OFF AND HE WORKED A MORNING SHIFT, HE HAD ME COME FOR LUNCH AND THEN STAYED TILL HE GOT OFF WHICH WAS ABOUT AN HOUR LATER. WE WENT BACK TO HIS PLACE FOR A WHILE TO MEET HIS DAUGHTERS AND OTHER FAMILY MEMBERS HE LIVED WITH. THEY ALL SEEMED REAL NICE AND HIS DAUGHTERS SEEMED TO LIKE ME OKM ALTHOUGH A LITTLE BACKWARDS. I SOON LEFT HIS PLACE TO GET HOME TO MY KIDS WHO WOULD SOON BE GETTING OFF THE BUS FROM SCHOOL, BUT MADE PLANS FOR HIM TO COME THE NEXT NIGHT FOR DINNER SINCE IT WAS THE WEEKEND AND MY KIDS COULD MEET HIM AND THE GIRLS AND HIM AND HIS GIRLS MEET MY KIDS. I TALKED TO ANGIE AS I WAS PREPARING SUPPER AND TOLD HER AND SHE SEEMED THRILLED FOR ME, AND I REALLY FELT GOOD ABOUT IT, BUT WASN'T SURE HOW THE BOYS WOULD FEEL. I MEAN IT WASN'T AS IF WE WERE GETTING MARRIED, MY DIVORCE WASN'T FINAL. IT WAS JUST A FRIENDSHIP FOR NOW AND I PRAYED THE BOYS WOULD BE OK WITH ANOTHER MAN AROUND OTHER THAN THEIR DAD.

FINALLY THE WEEKEND WAS HERE, I HAD BEEN NERVOUS ALL MORNING THINKING ABOUT THAT EVENING AND WONDERING WHAT TO PREPARE FOR SUPPER AND TO GET THRU MY WORK DAY. HE WAS WORKING TOO AND MADE AN EFFORT TO POP HIS

HEAD IN THE BAKERY TO SAY HEY WHEN HE ARRIVED. OF COURSE THERE WAS SOME TALK AT WORK, AND I WAS A LITTLE SCARED SOMEONE WOULD LET GEORGE IN ON THE FACT ANOTHER GUY WAS VYING FOR MY ATTENTION. BUT IT WAS MY LIFE RIGHT? NOT LIKE I WAS THE ONE WHO DID A CRIME, I WAS A VICTIM HERE AS WELL, BUT WHO KNOWS WHAT HE WAS SAYING BEHIND MY BACK. STILL UNBELIEVABLE AFTER 16 YEARS. I'M SURE HE WAS HURTING JUST AS WELL. IT WAS TOUGH FOR EVERYONE INVOLVED. I HAD DECIDED TO PREPARE SPAGHETTI FOR SUPPER, SO WHEN MY SHIFT WAS OVER I WENT AND DID THE NECESSARY SHOPPING AND THEN TO GET HOME TO THE KIDS AND START PREPARATIONS. I GOT HOME JUST AS THE BUS DROPPED OFF THE BOYS, ANGIE WAS ALREADY HOME AND WHEN I GOT IN THE HOUSE, THE KIDS SEEMED TO BE IN A GREAT MOOD SO IT CERTAINLY GAVE ME A CALMNESS I SO NEEDED TO GET THRU THIS NIGHT. I TOLD THEM OF MY PLANS TO HAVE WILLIE AND THE GIRLS OVER AND THEY SEEMED TO BE OK WITH IT.

SOON WILLIE AND THE GIRLS ARRIVED; DINNER WOULD BE A FEW MINUTES YET, SO WE ALL SAT IN THE LIVING ROOM TO GET AQUAINTED. MY KIDS SEEMED TO BE RECEPTIVE OF HIM AND THE GIRLS ALTHOUGH THEY WERE A LITTLE SHY AS THIS WAS CERTAINLY A NEW EXPERIENCE FOR THEM TOO. WE SAT DOWN TO EAT, MAKING SURE TO THANK GOD FOR OUR FOOD AND THE TIME WE HAD TOGETHER. AFTER WE ATE WE SAT IN THE LIVING ROOM AND WATCHED A MOVIE. AFTER IT WAS OVER I GOT THE BOYS SETTLED IN BED AND ANGIE HUNG OUT IN HER ROOM WHILE I TOOK WILLIE AND THE GIRLS HOME WHERE WE ENDING UP SETTING OUTSIDE AND TALK TO WELL AFTER

MIDNIGHT. ON THE DRIVE HOME, MY MIND PLAYED OVER AND OVER THE EVENTS OF THE NIGHT AND I PRAYED THINGS WOULD WORK OUT FOR US BECAUSE I REALLY LIKE HIM AND NEEDED HIM AT THIS POINT IN MY LIFE. THE NEXT WEEK WENT BY IN A BLUR, HAD A MEETING WITH THE DIVORCE ATTORNEY, MORE MEETINGS WITH ATTORNEY FOR THE CASE AGAINST GEORGE, WITH THE NEWS THAT THE CASE MAY BE TOUGH WITH THE FACT THAT ANGIE WASN'T PENETRATED, SHE FAILED THE LIE DETECTOR TEST AND HAD TO RETAKE. I HAD BEGUN TO HAVE DOUBTS AS TO THE NATURE OF THE INCIDENT. BUT WHY WOULD SHE TWIST THINGS? COUNSELING WAS HARD TO GET THRU, ESPECIALLY WITH THE KIDS TALKING ABOUT A NEW MAN IN MY LIFE.

ANOTHER WEEKEND WAS NOW UPON US AND THIS TIME WILLIE HAD SPENT THE NIGHT THAT FRIDAY NIGHT. HIS GIRLS HAD WENT TO THEIR MOMS FOR THE WEEKEND, AND HE CAME OUT TO SPEND SOME TIME WITH ME AND THE KIDS. I REMEMBER TALKING TO MY MOM ON THE PHONE, THAT BRIGHT SATURDAY MORNING AS I KICKED A SOCCER BALL AROUND THE BACK YARD, GIVING MY MOM EVERY DETAIL OF MY NEW FOUND LOVE. SHE SEEMED HAPPY FOR ME. HOWEVER, GEORGE ENDED UP STOPPING BY TO SEE IF HE COULD HAVE THE BOYS. IT WASN'T HIS WEEKEND AND USUALLY HE CALLED FIRST BUT I'M SURE HE GOT WIND OF THE RUMORS AT WORK THAT I WAS SEEING SOMEONE OR COULD HAVE BEEN FROM THE BOYS DURING THEIR MID WEEK VISIT WITH THEIR DAD. I HAD HOPED THAT WILLIE WOULD HAVE STAYED IN THE BEDROOM BUT HE CAME OUT AND JUST IN A PAIR OF PANTS, AND GEORGE GOT REAL UPSET. GEORGE

WENT BACK AND TOLD OUR PASTOR AND MY PASTOR CALLED TO ASK ME TO STEP DOWN FROM THE WORSHIP TEAM AND I WOULD NOT BE ALLOWED IN THE DRAMA PLAY AS WELL. I WAS CRUSHED, WHY DID HE FEEL HE NEEDED TO DO THAT, AFTER ALL HE WAS BEING ACCUSED OF A HENIOUS CRIME AND YET I WAS THE ONE BEING PUNISHED. MAYBE IT WASN'T RIGHT SEEING SOMEONE ELSE AND BEING MARRIED, BUT WE WERE SEPARATED 4 MONTHS BEFORE I MET WILLIE, GEORGE KNEW OUR MARRIAGE WAS OVER. MY LIFE SEEMED TO BE SINKING FAST, WHY COULDN'T ANYONE LEAVE ME ALONE AND ALLOW ME SOME HAPPINESS, I'D BEEN THRU HELL.

3 MONTHS INTO DATING WILLIE AND I NOTICED A CHANGE IN HIM, HE WAS SHOWING SIGNS OF WITHDRAWAL, AND BECOMING DEPRESSED. THERE WAS SOME BEHAVORIAL ISSUES SURFACING IN HIS YOUNGEST DAUGHTER AND WE WASN'T SURE IF IT CAME ABOUT WHEN HE MET ME OR SOMETHING THAT SHE HAD ALREADY BEEN DEALING WITH THAT HE WASN'T AWARE OF AND THOUGHT WAS ISSUES FROM BEING SEPARATED FROM THEIR REAL MOM, BUT SHE HAD STARTED BANGING HER HEAD AGAINST A WALL, AND IT WASN'T ON OCCASION, BUT WOULD DO IT EVERY TIME SHE GOT UPSET ABOUT SOMETHING. SHE HAD SOME DELAYS AND DEVELOPMENT ISSUES GOING ON AS IT WAS AND HE HAD SCHEDULED HER FOR A PHYSICAL AND TESTING TO SEE WHAT WAS GOING ON. ONE TIME SHE BANGED HER HEAD SO LONG AND SO HARD SHE PUT A HOLE IN THE WALL, AND RUBBED A BALD SPOT IN THE BACK OF HER HAIR.

WHEN IT CAME TIME FOR THAT APPOINTMENT, WE LEARNED THAT SHE WAS ADHD WHICH IS ATTENTION DEFICIT WITH HYPERATIVITY DISORDER, ODD WHICH IS OPPOSITIONAL DEFIANT DISORDER, FETAL ALCOHOL SYNDROME, AND MILDLY MENTALLY RETARDED BEING 3 YEARS BEHIND HER PEERS. MY GOODNESS WAS THERE ANYTHING ELSE GOING ON. THAT WAS ALOT TO ABSORB LET ALONE FOR A SINGLE FATHER TO HAVE TO DEAL WITH, I COULDN'T IMAGINE WHAT WAS GOING THRU HER LITTLE MIND. THERE WOULD BE MANY DOC VISITS, COUNSELING SESSIONS AND APPOINTMENTS WITH SOME SPECIALISTS TO HELP US BETTER UNDERSTAND THE CONDITIONS AND WHAT SHE WAS GOING THRU IN HOPES OF HELPING HER REMAIN CALM AND MEDICINES WERE GIVEN TO HELP WITH THIS TOO. CERTAINLY WOULD BE ALOT FOR ME TO TRY AND HELP HANDLE WITH ALL I WAS GOING THRU, BUT I FELT BAD FOR HIM AND WANTED TO BE THERE FOR SUPPORT.

THE NEXT WEEK SHE WAS SCHEDULED FOR AN APPOINTMENT TO SEE A SPECIALIST IN INDIANA. THE DAY OF THE APPOINTMENT I WAS CALLED INTO WORK AND ANGIE HAD STAYED WITH A FRIEND. WILLIE HAD OFFERED TO TAKE THE BOYS WITH HIM SO I DIDN'T HAVE TO WORRY ABOUT ANOTHER SITTER. WHILE AT THE APPOINTMENT, MY SON ERIC HAD APPARENTLY ACTED UP AND WAS BEING CORRECTED WHEN HE LOOKED AT WILLIE AND SAID YOU CAN'T TELL ME WHAT TO DO, YOU ARE NOT MY FATHER! WILLIE IN HIS FRUSTRATION OF ALL HE WAS DEALING WITH HIS DAUGHTER APPARENTLY JERKED ERIC OUT OF THE VAN AND WHIPPED HIM. A LADY DRIVING BY SEEN IT AND CALLED THE AUTHORITIES AND GAVE THEM THE

LICENSE NUMBER TOO. PRETTY SOON THERE WAS A KNOCK AT THE DOOR AND WHEN I OPENED IT, IT WAS STATE TROOPER FROM INDIANA AND HE EXPLAINED THE REASON FOR HIS VISIT. I THOUGHT TO MYSELF ARE YOU FREAKING KIDDING ME? DID I HAVE ENOUGH TO CONTEND WITH? THE OFFICER TALKED WITH ERIC AND WITH WILLIE AND ALTHOUGH WE GOT IT ALL STRAIGHTENED OUT, I STILL BROKE DOWN IN TEARS WONDERING IF I HAD MADE A HUGE MISTAKE GETTING INVOLVED WITH THIS GUY! I MEAN THE TRIAL WAS STILL OPEN, WE HADN'T EVEN BEEN TO COURT YES, THINGS WERE FRESH ON OUR MINDS, THE BOYS HAVING TO SEE THEIR DAD ONCE DURING THE WEEK AND EVERY OTHER WEEKEND AND YET THIS GUY WAS AROUND ALMOST EVERYDAY AND THINKING HE WAS THEIR FATHER NOW? IT WAS ALOT FOR THEM TO UNDERSTAND, I MEAN ERIC WAS ONLY 11 AND JASON WAS 8 - I COULDN'T IMAGINE THEIR CONFUSION. I HAD ALWAYS HEARD THE PHRASE GROWING UP THAT IF I KNEW THEN WHAT I KNEW NOW I WOULD HAVE DONE THINGS SO DIFFERENTLY.

FINALLY APRIL WAS HERE AND TIME FOR THE TRIAL. WILLIE HAD DECIDED TO COME WITH ME FOR MORAL SUPPORT, NOT SURE IF THIS WAS A GOOD IDEA, BUT I CERTAINLY NEEDED SOMEONE TO BE THERE FOR ME. THE TRIAL WHICH HAD A JURY, TOOK 3 DAYS, AND THE END RESULTED IN A HUNG JURY. 6 THOUGHT GEORGE WAS GUILTY, 6 THOUGHT HE WAS NOT GUILTY, SO BECAUSE OF THE LACK OF EVIDENCE IN THE CASE THE JUDGE RULED IN GEORGE'S FAVOR. WE BELIEVE THE PROSECUTER DID A LOUSY JOB PRESENTING THE CASE IN THAT HE DIDN'T ASK FOR THE JURY TO LOOK AT THE FACT THAT ANGELA KNEW

WHAT HER FATHERS PRIVATE PART LOOKED LIKE IN THE SENSE HE HAD A MOLE AND KNEW THE SHAPE OF THAT MOLE. SHE COULD HAVE IN NO OTHER WAY HAVE KNOWN THIS UNLESS SHE SEEN HIS PRIVATE AREA UP CLOSE! THIS WAS SUCH DEVASTATING NEWS, AND THERE WASN'T EVEN A CHANCE TO FILE AN APPEAL. HE COULDN'T BE TRIED AGAIN FOR THE SAME CRIME UNLESS HE DID IT AGAIN.

THE ONLY THING WE COULD DO NOW WAS GET THRU IT THE BEST WE COULD AND TRY AND PUT OUR LIVES BACK TOGETHER, BUT IT WAS GONNA TAKE TIME. THE TRIAL MADE THE FORNT PAGE OF THE LOCAL PAPER, NOT TO MENTION THAT FOR WHATEVER REASON THE SHERIFF'S DEPARTMENT SERVED GEORGE HIS DIVORCE PAPERS ON THE LAST DAY OF THE TRIAL. WHAT A SLAP IN THE FACE FOR GEORGE RIGHT? WELL THAT WAS NOT MY INTENT. THE SHERIFF WAS SUPPOSE TO SERVE HIM AT HOME BUT NEVER GOT AROUND TO IT WITH HIS SCHEDULE, SO SINCE HE FIGURED HE WAS ALREADY AT THE COURTHOUSE ON ANOTHER MATTER WHY NOT KILL 2 BIRDS WITH ONE STONE. THAT ONLY ADDED FUEL TO THE FIRE FOR ME AS A REMARK WAS THEN MADE THAT ANGELA AND I MADE THE WHOLE STORY UP SO I COULD BE RID OF GEORGE AND HAVE MY BOYFRIEND. REALLY!! WHO THE HELL GOES TO GREAT LENGTHS TO MAKE UP SUCH A HORRIBLE CRIME AS MOLESTATION, PUTTING SOMEONE THRU HELL LIKE THAT JUST SO THEY COULD GET DIVORCED AND HAVE A BOYFRIEND. HOW FLIPPIN WARPED IS THAT.

WITH ALL THE SEPARATION AND AFFAIRS AND THE WAY DIVORCE IS SO COMMON, ONE IS GOING TO

TRASH THE LIFE OF SOMEONE ELSE LIKE THAT AND PRINT IT ALL IN THE PAPER TO BOOT. IN THE NEWSPAPER ARTICLE IT READ THAT ANGELA HAD A FRIEND WHO WAS MOLESTED AT AGE 11 BY HER GRANDFATHER AND MAYBE ANGELA GOT SO INVOLVED IN THE STORY OF HER FRIEND THAT SHE BELIEVED IT HAPPENED TO HER. WHAT KIND OF A SICK JOKE IS THAT, TO STOOP TO SUCH A LEVEL AND CONCOCT A STORY, I WOULD NOT WISH THAT ON MY WORST ENEMY!!

I LEARNED A VALUABLE LESSON THAT DAY AS TO HOW OUR SOCIETY WAS AND I REGRETTED DATING WILLIE AT THAT TIME, ALTHOUGH I DIDN'T MEET HIM TILL 4 MONTHS AFTER THE ACCUSATIONS WERE MADE, I SHOULDN'T HAVE GOTTEN INVOLVED WITH HIM TILL THIS MESS WAS CLEARED UP, BUT I REALLY FELT THAT GOD BROUGHT HIM INTO MY LIFE TO HELP ME THRU A DIFFICULT TIME. I LOST SO MANY FRIENDSHIPS THRU THE TRIAL AND EVEN FELT LIKE AN OUTCAST IN MY OWN CHURCH, ONE PLACE YOU WOULDN'T THINK PEOPLE WOULD BE SO JUDGMENTAL. WILL HAD WANTED TO START COMING TO CHURCH BUT DEFINITELY WASN'T GOING TO BE THIS ONE WITH THEIR ATTITUDES, SO WE FOUND ONE THAT WE COULD START OUR NEW LIVES IN AND REALLY LIKE THE PASTORS AND THE PEOPLE MADE US FEEL AT HOME.

WILL AND I HAD BEEN DATING ONE YEAR, HIM MOVING IN THE MONTH BEFORE, WHEN I STARTED NOTICING A DIFFERENT SIDE TO HIM. HE BECAME OVERLY JEALOUS OF MY KIDS, ALWAYS QUICK TO CORRECT THEM YET NOT DISCIPLINING HIS OWN. WE BUTTED HEADS A FEW TIMES OVER THIS AND I

173

REMINDED HIM WHAT THE DOCTOR HAD SAID ABOUT HIS YOUNGEST NEEDED STRUCTURE AND RULES. WITH ALL THAT SEEMED TO BE AGAINST HER IT WAS IMPERATIVE THAT SHE HAVE BOUNDARIES, AND CONSISTENCY IN HER ROUTINE, ALL THE KIDS NEEDED THIS BUT HE ALWAYS FELT SORRY FOR HER AND LET HER DO WHATEVER MADE HER HAPPY.

IT'S OK TO FEEL SORRY OR FOR A BETTER WORD, COMPASSIONATE FOR A PERSON WITH DISABILITIES, BUT I BELIEVE YOU SHOULD DISCIPLINE AS WELL OR THEY WILL HAVE STRUGGLES AND GET INTO TROUBLE AS THEY GET OLDER AND LIVE ON THEIR OWN, NOT GET BY WITH STUFF AND USE THEIR DISABILITIES AS AN EXCUSE TO DO WHATEVER YOU WANTED AND BE A HOOLIGAN. THERE WERE SO MANY FIGHTS, SO MANY STRUGGLES, BUT I WAS ALWAYS TAUGHT NOT TO WALK AWAY FROM A SITUATION BUT TO STAND AND FIGHT FOR WHAT YOU BELIEVE IN AND WORK IT OUT. FIGHTING FOR WHAT YOU BELIEVE IS NOT PHYSICAL FIGHTING AS IN PUNCHING SOMEONE BUT DOING THE BEST YOU CAN TO RECTIFY THE CONFLICTS THAT ARISE. NOT ALWAYS IS THIS THE CASE HOWEVER, THEREFORE A CAUSE FOR A BREAK-UP.

ONE TIME IN THE MIDST OF A DISAGREEMENT, RATHER THAN HIM ANSWER A QUESTION I HAD, DECIDED TO PICK UP THE CORDLESS PHONE TO MAKE A CALL, I WENT TO REACH FOR IT AND HE BENT OVER AS IF TO HIDE IT SO I COULDN'T GET IT. I REACHED UNDER TO SEE IF I COULD GET IT THINKING IT WAS IMPORTANT TO SETTLE THE ISSUE AT HAND RATHER THAN HIM TALK TO SOMEONE ON THE PHONE, MY

OTHER HAND WAS ON HIS BACK AND AS MY ARM CAME DOWN FROM HIS BACK, I MUST HAVE SCRAPED HIS ARM ON AN ACCIDENT AND BEFORE I KNEW IT HE RARED UP AND THREW ME INTO THE WALL AND THE WALL BROKE HAVING THE IMPRINT OF MY BACK SIDE IN THE WALL. THE WIND WAS KNOCKED OUT OF ME AND WHEN I COULD MOVE, MY EYES MET WILLIE'S YOUNGEST DAUGHTER WHO HAD JUST GOTTEN HOME FROM KINDERGARDEN. WHEN SHE SEEN THE WALL SHE GOT SCARED AND STARTED TO CRY, I GRABBED THE PHONE AND CALLED THE SHERIFF'S OFFICE AND WHEN THEY CAME HE WAS ARRESTED FOR DOMESTIC VIOLENCE. I WAS DEVASTATED, THE MAN I HAD COME TO LOVE, WHO I THOUGHT WAS A GOD SEND FROM WHAT I WENT THRU WITH GEORGE, HAD NOW ABUSED ME HIMSELF. SINCE IT WAS HIS FIRST OFFENSE HE ONLY SPENT THE NIGHT IN JAIL AND A COURT DATE WAS SET, HE CAME BY AND GRAB SOME STUFF AND THE GIRLS AND WENT TO HIS MOM FOR A WHILE AND I WONDERED WHAT HAD HAPPENED TO ME.

WHY WAS WE GOING THRU ALL THIS? HE CALLED ME UP AFTER A WEEK WENT BY AND APOLOGIZED FOR WHAT HE DID. HE SAID HE DIDN'T WANT TO LOSE ME AND PROMISED HE WOULD BE A BETTER MAN AND NOT DO IT AGAIN AND TREAT MY KIDS BETTER. HE SEEMED SINCERE, SO I DECIDED TO WORK IT OUT. WITH ME BEING ON METROPOLITAN, THEIR RULES STATED THAT THERE COULDN'T BE MORE THAN 2 KIDS OF THE SAME SEX TO A ROOM. SINCE THERE WAS NOW 3 GIRLS, WE HAD TO SEARCH FOR A BIGGER HOUSE. IT DIDN'T SEEM TO TAKE LONG UNTIL WE FOUND A 4 BEDROOM INSIDE OF TOWN AND LOOKED FORWARD TO THE MOVE AND MAKING A FRESH START. I HAD SINCE LEFT MY JOB AT

THE BAKERY AND LANDED A RETAIL JOB AT KMART AND LOVED MY JOB.

ONCE MY DIVORCE FROM GEORGE BECAME FINAL, WILL AND I MADE PLANS TO GET MARRIED. I TOLD HIM IT WAS TIME WE GOT OUR LIVES RIGHT WITH GOD AND QUIT LIVING IN SIN FOR IT WASN'T A GOOD EXAMPLE TO BE SETTING FOR OUR KIDS. OUR NEW PASTOR HAD SUGGESTED WE GO THRU A MARRIAGE COUNSELING SESSION, BUT WILLIE DIDN'T WANT TO DO THIS AS IT WOULD REQUIRE US TO SEPARATE FOR ABOUT 6 MONTHS WHICH IS HOW LONG THE PROGRAM LASTED. INSTEAD WE SET THE DATE FOR THE NEXT MONTH AND SO THE PREPARATIONS BEGAN TO LOOK FOR A DRESS AND INVITATIONS AND ALL. I WAS VERY CRAFTY AND WANTED SOMETHING SIMPLE SO I DIDN'T THINK IT WOULD BE VERY DIFFICULT TO PUT SOMETHING TOGETHER. OUR PASTOR AGREED TO MARRY US AND THE DATE OF JULY 17, 1999 WAS SET. I FOUND A DRESS, MADE INVITATIONS, AND THE LADY WHO WAS TO BE MY MAID OF HONOR WAS VERY ARTISTIC AND MADE OUR BOUQUETS. ALL TOTAL I PUT TOGETHER A NICE WEDDING FOR AROUND 1200.00. I WAS SO PROUD OF MYSELF AND WILLIE WAS SURE ENOUGH HAPPY.

OUR BIG DAY ARRIVED AND I WAS EXCITED. WE'D BEEN TOGETHER ALMOST 2 YEARS AND ALTHOUGH IT WASN'T ALL BLISSFUL, THERE WAS NO OTHER PHYSICAL ALTERCATION SINCE THAT DAY THE YEAR BEFORE. WE KNEW THINGS WOULD BE HARD, HIS KIDS, MY KIDS, A BLENDED FAMILY WITH DIFFERENT PERSONALITIES, EACH CARRYING THEIR OWN BAGGAGE OF HURTS AND DISAPPOINTMENTS. FOR ME,I

TRUSTED THAT GOD WOULD HELP US THRU AND BLESS OUR LIFE TOGETHER, HOWEVER, IT WASN'T LONG BEFORE THE HONEYMOON WAS OVER AND THE TROUBLES BEGAN. ATTITUDES FLARED, MY KIDS COMPLAINING THAT WILLIE WAS BEING MEAN TO THEM, ALL OF WHICH HE DENIED WHEN CONFRONTED. I TIRED TO ENCOURAGE MY KIDS, THAT THIS WAS A NEW SITUATION FOR ALL OF US AND TO HANG IN THERE THE BEST THEY COULD, BUT THAT SOON CHANGED WHEN WILLIE LOST HIS JOB. THE VERBAL ABUSE SOON BEGAN, AND MY KIDS OFTEN TOLD ME WHEN I'D COME IN FROM WORK THAT HE WOULD LOCK MY KIDS IN THEIR ROOM WHILE I WAS GONE, AND THEN TELL ME I WAS WORTHLESS AND NOT A GOOD MOM. THAT HIS KIDS HATED ME AND I WAS NOTHING BUT A WITCH, ALL SORTS OF HATEFUL THINGS. I WAS SO HURT AND SEEMED TO CRY FOR HOURS. WHY WAS HE BEING LIKE THIS? WHEN I NEEDED TO GO TO BED EARLY CAUSE I HAD TO WORK THE NEXT DAY, HE'D HAVE HIS KIDS LAUGH AND JUMP AROUND AND KEEP ME AWAKE.

ONE NIGHT I'D HAD ENOUGH. I WENT DOWNSTAIRS AND TOLD HIM ABOUT THE RUCKUS HE WAS ALLOWING TO HAPPEN. WE HAD THIS REGISTER VENT IN THE CEILING THAT ALLOWED HEAT TO RISE INTO THE UPSTAIRS BEDROOM WE OCCUPIED, SO I COULD HEAR EVERYTHING THAT WENT ON IN THE LIVING ROOM BELOW. HE'S PURPOSELY TURN THE TV UP LOUD THEN HAVE HIS DAUGHTER WHO WAS MENTALLY HANDICAPPED LAUGH AT THE TOP OF HER LUNGS. WELL, AND ARGUMENT SOON ENTAILED, AND HE TOOK MY PURSE AND REFUSED TO GIVE IT BACK. I SEEN HIS WALLET AND GRABBED IT AND HE TOOK OFF AFTER ME. I RAN UPSTAIRS WITH HIM IN PURSUIT AND

DOWN THE HALL WE WENT. THE OLDER OF HIS DAUGHTERS, WHO WAS TRYING TO GET OUT OF THE WAY, TRIPPED OVER MY FOOT AND ALMOST FELL DOWN THE STAIRS.

I HAD GRABBED HER JUST IN TIME BEFORE SHE TUMBLED, BUT WILLIE BEING MAD, DIDN'T SEE IT LIKE THAT AND ASSUMED I WAS TRYING TO THROW HER DOWN THE STAIRS, AND HE STARTED PUNCHING ME. I RAN DOWNSTAIRS AND ASKED MY KIDS TO CALL THE COPS. HE WAS ABOUT TO GO OUT THE DOOR WHEN I STEPPED IN FRONT OF IT, PRETTY DUMB HUH? BUT HE HAD MY PURSE AND I DIDN'T WANT HIM LEAVING WITH IT, WHO KNOWS WHERE HE WOULD HAVE DUMPED IT AND MY LICENSE, MONEY AND CREDIT CARDS WAS IN THERE, SO I TRIED TO TALK TO HIM AND FIND OUT WHY HE WAS SO MAD? I WAS EXPLAINING THAT I NEVER TRIPPED HIS DAUGHTER ON PURPOSE, SHE WAS TRYING TO GET AWAY FROM THE YELLING AS HE WAS SHOVING ME DOWN THE HALLWAY AND I DIDN'T GET OUT OF THE WAY FAST ENOUGH AND SHE TRIPPED. THAT ONLY SEEMED TO MAKE HIM MADDER BY BLOCKING HIS EXIT DOOR BECAUSE HE GRABBED ME AND PUT ME IN A FULL NELSON CHOKE HOLD WHERE I ALMOST PASSED OUT.

THE POLICE FINALLY ARRIVED, I HAD REFUSED TO PRESS CHARGES. I FELT BAD FOR THE KIDS, KNOWING THAT IF I DID PRESS CHARGES AND HE WENT TO JAIL, IT WOULD HURT THEM AND HAVE A NEGATIVE AFFECT. YEAH, I KNOW LIKE SEEING HIM PUNCH ME AND PUTTING ME IN A CHOKE HOLD WOULDN'T RIGHT? BUT I WAS MORE CONCERNED FOR THEM AND HOW WE WOULD MAKE IT RIGHT THEN WITHOUT HIM WHEN I

178

SHOULD HAVE BEEN MORE CONCERNED OVER MY SAFETY AND THE FACT HE COULD HAVE KILLED ME BY ONE TURN OF MY NECK, THEN WHERE WOULD MY KIDS BE? AFTER THAT NIGHT THERE WASN'T ALOT OF PHYSICAL ALTERCATIONS, BUT THERE WAS VERBAL AND EMOTIONAL ABUSE. I JUST TOOK IT AS A PART OF LIFE, I MEAN NO ONE IS PERFECT AND YOU'LL HAVE STRUGGLES. WHEN 2 OR 3 MONTHS WENT BY AND HE WOULDN'T EVEN HAVE SEX WITH ME, OR SPEAK MUCH TO ME AT ALL, THEN WHEN HE DID IT WAS CUT DOWN AFTER CUTDOWN. HE WOULD TELL ME HOW BAD OF A MOM I WAS AND THAT HIS KIDS HATED ME AND MINE DIDN'T THINK MUCH OF ME EITHER. IT GOT TO BE TOO MUCH AND I HAD MET SOMEONE ON THE CB RADIO.

I KNEW IT WAS WRONG TO EVEN CARRY ON A CONVERSATION, NOT A VERY SMART THING TO DO AT THIS POINT BUT I FELT PUSHED OR SOMEHOW JUSTFIED WITH THE FACT THAT WILLIE WAS ABUSIVE AND MENTIONED HE WAS MOVING OUT SOON. AT THE TIME I WAS WORKING 2 JOBS, AND SO THIS CB GUY NAMED LONE WOLF ASKED TO MEET ME, BY BEING MARRIED I KNEW IT WASN'T RIGHT TO START GETTING INVOLVED WITH ANOTHER GUY, SO I WAS COMPELLED TO ASK WILLIE IF IT WAS OK TO MEET HIM. HE SAID THAT WAS OK WITH HIM AND I FELT GOOD IN AT LEAST TRYING TO DO WHAT WAS RIGHT BY GETTING THINGS IN THE OPEN. ONE NIGHT LONEWOLD CAME IN AND WE MET, HE WAS A HEFTY GUY AND NOT BAD LOOKING AND WE SEEMED TO HIT IT OFF. I WAS REALLY HOPING BY HAVING A FRIEND, WHICH WILLIE NEVER REALLY ALLOWED ME TO HAVE MANY OF, AND BE ABLE TO GET OFF THIS MERRY GO ROUND I WAS ON. BUT THAT SOON BACKFIRED, WHEN AFTER GETTING INVOLVED

FOR A WHILE AFTER WILLIE MOVED OUT, LONEWOLF TURNED OUT TO BE A THIEF AND A LIAR. NOTHING LIKE FEELING YOU ARE SINKING IN A POOL OF QUICK-SAND AND THAT GOD SEEMS FAR FROM YOU.

I SOON DITCHED HIM AFTER RECEIVING A 2000.00 PHONE BILL WHILE LONEWOLF WAS OUT ON THE ROAD. HE WAS A TRUCK DRIVER TO TRAVEL AROUND, I HAD ALLOWED HIM TO USE AN EXTRA PHONE I HAD AROUND AND HE MUST HAVE CALLED EVERY FRIEND HE HAD IN THE WORLD, YET NEVER COMMUNICATED WITH ME. HE ENDED UP LOSING THAT JOB AND CAME CRAWLING TO ME FOR HELP. HE HAD 3 KIDS, WHOM HE DIDN'T PAY SUPPORT FOR AND THE EX WAS ON HIS CASE ABOUT SCHOOL SUPPLIES AND OTHER THINGS THE KIDS NEEDED, SO I HELPED PURCHASE THE SUPPLIES FOR THEM. BUT IT WAS GETTING ME IN ONE BIG HOLE AND CAUSING ISSUE AFTER ISSUE, NOT TO MENTION GIVING ME A REPUTATION I DIDN'T CARE TO HAVE. I DID MY BEST TO TRY AND PICK UP THE PIECES AMND PREPARE MYSELF FOR SINGLE LIFE AND RAISING MY 3 KIDS.

NO MATTER WHAT I WAS DETERMINED TO DIG MY WAY OUT OF THE HOLE I HAD DUG FOR MYSELF AND ALMOST BURIED. BY THIS TIME ANGELA WAS 17, ERIC 13 1/2 AND JASON 11 AND I FELT BAD FOR THEM. WHAT IN THE WORLD WAS I THINKING? THE BOYS HAD BEEN SHUFFLED AROUND BETWEEN HOME, THEIR FATHERS HOUSE, HAVING A STEP FATHER TO CONTEND WITH THEN LEAVING ONLY FOR ME TO BRING ANOTHER GUY AROUND. I COULDN'T BEGIN TO IMAGINE WHAT THEY WERE THINKING OR FEELING AT THE TIME AS I WAS SO CAUGHT UP IN MY OWN MESS AND JUST COULDN'T DEAL. I LOVED MY KIDS WITH EVERYTHING IN ME YET I

FELT I COULDN'T HELP THEM CAUSE I COULDN'T EVEN HELP MYSELF. I TOOK CARE OF THEM THE BEST I COULD, TOLD THEM THINGS WOULD BE OK AND I PRAYED TO GOD THEY WOULD BE.

A MONTH LATER I RECEIVED DIVORCE PAPERS FROM WILLIE. WE HAD BEEN OFF AND ON SINCE THE DAY HE MOVED OUT, BUT IT SEEMED NO MATTER HOW HARD I TRIED TO MAKE THINGS WORK, HE JUST DISTANCED HIMSELF. I COULDN'T REALLY BLAME HIM TO A DEGREE, NO MAN WANTS A WOMAN TO CHEAT ON THEM, BUT I GUESS I LOOKED AT IT AS REVENGE AND WANTED HIM TO HURT JUST AS HE HAD HURT ME, PHYSICALLY, EMOTIONALLY, HE WASN'T THERE FOR ME LIKE I NEEDED HIM TO BE, ALL HE WANTED TO DO WAS HIT ON ME AND CUT ME DOWN, BUT 2 WRONGS DON'T MAKE A RIGHT. THE NEXT DAY WILLIE HAD STOPPED BY TO SEE IF I GOT THE DIVORCE PAPERS. I TOLD HIM I DID AND THE DIVORCE WAS SCHEDULED FOR AUG 19TH 2002. HE OPENED UP AND APOLOGIZED FOR THE WAY HE HAD TREATED ME AND HE DIDN'T WANT THE DIVORCE. HE SEEMED SINCERE, AND I LOVED HIM SO MUCH THAT I DECIDED TO TRUST HIS SINCERITY AND GIVE IT ANOTHER GO AT A LIFE TOGETHER. I WASN'T EXACTLY INNOCENT WHEN I WENT OUT WITH LONEWOLF ALTHOUGH I FELT JUSTIFIED AND SOMEHOW FORCED INTO IT BECAUSE HE SEEMED TO CARE SO MUCH FOR ME AND THE MAN I WAS MARRIED TOO SEEM TO HATE ME INSIDE AND BESIDES, I DID TAKE WILLIE FOR BETTER OR FOR WORSE.

I LET WILLIE MOVE BACK IN, AND FOR 2 OR 3 WEEKS THINGS WERE GREAT! THEN I FOUND THAT HE HAD STARTED DRINKING AGAIN AND THIS TIME

181

SMOKING POT, AND IT UPSET ME TO KNOW END AND WHEN I TRIED TO TALK TO HIM ABOUT, LOW AND BEHOLD THE VERBAL AND EMOTIONAL ABUSE STARTED AGAIN. WHAT WAS THIS GUYS DEAL? WAS HE DR JEKYL AND MR HYDE OR WHAT? HE DEFINITELY HD SOME SORT OF SPLIT PERSONALITY GOING ON OR DID HE HAVE NO WHERE TO GO WITH HIS 2 DAUGHTERS AND FEARED LOSING THEM, SO HE USED ME. ONE NIGHT WHEN HE CAME IN DRUNK, HE LAID INTO ME SOMETHING FIERCE AND THREATENED TO WIP THE STREET UP WITH MY FACE. I WAS SO SCARED I WENT AND LOCKED MYSELF IN THE CAR FOR A WHILE. WHEN I DECIDED TO GO BACK IN THE TRAILER I LEARNED THAT HE LOCKED ME OUT, THIS WAS GETTING MIGHTY RIDICULOUS IF YOU ASKED ME, SO I ENDED UP SLEEPING IN MY CAR.

THE NEXT DAY I LEFT AND FILED A CIVIL PROTECTION ORDER (CPO) AGAINST HIM. SOMEHOW HE GOT WIND I WAS FILING FOR ONE SO HE WENT TO THE COURT HOUSE AND FILED ONE AGAINST ME TOO. A COURT DATE WAS SCHEDULED AND WHEN WE WENT HE HAD BROUGHT HIS MOM, WHO KNEW NOTHING OF OUR SITUATION, OR SO I THOUGHT. SHE HADN'T SEEN THE THINGS HE DID TO ME AND MY KIDS YET LIED TO THE JUDGE ABOUT OUR RELATIONSHIP. BECAUSE OF THE FACT THAT WILLIE HAD NO DRIVER'S LICENSE, NO CAR HAD CUSTODY OF 2 YOUNG GIRLS AND TELLING THE JUDGE THAT HE HAD NO PLACE TO GO AND THE MOM VERFYING THEY COULDN'T LIVE WITH HER, THE JUDGE AWARDED HIM MY TRAILER WHICH MY MOM HAD CO-SIGNED FOR ME ON AND I WAS ON THE STREET WITH 2 BOYS AS MY DAUGHTER HAD SINCE MOVED OUT AFTER GRADUATION. THE JUDGE FELT SINCE I

182

HAD A CAR AND A VALID LICENSE I COULD LIVE OUT OF IT, BUT WITH 2 BOYS? IT DIDN'T SEEM TO MATTER TO THE JUDGE THAT THE TRAILER WAS IN MY NAME ONLY WITH MY MOM AS A CO-SIGNER. ON TOP OF THAT, CHILDREN SERVICES WAS CALLED ABOUT IT AND I WAS GIVEN 3 DAYS TO FIND A PLACE FOR THE BOYS AND I OR I WOULD LOSE THEM. REALLY? WHAT A NIGHTMARE!

AFTER THE 3 DAYS WENT BY, A FRIEND PUT US UP IN A HOTEL FOR A WEEK. I WAS SO GRATEFUL AS THAT GOT CHILDREN SERVICES OFF MY BACK, FOR THE TIME BEING ANYWAY. I KNEW I WOULDN'T BE ABLE TO PAY THE HOTEL PRICES ON WHAT I MADE. I WAS THANKFUL THAT IT WAS SUMMER AND SCHOOL WAS OUT, SO I DIDN'T HAVE TO WORRY ABOUT GETTING THE BOYS TO AND FROM SCHOOL ON TOP OF WORKING MY JOB. AT THE END OF THE WEEK, GEORGE, MY KIDS DAD ASKED US TO STAY WITH HIM. I WAS FLOORED, BUT KNEW IF I DIDN'T HAVE A PLACE I'D LOSE THEM AND I CERTAINLY DIDN'T WANT GEORGE GETTING CUSTODY. IT WAS NICE OF HIM TO WORK WITH ME AND NOT GO AFTER THE BOYS FOR CUSTODY BUT I STILL FELT AWKWARD STAYING WITH HIM AFTER ALL THAT HAPPENED WITH ANGELA BUT I KNEW I HAD TO DO SOMETHING SO I AGREED. I REALLY HOPED THERE WASN'T SOME ULTERIOR MOTIVE FOR HIS OFFER BUT WHAT CHOICE DID I HAVE? IT WAS ONE TRAP AFTER THE OTHER IT SEEMED. WOULD THERE EVER BE A WAY OUT? I ONLY PRAYED THERE WAS.

AFTER BEING AT GEORGE'S PLACE FOR ABOUT 3 MONTHS, WILLIE DROPPED THE CPO CHARGES AGAINST ME, SO I DECIDED TO DROP THE ONE I HAD

ON HIM. I WENT TO COURT AND WAS AWARDED MY TRAILER BACK AND I WAS ESTACTIC. WILLIE WANTED TO GET BACK TOGETHER AND SAID HE HAD CHANGED SINCE THE WHOLE CPO BIT, BUT I DIDN'T TRUST HIM SO I SAID MAYBE WE COULD GO TO COUNSELING AND WORK OUT SOME ISSUES. HE FELT THERE WAS NO TIME FOR HIM WITH HAVING THE GIRLS AND HE'D TOLD ME ABOUT LANDING A JOB IN THE LOCAL DINER AND DOING WELL. HE'D MET A GUY THERE WHO HE BECAME GOOD FRIENDS WITH AND SEEMED TO HAVE A POSTIVE INFLUENCE IN HIS LIF. THEY'D TALKED OF STARTING A MECHANIC'S BUSINESS TOGETHER AND I WAS ACTUALLY EXCITED FOR HIM. A MONTH WENT BY AND I DECIDED TO GIVE HIM ANOTHER CHANCE, SO HE MOVED BACK IN AND I PRAYED I WAS NOT GOING TO REGRET MY DECISION, BUT I TRULY LOVED HIM AND BELIEVED IN HIM.

A FEW MONTHS WENT BY AND THINGS WERE GOING WELL. I ACTUALLY STARTED RELAXING SOME. ANGELA WHO HAD BECOME PREGNANT HAD NOW GIVEN BIRTH TO OUR FIRST GRANDSON AND HE WAS SO PRECIOUS. GEORGE WHO HAD SINCE HAD A STROKE AND WAS IN A NURSING HOME WASN'T DOING TO WELL, SO SINCE ANGELA HAD THE BABY SHE COULDN'T HANDLE BEING THE POA FOR HER DAD, AND THE BOYS WERE TOO YOUNG. I THEN SWALLOWED MY PRIDE AND TOOK OVER THE RESPONSIBILITIES OF BEING GEORGE'S POA. NO MATTER WHAT HAPPENED IN OUR MARRIAGE THE BOYS STILL NEEDED THEIR FATHER AND I WOULDN'T FORGIVE MYSELF IF SOMETHING HAPPENED TO HIM AND I DIDN'T TAKE CARE OF HIM. GEORGE'S FAMILY WAS SCATTERED ABROAD, BOTH PARENTS LONG PASSED ON AND NO

ONE KNEW OF HIS MEDICAL STATE MORE THAN WHAT I DID, SO IT ONLY MADE SENSE FOR ME TO STEP IN TO HELP. ONE THING I ALWAYS TAUGHT MY KIDS WAS LEARNING TO FORGIVE. NO MATTER WHAT HAPPENED TO YOU AND IT WAS TIME I HAD TO EAT THOSE WORDS AND REALLY FORGIVE ALL THAT HAD HAPPENED IN OUR LIVES WHERE GEORGE WAS CONCERNED. WE HAD ALSO SOLD THE TRAILER THAT YEAR AND FOUND A NICE HOUSE WITH PLENTY OF SPACE AND YARD FOR THE KIDS AND HAD A NICE DECK, SO WE COULD HAVE GUESTS OVER. THE HOUSE WAS LOCATED BEHIND A GROCERY STORE, AND ALSO WAS CLOSER TO WILLIE'S WORK PLACE WHERE HE COULD WALK WHEN WEATHER WAS GOOD. THINGS WERE GREAT, SO WHY DID I HAVE THOS GNAWING FEELING SOMETHING WAS ABOUT TO GO WRONG.

WE GOT SETTLED IN OUR NEW PLACE AND BEEN THERE MAYBE 4 MONTHS WHEN WILLIE STARTED HAVING DRINKING PARTIES. I THOUGHT HE HAD STOPPED DRINKING AND HAD BEEN TRYING TO FINALIZE PLANS TO START A BUSINESS WITH HIS NEW FOUND BUDDY. I JUST DIDN'T LIKE IT AT ALL. I KNEW WHAT HE WAS LIKE WHEN HE DRANK, BUT I SUPPOSE IT WAS BETTER HE HAD THEM AT HOME RATHER THAN GOING TO THE BARS AND GETTING INTO TROUBLE AND HE ASSURED ME IT WOULDN'T BE AN ALL THE TIME THING. OF COURSE I SHOULD BETTER UNDERSTAND THE LIFE OF AN ALCOHOLIC, THEY TRY TO HOLD ONTO THEIR PROMISES, BUT ALCOHOLISM IS A SICKNESS.

ALTHOUGH THEY BELIEVE THEY HAVE NO PROBLEM AND HAVE THEIR DRINKING UNDER CONTROL, THERE IS SOMETHING THAT DRIVES THEM

TO DRINK THAT THEY ARE SOMETIMES AWARE OF CONSCIOUSLY AND THIS WAS THE CASE WITH WILLIE. IT WASN'T LONG WHEN HIM AND HIS FRIEND SENSING MY APPREHENSION ABOUT HIM DRINKING AT HOME STARTED GOING TO THE BAR AFTER WORK. THERE HE MET A WOMAN WHO LIVED UPSTARS FROM THE BAR AND OFTEN WENT TO HER PLACE. ONE NIGHT THE BOYFRIEND CAME IN AND CAUGHT THEM AND A FIGHT BROKE OUT. HE LEFT RIGHT BEFORE THE COPS GOT THERE AND I REMEMBER THEM DRIVING BY THE HOUSE LOOKING FOR HIM. HE'D THEN GO OUTSIDE WHERE THE OTHERS HAD FOLLOWED HIM HOME AND A FIGHT WOULD TAKE PLACE IN THE STREET. IT TOOK SEVERAL PEOPLE TO GET HIM IN THE HOUSE BEFORE BEING SRRESTED FOR PUBLIC INTOXICATION. THAT SEEMED TO BECOME WILLIE'S LIFESTYLE, GETTING DRUNK, SMOKING POT, GETTING INTO FIGHTS OR DRIVING DRUNK WITHOUT A LICENSE AND IN AND OUT OF JAIL. WHAT A LIF. WOULD I EVER LEARN!

ONE NIGHT WHILE WATCHING A MOVIE WITH FRIENDS, WILLIE'S CELL PHONE RANG AND I JUST HAPPENED TO ANSWER IT. IT WAS A WOMAN CALLING FOR HIM AND DIDN'T THINK MUCH OF IT AS I THOUGHT IT WAS A CO WORKER ASKING HIM TO WORK FOR HER. WHEN THE MOVIE WAS OVER, WILLIE STEPPED OUT FOR CIGARETTES, WHEN THE NEIGHBOR LADY CAME OVER COMPLAINING THAT WILLIE HAD BEEN GRABBING HER BREASTS AND SHE HAD BEEN AFRAID TO TELL ME FOR FEAR OF LOSING ME AS A FRIEND. WHEN WILLIE CAME BACK I QUESTIONED HIM ABOUT IT AND HE DENIED IT OF COURSE AND TOOK OFF FOR THE BAR. THERE I WAS ALONE AS THE KIDS WERE ALL GONE FOR THE WEEKEND, SO I DECIDED TO GET ON THE

186

COMPUTER AND PLAY A GAME TO GET MY MIND OFF OF THE EVENING. WHEN I TURNED IT ON WILLIE HADN'T LOGGED OFF AND I SEEN A PIC OF A GIRL ON THERE AND A MESSAGE THAT SAID SHE HAD TRIED CALLING HIM BUT THE BITCH ANSWERED. AS I WAS LOOKING THRU HIS MESSAGES I SEEN ONE THAT HE SENT TO HER THAT SAID FOR YOUR SWEETHEART, YOU BRING SUNSHINE TO MY LIFE. I WAS CRUSHED.

ALL THIS TIME TAKING HIM BACK CAUSE HE WAS SORRY AND HE LOVED ME WAS A BUNCH OF BOLOGNA. I HAD PUT UP WITH SO MUCH FROM HIM AND HE WAS CHEATING, SO FROM THAT DAY ON, AGAINST MY BETTER JUDGEMENT I STARTED GOING TO THE BARS WITH HIM TO KEEP HIM COMPANY. I FELT IF I COULD BE THE WOMAN HE DESIRED TO HAVE THEN HE WOULD STOP THIS NONSENSE AND TREAT ME LIKE A WOMAN AND NOT FEEL THE NEED TO MESS AROUND WITH SOMEONE ELSE. HE GOT USED TO THE IDEA AND EVEN LOOKED FORWARD TO IT, HOWEVER, IF I DIDN'T FEEL LIKE GOING, HE WOULD GET UPSET, CALL ME NAMES, AND THE FIGHTS WOULD START AGAIN, HE'D RESTRAIN ME AND THROW ME AROUND AND I WOULD SCRATCH HIM TO TRY AND GET AWAY WHICH ONLY MADE HIM MADDER. THEN HE'D BREAK AWAY, TAKE OUR BILL MONEY AND OFF TO THE BAR HE WOULD GO.

2 WEEKS WENT BY AND WILLIE CAME HOME ONE DAY AND SAID HE WAS FIRED FROM HIS JOB. HE SEEMED REALLY UPSET OVER IT AND SEEMED TO CALM HIM DOWN, FOR THE TIME BEING ANYWAY. THE NEXT DAY HE HAD A HEART TO HEART WITH ME AND SAID THERE WAS SOMETHING ABOUT GREENVILLE WHERE WE LIVED AT THE TIME THAT WASN'T RIGHT

AND ALL HE DID WAS GET IN TROUBLE HERE. HE FELT WE NEEDED A CHANGE AND WANTED TO MOVE ELSEWHERE, TO ANOTHER CITY. HE HAD BEEN OFFERED A JOB AT A GOOD RESTAURANT IN TROY AS PART OF THE MANAGEMENT TEAM AND WANTED US TO FIND A PLACE THERE. IT SEEMED LIKE A GOOD IDEA, AS THE GIRLS MOM LIVED IN PIQUA, AND MY MOM DID AS WELL AND I WOULD BE CLOSER TO HER. A CHANGED CERTAINLY SEEMED IN ORDER FOR US, A CHANCE FOR A BRAND NEW START AS A FAMILY. THE CHURCH WE HAD BEEN ATTENDING OFF AND ON HAD BEEN TALKING OF MERGING WITH ONE IN TROY, SO IT SEEMED AS IF GOD WAS TELLING US THIS WAS THE ANSWER FOR US. WE ALSO HEARD THE SCHOOL SYSTEM WAS BETTER AND WITH WILLIE'S YOUNGEST HAVING SOME LEARNING ISSUES THOUGHT THIS WOULD BE A GOOD AND POSITIVE THING FOR HER AS WELL. GREENVILLE SCHOOLS SEEMED TO BE BEHIND IN SOME OF THEIR CURRICULUM.

THIS TIME INSTEAD OF RENTING, I WANTED US TO PURCHASE OUR HOME. SOMETHING WE COULD CALL OUR OWN ALTHOUGH WE'D STILL HAVE A MORTAGE. I FELT IF WILLIE COULD SEE HIS HARD WORK PAYING OFF FOR SOMETHING HE WOULD BE MORE POSITIVE AND FEEL BETTER ABOUT HIMSELF AND STOP DRINKING AND DOING DRUGS. FOR 3 MONTHS I WORKED ON OUR FINANCES, AND OUR CREDIT. WHEN THINGS WERE IN ORDER WE WENT HOUSE HUNTING. WE FOUND A BEAUTIFUL 4 BEDROOM HOME, 2 FULL BATHS WITH BASEMENT, NICE FENCED IN YARD WITH A SWIMMING POOL AND DECK. IT WAS A LITTLE HIGHER THAN WHAT WE BUDGETED FOR BUT IF WE TIGHTENED OUR BELTS AND I GOT A JOB, WE

COULD MAKE IT. THE LOAD WENT THRU AND WE WERE PUMPED AND IN SEPT 2003 WE MADE THE MOVE TO OUR NEW HOME IN TROY OHIO.

SINCE THE PURCHASE OF OUR HOME, WILLIE SEEMED TO BE DOING A LOT BETTER. I HADN'T NOTICED SMOKING POT AND ALTHOUGH HE STILL DRANK HE HAD CUT IT DOWN TO A COUPLE IN THE EVENING. WE EVEN STARTED GOING TO CHURCH TOGETHER AND WAS ASKED TO BE DOOR GREETERS WHICH SEEMED TO PERK HIM UP. IT WAS GOOD SEEING HIM GET INVOLVED. WE STARTED HAVING EVENING DEVOTIONS IN WHICH HE WOULD TELL THE KIDS THE IMPORTANCE OF LIVING A LIFE FOR GOD AND THINGS WERE GOING TO START BEING ALOT DIFFERENT FROM NOW ON. HOWEVER, IT WAS ALL SHORT LIVED. I HAD GOTTEN A JOB AS A PAPER DELIVERY PERSON. WITH THE DISABILITES I HAD SINCE HAVING CARPAL TUNNEL AND ALL THE PREVIOUS ABUSE, MY DOC SAID THIS WAS ABOUT THE ONLY THING I COULD DO. I CAME HOME ONE DAY TO FIND HIM MASTURBATING TO PORNOGRAPHY ON THE INTERNET. I WAS SICKENED. I ASKED HIM WHAT HE WAS DOING AND HE ASSURED ME IT HAD NOTHING TO DO WITH ME AND WAS HARMLESS, YET IN MY MIND I WONDERED HOW HE COULD SAY THAT. I MEAN I'M A GOOD LOOKING WOMAN BUT CERTAINLY NOT BUILT LIKE A TOP MODEL.

HE HAD LEFT AND BEEN GONE QUITE SOME TIME, AND WHEN HE RETURNED, HE WAS STUMBLING AROUND AND I KNEW HE WAS DRUNK. I LAID THERE PRETENDING TO BE ASLEEP HOPING HE WOULDN'T BOTHER ME BUT INSTEAD STARTED MESSING WITH ME, WANTING SEX. I REALLY DIDN'T WANT TO BUT HIM

BEING DRUNK I WASN'T SURE IF HE WOULD BECOME ANGRY AT MY REFUSAL AND HURT ME, SO I LET HIM HAVE HIS WAY WITH ME. HE BEGAN USING THINGS ON ME AND I STARTED CRYING, TELLING HIM THAT IT HURT AND ALTHOUGH HE SAID SORRY, HE KEPT GOING. IT WAS LIKE HE DIDN'T CARE AS HE BEGUN TO WHIP ME WITH PIECES OF LICORICE. JUST AS I WAS ABOUT TO PUSH HIM OFF, HE WAS FINISHED AND I GOT UP AND RAN TO THE BATHROOM AND LOCKED MYSELF IN. AS I WAS CRYING AND CLEANING MYSELF UP, I COULDN'T BELIEVE HE HAD DONE THAT. I WONDERED WHERE HE HAD GOTTEN SUCH IDEAS TO DO WHAT HE DID, WE NEVER USED ANY THING TO HAVE SUCH KINKY SEX AND MY THOUGHTS WENT TO HIM ON THE INTERNET AND WONDERED SINCE SEEING HIM DOING THAT IF HE HAD SEEN THINGS ON THERE AND WAS THINKING OF THE WOMEN HE WAS MASTURBATING TOO AND THOUGHT I WOULD ENJOY ROUGH SEX AS THEY DID.

THE NEXT MORNING I WOKE UP IN PAIN AND HAD TROUBLE URINATING SO I CALLED THE DOCTOR AND THEY WAS ABLE TO SQUEEZE ME IN. THEY DETERMINED I HAD A URINARY TRACT INFECTION AND WENT AHEAD AND RAN A SCREEN FOR ANY POSSIBLE SIGNS OF AN STD, WHICH WOULD TAKE A FEW DAYS TO COME BACK.

A COUPLE DAYS LATER, I GOT THE CALL FROM THE DOCTORS OFFICE AND THE TESTS CAME BACK NORMAL. THERE WAS NO SIGNS OF AN STD AND I WAS SO GRATEFUL. AS I WENT ABOUT MY CHORES AFTER HANGING UP, I WAS PUTTING AWAY THE LAUNDRY WHEN I FOUND AN X-RATED MOVIE HE HAD APPARENTLY RENTED FROM THE VIDEO STORE AND IT

WAS OF TEENAGE GIRLS. I JUST LEFT IT THERE AND WENT TO DUST OFF THE COMPUTER. APPARENTLY, IT HAD JUST BEEN ON SLEEP CAUSE WHEN I MOVED THE MOUSE THE COMPUTER CAME ON. I SEEN WHERE HE WAS STILL LOGGED IN PROBABLY FORGETTING HE WAS EVEN ON THERE. HIS EMAILS CAME UP AND I SEEN HE HAD SEVERAL EMAILS FROM TEEN SEX SITES.

I WAS GROWING MIGHTY CONCERNED HE WOULD BE CAUGHT MESSING WITH UNDER AGE GIRLS AND BE LABELED A SEX OFFENDER THEREBY BRINGING SHAME TO THE FAMILY. HIS OLDER DAUGHTER CAME TO MIND JUST THEN. SHE HAD BEEN HAVING SOME ATTITUDE ISSUES LATELY AND I BEGAN TO WONDER IF THERE WAS SOMETHING TO THIS THAT ALSO INVOLVED HER. DESPITE ATTEMPTS TO TALK TO THEM WE FOUND OUR FAMILY SEEMED TO BE GROWING APART AS WILLIE HAD STARTED DRINKING HEAVILY AGAIN, GOT INTO DRUGS, AND STOPPED GOING TO CHURCH ALTOGETHER. THERE WAS A BAR DOWN THE STREET FROM WHERE WE LIVED AND WHEN HE DIDN'T COME HOME FROM WORK, I OFTEN FOUND HIM THERE. THE FIGHTING STARTED AGAIN AND MANY TIMES IN A DRUNKEN STUPER WOULD COME HOME WAKING ME UP BY TAKING A BALL BAT TO THE WOODWORK BUSTING IT ALL TO HELL. THREATS WOULD FLY, GETTING SHOVED AROUND. I WAS SO SCARED AND WANTED TO LEAVE, BUT WHY SHOULD I LEAVE MY OWN HOME? I COULDN'T UNDERSTAND WHY I STAYED WITH SOMEONE LIKE THIS, BUT KEPT THINKING IF I CONTINUED TO LOVE HIM AND STICK BY HIM FOR BETTER OR WORSE IT WOULD SOMEHOW SINK IN AND BE OK.

I KNOW IT WAS HARD FOR THE KIDS, BUT I DIDN'T WANT OUR FAMILY TORN APART. I LATER REALIZED IT JUST MADE MATTERS WORSE AND WAS ACTUALLY SHAPING THE LIVES OF MY CHILDREN. FOR THE GIRLS I FELT IT WAS TEACHING THEM TO STAY WITH AN ABUSER NO MATTER WHAT, FOR MY BOYS, IT WAS TEACHING THEM THAT WOMEN ARE TO BE TREATED THIS WAY. THIS WAS NOT THE WAY TO LIVE YET I FELT TRAPPED AND SCARED. I KNEW I COULDN'T MAKE THE MORTGAGE ON MY OWN. BEFORE I KNEW IT MY OLDER SON HAD STARTED SMOKING, AND DABBLING IN PORN. MY YOUNGEST BECAME WITHDRAWN AFTER WILLIE OFTEN ACCUSED HIM OF BEING A HOMOSEXUAL CAUSE HE KEPT TO HIMSELF AND DIDN'T DATE. WILLIE'S OLDEST DAUGHTER STARTED SMOKING AND THE YOUNGEST WAS ACTING OUT HER FRUSTRATIONS. IT WAS A MADHOUSE TO SAY THE LEAST.

ONE WED NIGHT WE ALL WENT TO CHURCH EXCEPT FOR WILLIE. I HAD AGREED AFTER MUCH PLEADING THAT IF WILLIE WOULD STAY OUT OF THE BAR AND NOT DRIVE DRUNK HE COULD DRINK AT HOME ALTHOUGH I DIDN'T LIKE IT. I SEEN WHAT IT DID WITH MY DAD OVER THE YEARS AND I SEEN WHAT IT WAS DOING TO US, BUT HE ASSURED ME IT WOULD ONLY BE A COUPLE OF BEERS AND AGREED IF HE WAS HOME HE COULD STAY OUT OF TROUBLE. WE ARRIVED HOME FROM CHURCH THOUGH HE WASN'T DRINKING BEER, HE WAS DRINKING JACK DANIELS WHISKEY AND THIS INFURIATED ME! HOW COULD HE TAKE ADVANTAGE OF MY KINDNESS AND GOOD INTENTIONS ONLY FOR HIM TO BREAK OUR AGREEMENT. I DIDN'T SEE IT AS TRYING TO CONTROL HIM, ONLY FOR HIM TO SEE WHAT HIS DRINKING WAS DOING TO HIM AND THIS FAMILY. I WAS

REALLY TRYING TO BE PATIENT AND SUPPORTIVE OF HIM THROUGH ALL THIS, BUT I SUPPOSE UNLESS THEY RECOGNIZE THEY HAVE A PROBLEM AND WANT TO SERIOUSLY GET HELP FOR THEIR ADDICTIONS AND ALLOW GOD TO DELIVER THEM AND HEAL THEM THEN WE ARE MERELY WASTING OUR TIME AND ENERGY.

NO MATTER HOW MUCH YOU LOVE THEM, THEY WON'T CHANGE FOR YOU, THEY HAVE TO CHANGE FOR THEMSELVES. IT WILL ONLY ADD FUEL TO THE FIRE AND INFURIATE THEM TO THE POINT THEY DRINK MORE OUT OF SPITE AND RESENT YOU EVEN MORE. I WAS SO ANGRY WITH HIM, NOT JUST FOR DESTROYING HIMSELF BUT FOR WHAT HE WAS DOING TO HIS FAMILY WHO LOVED HIM SO MUCH. I TOOK THE WHISKEY AND RAN TO THE BATHROOM AND DUMPED IT DOWN THE DRAIN. WOW, WHAT A MISTAKE THAT WAS. HE WAS SO ANGRY HE GRABBED THE BALL BAT AND STARTED SWINGING IT AT MY HEAD. I WAS BACKED INTO A CORNER AND WHEN HE SWANG IT HIT THE WOODWORK AND GOT WEDGED SO I RAN, BUT HE TRIPPED ME AND I FELL, WHEN I LOOKED AT HIM I COULD HAVE SWORE I SEEN THE DEVILS FACE. I WAS SO SCARED AND THOUGHT HE WAS GOING TO KNOCK MY BLOCK OFF.

THE KIDS CALLED THE POLICE AND WHEN THEY ARRIVED ALL THEY SAID WAS IT WAS HIS HOUSE TOO AND IF HE WANTED TO BREAK IT UP THAT WAS HIS BUSINESS THAT IT WOULD BE BEST IF I WENT SOMEWHERE FOR THE NIGHT. WHY ME? HE WAS THE DRUNKARD. I HAD MY GRANDSON, NOT SURE WHERE I WAS GOING TO GO. AT THAT POINT I'M NOT SURE WHERE MY BOYS WENT BUT I KNEW HIS GIRLS TOOK OFF UPSTAIRS. HIS OLDEST OFTEN TOLD ME SHE WAS

193

TIRED OF HIS DRINKING AND IT SCARED HER. I REMEMBER HER ASKING ME ON SEVERAL OCCASIONS WHEN I WOULD GO SOMEWHERE IF SHE COULD RIDE ALONG CAUSE SHE DIDN'T WANT TO BE THERE WITH HIM, ESPECIALLY WHEN HIS FRIENDS WERE OVER. THAT NIGHT HOWEVER, BECAUSE OF SCHOOL THE NEXT DAY, I LEFT THE KIDS, PACKED A FEW THINGS FOR THE NIGHT, TOOK MY GRANDSON AND LEFT. I FIGURED WILLIE WOULD SOON PASS OUT FROM HIS DRUNKENESS AND THINGS WOULD CALM DOWN. I CALLED A FRIEND FROM OUR CHURCH WHO WAS OUR CELL GROUP LEADER AND ASKED IF MY GRANDSON AND I COULD STAY THE NIGHT AND EXPLAINED WHY. SHE AGREED AND GAVE ME DIRECTIONS TO HER PLACE. WHEN I ARRIVED SHE HAD A PLACE SET UP FOR US, WE TALKED THEN FELL OFF TO SLEEP. MY GRANDSON AND I HAD A HARD TIME SLEEPING THOUGH, HE WAS FULL OF QUESTIONS. WILLIE AND HIM WAS CLOSE, AS MY GRANDSON CONSIDERED HIM A MALE ROLE MODEL AS HIS FATHER WASN'T IN THE PICTURE AND IN HIS YOUNG 4 YEAR OLD MIND JUST DIDN'T UNDERSTAND WHAT WAS HAPPENING.

THE NEXT MORNING WE PREPARED TO GO AND AFTER THANKING MY FRIEND WE LEFT. NOT SURE IF I WAS WANTING TO GO BACK HOME, BUT YET DIDN'T WANT OTHERS KNOWING MY BUSINESS SO WE HEADED BACK TO THE HOUSE. AS SOON AS I PULLED IN THE DRIVEWAY AN UNEASY FEELING SEEM TO ENGULF ME AND WONDERED WHAT HAD HAPPENED. I PARKED, SHUT THE CAR OFF, GRABBED SCOTT AND OUR THINGS AND WENT IN THE HOUSE. AS SOON AS I WALKED IN THE HOUSE, WILLIE'S OLDEST DAUGHTER CAME OUT OF OUR BEDROOM WITH HER PILLOW. I FREAKED OUT. I

MEAN SERIOUSLY? SHE SLEPT IN THE BED WITH HER FATHER? I HAD JUST WENT THRU A SIMILAR SITUATION WITH MY OWN DAUGHTER ALTHOUGH I NEVER CAUGHT THEM TOGETHER, CERTAIN EVIDENCE PROVED SOMETHING INDEED HAPPENED. NOW I WAS FACED WITH A SIMILAR SITUATION ONCE AGAIN WHEN HERE WILLIE'S OLDEST DAUGHTER WAS COMING OUT OF OUR BEDROOM WITH HER PILLOW. THANK GOODNESS SHE LOOKED SLEEPY AND WAS CLOTHED! I ASKED HER WHAT THE HELL SHE WAS DOING AND SHE CLAIMED WILLIE WAS HAVING BREATHING TROUBLE AND WANTED HER IN THERE TO KEEP AN EYE ON HIM. WILLIE HAD SLEEP APNEA AND WAS ON A C-PAP MACHINE TO HELP HIM SLEEP EASIER. THIS WAS SO ODD TO ME CAUSE HE NEVER SEEMED TO WORRY OVER THOSE ISSUES IN THE PAST, AND WHEN HE DID HAVE ISSUES IT WAS CAUSE HE REFUSED TO WEAR THE C-PAP MASK CAUSE HE DIDN'T LIKE IT. I JUST COULDN'T BELIEVE AFTER KNOWING WHAT I WENT THRU WITH ANGELA AND HER FATHER THAT HE WOULD EVEN GIVE THOUGHT TO ALLOWING HIS DAUGHTER IN THE SAME BED WITH HIM.

MY THOUGHTS RAN BACK TO A NIGHT THE MONTH BEFORE WHEN HE HAD BEEN DRINKING AND WHEN I CAME HOME AND LOOKED OUT THE PATIO DOOR HE HAD PICKED UP HIS OLDER DAUGHTER AND SHE HAD HER LEGS WRAPPED AROUND HIS WITH HER ARMS AROUND HIS NECK FOR SUPPORT AND THEY WERE DANCING, WHEN I LOOKED DOWN HE HAD A BULGE IN HIS PANTS. I CONFRONTED HIM OVER IT, BUT IT DIDN'T SEEM TO MATTER. ALL HE DID WAS ACCUSE ME OF BEING SICK IN THE HEAD AND BECAUSE ANGELA'S DAD WAS PERVERTED DIDN'T MEAN HE WAS

AND I WAS OVERREACTING. I FELT SO HUMILIATED, I REALLY BELIEVED THAT BY LOVING AND SUPPORTING HIM AND STAYING BY HIS SIDE, IT WOULD PROVE I WAS DEVOTED TO HIM AND HE WOULD WANT TO CHANGE.

WE HAD BEEN THRU SO MUCH AND MANAGED TO OVERCOME THE OBSTACLES AND FIND EACH OTHER AGAIN, BUT THE UPS AND DOWNS AS IF ON A ROLLERCOASTER WAS GETTING FOR THE BIRDS. I BELIEVE LOVE DOES CONQUER ALL AND THE MAN I FELL IN LOVE WITH WAS STILL THERE, HE WAS JUST BURIED SOMEWHERE IN HIMSELF. IT WAS LIKE WE WERE JUST GOING THRU THE MOTIONS, SOMETIMES HAVING FUN AND LAUGHING AND MY HOPES BEING BUILT UP THAT MAYBE THIS TIME THINGS WERE TURNING AROUND, ONLY FOR HIM TO HAVE A ROUGH DAY AT WORK OR WHATEVER THE REASON THAT SOMETIMES WE THOUGHT WERE SILLY REASONS TO GET TICKED AT, BUT HE WOULD GET SO MAD THEN HERE WE GO AGAIN, INSULTS FLYING OR SHOVING MATCHES THAT SEEMED TO GO ON FOR DAYS. I KNOW ALL COUPLES HAVE STRUGGLES, BUT GOING TO BED AND BEING AFRAID OF WHAT MAY OR MAY NOT HAPPEN ACCORDING TO WILLIE'S MOOD WASN'T WHAT I WOULD CALL A HEALTHY MARRIAGE, OR HAVING A LIFE AT ALL.

IT WAS NOW SEPT 2005, SUMMER HAD COME AND GONE AND ANOTHER SCHOOL YEAR STARTED. IT SEEMS AS IF WE HAVE MORE CONFLICT THAN FUN ANYMORE AND HERE WE ARE ANOTHER SUMMER WENT BY WASTED. THE ONE GOOD THING WE DID WAS GET A DOG. HE WAS PART TERRIER/PART CHIHUAHUA AND HIS NAME WAS CHICO. WILLIE HAD PURCHASED

HIM FROM A FAMILY WHO'S MAN OF THE HOUSE WAS NEEDING A KIDNEY TRANSPLANT AND THEY WERE TRYING TO RAISE MONEY TO HELP WITH EXPENSES. THE KIDS REALLY TOOK TO HIM AND IT SEEMED TO HELP TAKE THEIR MINDS OFF THE CHAOS GOING ON AROUND THEM.

THE NEXT WEEK, I TOOK A JOB WITH THE LOCAL NEWSPAPER MAKING HOME DELIVERIES. WITH WILLIE BEING IN AND OUT OF JAIL WE HAD ATTORNEY FEES AND COURT COST MOUNTING UP, NOT TO MENTION FINES AND WE NEEDED THE EXTRA MONEY, ESPECIALLY SINCE WE HAD JUST REFINANCED THE HOUSE WHICH RAISED OUR PAYMENT SOME. ONE DAY I HAD HIS DAUGHTERS HELPING ME AND THERE WAS A CUSTOMER WHO HAD A SIGN POSTED THEY WERE GIVING AWAY A FULL BLOODED BEAGLE. THE GIRLS FELL IN LOVE WITH HER IMMEDIATELY WHEN THEY SAW HER RUNNING AROUND IN THE YARD AND ASKED IF THEY COULD HAVE HER. AFTER GETTING SOME INFORMATION ON HER, LEARNING HER NAME WAS SNOOPY, WE WENT HOME AND TALKED TO THEIR DAD. SINCE SHE WAS FIXED AND HOUSE BROKE, HE AGREED TO TAKE HER SO WE DROVE BACK TO THE LADIES HOUSE AND PICKED UP SNOOPY.

WHEN WE GOT HOME WITH HER, CHICO WENT BONKERS AT HAVING A FEMALE COMPANION, HOWEVER SNOOPY WOULD HAVE NO PART OF HIM. THEY GOT ALONG PRETTY GOOD, BUT WHENEVER CHICO WANTED TO HAVE HIS WAY WITH HER, SHE WOULD SNAP AT HIM AND HE'S RUN OFF TAIL TUCKED BETWEEN HIS LEGS. IT WAS FUN WATCHING THEM PLAY TOGETHER AND OFTEN FILLED THE HOUSE WITH

LAUGHTER WHICH WAS SOMETHING THAT HAD REALLY LACKED OVER THE LAST FEW YEARS. SNOOPY FAR OUTWEIGHED CHICO BY A FEW POUNDS AND IT WAS FUNNY TO SEE THEN WRESTLE. CHICO BEING A SCAREDY CAT WOULD THEN ROLLOVER AND SNOOPY WOULD HOVER OVER HIM AND PINNING HIM TO THE FLOOR. NEITHER ONE OF THEM LIKE THUNDER STORMS, SNOOPY WOULD ALWAYS BURY HERSELF UNDER OUR COVERS AND CHICO WOULD HIDE UNDER THE BED, IT WAS A SIGHT TO SEE FOR SURE, SO FUNNY.

THE FUNNIEST THING TO SEE WAS WHEN THEY BOTH ATE AT THE SAME TIME. WE HAD THEIR BOWLS IN THE BATHROOM, WHICH WAS OFF OUR BEDROOM. WE SPENT ALOT OF TIME IN OUR ROOM WATCHING TV OR OPENING THE PATIO DOOR AND SITTING OUT ON THE DECK. SNOOPY NOT WANTING TO EAT ALONG SIDE CHICO WOULD LITERALLY PICK UP HER BOWL AND CARRY IT INTO OUR ROOM TO EAT. SOMETIMES SHE WOULD EAT CHICO'S FOOD TOO IF SHE WAS DONE AND HE HADN'T WENT TO EAT YET, SO WE HAD TO MONITOR HER EATING SO SHE DIDN'T GAIN ALOT OF WEIGHT. I REMEMBER ONE WEEK, MONEY WAS A LITTLE TIGHT, SO WE BOUGHT ANOTHER BRAND OF DOG FOOD WHICH HAD VEGI'S IN IT, THAT WAS ON SALE, PLUS I HAD A COUPON OFF.

SNOOPY SEEMED TO LIKE MOST OF IT BUT WHAT WAS FUNNY WAS WHEN SHE WOULD BRING IN HER BOWL FROM THE BATHROOM SHE WOULD DUMP HER BOWL OF FOOD AND ROOT HER NOSE THRU THE PIECES SHE LIKED AND LEAVE THE REST LOOKING AT CHICO AS SHE WALKED AWAY AS IF TO SAY THERE YOU GO CHICO, YOU CAN HAVE MY LEFTOVERS. CHICO

DIDN'T SEEM TO MIND, AS HE LIKED THE NEW FOOD AND ACTUALLY HAD SOME TO EAT WHEN HE WAS READY TO EAT RATHER THAN GOING AND FINDING HIS BOWL EMPTY. I'VE LEARNED DOGS ARE VERY SMART AND SO FUNNY TO WATCH WHICH BROUGHT SOME JOY AND COMFORT TO MY LIFE FOR SURE.

LATER THAT DAY AS WE LET THEM OUT TO DO THEIR BUSINESS, WILLIE AND I WERE SITTING ON THE DECK TALKING WHEN ALL OF A SUDDEN SNOOPY STARTED HOWLING. WHEN WE LOOKED OUT TO SEE WHAT WAS GOING ON SHE HAD CAUGHT THE SCENT OF SOMETHING, THE FUNNY THING ABOUT SNOOPY'S BREED IS WHEN THEY CATCH A SCENT THEY SNIFF, RAISE HEAD AND HOWL, SNIFF, RAISE HEAD AND HOWL. SHE DID THIS FOR ABOUT 10 MINUTES BEFORE SHE FINALLY CAUGHT SITE OF SOMETHING MOVING IN THE TREE. WHEN WE LOOKED THERE WAS A SQUIRREL AND SHE ACTUALLY GOT HERSELF UP ON THE BOTTOM BRANCH OF THE TREE TRYING TO REACH THAT SQUIRREL AND JUST A HOWLING AT IT AND THE SQUIRREL JUST SITTING A FEW BRANCHES UP AS IF DARING HER TO COME AFTER THEM, IT WAS THE CRAZIEST THING I HAD EVER SEEN, A DOG THAT CLIMBED A TREE AND IT HAD US LAUGHING SO HARD. I COULD HAVE KICKED MYSELF FOR NOT GRABBING THE CAMCORDER AND RECORD IT. THAT WOULD HAVE BEEN A GREAT VIDEO FOR AMERICA'S FUNNIEST HOME VIDEO SHOW.

IT WAS NOW THE FIRST WEEK OF OCT 2005, WE HAD JUST BURIED MY KID'S FATHER WHO PASSED AWAY A FEW DAYS BEFORE, OTHER THAN THAT THINGS HAD BEEN GOING PRETTY GOOD FOR THE

LAST MONTH AND WE WERE STARTING TO RELAX SOME. HOWEVER, CRISIS STRUCK AGAIN WHEN I GOT A CALL FROM THE TROY POLICE DEPARTMENT TO PICK UP WILLIES YOUNGEST DAUGHTER. I THOUGHT WHAT IN THE WORLD HAPPENED TO HER, SHE WAS SUPPOSE TO BE PICKED UP BY HER FATHER. I WAS THEN TOLD THAT WILLIE WAS PICKED UP FOR OVI AND THIS TIME IT WAS FOUND HE HAD DRUG PARAPHENIALIA. THE TRAGIC THING WAS, AT LEAST FOR ME IT WAS, HE HAD PICKED UP HIS DAUGHTER AND SHE WAS IN THE CAR WITH HIM AND IT REALLY FRIGHTENED HER. BESIDES BEING CHARGE WITH OVI AND PARAPHENELIA, HE WAS ALSO BEING CHARGED WITH CHILD ENDANGERING. I GUESS WHEN IT RAINS IT POURS. THE POLICE WAITED FOR ME TO GET THERE TO PICK HER UP BEFORE CARTING HIM OFF TO JAIL ONCE AGAIN.

WE GOT HOME AND I GOT HER SETTLED DOWN IN BED THEN WENT TO BED MYSELF AND BEGAN TO WEEP. I DIDN'T UNDERSTAND WHY THIS KEPT HAPPENING. WHY WASN'T MY LOVE ENOUGH. EVEN IF THERE WAS AN ISSUE HE HAD WITH ME, YOU WOULD THINK HE'D WANT TO BE THERE FOR THE KIDS. WHAT KIND OF EXAMPLE WAS HE SETTING FOR THEM? DID HE EVEN THINK ABOUT THAT? OR DID HE NOT EVEN CARE. MY THOUGHTS WENT TO THE WARNING MY FAMILY GAVE ME OF NOT MARRYING HIM IN THE FIRST PLACE, ESPECIALLY AFTER THROWING ME THRU A WALL LEAVING THE IMPRINT OF MY BACKSIDE IN THE PLASTER. ONE OF MY BROTHERS KNEW OF HIM AS THEY WORKED FOR A RENTAL COMPANY AND WILLIE AND HIS EX THAT HE WAS MARRIED TOO AT THE TIME RENTED FURNITURE FROM THIS COMPANY. MY BROTHER TOLD ME THAT WILLIE WAS TROUBLE, BUT

YOU HAVE TO FIND OUT THINGS FOR YOURSELF. CAN'T ALWAYS GO ON WHAT OTHER PEOPLE THINK OR SAY. I DIDN'T HEED THE WARNING, THIS SHOULD HAVE BEEN ONE TIME I SHOULD HAVE LISTENED TO SOUND ADVICE. I JUST BELIEVED WILLIE WAS SENT BY GOD DURING A VERY DIFFICULT TIME IN MY LIFE AND I WENT WITH IT.

THE NEXT DAY WILLIE APPEARED IN COURT, THE JUDGE, BECAUSE OF HIS FREQUENT COURT APPEARANCES SENTENCED HIM TO 6 MOS IN JAIL. SHE ASKED HIM IF HE HAD ANYTHING TO SAY FOR HIMSELF AND HE BROKE DOWN AND APOLOGIZED AHD SAID HE DIDN'T WANT TO GO TO JAIL AS HE WOULD LOSE HIS JOB. THE JUDGE THEN TOLD HIM THAT SHE WOULD STILL GIVE HIM 6 MOS BUT WOULD DO PROBATION PROVIDING HE ENTERED A TREATMENT PROGRAM WITH THE RECOVERY CENTER AND SEEK COUNSELING. BUT IF HE DIDN'T GET HELP OR IF HE VIOLATED HIS PROBATION BY DRINKING, OR HAVING PARAPHENIALIA OR EVEN DRIVING OUTSIDE OF THE PRIIVLEGES SHE GAVE FOR GOING TO WORK, OR ANY OTHER KIND OF TROUBLE WITH THE LAW, THEN SHE WOULD REINSTATE THE JAIL SENTENCE AND GIVE HIM ANOTHER 6 MOS ON TOP OF IT.

THE NEXT DAY SOME CALLS WERE MADE AND HE WAS ENROLLED IN A RECOVERY PROGRAM. THEY GOT IN CONTACT WITH A COUNSELOR WHO WAS WILLING TO DO HOME VISITS AND THEY THOUGHT IT BENEFICIAL TO HAVE FAMILY COUNSELING TO HELP US ALL SORT THINGS OUT IN HOW WE COULD HELP WILLIE OVERCOME HIS ADDICTIONS. OF COURSE MY KIDS THOUGHTS WERE, WE DON'T NEED COUNSELING, BUT

HIS DAUGHTERS AND I THOUGHT IT WOULD BE A GOOD THING, THIS WAY WE COULD SHARE OUR FRUSTRATIONS AND HOW HIS ADDICTIONS AND ABUSE AFFECTED US.

LATER THAT WEEK WE LEARNED THAT WILLIE'S MOM WAS DIAGNOSED WITH BREAST CANCER. HE TOOK IT HARD AND I FELT BAD FOR HIM, I THINK IT'S THE FIRST I'D SEEN HIM CRY. WE MANAGED TO GET THRU THE WEEKEND AND THAT FOLLOWING MONDAY WE STARTED COUNSELING. AT FIRST KIND OF INFORMAL, GETTING TO KNOW US, ASKING QUESTIONS. B THE NEXT WEEK THINGS WERE GETTING HEATED UP SOME. THE KIDS FINALLY STARTED OPENING UP ON HOW WILLIE'S DRINKING AFFECTED THEM. I COULD SEE WILLIE TENSING UP BUT IN ORDER TO HELP HE HAD TO SIT AND LISTEN TO IT.

WE LEARNED SO MUCH IN THAT ONE NIGHT OF THINGS THAT HAD BEEN BOTTLED UP FOR YEARS, IT JUST BLEW MY MIND. WE ALSO LEARNED THAT WILLIE'S OLDER DAUGHTER HAD SOME ANGER ISSUES AND WAS THE CULPRIT IN MANY DISTURBING THINGS THAT WAS HAPPENING INSIDE AND OUTSIDE OF THE FAMILY. WE HAD STUMBLED UPON A LETTER SHE HAD WROTE ABOUT HER DAD AND HOW SHE HATED HIM FOR ALL HE HAD DONE AND WANTED AWAY FROM HIM. WILLIE WAS STUNNED TO SAY THE LEAST AND I DIDN'T KNOW WHAT TO THINK OTHER THAN IT WAS GOOD TO GET IT OUT THERE. ONE THING WILLIE DID SHARE WAS THAT WHILE HE SAT IN JAIL OVER NIGHT THAT HE THOUGHT ONE OF THE REASONS WAS STRESS WAS THE BILLS. WE HAD THE HOUSE AND HE WORKED HIS TAIL OFF AND YET WE SEEMED TO LIVE PAYCHECK TO PAYCHECK.

I TOLD HIM I WOULD TAKE ANOTHER ROUTE IF THAT WOULD HELP HIM FEEL BETTER AND WOULD DO WHATEVER I COULD TO KEEP THINGS CALM, BUT HE HAD TO UNDERSTAND THAT EVERYTIME HE GOES ON A RAMPAGE OR A DRINKING BINGE AND WANTS TO DRIVE WITHOUT A LICENSE AND TAKEN TO JAIL, THERE ARE FINES, COURT COSTS AND ATTORNEY FEES TO BE PAID WHICH TAKES AWAY FROM OUR BUDGET. HE BROUGHT UP THE SUBJECT OF BANKRUPTCY. I WAS TOTALLY AGAINST THE IDEA, ESPECIALLY AFTER DEALING WITH THE CPO A FEW YEARS BACK AND GETTING INVOLVED WITH LONEWOLF THAT LEFT ME IN DEBT I FILED BANKRUPTCY THEN TO GIVE US A CLEAN SLATE. EVEN WITH THAT ON OUR RECORD WHEN TRYING TO GET A LOAN FOR A HOUSE, WE MADE EFFORTS TO BUILD OUR CREDIT AND IT PAID OFF WITH THEM APPROVING OUR HOUSE LOAN. WE NEEDED TO BE MOVING FORWARD NOT BACKWARDS. BUT HE BELIEVED IT WOULD HELP RELIEVE STRESS AND KEEP HIM FROM DRINKING AND THE COUNSELOR ASKED IF THAT WAS A POSSIBILITY AND I WANTED TO DO WHAT I COULD TO HELP, SO I RELUCTANTLY AGREED TO CHECK INTO ITBEFORE THE COUNSELOR LEFT HE GAVE US SOME POSITIVE GOALS TO WORK TOWARDS AS HAVING A BLENDED FAMILY AND AT THIS POINT ANYTHING WAS WORTH A TRY, NOTHING ELSE SEEMED TO WORK THUS FAR.

NOV 2005 WAS HERE AND A NATURAL DIASTER HIT LOUISIANA. HURRICANE KATRINA HAD DESTROYED PART OF A CITY AROUND NEW ORLEANS. WILLIE HAD BEEN COMING TO CHURCH WITH ME AND OUR CHURCH SET UP A DISASTER RELIEF PROGRAM AND WE WORKED MANY NIGHTS PUTTING TOGETHER SUPPLIES

AND CARE BOXES TO SEND OVER THERE. THEN THEY ASKED IF THERE WAS A GROUP THAT WANTED TO MAKE THE TRIP WITH THEM AND SOMEONE PAID FOR WILLIE AND 3 OF THE KIDS TO GO IF THEY WANTED. WILLIE WAS ESTACTIC ABOUT IT AND I THOUGHT WHAT AN AMAZING OPPORTUNITY IT WAS FOR HIM TO BE INOLVED IN SOMETHING AND GIVE GOD A CHANCE TO MOVE IN HIS LIFE. WILLIE HAD WENT WITH MY SON AND HIS 2 GIRLS, THEY HAD A GREAT TIME OTHER THAN WILLIE'S YOUNGEST RAN OFF AND THEN HE ALLOWED HER TO RIDE BACK FROM LOUISIANA WITH A STRANGER RATHER THAN STAY WITH THE CHURCH GROUP AND THIS SORT OF UPSET OUR PASTORS, BUT IT WAS GOOD THEY HAD A GREAT TIME AND WAS SUCH A BLESSING TO THE PEOPLE OF LOUISIANA. THANKSGIVING WAS HERE AND TURNED OUT TO BE THE BEST ONE WE'D HAD IN I DON'T KNOW HOW LONG. IT WAS 5 WEEKS TILL IT WOULD BE CHRISTMAS AND I WAS EXCITED THIS YEAR. I LOVE THE TOGETHERNESS THE HOLIDAYS BRING, THE FUN, THE REMINISCING AND ESPECIALLY GIVING TO OTHERS IN NEED!

WE ENDED UP FILING CHAPTER 13 BANKRUPTCY WHICH TOOK A SET AMOUNT OF MONEY FROM WILLIE'S CHECK AS AGREED UPON. COUNSELING WAS GOING WELL AND THINGS WERE STARTING TO LOOK UP FOR US. YET THOUGHTS SOMETIMES REFLECTED BACK TO THE SAME QUESTION, HOW LONG WOULD IT LAST? CALL IT PARANOIA IF YOU WILL, BUT IT SEEMED LIKE THE SAME SCENERIO, CRISIS, GET THRU IT, THINGS GO WELL, CRISIS. SAME CYCLE OVER AND OVER, ONLY THIS TIME THE CALM LASTED A LOT LONGER, SO I SHOOK THE FEELING OFF AS I ROOTED THRU THE DAYS MAIL FINDING LOTS OF CHRISTMAS CARDS FROM

MY NEWPAPER CUSTOMERS. THIS WAS MY 2ND YEAR AS A CARRIER AND WHEN IT CAME TO THE CHRISTMAS SEASON, WE GAVE OUT CARDS TO OUR CUSTOMERS THAT WISHED THEM WELL AND THANKED THEM FOR BEING A SUBSCRIBER. WITH THE DECLINE OF THE ECONOMY, THERE WAS A LOT OF THEFTS SO MANY PEOPLE DIDN'T LIKE TO LEAVE CARDS FOR THEIR CARRIER ON THEIR DOORS SO THEY'D ASK FOR OUR ADDRESS TO SEND ONE TO US THRU THE MAIL. THE CARDS WE GAVE INCLUDED OUR NAME AND ADDRESS WHERE IF THEY WANTED TO TIP THEIR CARRIER THEY COULD.

THE FIRST WEEK TIPS CAME FLOODING IN, I WAS AMAZED. WITH 4 WEEKS TILL CHRISTMAS WE HAD GOTTEN SO FAR IN TIPS ABOUT 700.00 WHICH WOULD MAKE FOR A VERY NICE CHRISTMAS FOR THE FAMILY. I WAS REALLY EXCITED AS CHRISTMAS IS MY FAVORITE TIME OF YEAR AND PRAYED WE'D GET THRU IT WITHOUT INCIDENT. HOWEVER, THAT ONCE AGAIN WAS WISHFUL THINKING WHEN I WAS AWAKEN THE NEXT MORNING BY A CALL FROM THE LOCAL POLICE ASKING ME IF I KNEW THAT WILLIE WAS IN JAIL. I TOLD THEM NO, AND ASKED WHAT HAPPENED, BECAUSE LAST I KNEW WILLIE WAS GOING TO STAY WITH HIS MOM OVERNIGHT. SINCE BEING DIAGNOSED WITH BREAST CANCER A COUPLE MONTHS BACK, HER KIDS WERE TAKING TURNS STAYING A NIGHT WITH HER TO HELP OUT AS SHE WAS WEAK FROM THE CHEMO. WELL, HE HAD LIED TO ME AND NEVER WENT TO SEE HIS MOM BUT WENT TO THE LOCAL BAR AND WAS DRINKING. HE HAD BEGUN TO FEEL GUILTY FOR GOING BACK ON HIS PROMISES THAT HE DECIDED TO DRIVE TO WALMART

TO BUY ME A PRESENT AND WAS PICKED UP FOR SPEEDING.

HE WAS CHARGED ONCE AGAIN FOR OVI AND BECAUSE HE WAS STILL ON PROBATION THERE WAS NO NEED TO SEE THE JUDGE THE NEXT MORNING, HIS SENTENCE WAS RE-INSTATED AND WAS TO SERVE HIS ONE YEAR SENTENCE AS WAS AGREED UPON WHEN HE SEEN HER THE END OF OCT. HERE IT WAS ABOUT 4 WEEKS BEFORE CHRISTMAS, AND HE WAS IN JAIL. I WAS BESIDE MYSELF WITH GRIEF. PRETTY SOON THERE WAS A COLLECT CALL FROM THE JAIL AND WHEN I ACCEPTED I LAID INTO HIM ASKING HIM WHAT HE WAS THINKING. I KNOW I SHOULDN'T HAVE BEEN SO HARSH BUT HE WAS BEING RIDICULOUS. HE SAID HE KNEW AND WAS REALLY SORRY AND TRIED TO EXPLAIN WHY HE DID IT BUT IT DIDN'T MAKE MUCH SENSE TO ME. HE HAD ALMOST EVERYTHING ONE COULD DREAM OF, OR SO I THOUGHT. HE SAID HE WAS GOING TO GET HELP WHILE IN THERE SINCE HE WOULD SERVE A YEAR. HE SAID THERE WAS A POSSIBILITY THAT IF HE DID WELL AFTER SERVING AT LEAST 6 MOS THEN HE HAD THE CHANCE TO SERVE THE OTHER 6 MOS AT HOME ON HOUSE ARREST AND BE ON PROBATION.

I PRAYED HE WAS SINCERE THIS TIME. SINCE HIS SENTENCE WAS REINSTATED HE ASKED ME TO CALL HIS WORK AND TALK TO HIS BOSS. I REALLY DIDN'T WANT TO DEAL WITH THAT BUT A BUSINESS WOULDN'T ACCEPT COLLECT CALLS SO I HAD TO SUCK IT UP. I MADE THE CALL AND HIS BOSS WAS NOT HAPPY AT ALL. HE INFORMED ME THAT WILLIE WAS FIRED, HE RAN A RESTAURANT NOT A KINDERGARDEN CLASS. WOW. NOW WHAT WAS WE TO DO? I DIDN'T MAKE ENOUGH

ON THE ROUTES AND WITH MY DISABILITY FROM MY PREVIOUS EMPLOYER TO MAKE THE MORTGAGE PAYMENT, LET ALONE ALL THE OTHER BILLS WE HAD.

WE MANAGED TO GET THROUGH THE WEEKEND, IT WAS SUNDAY AND THE KIDS AND I WENT TO CHURCH. AFTER CHURCH WAS OVER AND I TURNED MY PHONE ON AS USUALLY DO ON THE DRIVE HOME IN CASE AN EMERGENCY ARISES. AS SOON AS IT BOOTED UP A VOICEMAIL ALERT RANG. I LISTENED TO THE VOICMAIL AND IT WAS WILLIES EX WIFE, THE MOTHER OF THEIR 2 GIRLS AND SHE SAID SHE KNEW THAT WILLIE WAS IN JAIL AND SHE WANTED TO COME GET THE GIRLS AND WOULD I PUT UP A FIGHT. WILLIE IN HIS DRUNKEN STUPOR HAD CALLED HER COLLECT. FOR WHAT REASON I HAVE NO CLUE. WHEN I RETURNED HER CALL SHE WANTED TO KNOW WHAT HAPPENED AND I TOLD HER BRIEFLY WHAT HAD HAPPENED. SHE WANTED TO COME OVER TO TALK AND ASKED WHEN A GOOD TIME WAS, SO WE SET SOMETHING UP FOR THE FOLLOWING WEEK.

THE NEXT MORNING I WAS GETTING THE KIDS OFF TO SCHOOL WHEN THE PHONE RANG. IT WAS A COLLECT CALL FROM WILLIE AND HE ASKED HOW THINGS WENT WITH HIS BOSS. I TOLD HIM HE LOST HIS JOB AND ALSO ASKED HIM WHY HE FELT THE NEED TO CALL HIS EX, THAT SHE WANTED TO MEET WITH ME THIS WEEK ABOUT TAKING THE GIRLS. HE GOT REAL UPSET AND KEPT APOLOGIZING THEN ASKED IF I WAS LEAVING HIM. I TOLD HIM I HAD BEEN CONSIDERING IT AND HE BEGGED ME NOT TOO. IF HE WAS GONNA LOSE HIS GIRLS AND ME WHAT WAS THERE TO LIVE FOR. NOW HE WANTED TO PUT A GUILT TRIP ON ME? WE

HAD CONTINUED WITH THE FAMILY COUNSELING AND WHEN WE HAD OUR MEETING LATER THAT NIGHT I BROKE DOWN IN FRONT OF THE COUNSELOR. I JUST COULDN'T UNDERSTAND ALL THIS AND DID MY BEST TO BE THE BEST WIFE BUT ALWAYS SEEMED TO BE STUCK IN THE MIDDLE OF PEOPLES BAD DECISIONS. HE ASKED ME WHAT WILLIE SAID ABOUT ALL THIS AND I TOLD HIM I WASN'T TOTALLY SURE. HE SEEMED UPSET CONCERNING HIS ACTIONS AND SINCERE THIS TIME OF WANTING TO GET HIS ACT TOGETHER AND SAID HE WAS GOING TO CLASSES AND THE COUNSELOR SAID HE WOULD CHECK INTO IT. HE WANTED ME TO BE AWARE ALSO THAT HE HAD THE POWER TO MAKE ANY RECOMMENDATION OF ANY POTENTIAL CUSTODY CHANGE THAT WOULD BE IN THE BEST INTEREST OF THE GIRLS.

THAT NIGHT, WHEN THE KIDS CAME HOME FROM SCHOOL, I SPOKE WITH THE GIRLS AND TOLD THEM THERE WAS A POSSIBILITY THEIR MOM WAS FILING FOR A CUSTODY CHANGE AND WANTED TO COME GET THEM. I ASKED THEM WHAT THEY WANTED TO DO, I FIGURED THEY HAD A RIGHT TO VOICE THEIR OPINION, I WAS ONLY THE STEP PARENT AND ALTHOUGH WILLIE WANTED ME TO KEEP THEM, HE OPENED A CAN OF WORMS WHEN HE CALLED HIS EX. THE YOUNGEST WANTED TO STAY WITH ME, THE OLDER WANTED TO BE WITH HER MOM, HOWEVER THE YOUNGEST WANTED TO STAY WITH HER SISTER AS THEY WERE CLOSE SO SHE QUICKLY CHANGED HER MIND. JUST THEN THE PHONE RANG AND IT WAS WILLIE. HE ASKED TO SPEAK WITH THE GIRLS AND THEN SPOKE TO ME AND ASKED ME TO SEEK AN ATTORNEY. I TOLD HIM THERE WAS NO MONEY FOR THIS, WE DIDN'T NEED ANOTHER BILL, I

ALREADY HAD SPENT MONEY WE DIDN'T HAVE GETTING THE CAR OUT OF IMPOUND. WHY THEY NNEVER CALLED ME IN THE FIRST PLACE IS BEYOND ME, BUT INSTEAD THEY HAD THE CAR TOWED. HE JUST REPLIED AND SAID HE WOULD FIGURE IT OUT, JUST DO IT. FIGURE IT OUT? WHAT A JOKE I THOUGHT, SAID GOODBYE AND HUNG UP.

THE NEXT DAY I CALLED AN ATTORNEY AND MADE A CONSULT VISIT FOR LATER IN THE WEEK, HUNG UP ONLY TO RECEIVE A CALL FROM THE GIRLS MOM ASKING TO COME SEE ME AS SHE WAS IN TOWN SO I AGREED. I FIGURED IT BEST TO GET THIS OVER WITH BEFORE I HAD TO GO TO WORK. WHEN SHE CAME SHE HAD PAPERS FROM JUVENILE COURT, SHE HAD FILED FOR CHANGE OF CUSTODY OF THE 2 GIRLS JUST AS I SUSPECTED SHE WOULD DO. SHE SAID THAT WILLIE WOULD BE SENT PAPERS WITH THE COURT DATE WHICH WAS SCHEDULED FOR THE WEEK BEFORE CHRISTMAS, BUT WANTED TO SHOW ME AND ASKED TO PICK UP THE GIRLS. I THOUGHT WOW SO SOON? THEY DON'T MESS AROUND DO THEY? I TOLD HER THEY WERE NOT HOME FROM SCHOOL YET AND I HAD TO LEAVE FOR WORK. I TOLD HER THAT UNTIL HE RECEIVED HIS PAPERS I WASN'T RELEASING THEM JUST YET. OF COURSE SHE HAD HER BOYFRIEND WITH HER AND HE THREATENED TO TAKE US FOR EVERYTHING WE HAD OVER ALL OF THIS. I TOLD HIM I HAD NOTHING TO DO WITH IT, I WAS MERELY DOING MY BEST TO CARE FOR THE KIDS AND HE SEEMED TO CALM DOWN THEN THEY LEFT.

TWO DAYS LATER THE DREADED LETTER FROM JUVENILE COURT ARRIVED AND THE COURT HEARING

FOR CUSTODY CHANGE WAS INDEED A FEW DAYS BEFORE CHRISTMAS. I CALLED THE ATTORNEY AND ASKED IF WE COULD GET A CONTINUANCE AND WE SET UP A TIME FOR LATER THAT WEEK TO MEET AND DISCUSS OUR OPTIONS AND WHAT TO EXPECT. WE HAD ESTABLISHED POWER OF ATTORNEY FOR ME TO BE ABLE TO CARE FOR THE GIRLS IN THE EVENT THAT WILLIE WASN'T ABLE TO AND PRAYED THE JUDGE WOULD HONOR IT. WHAT STOOD IN OUR WAY THOUGH WAS THE FACT THEIR BIOLOGICAL MOTHER WAS STILL LIVING AND SHE WOULD HAVE TO GO THRU AN EVALUATION TO MAKE SURE SHE HADN'T BEEN IN TROUBLE WITH THE LAW AND SEE IF IT WOULD BENEFIT THE GIRLS GOING TO LIVE WITH HER. MORE THAN LIKELY WITH WILLIES HISTORY OF ALCOHOLISM AND BEING IN AND OUT OF JAIL IF THINGS CHECKED OUT WITH HER, SHE WOULD INDEED BE AWARDED CUSTODY. I ALSO PRAYED THAT WILLIE WOULD HAVE A REAL WAKE UP CALL WHILE SITTING IN JAIL AND DESIRE TO LIVE A MORE POSITIVE LIFE AND BE THANFUL FOR ALL HE HAD. WE REALLY NEEDED A MIRACLE IN ORDER FOR HIM TO KEEP CUSTODY OF THE GIRLS AND PRAYED THE COUNSELOR WOULD SEE THAT THE GIRLS WOULD BE OK REMAINING WITH US.

WHEN I MET WITH THE ATTORNEY AND LEARNED IN CUSTODY HEARINGS UNLESS A GOOD REASON, WE COULDN'T FILE FOR A CONTINUANCE. ALTHOUGH WE HAD POWER OF ATTORNEY THINGS HAD CHECKED OUT WITH THE MOM, THERE WAS NO RECORD OF HER BEING IN TROUBLE AND SHE HAD A GOOD STABLE JOB SO IT LOOKED REAL BLEAK FOR WILLIE, THE ONLY HOPE WAS THE OPINION OF THE COUNSELOR. I WENT LATER THAT DAY AND VISITED WILLIE IN JAIL AND I

TOLD HIM WHAT HAPPENED AND HE GOT REAL UPSET AND STARTED CRYING. I INFORMED HIM OF THE COURT HEARING AND WE PRAYED THEY WOULD LET HIM OUT TO ATTEND. I KIND OF FELT SORRY FOR HIM BUT HE DID THIS TO HIMSELF. IT GOES TO SHOW THAT YOU WILL REAP WHAT YOU SOW. ALL WE COULD DO NOW WAS PRAY AND STAND ON THE WORD OF GOD. WE DID HAVE A GOOD VISIT AND HE SEEMED TO HAVE CHANGED SOME, I WAS HOPEFUL SO I DECIDED TO SEE HIM THRU THIS. I HAVE LEARNED THAT WITH ALCOHOLISM, THE CHANCE OF A RELAPSE UNDER STRESSFUL CIRCUMSTANCES WAS SO GREAT AND WITH HIS MOM HAVING CANCER AND THE CUSTODY CHANGE, I WAS REALLY LEARY HE WOULD INDEED RELAPSE WHEN HE WAS RELEASED. I PRAYED TO GOD AND TOLD HIM I HOPE THIS WOULDN'T BE THE CASE AND HOPED WILLIE WOULD HAVE A REAL WAKE UP CALL OVER THIS AND GROW UP. WE REALLY NEEDED A MIRACLE IN ORDER FOR HIM TO KEEP CUSTODY OF THE GIRLS AND PRAYED THE COUNSELOR WOULD SEE THAT THE GIRLS WOULD BE OK REMAINING WITH US.

WILLIE WAS 13 WHEN HIS FATHER LEFT, HE WAS THE 3RD OLDEST OF 10 KIDS, ONE OLDER BROTHER HAD PASSED AWAY SO WILLIE WAS THE OLDEST OF THE BOYS AND HELPED HIS MOM RAISE THE YOUNGER SIBLINGS AS HIS OLDER HALF SISTER MOVED OUT THE YEAR BEFORE. I THINK THE PRESSURE OF HAVING THIS RESPONSIBILITY AT SUCH A YOUNG AGE EVENTUALLY LED TO ALCOHOL AND DRUG ABUSE BY AGE 15. AT AGE 16 AS HE FINISHED HIS FRESHMAN YEAR, HE DROPPED OUT OF SCHOOL ALTOGETHER. HIS MOM WAS ALL HE HAD AND NOW TRYING TO DEAL WITH HER HAVING CANCER WAS A LITTLE HARD FOR HIM TO SWALLOW,

NOT TO MENTION BEING ON THE VERGE OF LOSING CUSTODY OF HIS GIRLS THAT HE RAISED BY HIMSELF, FOR THE MOST PART, UNTIL HE MET ME.

THE MORE I THOUGHT ABOUT THIS THE MORE FRUSTRATED I BECAME WITH HIM. I'M SURE EVERYONE LOOKS FORWARD TO THE DAY THEY CAN MOVE OUT ON THEIR OWN AND GET MARRIED, HAVE A FAMILY, AND DREAM OF ONE DAY BUYING A HOUSE TO CALL THEIR OWN AND LEAVE FOR THEIR KIDS WHEN THEY DIE AND TO LIVE HAPPILY EVER AFTER. SOUNDS LIKE FAIRY TAIL THINKING HUH? MAYBE SO, BUT I BELIEVE YOU CAN HAVE AND ACHIEVE ANYTHING YOU WANT WHEN YOU HAVE A POSITIVE ATTITUDE AND SET YOUR MIND TO IT. I FELT I CONTRIBUTED WHAT I COULD AND WORKED REAL HARD SINCE MOVING ON MY OWN TO GET TO THE PLACE OF BUYING A HOUSE AND WHEN THE DREAM BECAME A REALITY, IT WAS SLIPPING AWAY IN ALMOST 3 SHORT YEARS SINCE MOVING IN. I REMEMBER ASKING GOD WHY, THRU TEARS STREAMING, AND REMINDED GOD THAT IN HIS WORD HE WOULDN'T PUT MORE ON US THAN WHAT WE COULD BEAR BUT AFTER ALL I HAVE COME THRU IN MY LIFE, WHAT I WENT THRU WITH THIS MAN WAS WAY TOO MUCH TO DEAL WITH ANY LONGER.

I PRAYED FOR STRENGTH, I PRAYED FOR WISDOM AS TO WHAT I NEEDED TO DO. JUST THEN I WAS INTERRUPTED WHEN THE PHONE RANG AND WHEN I ANSWERED IT WAS A COLLECT CALL FROM WILLIE AND I REALLY DIDN'T WANT TO EXCEPT THE CHARGES AT THAT POINT. I HAD BEEN CRYING, AND I FRANKLY DIDN'T WANT TO HEAR WHAT HE HAD TO SAY, BUT MANAGED TO ACCEPT THE CHARGES, I KNEW I

WAS ALL HE HAD RIGHT THEN. WHEN HIS VOICE CAME OVER THE LINE, HE SAID HELLO MY QUEEN, I'M SO SORRY FOR ALL I PUT YOU THRU. I GOT ALL CHOKED UP AND TEARS FLOWED AGAIN AS I ASKED HIM WHY. HE COULDN'T GIVE ME ALOT OF ANSWERS, BUT DID SAY HE NEEDED HELP, HE UNDERSTOOD ALCOHOLISM WAS A SICKNESS AND HE WOULDN'T BE ABLE TO BEAT IT ON HIS OWN.

HE UNDERSTOOD IF I WANTED TO LEAVE, AND WOULDN'T HOLD ON ME ANY BLAME IF I CHOSE TO DO SO, BUT PLEADED WITH ME OVER AND OVER TO STAY WITH HIM. I TOLD HIM THAT OBVIOUSLY I WASN'T THE ONE FOR HIM OR HE WOULD HAVE TRIED TO GET HELP LONG AGO TO STAY CLEAN AND SOBER, THAT HE WAS RUNNING FROM GOD. HE SEEMED TO UNDERSTAND AND WAS VERY UPSET WITH HIMSELF. HE SAID HE WASN'T PROUD OF THE MAN HE HAD BECOME BUT WAS SO GRATEFUL THAT HE HAD ME AND HOPED I WOULD HAVE A CHANGE OF HEART, ESPECIALLY SINCE HE MAY LOSE CUSTODY OF HIS GIRLS.

AS I HUNG UP THE PHONE, TEARS POURED, THERE WAS SO MANY THOUGHTS AND QUESTIONS AND NO ONE THERE TO COMFORT ME, HOLD ME AND TELL ME IT'S GONNA BE ALRIGHT. ALTHOUGH I KNOW GOD IS WITH US, FOR HE WILL NEVER LEAVE US OR FORSAKE US, I FELT SO ALONE, SO FAR FROM GOD AT THAT MOMENT. I DID HAVE MY YOUNGEST SON WHO STILL LIVED AT HOME, THEN THOUGHTS OF HOW I WOULD CARE FOR HIM OVER SHADOWED ME. MY OLDER SON HAD LONG SINCE MOVED OUT BEING ALMOST 19 NOW AND DIDN'T WANT TO LIVE WITH WILLIE SHOULD I DECIDE TO LET HIM COME BACK UPON HIS RELEASE

FROM JAIL. HE LIVED WITH A COUPLE BUDDIES BUT THEY COULD ONLY MANAGE TO PAY THEIR OWN BILLS AND ALTHOUGH MY YOUNGEST WAS WORKING, IT WOULDN'T BE ENOUGH WITH MY INCOME AND THE AMOUNT OF DEBT WE HAD TO STAY AFLOAT. I KNEW MY DAUGHTER WAS IN NO POSITION TO HELP OUT AS HER HUSBAND HAD JUST LOST A JOB AND SHE HAD HER SON TO CARE FOR. I WAS LOST AND I KNEW THAT ONLY GOD TO GET ME THRU THIS.

IT WAS THE DAY BEFORE THE CUSTODY HEARING AND AS I WAS GETTING THINGS IN ORDER THE PHONE RANG. AS I ANSWERED IT THE VOICE ON THE OTHER END WAS THAT OF THE GIRLS MOTHER. MY HEART CRINGED AND MY BODY STIFFENED. USUALLY WHEN SHE CAME TO PICK UP THE GIRLS FOR VISITATION, OR HAD CONCERNS ABOUT THE GIRLS SHE ALWAYS DEALT WITH WILLIE, THIS TIME IT WAS ME SHE HAD BEEN DEALING WITH AND I'M SURE AS WITH ALL COUPLES WITH KIDS THAT DIVORCE AND REMARRY, THERE IS USUALLY SOME JEALOUSY OR ANIMOSITY BETWEEN THE NEW SPOUSES. HOWEVER, I KNEW I HAD TO SET ASIDE MY OWN ATTITUDE TOWARDS HER AND WILLIE AND HELP MAKE THIS AS EASY ON THE GIRLS AS I POSSIBLY COULD, AND FOR THEIR SAKE JUST DEAL. THE GIRLS HAD BEEN THRU SO MUCH AND BEING 13,&14 THE TRANSITIONING FROM CHILDHOOD TO BEING A TEENAGER, BODY AND HORMONES RUNNING WILD, EMOTIONS UP AND DOWN, WAS HARD ENOUGH TO GET THRU AND NOW THIS WITH THEIR FATHER TOO. MY HEART WENT OUT TO THEM. MY THOUGHTS BROUGHT BACK TO HER SPEAKING, SHE ASKED ME IF I WAS GOING TO FIGHT HER IN COURT, SHE KNEW I HELPED RAISE THE GIRLS THE LAST 8 YEARS AND

THANKED ME FOR THE CARE AND LOVE I HAD SHOWN THEM, BUT DIDN'T WANT ANY TROUBLE AND THIS DRAGGED OUT FURTHER FOR EVERYONE'S SAKE INVOLVED. I TOLD HER WE WOULD SEE WHAT THE JUDGE SAID, IT WAS IN HER HANDS, NOT MINE BUT I WOULD COMPLY WITH WHAT EVER THE DECISION WAS.

I PICKED UP THE GIRLS FROM SCHOOL THAT DAY RATHER THAN HAVING THEM WALK HOME, AND WHILE I DID MY ROUTE I TALKED TO THEM ABOUT THE CUSTODY HEARING THAT WAS SCHEDULED FOR THE NEXT DAY. I ASKED THEM AGAIN IF THEY HAD MADE A DEFINITE DECISION AS TO WHAT THEY WANTED TO DO. THEY WERE FULL OF QUESTIONS ASKING ME IF I WOULD BE OK WITHOUT THEM, OR IF I WOULD BE ANGRY WITH THEM IF THEY DECIDED TO LIVE WITH THEIR MOM. THEY ASKED ABOUT THEIR THINGS AND WHAT THE HEARING WOULD BE LIKE. I EXPLAINED THINGS THE BEST I COULD TO THEM WITHOUT GETTING ALL CHOKED UP. OF COURSE I WOULD BE OK ALTHOUGH I WOULD MISS THEM, THEY WERE A PART OF MY LIFE FOR 8 YEARS, ALMOST AS IF THEY WERE MY OWN. I WOULDN'T BE ANGRY WITH THEM, THEY HAD A REAL MOM WHO LOVED THEM AND WANTED THEM WITH HER. AS FAR AS THEIR THINGS, THEY COULD TAKE WHATEVER THEIR MOM HAD ROOM FOR. THEY THANKED ME FOR CARING FOR THEM, BUT THEY WANTED TO LIVE WITH THEIR MOM. THEY WERE TIRED OF THEIR DAD'S DRINKING AND THE FIGHTS AND HIM GOING TO JAIL. I COULDN'T BLAME THEM ALTHOUGH HEARING THAT WAS AS IF A KNIFE HAD BEEN SLAMMED INTO MY HEART.

I HAD TROUBLE SLEEPING THAT NIGHT AND AT LAST MORNING WAS HERE, THE DAY OF THE CUSTODY HEARING. I COULDN'T HELP BUT HAVE THIS SINKING FEELING THINGS WERE NOT GOING TO GO IN OUR FAVOR, BUT SHOOK IT OFF AS I GOT THE KIDS OFF TO SCHOOL. I WAS HOPING THAT THE ATTORNEY WOULD BE ABLE TO GET THE JUDGE TO LET WILLIE ATTEND THE HEARING. WHEN I ARRIVED AT THE COURTHOUSE, I SEEN THE GIRLS MOM WITH HER ATTORNEY BUT NO SIGN OF WILLIE'S ATTORNEY YET. A SHORT WHILE LATER HE APPEARED AND SAID HE JUST LEFT THE ADULT COURT JUDGE AND SHE REFUSED TO ALLOW WILLIE TO ATTEND THE CUSTODY HEARING AND I COULD GO IN ON HIS BEHALF. THE ATTORNEY SAID THAT SINCE THE MOM HAD NO INSTANCES INVOLVING CHILDREN SERVICES, OR BEEN IN ANY TROUBLE THE JUDGE WOULD MORE THAN LIKELY OVERLOOK OUR POA AND AWARD HER CUSTODY AND MY HEART SANK.

WE WERE SOON CALLED IN BEFORE THE JUDGE AND SHE LOOKED AT THE POA, ASKED ME QUESTIONS, ASKED THE MOMS QUESTIONS AND THEN AFTER ASKING FOR A 30 MINUTES RECESS TO LOOK AT THE INFO AND MAKE HER DECISION WE PROCEEDED OUTSIDE TO THE WAITING ROOM MY FINGERS CROSSED. FINALLY WE WERE CALLED BACK IN TO THE COURTROOM AND THE JUDGE CAME FORTH WITH HER DECISION. AS HARD AS IT WAS FOR HER TO MAKE, SHE AWARDED CUSTODY OF THE 2 GIRLS TO THEIR MOTHER. I BEGAN TO CRY SILENT TEARS, I WAS HEART BROKEN THAT THE GIRLS I HAD COME TO LOVE AND HELP RAISE THE LAST 8 YEARS WERE BEING RIPPED FROM US BECAUSE OF THE BAD CHOICES OF THEIR FATHER. DIDN'T HE LOVE US?

THE REST OF THE DAY I WAS NUMB AS IF SHOT BY A STUN GUN. I WASN'T SURE HOW I GOT THRU MY ROUTE, ONLY BY THE GRACE OF GOD FOR SURE, I JUST SEEMED TO BE GOING THRU THE MOTIONS NOT EVEN GIVING THOUGHT TO STOPS AND TRAFFIC. THANK GOD FOR HIS GUIDANCE AND PROTECTION. I ARRIVED HOME JUST IN TIME FOR THE GIRLS AND AFTER GETTING THEM A SNACK SAT DOWN TO DISCUSS THE OUTCOME OF COURT THAT MORNING. I THEN GOT A CALL FROM WILLIE AND TOLD HIM THE NEWS AND HE DIDN'T TAKE IT WELL AT ALL. I PRAYED IT WOULD BE THE VERY BLOW THAT WOULD CAUSE HIM TO COME TO HIS SENSES AND CHANGE SOME THINGS. WE HAD BEGUN TO TALK MORE AND MORE AND IT WAS NICE TO HEAR HIM OPENING UP LIKE HE WAS. HE SAID HE HAD BEEN PRAYING MORE AND READING THE BIBLE AND ALTHOUGH I'D HEARD THAT OVER AND OVER BEFORE. THIS TIME HE REALLY SEEMED SINCERE. I KNEW HOW MUCH HIS GIRLS MEANT TO HIM AND THE VERY FACT OF LOSING CUSTODY SEEMED TO JOLT HIM BACK TO REALITY. WITH ALL HE'D LOST IT SEEMED CRUEL TO PUNISH HIM FURTHER BY LEAVING HIM MYSELF WITHOUT GIVING HIM THE CHANCE TO PROVE HE'D CHANGED AS HE SAID HE HAD.I WANTED TO SHOW HIM THAT HE HAD SOMEONE WHO WOULD SUPPORT HIM ON HIS ROAD TO RECOVERY.

THE NEXT COUPLE OF DAYS WAS ROUGH AS THE GIRLS AND I PACKED UP THEIR THINGS PREPARING FOR THEIR MOM TO PICK THEM UP. IT WAS A VERY EMOTIONAL TIME AND SEEMED UNFAIR I WOULDN'T HAVE THEM FOR CHRISTMAS WHICH WAS ONLY A FEW DAYS AWAY. WHEN THEIR MOM AND HER BOYFRIEND

ARRIVED, THEY LOADED UP THEIR THINGS IN THE TRUCK AND I FOUGHT TO HOLD BACK THE TEARS AS I GAVE THEIR MOM THE INSURANCE CARDS, AND IMPORTANT PAPERS. I GAVE THE GIRLS ONE FINAL HUG THEN THEY GOT IN THE TRUCK AND PULLED AWAY AND AS THEY DID I BEGAN TO SOB.

I DIDN'T THINK I HAD ANY TEARS OLEFT I HAD CRIED SO MUCH THE LAST FEW WEEKS. I FELT AS IF MY HEART HAD BEEN RIPPED OUT OF MY CHEST. I KNEW THEY WEREN'T LEGALLY MINE BUT I HELPED RAISE THEM AS IF THEY WERE AND I REMEMBER WHAT WE WENT THRU WITH THE YOUNGEST AND HER DISABILITIES. WHEN SHE WAS JUST 6 YEARS OLD SHE WAS DIAGNOSED WITH FETAL ALCOHOL SYNDROME, ADHD, ODD AND WAS DEVELOPMENTALLY HANDICAP WHICH MEANT SHE WAS 3 YEARS BEHIND HER PEERS. SHE REALLY STRUGGLED WITH ALOT OF CHANGE AND THIS WAS ONE MAJOR CHANGE FOR HER AND I PRAYED SHE'D BE OK THRU IT. AS CHRISTMAS CAME AND WENT AND IT JUST WASN'T THE SAME. WILLIE WAS STILL IN JAIL, THE GIRLS WITH THEIR MOM AND I WASN'T ABLE TO SEE THEM. I PRAYED AS THE NEW YEAR CAME UPON US IT WOULD BE A BETTER AND BRIGHTER YEAR FOR US. THIS LAST YEAR ESPECIALLY HAD BEEN HELL.

JANUARY CAME AND WENT. IT WAS WINTER 2006. I WAS LATE ON THE HOUSE PAYMENT AND WAS STARTING TO GET WORRIED. BECAUSE OF REFINANCING SO MUCH OUR PAYMENT WAS A TAD HIGH SO IT WAS SOMETHING YOU DID NOT WANT TO GET BEHIND ON IF YOU WAS TO SLACK ON ANYTHING. THAT NIGHT AS WILLIE CALLED I EXPRESSED MY CONCERNS WITH HIM AND HE TOLD ME NOT TO

WORRY. HE HAD THE OPPORTUNITY TO GET OUT ON HOUSE ARREST FOR GOOD BEHAVIOR AND FINISH HOIS SENTENCE AT HOME. HE WAS TO SEE THE JUDGE THE FOLLOWING MORNING AND FELT IF HE COULD GET ON HOUSE ARREST HE COULD GET A JOB WITH DRIVING PRIVILEGES AND HELP WITH THE BILLS. ALL I HAD TO DO WAS GET THE START UP FEE FOR THE EQUIPMENT, THIS WOULD MONITOR HIS COMING AND GOING BUT I WOULD HAVE TO GO SET IT ALL UP FOR HIM. THERE WOULD BE A MONTHLY FEE FOR THIS AS WELL AS COUNSELING WHICH HE SAID HE WAS WANTING TO DO SO HE COULD GET BETTER AND TREAT ME LIKE THE QUEEN I DESERVED TO BE TREATED LIKE. I DIDN'T EXPECT ROYAL TREATMENT, JUST TO BE LOVED AND NURTURED.

THE JUDGE WAS GRACIOUS AND RELEASED WILLIE ON HOUSE ARREST AND I WENT THRU THE PROPER CHANNELS FOR HIS RELEASE AND BY THE END OF FEB HE WAS OUT OF JAIL. HE WOULD BE ON HOUSE ARREST TILL THE END OF JUNE. AFTER 2 WEEKS, HE GOT A DELIVERY ROUTE WITH ME, THEN A WEEK LATER THE JUDGE GRANTED HIM DRIVING PRIVILEGES AND HE COULD NOW DRIVE HIMSELF. WE HAD TO GET SPECIAL YELLOW LICENSE PLATES FOR THE CAR AND SPECIAL BOND INSURANCE TOO. WE GOT THRU MARCH AND IT WAS NOW APRIL, THINGS WERE GOING WELL BUT MONEY GOT EVEN TIGHTER SO WE HAD TO CANCEL OUT HIS 401 K WHICH WAS ENOUGH TO COVER SOME BILLS AND PAY OUR PROPERTY TAXES BUT ONLY ONE MONTH OF OUR MORTGAGE, WE WERE STILL 3 MONTHS BEHIND THOUGH AND I FEARED THEY WOULD SOON START FORECOLSURE PROCEEDINGS. WE DECIDED TO PUT THE HOUSE UP

FOR SALE. I DIDN'T WANT ANY ADDED STRESS ON HIM, ALTHOUGH HE KNEW WHAT HE CREATED SOMETIMES IT CAN'T GET OVERWHELMING TO LIVE OUT THE REPERCUSSIONS OF THOSE BAD CHOICES OUTSIDE OF A JAIL CELL. SO BY GETTING OUT FROM UNDER THESE BILLS AND THE HOUSE AND MAKING A FRESH START SEEMED IN ORDER.

IN MAY 2006 WE FOUND AN APARTMENT WELL WITHIN OUR BUDGET AND MADE THE MOVE. ALTHOUGH WE COULD HAVE LIVED IN OUR HOUSE TILL IT SOLD OR FORECLOSED AND WE WERE CHASED OUT BY THE BANK, I DIDN'T FEEL RIGHT LIVING SOMEWHERE AND NOT PAYING, TO ME IT WAS LIKE STEALING FROM THE BANK. WE GOT SETTLED IN TO OUR NEW PLACE, IT WAS A 2 BEDROOM SO WHEN THE GIRLS CAME FOR THE WEEKEND THEY HAD TO CAMP OUT IN THE LIVING ROOM ON AN AIR MATTRESS. WILLIE WAS NOW FACE WITH CHILD SUPPORT PAYMENTS AND A LITTLE BEHIND NOW SO WE WAS LOOKING FOR WAYS WE COULD GENERATE EXTRA INCOME. WE TRIED SEVERAL WORK AT HOME PROJECTS, BUT NOTHING SEEM TO PAN OUT FOR US, SO WE ENDED UP TAKING ON MORE ROUTES TO COMPENSATE. THIS REQUIRED THE GIRLS HELPING US ON WEEKENDS THEY WERE THERE WHICH THEY HATED WITH A PASSION.

IT WASN'T LONG BEFORE THE OLDEST ONE BECAME REBELLIOUS AND REFUSED TO COME OVER FOR VISITATION. BECAUSE WILLIE WAS ON HOUSE ARREST, WE HAD TO WORK OUT A PLAN FOR TRANSPORTING GIRLS. WE WORKED IT OUT TO WHERE I WOULD PICK THEM OUT ON FRIDAYS AND THEIR MOM WOULD COME GET THEM ON SUNDAYS. I HAD TO

LITERALLY BEG THE OLDER GIRL TO COME EXPLAINING THAT WILLIE MAY HOLD HER IN CONTEMPT FOR NOT ENCOURAGING HER TO COME, BUT SHE HATED COMING AND I FELT BAD FOR HER. IT PUT ME IN THE MIDDLE OF SOMETHING THAT SHOULD HAVE BEEN BETWEEN THE 2 PARENTS OF THE GIRLS AND IT WAS VERY STRESSFUL FOR ME TRYING TO REASON WITH A TEENAGER. WHEN SHE DID COME WE TRIED TO MAKE HER VISIT PLEASANT, THEY WERE PAID FOR THEIR HELP WITH THE ROUTES. THERE WAS EVEN TIMES THAT WHEN WE RAN SHORT OF MONEY I WOULD RETURN TO THE STORE SOMETHING I BOUGHT FOR MYSELF JUST SO WE HAD MONEY TO DO THINGS FOR THEM. HOWEVER I LEARNED A VALUABLE LESSON IN DOING THAT. MONEY ISN'T EVERYTHING!

NO MATTER HOW MUCH YOU SPEND ON A PERSON , WHEN THERE IS NOTHING LEFT. TO SPEND, THEY TURN ON YOU. IT ONLY BUYS TEMPORARY HAPPINESS, THEN IT'S OVER AS QUICKLY AS IT COMES. THERE WAS NO APPRECIATION FOR WHAT I DID, NO THANK YOU, BUT NEVER COMPLAINED. I SET ASIDE MY FEELINGS AND DID MY BEST TO SHOW LOVE AND UNDERSTANDING IN HOPES OF SPARKING SOME FORM OF POSITIVE CHANGE TO MEND THINGS BETWEEN THEM AND THEIR FATHER IN GIVING A DIFFERENT OPINION AND PERSPECTIVE ON THINGS. HOWEVER THEIR MOM WASN'T THE EASIEST TO GET ALONG WITH NOW THAT SHE HAD CUSTODY OF THE GIRLS. MANY TIMES SHE WOULD SAY MEAN THINGS ABOUT ME, TO THE POINT OF CRITICIZING MY FAITH, TO THE GIRLS, AND TO THE COURT SYSTEM. THIS WHOLE ISSUE WASN'T ABOUT ME ANYWAY, IT WAS ABOUT THE GIRLS, AND ABOUT WILLIE, HIS ADDICTIONS AND THE WAY HE

HANDLED HIMSELF, TREATING OTHERS BADLY WHEN UNDER THE INFLUENCE OF DRUGS AND ALCOHOL. IT WASN'T AS IF I HELD A GUN TO HIS HEAD MAKING HIM DRINK, SMOKE POT AND DRIVE. BUT SOMEHOW I ENDED UP BEING THE BAD ONE, PORTRAYED AS A MONSTER, AND WHEN I TRIED TO BACK OFF, THEN I WASN'T A CHRISTIAN. I FELT BETWEEN A ROCK AND A HARD PLACE, THAT NO MATTER HOW HARD I TRIED I COULDN'T SO ANYTHING RIGHT.

IT WAS NOW SUMMER 2006, I HAD BEEN OFF A LITTLE OVER 5 YEARS FROM MY PLACE OF EMPLOYMENT FOR A WORK RELATED INJURY. I HAD BEEN DRAWING WORKER'S COMP AND IT WAS DETERMINED THE MONTH BEFORE THAT I COULDN'T RETURN TO MY JOB AND WAS OFFERED A SETTLEMENT WHICH I ACCEPTED BUT MEANT I WOULD BE TERMINATED FROM MY JOB. I RECEIVED MY SETTLEMENT THE NEXT MONTH AND ALSO APPLIED FOR SOCIAL SECURITY DISABILITY FOR THE 5TH TIME. THIS TIME I WOULD GO BEFORE A PANEL IN DAYTON TO DETERMINED IF I COULD DRAW DISABILITY. WE MANAGED TO GET SOME BILLS PAID OFF AND HAVE A SMALL SAVINGS. OUR HOUSE HAD SOLD ON QUICK SALE AND THANKFULLY WE WERE OUT FROM UNDER THAT MORTGAGE. THINGS WERE ONCE AGAIN COMING TOGETHER AND LOOKING UP FOR US AND I BREATHERD A SIGH OF RELIEF.

IT WAS NOW AUGUST 2006, JUST WHEN I THOUGHT THINGS WERE COMING AROUND AND US COMING TO SOME KIND OF NORMACY, I LEARNED WHEN WE GOT OUR CABLE BILL THAT WILLIE HAD ORDERED X-RATED MOVIES. I WAS SO HURT, I MEAN,

222

I'M SURE LOTS OF GUYS DO THAT, SO WHY WAS IT SUCH A PROBLEM FOR ME? WELL, I'M THE TYPE OF WOMAN THAT DOESN'T BELIEVE IN IT. IT'S LUSTING ACCORDING TO MY FAITH, COMMITTING ADULTERY IN HIS HEART AND IT MADE ME FEEL CHEAP AND WORTHLESS. I BECAME DISGUSTED TO BE HONEST THAT A MAN WOULD WANT TO RELIEVE HIMSELF OVER A PICTURE OF A NAKED WOMAN, OR EVEN WATCH FILTHY MOVIES. I FELT THAT I WASN'T GOOD ENOUGH OR EVEN WOMAN ENOUGH TO SATISFY MY MAN. EVEN THOUGH I HAD BEEN SEXUALLY ABUSED AT DIFFERENT TIMES OF MY LIFE AND HAD PAINFUL INTERCOURSE, I STILL HAD SEX ANYWAY AND ALWAYS ABLE TO PLEASE MY PARTNER THOUGH I ENDED UP IN PAIN FOR A COUPLE DAYS AFTERWARD. I COULDN'T HELP BUT WONDER, IF WHEN HE HAD IMAGES OF THE OTHER LADIES HE HAD SEEN NAKED IN THE FILMS OR THE BOOKS FLASHING THRU HIS MIND AND MADE HIM ABLE TO HAVE AN ORGASM SCREWING ME AND IT OFTEN BROUGHT ME TOO TEARS. WHEN I APPROACHED THE SUBJECT WITH HIM, HE DENIED IT, SAYING THE CABLE COMPANY MADE A MISTAKE. REALLY? WE HAD A BOX YOU HAD TO PUNCH A CODE INTO. I ASKED HIM IF HE EVEN GAVE THOUGHT TO HOW THIS MADE ME FEEL, AND HE BECAME ANGRY. I WAS SO UPSET I JUST GRABBED THE KEYS AND TOOK OFF TO RUN ERRANDS.

THE FIRST STOP I MADE WAS AT THE BANK TO CASH HIS PAYCHECK SO I COULD PAY ANOTHER BILL AND GET SOME GROCERIES. APPARENTLY WHILE I SAT IN THE DRIVE THRU OF THE BANK, HE HAD MADE A CALL TO THE BANK AND REPORTED I HAD STOLEN HIS CHECK AND NOT TO CASH IT FOR ME BECAUSE WHEN I PULLED UP TO THE WINDOW, THE LADY INFORMED ME

SHE COULDN'T CASH IT. I DIDN'T KNOW WHAT TO DO NOW. HOW WAS I GOING TO GET FOOD FOR THAT NIGHT'S DINNER? I WENT BACK HOME TO SPEAK WITH HIM ONCE AGAIN, ON THE WAY THINKING OF HOW RIDICULOUS HE WAS BEING. THINKING OF THE PROMISES HE MADE TO ME WHEN HE WAS LOCKED UP. THINKING WHAT A FOOL I WAS TO FALL FOR HIS LINE OF CRAP ONCE AGAIN. WHEN I ARRIVED I FOUND THE COPS THERE. THEY TOLD ME I HAD TO LEAVE AS WILLIE HAD TOLD THEM WE WERE IN A DISPUTE AND I HAD TAKEN HIS CHECK AND TRIED TO CASH IT WITHOUT HIS PERMISSION AND THINKING OF PRESSING CHARGES AGAINST ME YET HE WAS ON HOUSE ARREST AND NOT ALLOWED TO LEAVE ONLY TO GO TO WORK AND HOME OR TO DOCTORS APPT AND COURT. HOW WAS HIS CHECK TO GET CASHED AND IT WAS A JOINT ACCOUNT TO BOOT. HE SAID I WAS MEAN AND ABUSIVE TO HIS DAUGHTERS AND YET THEY WERE NOT EVEN THERE THAT WEEKEND. SOMETHING WAS SERIOUSLY WRONG IN THE HEAD CAUSE HE WAS ACTING LIKE A LUNATIC. WHAT A NIGHTMARE AND ALL I COULD DO WAS PRAY THIS WAS ALL A BAD DREAM AND I'D SOON WAKE UP AND IT WOULD BE OVER.

I CALLED OUR CHURCH ASKING FOR PRAYER AND BEGAN TO WEEP AS I EXPLAINED WHAT HAPPENED. I STILL HAD 2 HOURS BEFORE JASON GOT OUT OF SCHOOL AND I NEEDED TO TAKE HIM ACCORDING TO THE POLICE SINCE WILLIE WASN'T HIS REAL DAD. MY GOODNESS WOULD IT EVER STOP? MY LIFE HAD ONCE AGAIN SPUN OUT OF CONTROL. I BEGAN YELLING AT GOD, ASKING HIM WHY. I PRAYED HE WOULD DEAL MIGHTILY WITH WILLIE BECAUSE I CERTAINLY HAD NO ANSWERS AS TO HIS BEHAVIOR.

WHENEVER I'D COME UP WITH WAYS TO HANDLE THINGS AND BE FIRM, THEN I FELT GUILTY THINKING I WASN'T PORTRAYING THE LOVE OF CHRIST. THIS IS HOW WILLIE ALWAYS SEEMED TO WIN. HE STARTED BEING HATEFUL AGAIN AND CALL ME NAMES, LIE ON ME, THEN THE NEXT DAY HE'D BE NICE AND I WAS THE LOVE OF HIS LIFE. HE'D TWIST THINGS, MAKING BARGAINS AND I KNEW HE WAS ONLY MANIPULATING THINGS TO BENEFIT HIM, BUT WHEN YOU CALLED HIM ON IT, HE'D SAY IT WASN'T LIKE THAT AT ALL AND GIVE SOME CROPPED UP SCENERIO ON WHAT HE PERCEIVED IT TO BE.

JASON CAME HOME AND I PACKED SOME OF OUR THINGS AND WE LEFT. AFTER SPEAKING WITH OUR PASTOR AT THE TIME, THEY PUT US IN A HOTEL FOR A 3 DAYS TILL I GOT MY BEARINGS AND PLANNED OUR NEXT MOVE. WHEN WE GOT TO THE HOTEL I CALLED OUR LANDLADY AND EXPLAINED TO HER THE RENT MAY BE LATE AND TOLD HER WHY. SHE WASN'T VERY HAPPY TO HEAR WHY I WOULDN'T BE THERE AND ASKED WHY IT WAS THAT WILLIE COULDN'T BE THE ONE TO LEAVE. YOU SEE, SHE DIDN'T KNOW THAT WILLIE WAS ON HOUSE ARREST. WILLIE WAS AFRAID IF SHE KNEW THEN WE WOULDN'T GET THE APARTMENT. NOW HERE I WAS FACED WITH THE DECISION, DO I TELL HER OR DON'T I TELL HER THAT HE IS ON HOUSE ARREST. WHAT A MESS THIS WAS! WELL SINCE SHE ASKED, I FELT IT BETTER TO DEAL WITH WHATEVER REPERCUSSIONS WE WAS TO GET, SHE HAD TO KNOW THE TRUTH. WAS IT IN A SENSE REVENGE AGAINST HIM FOR WHAT HE DID TO ME? WELL, I WAS HURTING AND WANTED HIM TO PAY, BUT THEN AGAIN SHE EXPECTED ME OVER IN THE NEXT COUPLE DAYS TO PAY THE RENT

AND SHE HAD TO KNOW I'D BE LATE, SO I ENDED UP TELLING HER WILLIE WAS ON HOUSE ARREST AND HAD RUN INS WITH THE LAW.

SHE WAS NOT PLEASED AT ALL AND ASKED WHEN WE SIGNED THE LEASE WHY WE NEVER TOLD HER, SHE SHOULD HAVE BEEN INFORMED. WELL, THE LEASE SAID ANYTHING OF EXTREME NATURE, TO US EXTREME WAS LIKE BURGLARY, MURDER, THINGS OF THAT NATURE AND SINCE IT WAS FOR HIS DRINKING ISSUES I DIDN'T THINK IT WAS SEVERE ENOUGH TO BE REPORTED. THINGS HAD BEEN GOING REAL GOOD FOR US AND I REALLY BELIEVED THINGS WOULD BE DIFFERENT THAN WHAT THEY HAD BEEN SO WE CHOSE NOT TO TELL HER. I HATED MYSELF FOR NOT BEING HONEST AND THE FACT I HAD UPSET HER. THE LANDLADY INFORMED ME SHE RENTED IT TO US BECAUSE OF ME ANYWAY AND I WAS TO STAY THERE. SHE TRIED TO GET WILLIE OUT OF THERE, BUT NOT MUCH SHE COULD DO AT THE MOMENT. SHE LEFT THE SITUATION IN THE HANDS OF HER HUSBAND WHO WAS AN ATTORNEY PRACTICING IN TROY. SHE DID TELL ME THAT IF THE COPS WERE CALLED AGAIN FOR ANY REASON SHE WOULD HOLD ME RESPONSIBLE AND WE WOULD HAVE TO MOVE AND I AGREED ALTHOUGH UNSURE I WOULD EVEN RETURN THERE. I KEPT THINKING THAT MAYBE THINGS MAY CHANGE, ESPECIALLY NOW WITH THE ULTIMATUM GIVEN BY OUR LANDLADY. THERE IS ALWAYS HOPE.

I WAS DOING MY BEST TO KEEP A POSITIVE ATTITUDE AND NOT THINK NEGATIVELY. I FIRMLY BELIEVE SINCE BECOMING A CHRISTIAN THAT YOU CAN SPEAK THINGS INTO EXISTANCE. I WAS TRYING TO

RENEW MY MIND AND TRAIN MYSELF TO THINK AND SPEAK IN A MORE POSITIVE WAY. I TRIED TO LOOK FOR THE GOOD IN OTHERS AND WOULD BLAME MYSELF, I'M NOT PERFECT, I KNOW THERE WERE THINGS I NEEDED TO CHANGE ABOUT ME, SO I DEVELOPED THIS MINDSET THAT IF I CHANGED THEN THINGS WOULD BE BETTER. INSTEAD WHAT I NOTICED WAS IF I WENT WITH THE FLOW I WAS ACCEPTED, HOWEVER, IF I SHUT UP AND DIDN'T SAY ANYTHING, I WAS A WITCH AND HAD AN ATTITUDE. IF I SPOKE UP AND STOOD UP FOR MYSELF OR FOR OTHERS, THEN I WAS HATEFUL AND NOT A CHRISTIAN, AND THAT'S WHY I HAD NO FRIENDS. IT WASN'T THAT I DIDN'T HAVE FRIENDS, IT'S JUST NO ONE WANTED TO BE AROUND WILLIE AND THEY DIDN'T UNDERSTAND WHY I WAS STILL WITH HIM. THEY JUST LEFT ME ALONE PRAYING THAT ONE DAY I'D WAKE UP, SO THEY SAID, AND SEE THE LIGHT OF WHO HE REALLY WAS. THEY SAID THAT WILLIE WAS ALWAYS BAD MOUTHING ME TO HIS FAMILY AND OUR FRIENDS AND I WOULD HAVE TO DEFEND MYSELF ALL THE TIME TO PEOPLE. WILLIE SEEMED TO HAVE A WAY OF GETTING PEOPLE TO BUY INTO HIS LIES. MAYBE IT WAS JUST THEY FELT SORRY FOR ME AND JUST STAYED AWAY FOR FEAR OF TELLING HIM OFF OR GETTING INTO A FIGHT THEN HAVE HIM GET SO MAD HE ENDED UP HURTING ME WHEN THEY WOULD LEAVE.

AFTER THE 3 DAYS WAS UP IN THE HOTEL, WE ENDED UP MOVING BACK TO THE APARTMENT WITH HIM, I HAD NO WHERE TO GO. BECAUSE I DID, PEOPLE HAD STOPPED TALKING TO ME. THEY JUST COULDN'T UNDERSTAND WHY AFTER WHAT HE DID. SOME HAD THE IDEA I WAS JUST AFTER MONEY AND USING PEOPLE TO BE MY ESCAPE WHEN TIMES GOT TOUGH.

MY OWN CHURCH EVEN DISTANCED THEMSELVES AND IT WAS AWKWARD EVEN ATTENDING THERE. I THOUGHT OF COUNSELING BUT SHOOK IT OFF AS SOON AS I THOUGHT IT. IT SEEMED NO MATTER HOW MANY COUNSELING SESSIONS WE HAD, HOW MANY PEOPLE WE TALKED TO, WE DIDN'T GET ANSWERS, THOUGH IT WAS PROBABLY SMACKING ME IN THE FACE THE WHOLE TIME, I JUST DIDN'T PAY ATTENTION. I WAS HIT ON SO MUCH JUST FELT LIKE ANOTHER JAB TO ME. IT DID SEEM TO HELP ME FEEL BETTER WHEN I GOT THINGS OFF MY CHEST.

SOMETIMES I FOUND THAT IF YOU HEAR YOURSELF SPEAK OF ISSUES THE ANSWERS WILL COME OR AN IDEA TO TRY TO HELP YOUR SITUATION. IT WAS LIKE A JIG SAW PUZZLE AND I HAD MORE PIECES IN PLACE OF WHAT I NEEDED TO DO RATHER THAN THE PIECES OF NOT KNOWING WHAT TO DO, BUT I LOVED HIM AND IT HAD TO BE UNCONDITIONAL LOVE TO PUT UP WITH WHAT I DID. I WALKED AROUND AS IF BLINDED, GRASPING AT EVERYTHING I COULD GRAB ONTO TO MAKE SOME SORT OF SENSE OUT OF MY CHAOTIC LIFE. I WAS A FIGHTER AND I FOUGHT FOR WHAT I BELIEVED IN. THAT'S NOT A FIGHTER IN THE SENSE OF FIST FIGHT OR CREATING TROUBLE, BUT I DIDN'T GIVE UP EASY, I WASN'T A QUITTER. I WANTED HAPPINESS, I WANTED TO BRING HAPPINESS TO THE LIVES OF OTHERS, BUT NO MATTER HOW HARD I TRIED IT SEEMED TO MAKE THINGS WORSE, BACKFIRING IN MY FACE. I WAS SHUNNED, MISUNDERSTOOD, THERE WERE THOSE PEOPLE THAT DIDN'T WANT TO BELIEVE WHAT I WAS GOING THRU BECAUSE OF BEING SO UPBEAT. I WASN'T ONE TO WALK AROUND WITH A LONG

FACE, WANTING OTHERS IN OUR BUSINESS, SOME PICKED UP ON IT THEMSELVES.

YOU KNOW SOMETHING THOUGH? I HAD THE POWER ALL THE TIME TO CHANGE MY CIRCUMSTANCES, SO WAS IT LIKE I ENJOYED THE PROBLEMS? I DON'T THINK SO, I THINK I WAS BLINDED BY LOVE, MAYBE DESPERATION, I FEEL I WAS FORCED OUT OF MY LAST MARRIAGE BY THE LAW BECAUSE OF THE TRIAL WITH GEORGE AND ANGELA, SO I WASN'T GOING TO BE FORCE OUT OF THIS. I THINK I HAD A FEAR OF MAKING IT ON MY OWN TOO. AFRAID OF WHAT REPERCUSSIONS THAT MAY COME. FEAR IS A POWERFUL EMOTION. I BECAME WITHDRAWN AND DISTANCED MYSELF FROM PEOPLE. I WENT TO CHURCH TO WORSHIP GOD AND THEN LEFT AS SOON AS SERVICE WAS OVER. IT MAY HAVE APPEARED I WAS STUCK UP OR HAD AN ATTITUDE, BUT I DIDN'T THINK ABOUT THAT, I WAS TOO CAUGHT UP IN MY PAIN. I HATED CONFRONTAION, I HATED MAKING MISTAKES, I THINK I HATED MYSELF. I KNOW NO ONE IS PERFECT, BUT I STRIVED TO BE AS PERFECT FOR PEOPLE AS I COULD. I DON'T WANT TO BE A STUMBLING BLOCK FOR ANYONE CAUSING SOMETHING I DID OR SAY TO HURT ANOTHER AND CAUSE THEM TO FALL. I THINK I SMOTHERED OTHERS WITH KINDNESS AS I STRIVED TO REACH PERFECTION AND THAT ONLY PUSHED PEOPLE AWAY.

I THINK PEOPLE JUST WANT OTHERS TO BE THEMSELVES, NOT SOME PUPPETS PULLED BY STRINGS OR A ROBOT CONTROLLED BY A REMOTE. I BECAME A PEOPLE PLEASER, IT WAS SO EXTREME THAT IF I ENTERED SOMEWHERE AND SOMETHING

229

UNRELATED HAPPENED I WOULD BLAME MYSELF FOR IT HAPPENING CAUSE IF I HADN'T OF SHOWED UP THINGS WOULD HAVE BEEN BETTER. I'LL GIVE AN EXAMPLE AS TO HOW BAD I WAS DOWN ON MYSELF. A SALE RUNNING AT A STORE FOR THE LAST WEEK. THEY HAD A QUOTA THEY NEEDED TO MAKE AND SALES HAD BEEN OUTSTANDING ALL WEEK LONG TILL THE LAST DAY OF THE SALE AND I HAVING THE DAY OFF, DECIDE TO GO AND IT ENDS UP BEING THE WORST DAY FOR SALES AND THEY MISSED THEIR QUOTA. I WOULD ACTUALLY THINK IT WAS BECAUSE I SHOWED UP, THAT IF I WOULD HAVE JUST STAYED HOME THAT DAY THEY WOULD HAVE DONE AND MET THEIR GOAL.

I DIDN'T THINK ABOUT THE FACT IT HAD RAINED THAT DAY WHICH SOMETIMES HINDERS PEOPLE FROM GOING OUT OR THE FACT THAT MAYBE THEY HAD OTHER PLANS OR THAT THINGS WERE SO PICKED OVER NO ONE WAS INTERESTED IN WHAT WAS LEFT. BUT I ALWAYS BLAMED MYSELF, I WAS SO BOUND UP BY THE ENEMY IN NEGATIVITY I DIDN'T THINK I WOULD EVER BE ABLE TO BREAK FREE! I WAS IN A POOL OF QUICKSAND AND SINKING FAST. I COULDN'T PULL MYSELF OUT AND WHEN I CALLED FOR HELP IT WAS LIKE NO ONE WAS THERE. I FELT ABANDONED AND SO ALONE!

WHEN OUR CHURCH MOVED TO DAYTON, IT WAS HARD FOR ME TO MAKE THE DRIVE. I WAS WORKING ON SUNDAY MORNINGS DELIVERING PAPERS AND SERVICE STARTED THERE AT 10 AM, IT TOOK 45 MINUTES TO GET THERE SO I OFTEN COULDN'T GO. WE HAD LIFE GROUPS WHICH MET IN DIFFERENT CHURCH MEMBERS HOMES AND I LOOKED FORWARD TO GOING TO THOSE.

MAYBE IF I GOT MORE INVOLVED IN CHRISTIAN ACTIVITIES IT WOULD HELP ME HEAL AND BREAK THIS NEGATIVITY OFF MY LIFE. BUT ONCE AGAIN WHEN THINGS WOULD LOOK UP, SOMETHING CAME ALONG TO KNOCK YOU BACK. WE GOT THE CABLE BILL AGAIN AND THERE WAS ANOTHER X RATED MOVIE THAT APPEARED ON THERE, OBVIOUSLY ALL THE HELL WE WENT THRU THE LAST TIME AND THE POURING OUT OF MY HEART JUST WENT IN ONE EAR AND OUT THE OTHER.

I WAS OUTRAGED AND ASKED HIM IF HE EVEN LOVED ME AND CARED ABOUT WHAT HE WAS DOING TO ME OR US FOR THAT MATTER. HE SAID IT HAD NOTHING TO DO WITH ME, THEN WHAT WAS IT? I WAS A BEAUTIFUL WOMAN, NOT HEAVY, I TOOK PRIDE IN HOW I LOOKED AND YET HE WAS MASTURBATING TO NAKED WOMEN. HE WENT OUTSIDE THEN TO SMOKE, I COULDN'T BELIEVE HE WAS WALKING AWAY FROM ME, SO I FOLLOWED HIM OUTSIDE IN WHICH HE YELLED AT ME TO DROP IT, THEN LAID HIS CIGARETTE PACK ON THE RAILING WHICH WASN'T VERY STABLE. THE LADY DOWNSTAIRS HAD JUST COME HOME AND WAS UNLOCKING HER DOOR WHEN THE CIGARETTE PACK FELL OFF AND ALMOST HIT HER.

SHE CALLED THE POLICE AND REPORTED THAT WILLIE WAS ANGRY AND HAD THROWN HIS PACK AT HER AND THE FACT SHE WAS BLACK ACCUSED HIM OF BEING RACIST. SHE THEN CALLED THE LANDLADY AND TOLD HER ABOUT IT.THAT WAS IT FOR US, THE NEXT DAY THERE WAS A WRITTEN NOTICE ON OUR DOOR STATING WE HAD 5 DAYS TO VACATE THE PREMISES. SHE TOLD ME IF THE COPS WERE CALLED AGAIN WE

WOULD HAVE TO MOVE. THIS WASN'T MY FAULT, BUT SINCE SHE SAID SHE WOULD HOLD ME RESPONSIBLE, I WAS ONCE AGAIN BLAMES AND AT THE BLUNT END OF WILLIES ANGER ISSUES. EVERYONE ELSE WAS ALWAYS MADE TO BE RESPONSIBLE FOR WILLIE'S MISTAKES AND HE NEVER HAD TO DEAL WITH THEM, CAUSE SOMEONE ALWAYS CAME TO HIS RESCUE AND BAILED HIM OUT. I WAS REALIZING MYSELF THAT ANGER HAD BEGUN TO RULE ME AS WELL. MORE AND MORE I FOUND I HAD A SHORT FUSE, EASILYM UPSET OVER PETTY ISSUES, BUT I BELIEVED THEM TO BE OF IMPORTANCE. WHAT WAS WE GOING TO DO NOW? I HAD 5 DAYS TO FIND A PLACE TO LIVE. NEVER HAD I EVER IN MY LIFETIME BEEN EVICTED FROM A PLACE. I DEFINITELY WANTED OFF THIS MERRY GO ROUND RIDE.

2 DAYS WENT BY AND NOTHING, THEN MY MOM WAS TALKING ABOUT MY BROTHER AND IT DAWNED ON ME THAT MY SISTER IN LAW HAD A HALF DOUBLE IN PQUA AND ASKED MOM IF SHE HAD BOTH SIDES RENTED. MY MOM SAID THE ONE SIDE WAS EMPTY BUT IN NEED OF REPAIRS THAT MY SISTER IN LAW PUT ON HOLD FOR THE TIME BEING BUT THAT SHE THOUGHT THE OTHER SIDE JUST CAME OPEN, SO I CALLED MY SISTER IN LAW AND SURE ENOUGH SHE HAD AN OPENING AND SAID SHE'D LOVE TO RENT TO ME. PHEW!! THANK YOU LORD!! I WAS SO GRATEFUL. MOST PLACES WANTED RENTAL APPLICATIONS AND IT WASN'T VERY PROMISING THAT WE WOULD FIND A PLACE IN 3 DAYS TIME. WE WERE SO LUCKY SHE HADN'T RENTED IT YET, IT WAS A 3 BEDROOM AND HARD TO COME BY, I KNEW IT WAS GOD THAT KEPT THIS FOR US. SO HERE WE WENT MOVING AGAIN

AFTER ONLY 4 MONTHS, AND ONCE AGAIN I ALLOWED WILLIE TO COME. I KEPT PRAYING AND THINKING THAT WILLIE WOULD COME AROUND AND SEE THE WAYS GOD WAS MOVING IN OUR LIVES AND GET HIS LIFE ON TRACK. I WAS DEFINITELY TIRED OF MOVING AROUND, IT WAS HIGH TIME WE HAD SOME STABILITY IN OUR LIVES!

WE GOT MOVED AND SETTLED IN. IT WAS ALMOST OCT AND THE HOLIDAYS WOULD SOON BE HERE. THE NICE THING WAS I WAS PRETTY HANDY AT FIXING UP OUR POLACES WHERE WE LIVED AND THE OTHER SIDE OF THE HALF A DOUBLE HAD BEEN EMPTY FOR ALMOST 6 YEARS. SHE WAS WANTING TO GET IT FIXED UP AND HOPEFULLY RENTED BY THE FIRST OF THE YEAR, THEY HAD REAL BUSY SCHEDULES TO DO IT THEMSELVES AND MONEY WAS TIGHT SO IT WAS HARD TO HIRE THE HELP TO GET IT DONE, SO SHE ASKED MY MOM AND I IF WE WOULD HELP HER GET IT FIXED UP AND SHE WOULDN'T CHARGE US RENT FOR DOING IT. I WAS ESTACTIC AND ONLY TOO EAGER TO HELP HER, AND WILLIE SEEMED EXCITED TO NOT PAY RENT AND WOULD DEFINITELY HELP US CATCH UP ON OTHER BILLS, ESPECIALLY THE FINAL BILLS FROM PREVIOUS PLACE, MAYBE EVEN PAY SOME OFF.

THE NEXT DAY WE GOT STARTED. THERE WAS SOME THINGS WE WOULDN'T BE ABLE TO DO LIKE REPLACING THE TUB AND SOME PLUMBING, BUT WE WAS ABLE TO ACCOMPLISH ALOT OF OTHER THING AND GOT IT DONE BY MID DECEMBER WHICH PLEASED HER SO MUCH. I JUST PRAYED WE WOULD STAY SETTLED THIS TIME, WILLIE HAD DONE WELL NOT DRINKING, AND BEEN THAT WAY SINCE BEING

233

RELEASED FROM JAIL AND PUT ON HOUSE ARREST. HE HAD TO CHECK IN ONCE A WEEK FOR SCREENING AND SEE HOW HE WAS DEALING WITH THINGS. MAYBE THIS IS WHAT CAUSE HIS ANGER ISSUES TO RE-SURFACE, NOT BEING ABLE TO DRINK, BUT I PRAYED THAT HE WOULD FIND COMFORT IN PEACE SOMEHOW. WE GOT THRU THE HOLIDAYS AND IT WAS REALLY NICE. WE LAUGHED AND HAD FUN AND I COULDN'T HELP BUT MUTTER AND THANK YOU TO GOD FOR HELPING US THRU. WILLIE HAD GOTTEN ME A DOG, WELL, IT WAS FOR ALL OF US AND THAT SEEMED TO HELP BRING A CALM TO HIS LIFE. HER NAME WAS SCOOT AND WAS A TERRIER/PUG MIX. AND SHE WAS ALOT OF FUN TO HAVE AND SOON TOOK TO WILLIE ALTHOUGH WAS GOTTEN FOR ME.WHEN WE HAD PUT OUR HOUSE UP FOR SALE AND MOVED TO THE APARTMENT WE WASN'T ALLOWED TO HAVE PETS, SO WE HAD TO FIND THEM HOMES. THAT WAS HARD CAUSE WE CAME TO LOVE THEM VERY MUCH AND WAS A HUGE PART OF OUR FAMILY. SO IT WAS NICE HAVING A PET AROUND AGAIN.

THE NEW YEAR CAME AND WENT WITHOUT INCIDENT AND I WAS FINALLY STARTING TO RELAX. MY SON WAS THE ONLY ONE LEFT AT HOME AND THE 2 GIRLS CAME EVERY OTHER WEEKEND, SO WE HAD ALOT OF TIME TO WORK ON US. WE BOTH WORKED FOR THE NEWSPAPER AND DID OUR ROUTES TOGETHER. THEN A COUPLE ROUTES CAME OPEN FOR DAYTON DAILY NEWS SO WE TOOK ROUTES THRU THEM. HE HAD ONE AND I HAD ONE WHICH WE DELIVERED AT 2;30 AM, WOULD COME HOME GO BACK TO BED THEN UP FOR OUR AFTERNOON ROUTE FOR TROY DAILY NEWS. IT WAS WORK, AND WE WAS OFTEN TIRED BUT IT MADE FOR A NICE INCOME, AND WAS

FINALLY MAKING A DENT IN THE MOUNTAIN OF DEBT WE HAD. SINCE WE HAD TO CANCEL THE BANRUPCTY CAUSE HE LOST HIS JOB, MOST OF THE BILLS WAS RE-INSTATED SO WE WAS NECK HIGH IN DEBT. OUR SLEEP HABITS CHANGED TOO, GOING TO BED AT ABOUT 9 PM AND UP AT 2 AM, HOME BY 5 AM TO 6 AM DEPENDING ON THE DAY OF THE WEEK AND WHETHER THE TRUCK WAS LATE OR NOT, THEN TAKE A NAP ONLY TO HAVE TO LEAVE TO DO OUR OTHER ROUTES IN THE AFTERNOON. THANKFULLY JASON WAS THE ONLY ONE LEFT AT HOME AND HE WAS A SENIOR IN HIGH SCHOOL, SO DEFINITELY ABLE TO TAKE CARE OF HIMSELF. IT WAS DEFINITELY AN ADJUSTMENT PERIOD.

SOON IT WAS CHRISTMAS 2006, THE TIPS WAS VERY NICE THIS YEAR AND MADE FOR AN AWESOME CHRISTMAS FOR THE FAMILY. WE EVEN GOT INVOLVED WITH ANGEL TREE THIS YEAR WHICH BOUGHT GIFTS FOR THOSE IN NEED, THAT WAS ONE THING THAT WILLIE AND I ALWAYS AGREED ON WAS SPREADING JOY AND HAVING PEACE FOR THE HOLIDAYS NO MATTER WHAT. THE KIDS WAS OVERJOYED, WILLIE WAS RELEASED OFF HOUSE ARREST, HIM AND THE GIRLS WAS WORKING ON THEIR RELATIONSHIP, MY DAUGHTER WAS PREGNANT AND EXPECTING IN APRIL 2007. AS I REFLECTED BACK ON THE LAST YEAR, THE HURTS AND THE STRUGGLES YET SEEING US ALL TOGETHER AT THIS TIME AND NO TENSION, AND HOW WILLIE AND I REMAINED TOGETHER. IT WAS DEFINITELY THE BEST CHRISTMAS WE'D HAD IN A LONG WHILE. WE WAS THANKFUL OUR HOUSE HAD SOLD AVOIDING A FORECLOSURE. THAT WAS ONE LESS NEGATIVE THING TO APPEAR ON OUR CREDIT REPORT. WE WERE BLESSED AND I THANKED GOD FOR CARRYING US

THRU AND PRAYED 2007 WOULD BE A BETTER AND PROSPEROUS YEAR FOR US.

FINALLY THE NEW YEAR WAS UPON US, BUT IT WAS MET WITH THE REPOSSESSION OF BOTH OF OUR CARS. WE TRIED TO CATCH UP ON WHAT WE COULD BUT THEY WANTED TOO MUCH MONEY AND DIDN'T WANT TO WORK WITH US. OUR CREDIT WAS IN THE TOILET AND WITH THE HOUSE SOLD, THERE WAS NO CHANCE OF REFINANCING TO GET OUT FROM UNDER THE CREDITORS. HIS COURT FINES WAS THRU THE ROOF AND HAD TO MAKE REGULAR PAYMENTS ON THAT OR HE COULD HAVE WENT BACK TO JAIL FOR NON PAYMENT. ATTORNEY FEES WERE CRAZY TOO. THEN WILL STARTED TO NOTICE HIS OLDER DAUGHTER HAVING SOME REBELLOUS TENDENCIES AGAIN. SHE OFTEN FOUGHT WITH HIM ABOUT COMING OVER, WOULD YELL AND SCREAM AT HIM AND I JUST COULDN'T UNDERSTAND WHAT HAD GOTTEN INTO HER. MUCH OF IT IS STILL A BLUR TO ME, BUT AS I SIT AND TYPE THE SCENES FROM MY LIFE, I REMEMBER HOW I ONCE LOVED ROLLERCOASTERS.

I LOVED THE RIDES THAT WENT ROUND AND ROUND OR SPUN YOU IN CIRCLES GIVING YOU PLEASURE, YET SOMEHOW AS MY LIFE AT TIMES SEEMED TO SPIN OUT OF CONTROL, IT CREATED SADNESS, ANXIETY, HURT, PAIN, ALL KINDS OF EMOTIONS. WHEN WOULD THE PEACE COME? YES WE ALL FACE THINGS AND LIFE HAPPENS, BUT TO ME IT COULD GIVE US TIME TO GET THRU ALL WE'D BEEN THRU AND HAVE A TIME WHERE IT WAS CALM AND PEACEFUL. I THINK THOUGH MAYBE IT WAS OUR ATTITUDES ON HOW WE PERCEIVED THESE LIFE MIS-

HAPS THAT WAS THE KEY, KNOWING THAT LIFE WILL NEVER BE PERFECT, PEOPLE WILL NEVER BE PERFECT, BUT GOD BEING PERFECT COULD HELP US STRIVE FOR THAT PEACE IN THE MIDST OF THE STORMS LIFE BRINGS. I WAS DEFINITELY READY TO GET OFF THIS ROLLERCOASTER I WAS ON. I WAS TIRED OF THE TWISTS AND TURNS, TIRED OF SPINNING AROUND AND WAS READY FOR SMOOTH SAILING.SOMETIMES I FELT MYSELF SCREAMING INSIDE, YET NO NOISE WOULD COME OUT AS IF IN A DEEP HOLE, COVERED UP, NO WAY OUT, NO ONE TO HEAR ME OR AROUND TO PULL ME OUT. I KNOW GOD WAS WITH ME, HE NEVER LEAVES US OR FORSAKES US, BUT SOMETIMES WE DISTANCE OURSELVES FROM HIM AND GET SO CAUGHT UP IN OUR CRAP THAT WE LOSE SIGHT OF HIM.

HIS DAUGHTER EVENTUALLY STOPPED COMING OVER, THIS REALLY BOTHERED WILLIE, ALTHOUGH HE DIDN'T COME RIGHT OUT AND SAY THAT, HE WOULD DROP HINTS. HE TRIED TO HIDE HIS HURT THRU ANGER OUTBURSTS, LIKE IT DON'T BOTHER ME, SHE WANTS TO ACT LIKE THAT IT'S HER PROBLEM, I DON'T CARE ONE BIT. HE WOULD SAY SHE WAS A BRAT AND BEING BRAIN WASHED. HE ENDED UP SPENDING MORE TIME WITH THE YOUNGEST GIRL, BUYING HER THINGS, TAKING HER PLACES AND I WONDERED IF IT WASN'T JUST A PLOY TO MAKE THE OLDER GIRL JEALOUS. BUT HEY! WHO WAS I TO JUDGE? I DIDN'T AGREE WITH HIS BEHAVIOR BUT I WASN'T ABOUT TO MAKE WAVES OVER IT. I COULDN'T HELP BUT WONDER IF HE SOMEHOW THOUGHT I WAS TO BLAME FOR THE DISTANCE THAT WAS BETWEEN HIM AND HIS OLDEST GIRL, AS HE HAD BEGUN HIS ANGRY OUTBURSTS TOWARDS ME ONCE AGAIN. IT WAS HARD TO KNOW WHAT WAS IN HIS

HEART THAT WAS BEING COVERED UP WITH ANGER, HE WASN'T ONE WHO REALLY SHARED ALL HIS DEEP FEELINGS. HE KEPT THINGS BOTTLED UP, BUILT WALLS AND I BELIEVE HE THOUGHT THAT BY OPENING UP AND SHARING HIS TRUE FEELINGS SOMEHOW MADE HIM WEAK AND VULNERABLE.

IN PHIL 2:4, SCRIPTURE SAYS TO LOOK OUT NOT FOR YOUR OWN INTERESTS BUT THE INTERESTS OF OTHERS. I SUPPOSE I WAS LIVING BY THIS SCRIPTURE BY STAYING WITH HIM, AS I TRIED TO PUT MYSELF IN OTHERS SHOES AND IMAGINE HOW THEY FELT ABOUT THINGS, WHY THEY FELT IT AND WHAT CAN I DO TO HELP AND MAKE IT EASIER FOR THEM TO COPE, THINKING THAT IF I HAD THE ANSWERS, OR APPEARED AS IF I DID THEY WOULD LOVE ME AND SEE HOW VALUABLE AND IMPORTANT I WAS TO HAVE IN THEIR LIFE. YOU KNOW, DO UNTO OTHERS AS YOU WOULD HAVE THEM DO TO YOU. I LOVED HIM AND THE 2 GIRLS AND WANTED THE BEST FOR THEM. I FELT I HAD WENT OUT OF MY WAY NUMEROUS TIMES TO PROVE THIS TO THEM AND THAT THEY WERE ACCEPTED NO MATTER WHAT JUST AS CHRIST ACCEPTS US NO MATTER WHAT.

AFTER ALL WE ARE TO DO OUR BEST TO PORTRAY THE LOVE OF OUR FATHER IN HEAVEN RIGHT? BUT WILLIE ALWAYS SEEMED TO SEE IF AS CONTROLING HIM OR AS MANIPULATION AND I THINK HE HAD RESENTED ME FOR MANY THINGS, BUT YET WAS USING ME TOO, ALTHOUGH HE NEVER LED ON TO THAT FACT. THROUGH ALL THE TIMES I STAYED WAS ONLY FEEDING HIS ANGER, HIS CONTROL THAT HE FELT HE HAD LOST EVERYWHERE ELSE BUT BY ME AND HE WANTED TO HANG ON, AT WHATEVER COST, TO

MAKE HIM FEEL LIKE A MAN. BUT I WAS BLINDED BY THIS, WHAT OTHERS WERE SEEING I COULDN'T SEE. I LIED FOR HIM, TOOK THE FALL FOR HIM WHEN HE WOULD DRIVE WHILE HAVING A SUSPENDED LICENSE AND THE COP BEING FAR BEHIND WOULD SWITCH SEATS AS IF I WAS DRIVING AND I WOULD GET THE TICKET SO HE WOULDN'T GET IN TROUBLE FOR DRIVING UNDER SUSPENSION. OTHERS STARTED TO CRITICIZE ME AND TELL ME I SHOULD LEAVE AND WHY WAS I PUTTING UP WITH IT, YET I WANTED THE CONTROL OVER MY OWN LIFE AND CLOSED MY MIND AND MY EYES TO THE RIDICULE. MY FAMILY QUIT COMING AROUND SO OFTEN HOPING THAT ONE DAY I WOULD WAKE UP AND SEE HIM FOR WHO HE TRULY WAS WHICH WAS AN ANGRY, BITTER AND RESENTFUL MAN THAT BROUGHT ROTTENNESS YOUR BONES. WHEN THEY DID COME, YOU COULD SENSE THE TENSION BETWEEN THEN AND ALMOST CUT IT WITH A KNIFE IT WAS SO THICK. MAYBE HE FELT ASHAMED FOR THE WAY HE WAS AND WOULD OFTEN STAY IN THE BEDROOM AND NOT EVEN ASSOCIATE WITH THEM. WHEN I WAS ASKED WHAT HIS ISSUE WAS I'D MAKE EXCUSES FOR HIM AND TRIED TO MAKE THE BEST OF IT.

IT WAS REALLY EATING AT ME AND WAS SO AWKWARD TO DEAL WITH. WHY COULDN'T PEOPLE JUST GET ALONG? NO ONE EVER SEES EYE TO EYE ON EVERYTHING, IF WE WAS ALL ALIKE I THINK THIS WORLD WOULD BE BORING. WE WOULDN'T APPRECIATE EACH OTHERS UNIQUENESS, GIFTS AND TALENTS. AND BECAUSE THERE MAY BE CONFLICT OR FEELINGS OF SHAME FOR MISTAKES MADE DOESN'T

MEAN WE SHOULD BE HARD NOSED TOWARDS OTHERS AND UNWILLING TO WORK THRU OUR DIFFERENCES.

BECAUSE I'M A THINKER AND LIKE TO PROBLEM SOLVE, THERE'D BE MANY TIMES I'D HAVE AN IDEA ONLY FOR WILLIE TO SHOOT IT DOWN. THERE NEVER SEEMED TO BE A COMPROMISE ON ANYTHING AND IF BY CHANCE THERE WOULD BE A COMPROMISE AND PUT IT INTO MOTION, IT WOULD BE CHANGED BY HIM AFTER A COUPLE WEEKS OR SO. SOME THINGS TAKE TIME TO IMPLEMENT. I HAD HEARD BEFORE THAT IT TAKES 21 DAYS DOING SOMETHING CONSISTENTLY BEFORE IT BECOMES A HABIT. I BELIEVE THIS TO BE TRUE IN MANY AREAS, CONSISTENCY BEING THE KEY FACTOR, HOWEVER WILLIE COULDN'T BE CONSISTENT WHERE IT MATTERED MOST. I'M NOT A MIND READER OF ANY KIND BUT I GOT THE IDEA THAT THE REASON WILLIE CHANGED THINGS ALL THE TIME WAS AS IF HE WAS SOMEHOW LOSING CONTROL AND DIDN'T LIKE THE IDEA OF A WOMAN'S IDEA ACTUALLY WORKING AND IT ANGERED HIM THAT HE DIDN'T THINK OF IT HIMSELF. BUT THIS WASN'T MEANT TO BE A POWER STRUGGLE. IT WASN'T SOME KIND OF CONTEST TO SEE WHO WAS BETTER THAN THE OTHER OR WHOSE IDEA WAS GREATER. IT SHOULD HAVE BEEN 2 PEOPLE, EACH HAVING THEIR OWN SET OF KIDS BRINGING EACH OF THEIR IDEAS TO THE TABLE AND FINDING A PIECE OF EACH ONES IDEA AND FORMING RULES THAT WOULD WORK FOR ALL AND BE CONSISTANT WITH IT.

THE BIBLE EXPLAINS IN EPHESIANS 5:22-33 THAT THE MAN IS THE HEAD OF THE HOUSE AND ARE SUPPOSE TO LOVE THEIR WIVES AS CHRIST LOVED THE CHURCH AND GAVE HIMSELF FOR IT, THEREBY

THE WIFE IS TO BE SUBMISSIVE TO THE MAN, LOVE AND HONOR HIM. I DON'T BELIEVE WILLIE LOVED ME ENOUGH IN THIS MANNER, AND ALTHOUGH I TRIED BEING SUBMISSIVE ON MY OWN, I CERTAINLY DIDN'T WANT TO HONOR HIM FREELY BUT FELT I HAD TO HONOR HIM IF I DIDN'T WANT TO REAP THE REPERCUSSIONS THAT WOULD FOLLOW IF I DIDN'T. MANY TIMES HE WOULD SAY PEOPLE WERE DECEITFUL AND GOING BEHIND HIS BACK TRYING TO CHANGE THINGS AND WOULD PACE BACK AND FORTH LIKE A CAGED ANIMAL BEING LOCKED UP JUST LOOKING FOR A WAY TO GET OUT AND ATTACK, HE WAS OUT OF CONTROL AND I JUST KNUCKLED UNDER TO KEEP THE PEACE. WHEN I WOULD TRY TO REASSURE HIM THAT NO ONE WAS MANIPULATING HIM, HE'D CALL US A LIAR AND TELL US TO SHUT UP. NOTHING LIKE FEELING BETWEEN A ROCK AND A HARD PLACE AND COMPLETELY WORTHLESS. HE WOULD COMPLAIN AGAIN ABOUT NO MONEY, AND I WOULD TELL HIM THEN SIT DOWN WITH ME WHEHN I DO THE BILLS AND YOU WILL SEE FIRST HAND WHAT WE ARE DEALING WITH, YET HE SAID NO, YOU DEAL WITH IT, THEN WHEN I DID AND TRIED TO DO THE BEST I COULD, HE DIDN'T LIKE THAT EITHER. IT WAS LIKE WALKING ON EGG SHELLS, WAS HE EVER HAPPY? I HAD BECOME RESENTFUL AND ANGRY. I FOUND MYSELF IN A DEEP WELL AND THE WALLS HAD NO GAPS IN THEM TO GAIN ANY KIND OF FOOT HOLD SO I COULD START CLIMBING OUT. IT WAS DARK AND I WAS ALONE AND FELT LOST AND HOPELESS.

WILLIE HAVING LOSING HIS MOM TO BREAST CANCER HAD A HARD TIME COPING WITH HER DEATH AND NOW HAD BEEN HURT OVER THE FACT HIS OLDER

241

DAUGHTER WASN'T WANTING TO COME SEE HIM. IN THE MAIL ONE DAY HE RECEIVED A LETTER FROM HER. HE READ IT AND I COULD SEE THE PAIN IN HIS EYES WHEN HE FINISHED SO IT MUST NOT HAVE BEEN GOOD. HE SAID HE WANTED ME TO READ IT ALTHOUGH THE LETTER STATED SHE DIDN'T WANT ME TOO. I WONDERED WHAT I EVER DID TO HER THAT WARRANTED HER BEING COLD AND DISTANT TO ME. I WASN'T A MEAN PERSON NOR DID I HAVE A SELFISH BONE IN MY BODY BUT WOULD OFTEN DO WITHOUT TO HELP SOMEONE ELSE. THEN THE THOUGHT CAME TO MIND THAT MAYBE WILLIE WAS STARTING TROUBLE BY WANTING ME TO READ IT INSTEAD OF KEEPING IT TO HIMSELF.

WHAT WAS HIS MOTIVE? DID HE THINK IT WOULD BE REVENGE OR HIM SHIFTING ALL THE BLAME ONTO ME AND OFF HIMSELF? AS I READ THE LETTER, SOME THINGS WERE CONFIRMED FOR ME THAT I HAD FEARED FOR A LONG TIME. HE HAD BLAMED ME FOR THE DISTANCE BETWEEN HER AND HER FATHER, BUT NOT BECAUSE I WAS MEAN, IT WAS BECAUSE I HAD COME INTO THEIR LIVES. SHE WAS HAPPY WITH HAVING HIM TO HERSELF AFTER HE GAINED CUSTODY AND SHE NEVER LIKED ME FROM THE BEGINNING, MAYBE IN HER YOUNG MOND SHE HAD ALWAYS HOPED HER PARENTS WOULD GET BACK TOGETHER, BUT WITH ME IN THE PICTURE HAD RUINED THE CHANCES AND SHATTERED HER DREAM.

SHE THOUGHT I WAS CONTROLLING HIM AND MAKING HIM CHOOSE ME OVER HER, AND SAID SOME OTHER HORRIBLE THINGS ABOUT ME, WHICH WASN'T TRUE, BUT PEOPLE PERCEIVE THINGS DIFFERENT SO I

SAT DOWN TO WRITE HER A LETTER IN RESPONSE TO HERS. I DIDN'T KNOW IF IT WOULD EVEN HELP OR IF SHE WOULD EVEN READ IT FOR THAT MATTER, BUT FELT I NEEDED TO EXPLAIN MY VERSION TO THE SITUATION AS THERE ARE ALWAYS 2 SIDES TO EVERY STORY. I BELIEVED I DID THE BEST I COULD IN THE SITUATION I WAS IN AND TRULY HAD EVERYONE'S BEST INTEREST AT HEART. IF SHE DIDN'T LIKE ME, WHY CALL ME MOM? WHY WANT TO GO PLACES WITH ME TO GET AWAY FROM HER FATHERS DRINKING? I WASN'T PERFECT BY ANY MEANS. I MADE MANY MISTAKES, BUT I COULD ONLY STRIVE TO LEARN FROM THOSE MISTAKES AND MAKE THINGS BETTER NOT JUST FOR MYSELF BUT THOSE AROUND ME.

I DEBATED FOR A COUPLE DAYS OF WHETHER TO MAIL THE LETTER, BUT DECIDED TO TAKE IT TO POST OFFICE. I'M NOT EXACTLY SURE WHAT HAPPENED TO THE LETTER, WHTHER SHE READ IT HERSELF OR WHETHER HER MOM READ IT AND JUST TOLD HER THAT HER FATHER LET ME READ THE LETTER. IT'S HARD TO TELL WHETHER HER MOM EVEN TOLD HER THE CONTENTS OF THE LETTER. ALL I DO KNOW IS CALLED HER DAD AND TOLD HIM IS WASN'T RIGHT HE LET ME READ IT AS SHE THOUGHT IT WAS A PRIVATE MATTER BETWEEN HER AND HIM AND SHE WALKED OUT OF HIS LIFE. I DIDN'T KNOW WHAT TO THINK, WHETHER HE WAS TRYING TO HURT ME BY SHOWING IT TO ME OR IF HE WAS ACTUALLY WANTING ME TO HELP HIM DEAL WITH IT BY SHARING AS HUSBANDS AND WIVES SOMETIMES DO DURING HURTFUL TIMES. WILLIE WAS SO GOOD AT COVERING THINGS AND MANIPULATING THINGS TO CAUSE HIM TO COME OUT

SMELLING LIKE A ROSE IT HAD ME CONFUSED ON WHO HE WAS. IT WAS HARD NOT TO DOUBT HIS INTENTIONS.

LATER THAT YEAR, IT WAS PARTICULARLY ICY OUTSIDE, AND WHILE ON MY ROUTE, A CAR COMING AROUND THE CURVE, SLID AND HIT ME ALONG THE DRIVER SIDE OF CAR KNOCKING ME PARTIALLY IN A DITCH. I WAS HURT BUT NOT SERIOUSLY ENOUGH TO GO TO THE HOSPITAL, BUT MESSED UP MY CAR. ONCE THE SHERIFF GOT THERE AND WE EXCHANGED NAMES AND INSURANCE COMPANIES. WHEN I CALLED MY INSURANCE COMPANY TO MAKE A REPORT AND GIVE THEM THE OTHER GUYS INFO, I WAS PUT ON HOLD. AFTER ABOUT 15 MINUTES THE AGENT CAME BACK ON THE LINE AND I WAS TOLD THIS GUY LIVED AT THE SAME ADDRESS AS HIS PARENTS AND HIS INSURANCE HAD BEEN CANCELED 3 MONTHS PRIOR TO THE ACCIDENT. GREAT! JUST WHAT WE NEEDED. HOW WAS WE TO GET OUR CAR FIXED? SINCE WE OWED ON MY CAR WE HAD FULL COVERAGE INSURANCE SO THEY WOULD COME OUT AND ACCESS THE DAMAGE AND DETERMINED IF FIXABLE OR NOT AND SEE IF WE COULD GET A RENTAL CAR. THE NEXT DAY AN INSURANCE ADJUSTER CAME OUT AND DETERMINED MY CAR WAS TOTALED. ALTHOUGH DRIVABLE, THE COST OF REPAIR WOULD BE OVER THE VALUE OF CAR THEREFORE BEST TO TOTAL IT OUT. I WAS ALSO EXPERIENCING BACK PAIN AND STARTED SEEING A CHIROPRACTOR, SO THERE WOULD BE A POSSIBLE LAWSUIT AGAINST THE DRIVER. WHO KNEW HOW LONG THAT WOULD TAKE, BUT WE DID GET A RENTAL CAR FOR A WEEK, TILL WE FIGURED OUR NEXT MOVE, AS OUR JOB REQUIRES HAVING A CAR.

ALMOST A YEAR WENT BY AND WILLIE SEEN HIS OLDER DAUGHTER MAYBE 3 TIMES. I KNEW HE WAS HURT OVER IT, AND WHEN I TRIED TO TALK TO HIM AND COMFORT HIM, HE'D HAVE NO PART OF IT. HE HAD SUNK WITHIN HIMSELF SHUTTING THE DOOR WHEN IT CAME TO HER AND KEPT TO HIMSELF UNLESS HE FELT LIKE DEALING WITH ANYTHING AND KEPT BUSY, BUT ONE THING I WAS PROUD OF HIM FOR WAS HE HADN'T STARTED DRINKING AGAIN SINCE GOING TO JAIL IN 2006 AND I OFTEN TOLD HIM I WAS PROUD OF HIM, I GUESS HE JUST SHOOK IT OFF, CAUSE I DIDN'T GET AS MUCH AS A THANK YOU OR ANYTHING AND IT HURT DEEPLY BUT THE HOLIDAYS WAS HERE AND I KNEW IT WOULD BE DIFFICULT THIS YEAR. HE DIDN'T WANT STRIFE FOR THE HOLIDAYS WHICH I WAS GRATEFUL FOR. NO MATTER HOW BAD THE YEAR WAS, WE WERE DETERMINED TO MAKE THE HOLIDAYS A JOYFUL TIME AND THIS YEAR WOULD BE NO DIFFERENT JUST CAUSE PEOPLE HAD BURRS UP THEIR FANNY.

RIGHT BEFORE CHRISTMAS 2008 MY SON ERIC MARRIED JESSICA AND THEY WERE EXPECTING A BABY THE FOLLOWING MONTH. ERIC MET HER THRU WILLIE'S FRIENDS HE KNEW IN HIS YOUNGER YEARS AND GOT RE-AQUAINTED WITH IN 2002. THEY DATED OFF AND ON AND THEN LOST CONNECTION FOR A WHILE, UNTIL THE DEATH OF WILLIES MOM WHEN THEY SEEN EACH OTHER AGAIN AT THE FUNERAL. AT THAT TIME JESSICA WAS PREGNANT WITH HER FIRST CHILD FROM A PREVIOUS RELATIONSHIP AND DUE VERY SOON. HE WAS WITH HER THRU THE BIRTH AND ALTHOUGH HAVING SOME DIFFICULTIES IN THE RELATIONSHIP, DECIDED TO MARRY HER BEFORE THE BIRTH OF HIS FIRST CHILD BUT HER SECOND.

IT WAS NOW 2009 WHICH BROUGHT THE BIRTH OF MY 8TH GRAND CHILD, 4 BEING STEP BUT CONSIDERED THEM MY OWN AND MY FIRST GRANDDAUGHTER MADALYNN ON JAN 2ND JUST MISSING BEING A NEW YEARS BABY BY A FEW HOURS. I GOT TO BE IN THE DELIVERY ROOM AND WATCH HER BE BORN AND SHE CAME SO FAST. THE DOCTOR HAD BARELY GOTTEN PREPPED AND STOOD BEFORE JESSICA WHEN MADALYNN CAME AND SHE WAS SO PRECIOUS. WE DIDN'T GET ALOT OF TIME WITH THE GRANDKIDS AS ANGELA AND HER FAMILY LIVED IN GREENVILEE AND ERIC AND JESSICA LIVED IN COVINGTON AND I MISSED THEM GREATLY. 2009 ALSO BROUGHT US A NEW PRESIDNET. OBAMA WHO WON THE 2008 PRESIDENCY, HAD JUST TAKEN OFFICE. SOMETHING ABOUT HIM WHEN HE RAN FOR PRESIDENT THAT I DIDN'T LIKE. I ACTUALLY FELT IN MY SPIRIT HE WAS THE ANTI-CHRIST SO I DIDN'T VOTE FOR HIM.

A COUPLE MONTHS OR SO AFTER HE TOOK OFFICE, THE ECONOMY HAD STARTED ON A DECLINE. THE NEWS STATIONS WAS STATING THAT A PENDING RECESSION COULD HAPPEN IF THINGS DIDN'T TURN AROUND ECONOMICALLY. PEOPLE WERE LOSING JOBS RIGHT AND LEFT, GAS PRICES SKYROCKETING, THIS WAS THE WORST I HAD SEEN IT. MY DAUGHTER AND SON IN LAW WERE STRUGGLING AS WELL WITH THE JOB LOSSES THEY EXPERIENCED AND ENDED UP BEING EVICTED FROM THEIR HOUSE, JUST A MONTH AFTER THE BIRTH OF THIER SON SO THERE WAS NO WHERE TO GO BUT MOVE HOME WITH US. WILLIES YOUNGEST WAS ONLY THERE EVERY OTHER WEEKEND SO WE GAVE MY DAUGHTER AND FAMILY HER ROOM

246

AND BOUGHT WILLIES YOUNGEST AN AIR MATTRESS AND WOULD CAMP HER OUT IN THE LIVING ROOM WHEN SHE CAME OVER. IT WAS A TOUGH SITUATION FOR ALL, SOMETHING THAT WOULD TAKE SOME GETTING ADJUSTED TOO WITH ALL OF US IN THE SAME HOUSE, ONE BATHROOM, PHEW! THE FACT THAT WILLIE AND I HAD TO GET UP SO EARLY FOR WORK, WE HAD TO BE IN BED MY 9 PM. THE ROOM ANGELA AND HER FAMILY WOULD SHARE WAS ABOVE OURS AND PRAYED THEY SETTLED IN EARLY SO WE DIDN'T HEAR A BUNCH OF FOOTSTEPS TO KEEP US A WAKE OR WILLIE WOULD BE A BEAR TO DEAL WITH. OF COURSE THIS GAVE WILLIE A PERFECT PLACE OF THROWING HIS WEIGHT AROUND AS HE LAID DOWN SCHEDULES AND GUIDELINES, WHICH DIDN'T EXACTLY GO OVER WELL WITH MY SON IN LAW, BUT HE RESPECTED WILLIE'S RULES AS THEY WERE UNDER OUR ROOF. THE ONLY THING WE ASKED OF THEM WAS TO HELP WITH FOOD AND WHATEVER THE ELECTRICITY AND WATER WENT UP, THEN THEY COULD START SAVING FOR THEIR OWN PLACE AS THEY FOUND JOBS.

I REALLY ENJOYED MY GRANDBABIES AND WITH ANGELA LIVING THERE, I GOT TO SPEND ALOT OF TIME WITH HER 3 BOYS AND WATCH THEM LEARN AND GROW AND ALSO LARRY'S 3 BOYS WHEN THEY CAME EVERY OTHER WEEKEND FOR VISITATION. I MISSED OUT ON ALOT WITH MY OWN KIDS GROWING UP WITH BEING ILL AND ALOT STUFF GOING ON AND IT HURT ME DEEPLY. I HAD BEEN A SMOKER FOR 10 YEARS, AND DIDN'T REALIZE THAT I WAS ALLERGIC TO CIGARETTE SMOKE AND I WAS CONSTANTLY SICK WITH ONE THING OR ANOTHER AND SPENT TIME SLEEPING WHEN NOT WORKING OR THERE WASN'T FIGHTING GOING ON.

SOMEHOW I LOOKED AT HAVING TIME WITH MY GRANDKIDS AND WATCHING THEM GROW HELPING TO REGAIN SOME OF WHAT I MISSED WITH MY OWN THREE.

IN MARCH 2009, ERIC CAME TO ME AND SAID THEY WERE STRUGGLING AND NOT SURE WHAT THEY WAS GOING TO DO. JESSICA HAD HER OWN APARTMENT WHEN SHE WAS SINGLE AND ONLY PAID 5.00 A MONTH FOR RENT AS IT BASED HER RENT ON HER INCOME. WHEN HER AND ERIC GOT MARRIED AND HE MOVED IN THEY GOT NOTICE IT WOULD RAISE HER RENT FROM 5.00 TO 595.00 A MONTH WITH 2 KIDS TO SUPPORT AND NOT RECEIVING CHILD SUPPORT FOR THE OLDER CHILD, THIS WOULD REALLY STRAP THEM, SO THEY WOULD HAVE TO FIND SOMETHING CHEAPER. WILLIE AND I HAD DISCUSSED THEM MOVING IN WITH US DUE TO THE RECESSION THAT NOW HIT, BUT KNEW OUR CURRENT PLACE WOULD NOT BE BIG ENOUGH TO HOLD EVERYONE, SO WE OURSELVES BEGAN TO SEARCH FOR A BIGGER PLACE THAT WOULD ACCOMODATE 116 PEOPLE COUNTING THE CHILDREN THAT WOULD COME EVERY OTHER WEEKEND.

IN APRIL 2009, WE FOUND A 4 BEDROOM RIGHT DOWN THE STREET FROM WHERE WE WERE CURRENTLY. AFTER GOINT THRU ALL THE CHECKS AND APPLICATION PROCESS WE WERE APPROVED. THE RENT WAS 200.00 A MONTH HIGHER BUT THAT WOULD BE SPLIT BETWEEN ANGELA AND ERIC ALONG WITH THE AGREEMENT OF HELP WITH ELEC, FOOD AND WATER. IT HAD 1 FULL BATH AND 1/2 BATH WHICH WAS GREAT. IT HAD A BASEMENT AND A FULL SIZED FENCED IN YARD, WITH A ONE CAR GARAGE AND THEY SAID WE

248

COULD KEEP OUR DOG SINCE SHE WAS SMALL WHICH WE WERE GLAD FOR. THE UTILITY ROOM HAD A CLOSET THAT WAS BIG ENOUGH FOR A SMALL DRESSER. THE ROOM ITSELF AFTER PUTTING A WAHSER AND DRYER IN THERE WAS BIG ENOUGH FOR A SINGLE BED WHICH WOULD BE PERFECT FOR JASON SINCE HE WAS BY HIMSELF, ALL WE HAD TO DO WAS BUY A SLIDING DOOR SO HE'D HAVE SOME PRIVACY.

FOR 2 WEEKS MY MOM AND I WENT AND PAINTED THE PLACE AND CLEANED IT UP. BYDOING SO THE LADLORD WORKED WITH US ON THE DEPOSIT WHICH WAS NICE BEING THAT WE HAD TO FIND A PLACE SORT OF QUICKLY AND DIDN'T HAVE MONEY TO COME UP WITH THAT FAST FOR A DEPOSIT. WILLIE OF COURSE STAYED AT THE OLD PLACE AND ONLY CAME DOWN ONCE OR TWICE TO SUPERVISE AS HE STATED AND SEE HOW WE WERE COMING. HE DID MANAGE TO PAINT ONE WALL IN THE SEVERAL ROOMS WE HAD TO DO THEN LEAVE, BUT AT LEAST HE DID HELP WITH SOMETHING. I FIGURED HE'S BE DOING MOST OF THE LIFTING ANYWAY, BUT AT LEAST IT WAS DOWN THE STREET AND WE DIDN'T HAVE FAR TO CARRY THINGS. THE PLACE WAS FINALLY FINISHED AND READY TO MOVE INTO. THE OLDER KIDS PICKED WHICH ROOMS THEY WANTED, WE SET UP A SPOT IN THE BASEMENT FOR WILLIES YOUNGEST DAUGHTER AND SHE HAD HER OWN PRIVACY TOO. MY YOUNGEST JASON HAD A FRIEND WHO WAS HOMELESS AT THE TIME SO WE HAD AN ENCLOSED BACK PORCH THAT WE SET UP FOR HIM AND A BACK ENTRANCE HE COULD COME AND GO FROM. SINCE IT WAS WARM OUTSIDE THERE WAS NO WORRIES ABOUT HEATING AND IT WOULD BE TEMPORARY ANYWAY TILL HE FIGURED OUT WHAT TO

DO. SO IN MAY OF 2009 THE 13 OF US WITH THERE BEING 17 EVERY OTHER WEEKEND HAD BEGUN OUR NEW JOURNEY AT 827 W HIGH ST. WHAT A HOUSE FULL. WE SOON SETTLED IN. WE HAD TO EAT IN SHIFTS TO ALLOW ROOM IN THE KITCHEN FOR EVERYONE. SOMETIMES THE ADULTS ATE IN THE LIVING ROOM OR IN THEIR BEDROOM. WE HAD OUR MOMENTS, BUT FOR THE MOST PART WE MANAGED QUITE WELL AND MADE IT WORK.

ONE MORNING WHEN WILLIE AND I HAD RETURNED FROM OUR ROUTES, WE WERE READING THE PAPER OVER BREAKFAST. SUDDENLY AN ARTICLE CAUGHT MY ATTENTION. IT READ HAVE YOUR ADULT CHILDREN MOVED BACK HOME? IF SO WE'D LIKE TO DO A STORY FOR AN UPCOMING EDITION OF THE DAYTON PAPER. I SAID SOMETHING TO WILLIE ABOUT IT AND ASKED IF IT WOULD BE OK TO DO IT AS IT SOUNDED LIKE FUN AND WOULD BE SOMETHING WE COULD TREASURE AS WE GOT OLDER. HE SAID IT WAS OK SO I EMAILED THE REPORTER WITH OUR STORY. HE EMAILED BACK A LITTLE WHILE LATER AND SAID THEY WERE AMAZED AND DEFINITELY INTERESTED IN INTERVIEWING US. I WAS SO EXCITED, YOU JUST NEVER KNOW WHAT OPPORTUNITIES MAY ARISE FROM SOMETHING LIKE THIS OR HOW SOMETHING THAT MAY SEEM TRIVIAL TO SOME, MAY ENCOURAGE THE LIFE OF SOMEONE ELSE. I NEVER DREAMED IT WOULD GO IN THE DIRECTION IT DID BUT WILL SHARE THAT A BIT LATER.

WE FELL ASLEEP FOR A WHILE AND WHEN I WOKE I TOLD THE OTHERS WHAT I HAD DONE AND THEY ARE SEEMED INTERESTED AND SAID IT WOULD

BE FUN TO DO. JUST THEN THE PHONE RANG AND IT WAS THE REPORTER CALLING TO SET UP A TIME TO COME OUT AND INTERVIEW US. WE CHECKED OUR SCHEDULES AND AGREED ON A TIME FOR FRIDAY EVENING WHEN WE'D ALL BE HOME TOGETHER AND WILLIE'S DAUGHTER WOULD BE THERE AS HE WANTED HER A PART OF THE INTERVIEW TOO ALTHOUGH SHE DIDN'T LIVE WITH US. I DIDN'T ARGUE WITH HIM AND WENT BACK TO SPEAKING WITH THE REPORTER TO LET HIM KNOW OF THE DAY AND TIME. AFTER I HUNG UP, WE ALL WERE REALLY EXCITED AND THAT WAS PRETTY MUCH OF THE CONVERSATION FOR THE NEXT COUPLE OF DAYS AS WE BUZZED AROUND DOING SOME THOROUGH CLEANING AND RE-ARRANGING WHILE TALKING ABOUT HOW WE MAY JUST MAKE IT BIG FROM THIS. AS THOUGHTS RACED THRU MY MIND AS TO MAYBE GOOD COMING FROM THIS I WAS SORT OF NERVOUS, YET THANKED GOD FOR AN OPPORTUNITY SUCH AS THIS. I PRAYED ATTITUDES WOULD BE IN CHECK AND EVERYONE IN A GOOD MOOD, NOT POINTING ANY FINGERS BUT EVERYONE KNEW WHO I MEANT.

FINALLY FRIDAY WAS HERE, WILLIE'S DAUGHTER HAD CAME OVER AND WE HAD EATEN EARLY AND GOT THE DISHES IN THE DISHWASHER. I WENT THRU MAKING SURE HOUSE WAS IN ORDER. I WAS VERY PICKY ABOUT HOW THE HOUSE LOOKED ESPECIALLY WHEN GUESTS CAME OVER AND FIRST IMPRESSIONS ARE EVERYTHING TO ME. THIS WAS A SPECIAL TIME AND I WANTED IT TO BE MEMORABLE FOR MYSELF AND THE OTHERS. WHEN THE DOORBELL RANG, I TOOK A DEEP BREATH TO TRY AND CALM MY NERVES THEN ANSWERED THE DOOR. IT WAS THE REPORTER AND WE

251

ALL GATHERED IN THE LIVING ROOM AS HE ASKED US SOME QUESTIONS AND TOOK SOME PICTURES. IT WAS THE HIGHLIGHT OF MY WEEK AND I COULDN'T WAIT TO SEE OUR ARTICLE IN THE DAYTON PAPER. AFTER THE REPORTER LEFT, WE TALKED ABOUT HOW WELL IT WENT AND AGAIN MENTIONED WHAT POSSIBILITIES MAY ARISE FROM THIS ARTICLE. YOU HEAR OF THE CELEBRITIES WITH THE BIG BROODS, SOME EVEN HAVING THEIR OWN TV SHOWS AND WE GREW EVEN MORE EXCITED THINKING THIS COULD BENEFIT US IN MANY WAYS. WE CAN DREAM RIGHT? OF COURSE WE CAN CAUSE NOTHING IS IMPOSSIBLE WITH GOD!

THAT SUNDAY WHEN WE WENT INTO PICK UP OUR PAPERS, WE WERE MET BY PEOPLE WHO CALLED US CELEBRITIES AND WE WERE IN THE BIG TIME NOW. I FIGURED OUR ARTICLE WAS IN THE PAPER BUT NEVER IMAGINE OUR PICTURE WOULD MAKE THE FRONT PAGE!! I COULDN'T BELIEVE IT, WOW, THE FRONT PAGE, I WAS STOKED. I COULD HARDLY MAKE IT THRU MY ROUTE, AND I HAD TO HAVE THANKED GOD A HUNDRED TIMES. WHEN WE GOT HOME I SHOWED IT TO MY KIDS AND THEY WERE JUST AMAZED! WE FELT LIKE BUMBLE BEES WITH ALL THE BUZZ GOING ON.

THE NEXT DAY I GOT A CALL FROM THE REPORTER SAYING A LADY HAD CALLED IN THERE CONCERNING OUR ARTICLE AND ASKED IF THEY COULD GET MY NUMBER AS THEY HAD A TV THEY WANTED TO GIVE TO US. HOW AMAZING THAT PEOPLE WANTED TO BRING THINGS TO US AND WONDERED WHAT OTHER DOORS MAY SOON OPEN AS A RESULT OF A SIMPLE RESPONSE TO AN ARTICLE IN THE PAPER. BAM! WHAT HAPPENED A WEEK LATER THOUGH WAS

THE ICING ON THE CAKE. I NEVER DREAMED IT COULD HAPPEN TO US ALTHOUGH WE OFTEN TALKED ABOUT IT IN A JOKING MATTER. WE GOT A CALL FROM A REPORTER FOR PEOPLE MAGAZINE! YES, YOU READ THAT RIGHT. PEOPLE MAGAZINE WAS INTERESTED IN DOING A STORY ON US! I ALMOST FAINTED AND RAN TO TELL THE OTHERS. AT SOME POINT IN PEOPLE'S LIVES I THINK THEY'D LIKE TO BE A PART OF SOMETHING GREAT LIKE THIS, WITH THE POSSIBILITY OF LANDING A TV SHOW, OR MAYBE DOING A COMMERCIAL AND EARNING GOOD MONEY.

I PINCHED MYSELF TO MAKE SURE THIS WAS REAL AND I WASN'T JUST DREAMING. WHAT AN AMAZING OPPORTUNITY FOR MY FAMILY! OH THANK YOU LORD! WE COULD POSSIBLY RECEIVE ROYALTIES THAT COULD HELP US GET OUT OF DEBT, BUY ANOTHER HOUSE AND HELP MY FAMILY. WAS IT WISHFUL THINKING THOUGH? I MEAN I WAS A WOMAN OF GREAT FAITH AND BELIEVED NOTHING IS IMPOSSIBLE FOR THOSE THAT BELIEVE. I MARVELED AT THE GOODNESS OF GOD. TEARS BEGAN TO FLOW AT HIS GOODNESS AND ALL THE TIME, NO MATTER WHAT WE WENT THRU AS A FAMILY OR INDIVIDUALLY HE WAS RIGHT THERE IN THE MIDST OF US. I ASKED HIM TO LET HIS WILL BE DONE IN US AND NOT ALLOW ANYTHING TO STAND IN OUR WAY OF WHAT HE HAD FOR US, MAINLY WILLIE'S MOOD SWINGS.

WELL THE NEXT COUPLE OF WEEKS WAS BUSIER THAN A CAT ON A HOT TIN ROOF COVERING UP IT'S DOO DOO. THERE WAS A PROCESS THAT WE HAD TO GO THRU IN ORDER TO SCHEDULE THE TIME FOR THE INTERVIEW AND PICTURES. WE HAD TO GIVE THE

NUMBER OF PEOPLE IN THE HOUSE ALONG WITH EVERYONE'S NAME, AGE, HOW MANY WERE ADULTS, HOW MANY WERE CHILDREN AND FOR THE CHILDREN THE PARENTS HAS TO SIGN A RELEASE FORM FOR PERMISSION TO PUBLISH THE CHILDREN'S PHOTO. THEY WANTED US TO TAKE SOME SAMPLE PICS OF THE INSIDE OF THE HOUSE AS TO LIVING ARRANGEMENTS, WITH RANDOM PICS OF US IN OUR DAILY ROUTINE JUST TO GET A GENERAL IDEA OF THE LAYOUT OF OUR HOUSE AND HOW TO DO THE STORY. NOW, IT'S ONE THING TO RANDOMLY TAKE SOMEONE'S PIC WITHOUT THEM BEING AWARE, BUT TO KNOW YOU HAVE TO DO SOMETHING FOR A PIC TO BE TAKEN WAS NERVE RACKING. HOW COULD ONE BE NATURAL? I WAS HAVING THE TIME OF MY LIFE THOUGH, IT WAS SO MUCH FUN AND THE LAUGHTER IN TRYING TO GET PICS JUST MELTED MY HEART. I PRAYED THAT THE PAST WOULD BE BURIED AND BRIGHTER DAYS WOULD BE IN STORE FOR US, DAYS FILLED WITH LOTS OF FUN AND LAUGHTER.

WE GOT OUR PAPERWORK FINISHED AND TURNED IN BY THE 2 WEEK DEADLINE. THEY HAD TO GO THRU IT AND GET EVERYTHING FINALIZED THEN CALLED WITH A DATE. IT WAS SET FOR AUGUST 2, 2009 WHICH WAS IN JUST 2 WEEKS. THE CREW FROM PEOPLE'S MAGAZINE WOULD COME TO OUR HOUSE AND SET UP, BRINGING A MAKE UP CREW AND OUTFITS FOR US TO WEAR. THEY WOULD DO ONE FINAL ASSESSMENT OF WHERE THEY WANTED TO POSITION EVERYONE AND WE WOULD RECEIVE 5 COMPLIMENTARY COPIES OF THE MAGAZINE TO KEEP. WHAT AN AWESOME TIME IT WAS FOR US, AND SOMETHING WE WOULD BE ABLE TO TREASURE FOR

YEARS TO COME EVEN IF NOTHING ELSE EVER CAME OF IT. I THOUGHT OVER THE LAST COUPLE OF MONTHS SINCE DOING THE INITIAL ARTICLE FOR THE DAYTON PAPER AND NOTICED HOW HAPPY I HAD BEEN. FOR JUST A LITTLE WHILE I SEEM TO FORGET THE HEARTACHE I HAD EXPERIENCE MY WHOLE LIFE. I TRULY BELIEVED AT THAT MOMENT THINGS WERE GOING TO GET BETTER FOR US THIS TIME AROUND. FINALLY!

AT LAST THE BIG DAY ARRIVED! AUG 2, 2009 HAD COME. THEY WERE DUE TO ARRIVE AT 3 PM THAT DAY AND THERE WAS MUCH I NEEDED TO DO TO GET READY. WE WERE ALL SO NERVOUS, BUT MANAGED TO GET THE YARD WORK DOWN AND THE HOUSE IN ORDER. WE HAD LAID THE KIDS DOWN FOR A NAP AFTER AN EARLY LUNCH HOPING THEY WOULD SLEEP AN HOUR AS THE MAKEUP CREW AND THE DESIGNER WAS COMING FROM NEW YORK AND DUE TO ARRIVE AT 1:00 SINCE THERE WAS 12 OF US TO WORK ON FOR THE SHOOT AT 3. WE DIDN'T WANT THE KIDS TO BE CRANKY. I STILL COULDN'T BELIEVE THIS WAS HAPPENING AND HAD TO PINCH MYSELF SEVERAL TIMES TO MAKE SURE I WASN'T DREAMING, I MEAN I COULD HAVE BEEN SLEEPWALKING WITH MY EYES OPEN FOR ALL I KNEW. I MEAN PEOPLE MAGAZINE!! COMING TO MY HOUSE!! IN OUR LITTLE TOWN OF PIQUA, OHIO!! WHAT AN HONOR IT WAS.

THE MAKEUP ARTIST ARRIVED FIRST AND SHE WAS WONDERFUL. VERY PROFESSIONAL AND SO PATIENT, BUT I IMAGINE SHE HAD TO BE AS SHE DID THIS FOR A LIVING EVERYDAY. SHE BROUGHT TONS OF STUFF WITH HER, STYLERS, FLAT IRONS, SPRAYS AND

MORE MAKE-UP THAN A CONVENIECE STORE. WELL, MAYBE NOT THAT EXTREME BUT IT WAS QUITE ALOT IN MY EYES. AS I SAT DOWN TO HAVE MY MAKEOVER, I NOTICED THE NEIGHBOR'S PEERING OUT THEIR WINDOWS, SOME HAD BEEN WALKING DOWN THE STREE AND SLOWED THEIR PACE, WONDERING WHAT WAS GOING ON. JUST WAIT TILL THE CAMERA CREWS ARRIVED, THERE WOULD DEFINITELY BE A BUZZ IN THE NEIGHBORHOOD, BUT THIS WASN'T MR ROGERS HOUSE.

I WAS FEELING A LITTLE AWKWARD, OR MAYBE OVERWHELMED IS A MORE PROPER WORD NOT TO JUST HAVE PEOPLE WATCHING US, BUT TO HAVE SOMEONE ELSE DOING MY MAKE-UP. I CAN'T DESCRIBE INTO WORDS EXACT;LY HOW I WAS FEELING AT THAT MOMENT, BUT I KNEW IT WAS LIKE A QUEEN AND I DIDN'T WANT IT TO END AS I HAD NEVER FELT SO SPECIAL. TO BE PAMPERED AND CARED ABOUT FOR EVEN THE HALF HOUR SHE SPENT ON MY MAKE-UP AND HAIR BROUGHT TEARS TO MY EYES THAT I HAD TO TRY AND FIGHT BACK SO MY MAKE-UP WOULDN'T RUN. SHE MUST HAVE SEEN, OR AT LEAST SENSED IT BECAUSE SHE BEGAN TO SHARE STORIES OF PEOPLE SHE HAD WORKED ON IN THE PAST. IT WAS DEFINITELY AN AWESOME EXPERIENCE AND GLAD MY FAMILY WAS THERE TO SHARE IN IT TOO. GOD TRULY BLESSED ME AND CARES ABOUT HOW WE FEEL AND IT AMAZES ME HOW THINGS COME ABOUT IF ONLY THERE FOR JUST A SEASON. GOD HAS BROUGHT SO MUCH JOY TO MY LIFE, THAT EVEN IN MY DARKEST DAYS, HE SHOWED THAT FLICKER OF LIGHT ALTHOUGH A TEENY FLICKER THAT GUIDED ME AND HELPED ME TO HOLD ON, SO MANY TIMES I JUST WANTED TO DIE. I WAS SO TIRED

OF THE ABUSE, FEELING AS THOUGHT MY LIFE WAS WORTHLESS AND I DIDN'T MATTER. BUT THIS DAY, AUGUST 2, 2009, I MATTERED AND I WAS GOING TO BE IN A WORLD-WIDE MAGAZINE!!

BY 2:45 WE WERE ALL READY AND WAITING THE ARRIVAL OF THE CAMERA CREW. THEY HAD CALLED TO REPORT THEIR FLIGHT WAS DELAYED AND TRYING TO GET A RENTAL AND WOULD BE HERE SOON. THE KIDS WERE STARTING TO GROW IMPATIENT,AS NONE OF THEM TOOK A NAP, WHICH MADE THE ADULTS A LITTLE ANTSY AND I MUTTERED A PRAYER THAT EVERYONE WOULD HANG IN THERE AND THE KIDS WOULD NOT BE CRANKY AND WORK WITH THE CAMERA CREW, I DIDN'T WANT THIS DAY TO BE RUINED, ALTHOUGH THE ENEMY TRIED OVER AND OVER TO CONVINCE ME THIS WAS A MISTAKE. IT WOULDN'T MATTER IF I'D STRUCK OIL BECOMING A RICH WOMAN, MY FAMILY WOULD JUST STEAL MY JOY. HE WHISPERED THAT THEY'D FIND SOME WAY TO RUIN THINGS AS THEY'D HAD IN THE PAST, WHY SHOULD THIS BE ANY DIFFERENT, JUST THROW IN THE TOWEL NOW WHILE I HAD THE CHANCE, BUT I FOUGHT IT OFF AND SAID NO WAY!! IT WAS LIKE SOMETHING ROSE UP INSIDE OF ME AND WAS DETERMINED THAT NOTHING WAS GOING TO RUIN THIS DAY!!

THE PHOTOGRAPHERS FINALLY ARRIVED, SET UP THE CAMERA'S AND WE WERE ROLLING! IN OUR HOUSE WE HAD AN UPSTAIRS AND THEY WANTED TO TAKE OUR PICS PEERING OUT THE WINDOWS. ANGELA WITH ONE OF THE BOYS WAS IN ONE WIDOW AND LARRY WITH THE OTHER BOY WAS IN THE OTHER UPSTAIRS WINDOW WITH THE SCREENS UP. JESSICA AND ERIC

ALONG WITH THEIR 2 WAS ON THE FRONT PORCH AND WILLIE AND I ALONG WAS IN A DOWNSTAIRS WINDOW AND JASON AND ANGELA'S SON SCOTT WAS IN THE OTHER DOWNSTAIRS WINDOW. THE KIDS WERE A TAD CRANKY BUT HELD UP WELL. THEY TOOK A FAMILY PICTURE WITH ALL OF US ON THE STAIRS, AND THEN ONE FINAL ONE OUTSIDE ALONG THE BANISTER, PACKED UP AND LEFT AFTER TELLING US THE ARTICLE WOULD APPEAR IN THE SEPTEMBER ISSUE OF PEOPLES MAGAZINE. IT MADE FOR ONE FANTASTIC DAY AND I WAS SO PROUD OF MY FAMILY, ESPECIALLY MY GRANDBABIES FOR HANGING IN THERE LIKE THE TROOPERS THEY WERE.

FOR THE NEXT WEEK WE WERE FLOODED BY CALLS FROM PEOPLE EXPRESSING INTEREST IN OUR STORY. THE ONE CALL IN PARTICULIAR I WAS SUPER STOKED ABOUT WAS THE OPPORTUNITY TO APPEAR ON THE ELLEN DEGENERATE SHOW, THE DISCOVERY CHANNEL, AND A PRODUCTION COMPANY FROM CALIFORNIA WAS INTERESTED IN A DOING A SHOW! THEN A COMPANY IN FLORIDA CONTACTED US WANTING TO DO A PLAQUE FOR US AND WANTED TO SEND INFORMATION ON IT AND THE COST. I THOUGHT IT WAS A NEAT IDEA AND SOMETHING WE COULD HANG IN OUR HOME TO TREASURE FOR A LONG TIME! I WAS IN AWE, I MEAN BACK WHEN WE FIRST DID THE ARTICLE WITH THE DAYTON PAPER I REMEMBER US HAVING MANY CONVERSATIONS TO WHAT THE POSSIBILITIES COULD PRODUCE AS A RESULT AND NOW HERE WE WERE, DOORS OF OPPORTUNITIES WERE BEING OPENED RIGHT BEFORE US. I WAS SO HUMBLED AND GAVE THANKS TO GOD FOR ALLOWING ME THIS TIME OF PLEASURE AND GOOD FORTUNE. MANY PEOPLE

THOUGHT THIS FAMILY? REALLY? IT WON'T LAST, BUT I JUST SHRUGGED IT OFF. I KNOW THERE ARE THOSE WHO BECOME JEALOUS OF ANOTHERS SUCCESS AND WITH IT BRINGS THOSE NEGATIVE PEOPLE INTO THE OPEN WHO HAVE NOTHING BETTER TO DO THAN BRING OTHERS DOWN CAUSE THEY AREN'T HAPPY WITH THEIR LIVES. BUT I BELIEVED OUR BREAK HAD COME AND IT WAS ONLY GOOD THINGS FOR MY FAMILY NOW! THE SKY WAS THE LIMIT TO THE THINGS GOD HAD FOR MY FAMILY.

HAVE YOU EVER HEARD THE PHRASE ALL GOOD THINGS COME TO AN END? WELL OURS CAME TO AN ABRUPT HALT THE NEXT WEEK WHEN WILLIE UNDER THE INFLUENCE OF DRUGS, BECAME ANGRY AT ME FOR HAVING A CAMERA BELONGING TO HIS YOUNGEST DAUGHTER, AND STARTED CURSING ME AND THREATENING MY LIFE. I DIDN'T TAKE IT AS HE ACCUSED ME OF, SHE LEFT IT AT THE PAPER PLANT AND I DIDN'T WANT IT TO GET STOLEN, SO I PICKED IT UP. WHEN I DID I ACCIDENTLY BUMPED THE ON/OFF BUTTON AND IT CAME ON. WHEN I WENT TO SHUT IT OFF MY EYE CAUGHT SITE OF A PIC SHE HAD TAKEN OF HERSELF. I COULDN'T BELIEVE WHAT I HAD SEEN, SHE HAD BEEN TAKING SOME SEDUCTIVE LOOKING PICS OF HERSELF WHILE AT THE PLANT DOING OUR PAPERS AND SOME WAS OF HERSELF STRADDLING A LIGHT POLE AS IF SHE WAS A POLE DANCER. WHEN I GOT HOME FROM MY ROUTE, I GAVE THE CAMERA TO WILLIE AND ASKED HIM TO TAKE A LOOK AT WHAT WAS ON THERE AND HE BECAME ANGRY, TELLING ME I WAS INVADING HER PRIVACY. HE LOOKED AT THE PICS AND SEEN NOTHING WRONG WITH WHAT SHE TOOK. I THOUGHT REALLY? IT ONLY CONFIRMED MY SUSPICION

259

THAT HE STILL HAD A FETISH WITH PORNOGRAPHY. I DIDN'T UNDERSTAND WHY HE WAS SO ANGRY, BUT I KNOW I WAS AFRAID TO GO TO SLEEP. I HAD TO TAKE A NAP AS IT WAS SUNDAY MORNING AND I HAD TO BE UP TO GET READY FOR CHURCH IN A COUPLE HOURS.

HE GOT UP AND LEFT THE ROOM AND I SEEN HIM FLIP ON THE TV IN THE LIVING ROOM. I THOUGHT GOOD, HE WOULD LEAVE THINGS ALONE AND I COULD GET A NAP IN. I MUST HAVE DOZED OFF BECAUSE I WAS SUDDENLY AWAKENED BY LOUD MUSIC. I LOOKED AT THE CLOCK AND I WAS ONLY ASLEEP MAYBE 15 MINUTES. I TRIED TO GO BACK TO SLEEP BUT COULDN'T AS HE WAS BANGING AROUND IN THE KITCHEN AS HE MADE HIMSELF BREAKFAST. HE OFTEN GOT LIKE THAT WHEN HE WAS ANGRY AND I THOUGHT OH BOY HERE WE GO. I DIDN'T WANT TO SAY ANYTHING BUT I WAS SO TIRED SO AFTER ANOTHER HALF HOUR WENT BY AND THE MUSIC WAS STILL BLARING, I WENT TO SAY SOMETHING. HE JUST IGNORED ME AND WENT ABOUT COOKING HIS BREAKFAST AS IF I WASN'T EVEN THERE. I WENT OVER AND TURNED IT DOWN AND THEN WENT BACK TO THE BEDROOM AND LAID DOWN. I DOZED BACK OFF AND BOOM, HE TURNED IT BACK UP. I WENT BACK OUT AND WENT TO TURN IT DOWN WHEN HE GRABBED ME FROM BEHIND AND STARTED SHOVING ME AROUND THE KITCHEN.

I GOT MY BEARINGS AND GRABBED THE BOOM BOX AND WENT TO RUN WHEN HE GRABBED ME AGAIN AND THREW ME INTO THE DEEP FREEZE. I DROPPED THE BOOM BOX AND LEANED OVER THE TABLE IN PAIN WHEN HE CAME UP BEHIND ME AND PICKED ME UP AND STARTED SQUEEZING ME. JUST AS HE WENT TO

THROW ME ACROSS THE ROOM MY SON CAME INTO THE KITCHEN WONDERING WHAT ALL THE RUCKUS WAS ABOUT. APPARENTLY WILLIE THOUGHT EVERYONE WAS STILL ASLEEP BUT HOW COULD THEY BE WITH AS LOUD AS HE HAD THE MUSIC BLARING. I TOLD MY SON TO CALL THE POLICE AND AS I BROKE FREE WENT TO THE BEDROOM AND LOCKED THE DOOR BEHIND ME. I BREATHED A SIGH OF RELIEF AS THIS WAS THE FIRST TIME ANYONE HAD WITNESSED THE THINGS WILLIE DONE TO ME. WILLIE CAME AND TRIED TO GET IN THE ROOM, BEATING ON THE DOOR WITH ALL HIS MIGHT, BUT TO NO AVAIL, SO HE DECIDED TO GO AFTER MY SON AND THREATENED TO TAKE HIM OUTSIDE AND WHOOP ON HIM.

JUST THEN THE DOORBELL RANG, I WASN'T SURE WHO IT WAS BUT AFTER A FEW MINUTES THERE WAS A KNOCK ON MY BEDROOM DOOR. I WAS SCARED TO OPEN THE DOOR, I DIDN'T KNOW IF IT WAS A PRANK BY WILLIE OR NOT. YOU NEVER KNOW WHAT HE WOULD BE UP TOO WHEN UNDER THE INFLUENCE AND HE COULD HAVE VERY WELL RANG THE BELL AS A PRANK TO GET ME TO OPEN THE DOOR AND ATTACK ME. JUST THEN I HEARD A FEMALE VOICE IDENTIFYING HERSELF AS A POLICE OFFICER, SO I OPENED THE DOOR SLOWLY AND PEERED OUT. SEEING THAT THERE WAS 2 OFFICERS THERE, I OPENED THE DOOR, SHAKING LIKE A LEAF AND WAS ASKED WHAT HAD HAPPENED. I EXPLAINED WHAT HAPPENED AND ASKED TO WRITE A STATEMENT WHILE THEY WENT TO DIFFERENT AREAS TO TALK TO WILLIE AND MY SON WHO WAS A WITNESS TO HIM HAVING ME IN A BEAR HUG AND GET THEIR STATEMENTS AS WELL.

AFTER COLLECTING THE STATEMENTS AND READING THEM OVER, TALKING AMONGST EACH OTHER, THEY DECIDED TO ARREST WILLIE FOR DOMESTIC VIOLENCE. WHEN THEY PUT THE CUFFS ON HIM HE SNARLED AT ME AND SAID I HOPE YOU ARE HAPPY, YOU KNOW I'M GOING TO JAIL RIGHT? THE FEMAIL OFFICER LOOKED AT HIM AND TOLD HIM TO KEEP QUIET AND NOT TALK TO ME, AND THEY LED HIM OUT THE DOOR INTO THE COP CAR AND OFF THEY WENT.

I WILL STILL SHAKEN UP, SO I CALLED MY PASTORS FOR PRAYER. I WAS ON THE WORSHIP TEAM AND DIDN'T WANT ANYTHING TO HINDER GOD'S SPIRIT FROM MOVING IN SERVICE, AND I DIDN'T WANT TO MISS. I LOVE SINGING AND WORSHIPPING THE LORD. MUSIC IS MY PASSION AS WELL AS BEING A BLESSING TO OTHERS, SO I MANAGED TO PULL MYSELF TOGETHER, GOT READY AND LEFT FOR CHURCH. IT WAS A GOOD SERVICE, ONE I SO NEEDED AND FELT THE PRESENCE OF GOD SO STRONG THAT MORNING. AFTER CHURCH WAS OVER AND I GOT HOME, I WAS MET WITH WILLIE'S YOUNGEST DAUGHTER WHO HAD LEFT THE HOUSE AFTER OUR ARGUMENT AND APPARENTLY STAYED WITH A FRIEND.

I TOLD HER WHAT HAD HAPPENED AND WAS TAKEN BY SURPRISE WHEN SHE GAVE ME A HUG. USUALLY THE GIRLS WERE ON HIS SIDE, BELIEVING THINGS WERE MY FAULT, BUT MAYBE THAT'S WHAT HE WANTED ME TO THINK SO HE WOULDN'T LET ON HE WAS LOSING CONTROL. SHE CALLED HER MOM AND HAD HER COME TO HELP PACK UP HER THINGS WE HAD GOTTEN HER FOR HER ROOM AND I WAS CHOKED UP

WITH EMOTION. HERE WE WAS AGAIN PACKING UP THEIR BELONGINGS, BUT THIS TIME I MAY NEVER SEE THEM AGAIN AS I HAD DECIDED THIS TIME TO HAVING NOTHING MORE TO DO WITH WILLIE. I WAS DONE NOW AFTER 12 YEARS, AND BELIEVED THIS WAS THE WAKE UP CALL I NEEDED ONCE AND FOR ALL. I WAS SCARED FOR MY LIFE, BUT ALL THOSE TIMES BEFORE NOTHING EVER SEEM TO STICK AS THERE WEREN'T ANY WITNESSES, BUT THIS TIME I HAD ONE AND OUR STATEMENTS ALMOST MATCHED TO THE T AND WE WERE IN SEPARATE ROOMS. I HAD FINALLY BROKEN FREE AND I'M SURE HE WOULD GET SENTENCED TO SOME JAIL TIME!

THE NEXT WEEK I WAS CONTACTED BY A COUNSELOR FROM THE ABUSE CENTER, WHO TOLD ME SHE WAS ASSIGNED AS MY COACH. WILLIE WOULD GO ON TRIAL DUE TO THE NATURE OF THE CHARGES THE OFFICERS GAVE HIM AND THERE COULD BE A JURY PANEL INVOLVED. I WAS SO THANKFUL TO HAVE MY PASTORS AND MY FAMILY THERE FOR SUPPORT AND PRAYER AS WELL AS I DIDN'T KNOW WHAT EXACTLY TO EXPECT. THE COUNSELOR ALSO TOLD ME THAT I WOULD BE ABLE TO GET AN ATTORNEY THAT WOULD BE PAID FOR THRU THE CENTER BY GRANTS THEY RECEIVED.

SHE ALSO TOLD ME I SHOULD BE ELIGIBLE FOR LEGAL AID IF I WANTED TO PURSUE THE FILING OF A DIVORCE, AND THEY WOULD BASE THE COST ON MY INCOME, AND IF MY INCOME WAS LOW ENOUGH IT COULD BE FREE. I ALREADY KNEW I WANTED AWAY FROM HIM, I SHOULD HAVE DONE IT LONG AGO AND I WAS GRATEFUL FOR PROGRAMS OUT THERE THAT

WOULD HELP ME DO JUST THAT. IT WAS A HUGE STEP FOR ME AND GOING TO BE HARD TO MAKE IT ON MY OWN, BUT I WAS THANKFUL TO HAVE MY KIDS WITH ME TO HELP WITH THE BILLS TILL THINGS WAS FIGURED OUT. I BELIEVE THIS WAS GOD SETTING US UP AND PREPARING US FOR THIS MOMENT, ALTHOUGH WE WENT THRU HARDSHIPS TO GET TO THIS POINT, IT WAS GOING TO TURN OUT FOR GOOD IN THE END. GOD ALWAYS CARES FOR THE FINEST DETAILS OF OUR LIFE AND SOMETIMES THE LESSONS ARE HARD, SOME BY OUR OWN CHOICE, SOMETIMES NOT, BUT IF WE KEEP THE FAITH AND LOOK TO HIM, WE WILL GET THRU IT!

THAT FOLLOWING WEEK WE HAD A PRELIMINARY HEARING. THIS WAS WHERE I WAS TOLD WHAT MY OPTIONS WERE. SINCE HE WAS CHARGED WITH DOMESTIC VIOLENCE BEFORE WHILE WE LIVED IN GREENVILLE, HE COULD FACE UP TO 18 MONTHS IN PRISON, NOT JAIL, GET A FINE AND IT WOULD GO BEFORE A JURY TO DECIDE, BUT THEN AGAIN HE COULD GET A SLAP ON THE WRIST AND WALK TO IF THEY FEEL THERE ISN'T ENOUGH EVIDENCE. OR I COULD AGREE TO A LESSER CHARGE WHICH WOULD GIVE HIM AN AUTOMATIC 6 MONTHS IN JAIL, MANDATORY COUNSELING, AND A FINE OF 1000.00. I AGREE TO THE LESSER CHARGE SINCE IT WAS GUARANTEED, I DIDN'T WANT TO TAKE THE CHANCE OF HIM GETTING OFF AND COME AFTER ME. THEY ASSURED ME I COULD GET ANOTHER CIVIL PROTECTION ORDER WHICH WOULD KEEP HIM FROM BEING ALLOWED NEAR ME, BUT I WAS SCARED, SINCE WHEN DID HE EVER ABIDE BY ANYTHING. AND I DIDN'T WANT TO HAVE TO SIT THRU A TRIAL AND FACE HIM. AFTER ABOUT 30 MINUTES OF THE ATTORNEY'S FOR

BOTH OF US MEETING WITH THE JUDGE DELIBERATING, IT WAS SETTLED.

HE WOULD SPEND THE NEXT 6 MONTHS IN JAIL AND I WAS AWARDED A TEMPORARY CIVIL PROTECTION ORDER (CPO) FOR 2 YEARS. I COULD GET UP TO 5 YEARS PROTECTION IF NEEDED WHICH PREVENTED HIM FROM CONTACTING ME, A FAMILY MEMBER OR MAILING LETTERS. WHEN IT WAS ALL OVER I BREATHED A HUGE SIGH OF RELIEF AS I LEFT THE COURTHOUSE, BUT YET WAS WORRIED ABOUT HOW I'D MAKE IT FINANCIALLY. IT'S AMAZING WHEN YOU THINK ABOUT IT HOW MUCH MONEY CAN BECOME A CRUTCH AND CAUSE YOU TO DO THINGS OR STAY IN A RELATIONSHIP THAT'S TOXIC JUST TO BE ABLE TO LIVE. BUT I KNEW THAT I SERVED A MIGHTY GOD WHO HAD CARRIED ME THUS FAR AND WOULD BE FAITHFUL TO BRING TO COMPLETION ALL THINGS HE HAS PURPOSED FOR MY LIFE!

THAT NIGHT WHEN MY KIDS GOT HOME FROM WORK, WE HAD A FAMILY MEETING. I TOLD THEM ABOUT THE COURT HEARING THAT DAY AND THAT FOR THE TIME BEING I REALLY NEEDED US TO PULL TOGETHER. AS WE WERE TALKING MY KIDS OPENED UP AND SHARED THINGS THEY HAD DEALT WITH FROM WILLIE, MOST OF IT HAPPENING WHEN I WAS AT WORK. I ASKED THEM WHY THEY NEVER TOLD ME AND THEY SAID THEY WERE THREATENED HARM IF THEY OPENED THEIR MOUTHS TO ME. THEY DIDN'T WANT TO CAUSE TROUBLE FOR ME, AND IN A SENSE THEY THOUGHT SINCE I STAYED WITH HIM, THEY DIDN'T THINK I WOULD CARE. I COULDN'T BELIEVE WHAT I WAS HEARING, THEY WERE BEING ABUSED THEMSELVES AND

THOUGHT I DIDN'T CARE ENOUGH FOR THEM TO DO ANYTHING ABOUT IT! I SAT THERE NUMB AND IN SHOCK AS THEY EACH TOOK THEIR TURN SHARING THEIR STORY WITH ME AND MY HEART SANK. TEARS FILLED MY EYES AND I CHOKED ON MY WORDS AS I APOLOGIZED TO EACH OF THEM. I TOLD THEM I LOVED THEM VERY MUCH, AND HAD I KNOWN ALL THEY WERE ENDURING, WOULDN'T HAVE SUBJECTED THEM TO THAT, I REALLY DIDN'T KNOW ALL THAT WAS HAPPENING. WOW, HOW COULD I NOT KNOW, WAS I BLIND OR DEAF?

I THANKED ALL MY KIDS FOR BEING THERE, NOT THAT I WANTED ANY OF THEM TO GO THRU THE STRUGGLES HEARTACHES THEY WENT THRU BEING ON THEIR OWN, BUT THE FACT THAT IF THOSE STRUGGLES DIDN'T COME BRINGING US TO THE PLACE WE WERE AT THAT POINT AND TIME, I COULD HAVE BEEN SERIOUSLY HURT THIS TIME. I REMEMBER LAYING IN BED THAT NIGHT WEEPING BEFORE GOD, PLAYING OVER AGAIN THE SCENES FROM MY LIFE, ESPECIALLY THE EVENTS OF THE LAST FEW WEEKS, THINKING HOW CRAZY THIS GUY WAS AND THANKING GOD FOR PROTECTING US, HOW SORRY I WAS THAT MY KIDS HAD SUFFERED TOO. I JUST DIDN'T KNOW HOW DEEP THIS WAS HURTING THEM, SEEMED TO BE CONCERNED JUST FOR ME.

I THOUGHT WHAT WILLIE DID AS FAR AS CORRECTING THEM WAS JUST A PART OF WHAT I WOULD CALL NORMAL DISCIPLINE MEASURES, NOT WHAT WAS HAPPENING BEHIND THE SCENES, DOING MY BEST TO BE A SUBMISSIVE WIFE AND BRINGING MY CHILDREN UP IN THE LOVE AND ADMONITION OF THE LORD. MAYBE THRU FEAR OF HIM I HAD BECOME

266

BRAINWASHED AS TO HIS TRUE NATURE, BUT I CAME TO THE REALIZATION AT THAT MOMENT IT WAS AN EVIL SPIRIT RIGHT FROM THE PITS OF HELL THAT HAD BEEN WORKING THRU HIM AND I DON'T THINK HE EVEN RECOGNIZED IT. AT LEAST NOW WE WERE HEADED IN THE RIGHT DIRECTION, KNOWING WE HAD A ROUGH ROAD AHEAD THAT WOULD BE A TOTAL WALK OF FAITH, BUT WE ARE MORE THAN A CONQUEROR THRU CHRIST, SO I KNOW THAT IF WE WERE BROUGHT TO THIS SITUATION, HE WOULD SEE US THRU IT AS WELL!! I WASN'T HAPPY TO HAVE ANOTHER FAILED MARRIAGE, BUT HAD I CONTINUED IN A MARRIAGE WITH WILLIE, THIS TIME I MAY HAVE DIED. I KNEW I HAD A TOUGH ROAD AHEAD, BUT TRUSTED THAT GOD WOULD BE WITH ME EVERY STEP OF THE WAY.

LATER THAT WEEK WE RECEIVED IN THE MAIL OUR COPIES OF THE PEOPLE MAGAZINE, IN IT WAS OUR ARTICLE, CALLED UNDER ONE ROOF, AND THEY DID AN AMAZING JOB PUTTING IT TOGETHER AND THE ARTICLE WAS NICE. ONE STATEMENT THEY PUT IN THERE WAS SOMETHING MY SON IN LAW SAID THAT I HAD FORGOTTEN ABOUT, AND THAT WAS THE JOKE THAT FOR CHRISTMAS THEY WAS GETTING ME A DOORMAT THAT SAID WELCOME TO THE JUNGLE. WE DEFINITELY HAD A HOUSE FULL FOR SURE, BUT WOULDN'T HAVE CHANGED A THING. LATER THAT DAY WE GOT A PACKAGE FROM UPS AND IT WAS OUR PLAQUE, IT WAS HUGE, A CHERRY WOOD AND THEY HAD OUR PIC INGRAVED IN THERE. WHAT A TREASURE TO HAVE, JUST HAD TO FIND A PLACE TO HANG IT. WHEN I WENT TO CHURCH THAT SUNDAY, MOST HAD PICKED UP A COPY OF THE MAGZINE AND AN ANNOUNCEMENT WAS MADE OF HAVING A CELEBRITY

IN THE HOUSE AND I WAS TOUCHED BY THEIR KIND WORDS.

THE NEXT MONTH WAS A LITTLE ROUGH TO GET THRU BEING WITHOUT WILLIE'S INCOME. I LEARNED AFTER GOING THRU THE BILLS THOROUGHLY, THAT I WAS LEFT WITH 11,280.00 OF DEBT. SINCE MY NAME WAS ON THE MAJORITY OF THE BILLS, I KNEW I'D HAVE TO PAY THEM MYSELF CAUSE HE SURE WOULDN'T DO ANYTHING TO HELP ME WITH THEM. THE OTHER WORKING MEMBERS OF THE HOUSE HAD TO REALLY PITCH IN TO HELP WITH THE RENT AND OTHER BILLS AND I PRAYED GOD WOULD HELP US. WE DECIDED TO HAVE A YARD SALE TO MAKE MONEY TO HELP PAY THINGS AS CHRISTMAS WAS A COUPLE MONTHS AWAY. WE SOLD SOME OF THE FURNITURE, AS MOST OF US STAYED IN OUR BEDROOMS ANYWAY AND WE HAD A SMALLER TABLE TO USE FOR THE KIDS, SO WE SOLD OUR BIG DINETTE AND WAS ABLE TO COVER THE RENT, WHICH WAS A BLESSING. I ALSO BEGAN PACKING UP WILLIES THINGS AND LOADING IT ALL IN HIS VAN WHICH WAS STORED BACK BEHIND THE GARAGE. WE MAINLY USED THE GARAGE FOR STORAGE, SO NOT MUCH ROOM TO HOLD A VEHICLE SO IT WAS LOCKED AND PARKED OUTSIDE. I HAD MANAGED TO PAY IT OFF USING UP HIS CREDIT LIMIT ON HIS CREDIT CARD SO HE'D AT LEAST HAVE TRANSPORTATION UPON RELEASE FROM JAIL. I JUST NEEDED TO FIND A PLACE TO PARK IT FOR HIM TO GET SINCE I HAD THE CPO AGAINST HIM AND HE WASN'T ALLOWED THERE. TO ADD TO THE HEARTACHE, WAS WHEN ALL CHANCES OF A TV INTERVIEW AND ANY SHOWS THAT MAY HAVE COME FROM OUR ADVENTURE WAS PUT TO AN END. WHEN THE PRODUCTION COMPANY HAD CALLED I HAD

TO BE HONEST WITH THEM OF THE SITUATION AND THEY WERE DISAPPOINTED.

ALTHOUGH IT MADE FOR GOOD DRAMA IN SOME CASES, IT WASN'T AT THIS POINT IN TIME WHAT THEY WANTED. SO. NO DOCUMENTARY, NO MODELING OPPORTUNITIES, NO INTERVIEWS, NO STORIES AND I CRIED. WHAT AN AWESOME CHANCE AT A BETTER LIFE, BUT IT WASN'T MEANT TO BE I GUESS. GOD OBVIOUSLY HAD BETTER PLANS FOR ME. WHAT I DID HAVE THAT NO ONE COULD TAKE AWAY WAS THE MEMORIES OF THE EXPERIENCE. I DON'T MEAN TO GO ON AND ON AND BE SO DRAB, BUT FOR SO LONG I WAITED FOR THINGS TO GET BETTER, KEEPING MY TRUE FEELINGS BOTTLED UP, NOT ALLOWING MYSELF TO RELEASE THEM TO KEEP FROM BEING A STUMBLING BLOCK FOR SOMEONE ELSE.

I HAD FELT LIKE A CAGED ANIMAL FOR SO LONG AND COULDN'T SEEM TO BREAK COMPLETELY FREE. NOW THAT I WAS FREE, I WAS SORT OF LOST. OUR PASTOR HAD BEGUN A NEW SERIES OF MESSAGES ON GETTING OUT OF OUR COMFORT ZONES. OUT OF THE BOX WE KEPT OURSELVES IN AND TAKING OFF THE FIG LEAVES, WE FOUND OURSELVES HIDING BEHIND. THESE MESSAGES WAS MY WAKE-UP CALL, AND AS I STARTED STUDYING GOD'S WORD, I BEGAN TO HEAL AND GROW AND GOD STARTED TO OPEN NEW DOORS FOR ME. IT'S IRONIC HOW WHEN YOU SEEM TO GROW IN THE THINGS OF GOD AND GET YOURSELF ON THE RIGHT TRACK, HOW THE ENEMY WILL TRY AND SNEAK IN THERE TO TIGHTEN THE APRON STRINGS SO YOU DON'T GET TOTALLY FREE. THERE ENDED UP BEING A BLOW-UP IN THE HOUSE BEWEEN MY DAUGHTER AND

DAUGHTER IN LAW, EVERYONE JUMPING IN AND GETTING ON EACH OTHER'S NERVES. MY DAUGHTER AND SON IN LAW ENDED UP MOVING OUT BECAUSE OF IT AND SAID SOME VERY HURTFUL THINGS TO ME. IT WAS DEFINITELY SOMETHING I SHOULDN'T HAVE HAD TO DEAL WITH ON TOP OF EVERYTHING ELSE ON MY PLATE. BUT I LEARNED I COULD NO LONGER CONTROL EVERY SITUATION. I HAD TO, FOR ONCE, TAKE CARE OF ME.

IT WAS NOW NOVEMBER 2009 AND THIS YEAR WINTER WAS APPROACHING FAST. WE USED TO SPLIT THE BILLS 3 WAYS WITH JASON HELPING WHEN HE COULD, BUT NOW IT WAS HALF AND HALF AND WITH CHRISTMAS AND THE HEAT BILLS KICKING IN WE DIDN'T KNOW WHAT WE'D BE IN STORE FOR. I WAS DETERMINED HOWEVER, THAT I WASN'T GOING TO LET IT GET ME DOWN, I HELD ONTO MY PROFESSION OF FAITH THE GOD WOULD PROVIDE AND HAD GREAT FRIENDS WHO WAS BEHIND ME AND ENCOURAGED ME. THAT WEEK I HAD GOTTEN A LETTER FROM LEGAL AID TELLING ME THAT THEY WOULD PAY FOR MY DIVORCE IN FULL. THAT WAS SUCH A RELIEF FOR ME. I MADE A VOW TO GOD THAT I WOULD NOW DEVOTE MY LIFE TO HIM, TO WRITING AND NOT MARRY AGAIN. I WAS DONE WITH MEN AND NEVER WANTED TO EXPERIENCE AGAIN WHAT I HAD BEEN THRU IN MY LIFE. DURING THIS TIME I DISCOVERED FACEBOOK. I WAS ABLE TO COME IN CONTACT WITH FAMILY MEMBERS I HADN'T SEEN OR EVEN TALK TO IN YEARS AND FOUND THAT MANY PEOPLE FROM MY CHURCH AND ONE'S I PREVIOUSLY ATTENDED ALSO HAD FACEBOOK PAGES, SO I WAS EXCITED AND LOOKED FORWARD TO INTERACTING WITH FRIENDS AND ALSO THOUGHT IT WOULD BE A

GREAT MINISTRY OPPORTUNITY TOO AS I COULD POST SCRIPTURE AND ENCOURAGING THOUGHTS FOR OTHERS.

SOON THANKSGIVING WAS HERE AND MY MOM HAD COME TO HELP PREPARE THE MEAL AS SHE HAD DONE IN YEARS PAST SINCE MY FATHER PASSED AWAY. I HAD TAKEN A BREAK AFTER GETTING THE TURKEY IN AND LOGGED INTO FACEBOOK. I HAD RECEIVED A COUPLE PRIVATE MESSAGES AND SOME POSTS ON MY FACEBOOK PAGE THAT REALLY TOUCHED AND UPLIFTED ME. I WAS SO THANKFUL FOR THIS NEW DISCOVERY OF MINE AND INSTEAD OF RUNNING IN FEAR, LOOKING FOR PLACES TO CRAWL UNDER AND HIDE, I WAS GAINING STRENGTH TO FACE THOSE FEARS HEAD ON AND IT HELPED ME BEAR THE THINGS I NEW I HAD TO FACE YET IN MY FUTURE. I WAS TAKING TIME FOR ME, SLOWING DOWN TO SMELL THE ROSES AND NOTICE THINGS. THE WAY WAS OPENING FOR ME, I WAS LEARNING SO MUCH AND LOOKING TO THE FUTURE WITH EXCITEMENT. EVEN WHEN I HAD TIMES OF DIFFICULTY AND NO ENERGY FOR ANYTHING, NOT EVEN TO GET INTO GOD'S WORD, I'D LOG INTO FACEBOOK AND WHAT I NEEDED FOR THAT PARTICULIAR MOMENT WAS RIGHT IN FRONT OF ME. GOD SEES ALL AND KNOWS ALL AND MEETS US RIGHT WHERE WE ARE AT THE MOMENT. WHAT AN AMAZING FATHER HE IS!

DECEMBER WAS NOW HERE, AND CHRISTMAS WOULD SOON BE HERE. IT WOULD BE A LITTLE SAD, ONLY CAUSE I KNEW IT WAS WILLIE'S FAVORITE TIME OF YEAR AND WE ALWAYS SEEMED TO HAVE THE BEST TIME TOGETHER. BUT I WOULD GET THRU IT AND MAKE

IT THE BEST WITH THE NEW ME. GOD BEGAN SPEAKING TO ME THRU FACEBOOK AND I GAINED MANY FRIENDS FROM ALL OVER THE STATES AND A FEW IN OTHER COUNTRIES AS WELL. NOT ONLY WAS I BEING MINISTERED TO BUT GOD USED ME TO RECIPROCATE LOVE AND EMCOURAGEMENT TO OTHERS TOO! YEE HAW! I READ MANY STORIES OF PEOPLE BEING HEALED, MANY BEING TOUCHED AND GIVEN DIRECTION TO WHAT THEY NEEDED TO DO. I PRAYED FOR PEOPLE AND 2 WERE INSTANTLY HEALED FROM THEIR AILMENTS. EVEN READ WHERE ONE GAVE THEIR LIFE TO CHRIST. HALLELUJAH! THEN I NOTICED A POST FROM A FRIEND OF MINE WHO I HAD WENT TO CHURCH WITH BUT HAD BEEN CALLED TO GEORGIA. SHE MENTIONED HEADING TO A PRAYER MEETING THAT NIGHT AT HER CHURCH. I WAS IN NEED OF PRAYER MYSELF AND KNEW SHE WAS A PRAYER WARRIOR SO I COMMENTED TO PLEASE LIFT ME UP IN PRAYER. THE NEXT DAY SHE SENT ME A MESSAGE AND WHEN I OPENED IT, SHE TOLD ME AS SHE WAS STANDING IN THE PRAYER LINE THE NIGHT BEFORE, HER PASTOR CALLED HER OUT.

HE TOLD HER SHE HAD A FRIEND IN OHIO WHO SHE WAS STANDING IN PRAYER FOR. HE WASN'T SURE OF ALL THE DETAILS OF WHAT THIS FRIEND IN OHIO WAS GOING THRU, BUT TO TELL HER IT'S TIME TO MOVE. HE GAVE HER THAT WORD FOR ME! I DIDN'T KNOW EXACTLY WHAT IT MEANT, BUT EXCITEMENT ROSE UP IN MY SPIRIT. MY LIFE WAS IN SUCH A TRANSITION RIGHT NOW IT COULD MEAN ANY NUMBER OF THINGS. I HAD BEEN CONTEMPLATING WRITING A BOOK THAT WOULD MINISTER TO OTHER WOMEN IN SIMILAR SITUATIONS AS MYSELF, HAD FELT THE CALL

TO MAYBE DO SOME TRAVELING TO MIINSTER TO OTHER WOMEN IN SOME SORT OF ABUSE SITUATION OR MAYBE HAD COME OUT OF AN ABUSE RELATIONSHIP AND HAD THOUGHT OF MOVING TO ANOTHER PLACE A LITTLE SMALLER FOR A FRESH START AND THAT WOULD BE A LITTLE CHEAPER THAN WHERE WE WERE. I KNEW ALL THESE THINGS WOULD TAKE MONEY, SOMETHING WE DIDN'T HAVE MUCH OF AS I STILL HAD ALOT OF DEBT.

IT WAS A WEEK BEFORE CHRISTMAS AND WE HADN'T DONE MUCH SHOPPING FOR GIFTS, I WAS GETTING A LITTLE PANICKY AND I WANTED THIS CHRISTMAS TO BE NICE AND ALTHOUGH THE REAL REASON FOR THE SEASON IS JESUS, IT IS ABOUT GIVING AND I GET SO EMOTIONAL AND FELL SO GOOD TO SEE THE SMILES ON THE FACE OF OTHERS WHEN THEY RECEIVE SOMETHING, AND BUT DON'T ALWAYS UNDERSTAND THE WHOLE CONCEPT OF WHAT CHRISTMAS TRULY MEANS, THEY JUST WANT PRESENTS. THANKFULLY SOME TIPS HAD STARTED COMING IN FROM MY ROUTES AND HADN'T GIVEN MUCH THOUGHT TO HOW MUCH WAS THERE, I HAD JUST STUCK IT ALL IN THE SAFE. WHEN I PULLED IT OUT AND COUNTED IT THERE WAS 800.00 THERE. I DIDN'T REALIZE I HAD GOTTEN SO MUCH, I HAD PANICKED FOR NOTHING AND MUTTERED AN I'M SORRY TO GOD FOR MY LACK OF FAITH HE WOULD CARRY ME THRU. I WAS DEFINITELY LOOKING FORWARD TO A STRESS FREE CHRISTMAS WITHOUT EVERYONE FEELING TENSE AND WALKING AROUND ON EGG SHELLS WONDERING IF WILLIE WAS GOING TO CRITICISE THEM OR SOMETHING WE DID. SOON CHRISTMAS DAY CAME AND WHAT AN EXCITING DAY IT WAS.

IT'S AMAZING HOW WHEN YOU THINK YOU CAN'T DO MUCH, GOD INTERVENES AND THE KIDS ALWAYS MAKE OUT LIKE BANDITS. THE SAD PART OF CHRISTMAS BEING OVER WAS YOU GET ALL HYPED UP FOR THE HOLIDAY AND WHEN IT'S OVER IT SORT OF BRINGS YOU DOWN SOME. IT'S LIKE BEING ON A HIGH AND WHEN YOU COME DOWN IT MAKES YOU FEEL KIND OF EMPTY. THE THRILLS AND WARM SENS OF BELONGING, YOU JUST DON'T WANT TO LET GO OF. I ALSO BELIEVE PEOPLE ARE MORE CARING AND SENTIMENTAL DURING THE CHRISTMAS SEASON, AT LEAST FROM WHAT I SEEN AND IT WAS HARD TO MOVE ON FROM THAT. ALTHOUGH THIS YEAR BROUGHT ABOUT HEARTACHE, MANY GREAT THINGS TOOK PLACE THAT FAR OUTWEIGHED THE ROUGH COUPLE MONTHS I WENT THRU WITH WILLIE'S GOING TO JAIL. I LOOKED FORWARD TO NEW BEGINNINGS IN THE NEW YEAR! 2010 ALL THINGS WOULD BE MADE NEW. I WAS ANTICIPATING ALL THAT GOD WOULD DO AND HAVE IN STORE FOR ME AND THE FAMILY!

AS I WAS PREPARING FOR THE LAST SERVICE OF 2009, MY MIND WAS FILLED WITH MANY THOUGHTS. WE WERE HAVING A GUEST SPEAKER AND I REALLY HIM. HE WAS GOING TO DELIVER A FRESH WORD FOR 2010 AND I WAS LOOKING FORWARD TO IT. HOW I NEEDED A FRESH WORD FROM GOD! I NEEDED DIRECTION AND I NEEDED CLARITY FOR WHAT 2010 WAS TO HOLD FOR ME. I WAS EXCITED TO BE STARTING THIS NEW YEAR ALTHOUGH ALONE AND NOT EXACTLY SURE WHERE THE ROAD WOULD LEAD AND I ADMIT I WAS SCARED TOO. I HAD NEVER REALLY BEEN ALONE FOR THIS LONG, BUT I WAS LOOKING FORWARD TO THIS NEW

JOURNEY WITH THE LORD AS A SINGLE WOMAN. GOD SAID IN HIS WORD THAT HE WOULD NEVER LEAVE US OR FORSAKE US AND THAT HE WHO BEGAN A NEW WORK WILL BE FAITHFUL TO BRING TO COMPLETION ALL THINGS AND IS A FRIEND WHO STICKS CLOSER THAN NAY BROTHER! THIS ALSO REMINDED ME OF THE FOOTPRINTS POEM, THAT DURING TIMES WHEN WE SAW ONLY ONE SET OF FOOTPRINTS IN THE SAND INSTEAD OF 2 IT WAS DURING THOSE TIMES THAT GOD WAS CARRYING US.

OUR PASTORS, BEING SOMEWHAT NEW TO MINISTRY, HAD A WONDERFUL FAMILY AS THEIR SPIRITUAL PARENTS SO TO SPEAK. THEY WERE AN AWESOME COUPLE THAT SPOKE FREQUENTLY AT OUR CHURCH AND WERE THERE TO ENCOURAGE OUR PASTORS AND WHO OUR PASTORS COULD BE ACCOUNTABLE TOO. I ALWAYS ENJOYED WHEN HE CAME TO SPEAK. THAT PARTICULIAR SUNDAY WHEN OUR GUEST SPEAKER SPOKE, HE DELIVERED A CHALLENGE TO THE CONGREGATION TO DIG DEEPER AND GO ABOVE AND BEYOND FOR 2010 THAN WHAT WE MAY HAVE DONE IN 2009. TO TRY GOD AND SEE IF HE WOULD NOT DO ALL HE SAID IN HIS WORD HE WOULD DO AND THAT WAS TO POUR OUT A BLESSING THAT WE WOULDN'T BE ABLE TO CONTAIN. OUR PASTOR THE WEEK BEFORE HAD PREACHED A MESSAGE THAT 2010 WOULD BE THE YEAR OF FRUITFULNESS AND OUR GUEST SPEAKER'S MESSAGE WENT RIGHT ALONG WITH OUR PASTORS AND CONFIRMED SOME THINGS. HE ASKED US TO GIVE SOMETHING EXTRA IN OUR OFFERING FOR 2010, WHETHER IT BE 5.00 A WEEK ABOVE OUR TITHE OR 10.00 A MONTH, TO BE IN PRAYER ABOUT IT. WELL I FELT IMPRESSED OF THE

LORD TO GIVE 15% OF MY INCOME AS A TITHE RATHER THAN 10% LIKE THE MENTIONED IN THE BIBLE. IMMEDIATELY I QUESTIONED IT THINKING IT WAS THE ENEMY SPEAKING.

IT'S IRONIC HOW WHEN GOD IS SPEAKING TO US HOW WE AUTOMATICALLY ASSUME IT'S THE ENEMY. I SUPPOSE IT'S DUE TO OUR CARNAL MINDS AND SINFUL NATURE. WE WANT THINGS EASY AND COMFORTABLE, WANT THIS CHEAP OR FOR NOTHING. CONVENIENCE IS WHAT COMES TO MIND. BUT IF YOU WANT THE BLESSING OF GOD IN YOUR LIFE, IT WILL INDEED COST YOU SOMETHING! EVEN SO, I STILL QUESTIONED GOD AND ASKED HIM HOW I WAS TO DO THIS, I WAS JUST A MERE PAPERGIRL AND WAS LEFT ALOT OF DEBT FROM THE DIVORCE, SURELY LORD I DIDN'T HEAR YOU RIGHT. THEN HE SPOKE AS CLEAR AS A BELL AND SAID TRY ME AND SEE IF I WON'T DO WHAT I SAID I WOULD DO, SO I FILLED OUT A PAPER AS INSTRUCTED STATING THAT THE FIRST SUNDAY OF JANUARY 2010 I WOULD GIVE 15% OF MY INCOME AS MY TITHE AND I DROPPED IT IN THE OFFERING BASKET! AS THE SAYING GOES, OBEDIENCE IS BETTER THAN SACRIFICE, AND I WAS TRUSTING THINGS WOULD LOOK UP.

THE NEXT SUNDAY ALTHOUGH STILL UNSURE OF THE PROMISE I MADE, I HONORED MY COMMITMENT I MADE TO GOD AND GAVE 15% OF MY INCOME. NOW, HOW MANY KNOW THAT WHEN YOU STEP OUT IN FAITH ON SOMETHING THE ENEMY IS RIGHT THERE TO TRY AND STEAL THE WORD AND TO TRY AND DESTROY AND WRECK HAVOC IN OUR LIVES. WE HAD GOTTEN A MONTH BEHIND IN THE RENT AND HAD TO TRY AND MOVE TO DOWNSIZE, HOPEFULLY FINDING A CHEAPER

PLACE AND JANUARY WAS DOWN ON INCOME AS CUSTOMERS HAD DROPPED THE PAPER INVOLVING MY YOUNGEST SONS AND MY INCOME AND MY OTHER SON'S JOB CUT HOURS. BUT I STILL TOOK THAT STEP OF FAITH AND HONORED MY COMMITMENT KNOWING THAT IF GOD BROUGHT YOU TO IT HE WOULD SEE YOU THRU IT.

THE NEXT WEEK WE FOUND A HOUSE THAT WAS 100.00 CHEAPER AND ALSO A 4 BEDROOM. WE PRAYED THAT IT WOULD BE CHEAPER TO HEAT THIS NEW PLACE TOO THAN WHAT THE OTHER HOUSE WAS. ALL OF US BUT ANGIE, AND HER HUSBAND AND KIDS MADE THE MOVE ALTHOUGH WE GOT ALOT OF SNOW THAT WEEK. WE GOT SETTLED BUT THEN HAD ALL THE FINAL BILLS FROM THE OTHER HOUSE AS WELL. IT WAS NOW FEB WHICH WAS ANOTHER SLOW MONTH FOR US, THEN WE WERE MET WITH CAR REPAIRS. I REMEMBER WHEN I WAS PRAYING ONE MORNING, I TOLD GOD THAT HE WOULDN'T PUT MORE ON US THAN WHAT WE COULD BEAR, BUT I'D HAD ENOUGH! THROUGH IT ALL I STILL REFUSED TO ALLOW THE ENEMY TO DISCOURAGE ME AND I STILL CONTINUED TO GIVE THE 15% EXPECTING BREAK THRU TO COME!

THE NEXT WEEK AT CHURCH I RECEIVED 2 WORDS, BOTH FROM DIFFERENT LADIES. ONE LADY SPOKE TO ME AND SAID THAT AS SHE'D BEEN PRAYING FOR ME, GOD TOLD HER TO TELL ME THAT HE'D SEEN MY TEARS AND CRIES FOR HELP AND WANTED TO ASSURE ME EVERYTHING WAS GONNA BE OK. THIS WAS A NEW JOURNEY THAT I'M BEGINNING AND IT WOULD TAKE ME PLACES I'VE NEVER BEEN AND SOMEONE WAS COMING INTO MY LIFE, TO HELP ME

FULFILL WHAT GOD HAD FOR ME! GOD COULD HAVE SPOKEN THIS TO ME HIMSELF, HE ALREADY PUT IN MY HEART TO WRITE A BOOK AND MINISTER TO THE LIVES OF OTHER WOMEN WHO EXPERIENCED ABUSE, EVEN CALLED APUBLISHING COMPANY TO FIND OUT WHAT THE COSTS WERE TO PUBLISH MY BOOK WHEN FINISHED AND WHAT THE REQUIREMENTS WERE FOR PUBLISHING. GOD ALSO HAD GIVEN ME A HEART FOR MISSIONS. HOWEVER SOMETIMES WE CAN HAVE DOUBTS AS TO WHAT GOD'S WILL IS FOR OUR LIFE AND HE WILL CONFIRM WHAT HE PUTS IN OUR SPIRIT THRU OTHERS TO BOOST OUR FAITH AND ENCOURAGE US. I BELIEVE THAT IS WHAT HE DID THRU THIS LADY, AND THE NEXT ONE THAT I WILL SHARE IN A MOMENT!

THE END OF FEB FIRST PART OF MARCH TIME FRAME ANOTHER LADY HAD COME TO ME WHILE AT CHURCH AND SPOKE A WORD TO ME. SHE SAID THAT GOD WANTED ME TO KNOW THAT A MAN WAS COMING INTO MY LIFE IN THE FUTURE THAT WAS A PART OF THE CALLING GOD HAD FOR MY LIFE, THAT WOULD INSPIRE ME AND SUPPORT ME IN MY ENDEAVOURS TO REACH OUT TO OTHERS. I THANKED HER FOR THE WORD AND ALTHOUGH EXCITEMENT WAS RISING IN MY SPIRIT, I THOUGHT LORD I DON'T WANT ANOTHER MAN. I DON'T WANT TO EVER EXPERIENCE THE KIND OF PAIN I HAD ENDURED EVER AGAIN. BUT I TOLD GOD THAT IF IT WAS HIS WILL, I WANTED TO BE OBEDIENT TO HIM AND WHAT HE HAD FOR MY LIFE OR WHEREVER HE WANTED ME TO GO.

2 WEEKS LATER AND I HAD RECEIVED A FRIEND REQUEST FROM A GENTLEMAN WHO LIVED IN NADI FIJI. HE WAS A PART OF A GROUP ON FACEBOOK. HIS

PROFILE STATED HE WAS A BORN AGAIN CHRISTIAN WHO WAS WIDOWED THE YEAR BEFORE AND HAD 5 CHILDREN. I ACCEPTED HIS FRIEND REQUEST THINKING IT WAS NEAT TO HAVE FRIENDS FROM ALL OVER THE WORLD. YOU NEVER KNOW WHERE GOD CAN USE YOU TO TOUCH THE LIFE OF SOMEONE ELSE. HE THANKED ME FOR ACCEPTING REQUEST THEREBY HAVING DISCUSSIONS ABOUT WRITING AND MINISTRY. I LEARNED ABOUT THE ISLAND OF FIJI AND THE CHURCH THEY WERE APART OF THERE, AND THEN HE MADE THIS STATEMENT THAT HIS PASTOR HAD PRAYED OVER HIM ONE SUNDAY MORNING. HIS PASTOR SAID THERE WAS A CATALYST COMING TO THE ISLAND OF FIJI THAT WAS CARRYING THE THINGS OF GOD FOR WHAT THEY NEEDED IN THIS SEASON. SUDDENLY WITHIN MY SPIRIT SOMETHING ROSE UP. THINGS WERE BEING CONFIRMED OF WHAT HAD BEEN SPOKEN OVER ME AND I ASKED GOD, LORD? ARE YOU CALLING ME AS A MISSIONARY AND I'M TO GO TO THE ISLAND OF FIJI? I FIGURED IF I WAS TO DO MISSIONS WORK IT WOULD BE HERE IN THE STATES. WE HAVE MANY DIFFERENT PROGRAMS AND AREAS NEEDING VOLUNTEERS.

IT WAS NOW APRIL 2010, AND FOR THE LAST MONTH I HAD BEEN RECEIVING TID-BITS OF THINGS THAT GOD WAS DIRECTING ME TO DO. I HAD VIDEO CONTACT WITH THE FAMILY IN FIJI AND HAD MANY DISCUSSIONS ABOUT MINISTRY. WE OFTEN PRAYED TOGETHER AND I THANKED GOD FOR BRINGING SUCH A GODLY MAN AND FAMILY INTO MY LIFE. GOD WAS ALSO CONFIRMING SOME THINGS IN MY SPIRIT, YET I WAS STILL APPREHENSIVE AND HAD SOME DOUBTS, THIS WAS DEFINITELY A HUGE OPPORTUNITY FOR ME, BUT I HAD NEVER BEEN FROM HOME. I BEGAN TO DO

SOME SEARCHING TO SEE WHAT ALL THIS ENTAILED. I CHECKED THE MAP TO SEE WHERE FIJI EVEN WAS, CHECKED OUT FLIGHTS, I MEAN I HAD NEVER BEEN ON A PLANE BEFORE. I WOULD BE LEAVING MY FAMILY. HOW ON EARTH WOULD MY SONS MANAGE WITHOUT MY INCOME? WOULD I NEED SHOTS? WHERE DID THIS FAMILY FIT INTO THE PICTURE AND WHAT ABOUT THE PASTOR AND THE CHURCH I WOULD BE A APART OF? ALL SORTS OF THOUGHTS RUNNING THRU MY MIND, AND IT WAS SCARY, BUT EACH TIME I WOULD LOG INTO FACEBOOK THERE WOULD BE A WORD THAT SEEMED TO CONFIRM FOR ME WHAT GOD HAD PLANNED FOR ME, AND I KNOW HE HAD ALREADY ORDERED MY STEPS AND IF HE BROUGHT ME TO IT WOULD PREPARE ME TO WALK IT OUT! I KEPT A JOURNAL AND STARTED WRITING THESE THINGS DOWN AND IN MY PRAYER TIME WOULD TALK TO GOD ABOUT IT OR THE CONTACT I HAD IN FIJI. ALTHOUGH THE WORDS I HAD GOTTEN WERE DIFFERENT WORDS, IT ALL BOILED DOWN TO ONE THING, THE WORD THAT WAS PUT IN MY HEART FROM A DEAR FRIEND FROM GEORGIA BACK IN NOVEMBER, "GET READY TO MOVE"! I WAS TO GET OUT OF MY COMFORT ZONE AND GET READY FOR THE RIDE OF MY LIFE!

MAY WAS NOW HERE. IT WAS PRETTY MUCH SET IN MY SPIRIT THAT GOD HAD CALLED ME TO DO SOME MISSIONARY WORK AND I DON'T BELIEVE IT WAS BY ACCIDENT THAT WHAT GOD PLACED IN ME WAS FOR THE PEOPLE OF FIJI FOR THIS SEASON THEY WERE IN. GOD HAD DONE SUCH A HEALING IN ME IN A FEW SHORT MONTHS SINCE BREAKING FREE FROM THE CHAINS OF AN ABUSIVE LIFESTYLE AND I HAD A FIRE AND ZEAL LIKE I HAD NEVER EXPERIENCED. WHAT IF?

THAT WAS THE QUESTION BURNING IN MY SPIRIT. WHAT IF WHAT GOD PLACED IN ME WOULD CAUSE A REVIVAL TO BREAK OUT IN THE ISLAND OF FIJI? BUT I KEPT THINKING, WHY FIJI? WHY NOT SOMEWHERE HERE? BUT WE DON'T QUESTION GOD. HIS WAYS ARE NOT OUR WAYS, HIS THOUGHTS ARE NOT OUR THOUGHTS. HE CALLS US OUT TO BE A BLESSING AND A LIGHT IN THE MIDST OF DARKNESS.

ALTHOUGH THE PASTOR OF THE CHURCH IN FIJI WAS EXCITED TO HEAR SOMEONE FROM AMERICA WOULD POSSIBLY BE COMING, I STILL HAD TO SPEAK WITH MY PASTORS. I WANTED TO MAKE CERTAIN THAT I WAS HEARING FROM GOD AND IT WAS THE LORD LEADING ME, AS THIS WAS A HUGE STEP TO MAKE! THE FAMILY I HAD BEEN SPEAKING WITH WAS GOING TO BE MY HOST FAMILY WHILE I WAS THERE, AND WOULD DRIVE ME AROUND TO WHEREVER WE WAS TO MINISTER SAVING COST OF A RENTAL CAR OR CABS. A PLACE TO STAY WOULD BE ARRANGED AND PAID FOR AS WELL. I WAS DEFINITELY EXCITED AND WAS BEGINNING TO DO MY HOMEWORK AS TO THE CULTURE THERE AND WHAT TO EXPECT. WHEN I WAS A TEEN AND YOUNG IN THE FAITH, WE OFTEN HAD MISSIONARIES COME AND SPEAK AT OUR CHURCH. I KNEW SOME OF WHAT THEY WENT THRU AS TO LIVING CONDITIONS, WATER SUPPLY, FOOD, IMMIGRATION LAWS, TIME DIFFERENCES, THINGS OF THAT NATURE. AFTER ALL FIJI WAS ON THE OTHER SIDE OF THE WORLD. I WOULD HAVE TO FLY TO CALIFORNIA, THEN GO TO THE INTERNATIONAL AIRPORT, AND CATCH THE FLIGHT TO FIJI, TOTAL FLIGHT OF ABOUT 27 HOURS. PHEW!

ALL THESE THINGS OF MY LIFE WAS BROUGHT TO REMEMBRANCE AS THE LORD WAS BRINGING DIFFERENT SCENES OF MY LIFE TO ME. IT WAS AS IF HE WAS SAYING TERESA, REMEMBER ALL YOU LEARNED ABOUT MISSIONARIES. TERESA REMEMBER WHEN YOU WENT THRU THIS SITUATION. WHAT I THOUGHT WAS TIMES OF DESPERATION AND ABANDONMENT, TIMES OF PAIN AND SUFFERING, TIMES OF FEELING, WORTHLESS AND HAVING NO MEANING, HAD ALL BEEN A LEARNING EXPERIENCE AND A GROWING PERIOD TO MAKE ME THE WOMAN I WAS AT THIS POINT IN TIME! AN OVERCOMER! GOD WAS WITH ME THEN, AND HE WAS WITH ME AT THIS MOMENT! ALL THAT I WENT THRU I NOW BELIEVE WAS TO GIVE ME INSIGHT AND BETTER UNDERSTANDING THAT THERE IS WOMEN OUT THERE, AND EVEN MEN TOO WHO HAVE BEEN OR ARE BEING ABUSED AND FEELING THE SAME WAY I HAD. SOME MAY HAVE EVEN CONTEMPLATING SUICIDE THINKING THAT IS THE ONLY ROUTE OF ESCAPE!

IT WAS THE END OF MAY 2010, I HAD JUST SET UP A MEETING TO SPEAK WITH MY PASTORS. I TRUSTED THEM AND VALUED THEIR OPINION. THEY HAD NEVER STEERED ME WRONG AND WERE VERY UPFRONT PEOPLE, SO IF THERE WOULD HAVE BEEN A CHECK IN THEIR SPIRIT OR ANY UNSURETY AT ALL AS TO WHAT I WOULD BE SHARING WITH THEM AS TO THE TIMING, I WOULD HAVE RE-THOUGHT SOME THINGS, CONTINUED IN PRAYER, AND WAITED. AFTER SHARING WITH THEM, THEY FELT A PEACE THEMSELVES. IN FACT, PASTOR TOLD ME THAT WHEN I FIRST SET UP THE MEETING, HE LOOKED AT HIS WIFE AND SAID, COULD TERESA BE THE FIRST MISSIONARY FROM OUR CHURCH?

I KNEW THEN I HAD HEARD GOD CORRECTLY AND FOR THE FIRST TIME I HAD COME TO UNDERSTAND THE PEACE OF GOD, THE PEACE THAT PASSES ALL UNDERSTANDING. OF COURSE THE ENEMY TRIED HIS TACTICS, HE IS RELENTLESS WHEN IT COMES TO THE THINGS OF GOD, AND DOESN'T WANT THE KINGDOM OF GOD TO ADVANCE. BUT WHEN IT'S OF GOD, THERE IS NO STOPPING, GOD ALWAYS PREVAILS. THE ENEMY IS A DEFEATED FOE ANYWAY! WELL THERE WAS PREPARATIONS TO MAKE NOW, PASSPORT, WHAT TO DO CONCERNING MY JOB, MY SONS AND HOUSEHOLD BILLS AS I STILL HAD THE DEBT TOO FROM THE DIVORCE. I WOULD THEN NEED A PHYSICAL AND SHOTS, AIRFARE AS I LEARNED I WOULD NEED A RETURN TICKET.

I WASN'T SURE AT THE TIME HOW LONG I WOULD BE GONE AND WAS GOING TO BUY A ONE WAY AND THEN WHEN MY TIME THERE WAS FINISHED PURCHASE A TICKET FOR HOME. HOWEVER, ACCORDING TO FIJI CUSTOM AND THE NUMBER OF TOURIST THAT ENTER THE COUNTRY, THEY REQUIRED AND ROUND TRIP TICKET TO ENSURE WE WERE PLANNING ON LEAVING THE COUNTRY AND KEEP FROM HAVING PEOPLE STUCK IN THE COUNTRY AND UNABLE TO GET OUT THEN HAVING TO DEPORT PEOPLE COSTING A GREAT DEAL OF MONEY FOR THE COUNTRY. SO I WENT TO GOD AND ASKED HIM TO CONFIRM FOR ME A TIME HE WOULD NEED ME IN FIJI SO I COULD KNOW WHAT MY COST WOULD BE FOR THE ROUND TRIP TICKET. HE CONFIRMED FOR ME 9 MOS. SO I STARTED CHECKING DATES FOR THE MOST ECONOMICAL FLIGHT I COULD GET. EVEN THOUGH IT WAS ONLY MAY I KNEW IT WOULD TAKE A LITTLE TIME TO GET THE MONEY

RAISED THAT WOULD BE NEEDED NOT JUST FOR MY PREPARATIONS TO GO BUT MY STAY OVER THERE FOR 9 MOS. AND THE HOLIDAYS WOULD BE COMING SOON AS WELL MAKING FLIGHTS MORE EXPENSIVE AS PEOPLE TRAVELED HOME TO FAMILY. THANKFULLY MY ROOM AND BOARD AND TRAVELS WHILE IN THE COUNTRY WERE COVERED SAVING ME QUITE A BIT OF EXPENSE.

JUNE WAS HERE. AFTER 2 1/2 YEARS OF WAITING FOR A SETTLEMENT FROM A CAR ACCIDENT I HAD IN DEC 2007, I GOT A CALL FROM MY ATTORNEY I HAD TO HIRE SINCE THE GENTLEMAN HAD NO INSURANCE AND WE HAD TO SUE AND TOLD ME THAT AFTER HIS FEES AND PAYING ALL MY MEDICAL EXPENSES, I WOULD RECEIVE A SETTLEMENT FOR 3200.00 AND IT WAS READY FOR PICKUP. AFTER I MADE ARRANGMENTS TO COME IN TO SIGN FOR IT, I HUNG UP THE PHONE AND WHOOPED AND HOLLERED THE REST OF THE DAY GIVING GOD PRAISE AND THANKS. IT MADE SENSE NOW WHY I HAD TO WAIT SO LONG, GOD HAD BIG PLANS FOR THAT MONEY AND IT WOULD HAVE BEEN SPENT HAD IT COME SOONER. THIS DEFINITELY CAME IN HANDY TOWARDS THE EXPENSES I HAD, BUT I KNEW IT WAS A FAR CRY YET FROM WHAT I NEEDED, BUT I TRUSTED GOD AND KNEW THINGS WOULD WORK OUT! I TOOK THE MONEY AND SAT DOWN AND PRAYED.

AS I WAS GOING THRU MY CHECKLIST OF THINGS THAT NEED PAID AND WHAT I HAD TO DO, I ASKED GOD TO HELP ME PUT THE MONEY WHERE IT WAS MOST USEFUL. AFTER THE ACCIDENT THAT DEC 2007, I HAD GOTTEN ANOTHER CAR BUT HAD TO FINANCE IT, IT WAS A LITTLE OVER 2 YEAR LOAN AND WAS DUE TO BE

PAID OFF IN JULY. I WANTED TO GET THAT PAID OFF, OWING ONLY ABOUT 700.00, SO I PUT THAT ON THE LIST OF PRIORITY THINGS TO DO. I PAID DOWN 2 OF THE CREDIT CARDS I HAD. I THEN CALLED TO ORDER MY PASSPORT AND LEARNED IT WOULD TAKE 6 TO 8 WEEKS TO GET. I HAD MADE PLANS TO FLY OUT OF DAYTON ON AUG 10TH SO THIS WOULD DEFINITLY BE A PRIORITY TO GET DONE. THEN I HAD TO GET MY PHYSICAL AND SHOTS. I WOULD NEED A POLIO, UPDATED TETANUS SHOT, TYPHOID FEVER SHOT AND HEPATITIS A&B. HOWEVER, THEY TOLD ME THE HEPATITIS SHOTS WAS A LONG PROCESS AND WASN'T SURE IF I COULD GET DONE IN TIME TO FLY OUT ON THE 10TH OF AUG. I JUST GAVE IT TO GOD AND PRAYED HE WOULD WORK IT OUT FOR ME, AFTER ALL HE CALLED ME TO THIS.

I WAS SO SCARED, I COULDN'T IMAGINE ME TRAVELING ON A PLANE NEVER BEING ON ONE BEFORE. I USUALLY WORRIED ABOUT GOING FAR FROM HOME WHEN I TRAVELED OUT OF TOWN LET ALONE OVERSEAS. BUT I STILL HAD THIS OVERWHELMING PEACE, AND EXCITMENT ROSE UP WITHIN ME THAT IN 2 MONTHS I WOULD BE ON THE ISLAND OF FIJI, I KNEW IT WAS GONNA BE OK. WHAT EXCITED ME THE MOST OF ALL THAT GOD HAD DONE AND PROVIDED FOR AT THIS POINT THAT AS I WAS FINISHING GOING OVER MY BILLS AND SEEING HOW MUCH MORE I NEEDED WAS THE FACT OF MY TOTAL DEBT. AT THE TIME I WENT THRU THE DIVORCE I WAS 11,280.00 IN DEBT. SINCE JAN OF 2010 WHEN I HONORED MY COMMITTMENT OF GIVING 15% OF MY COME AS A TITHE, I HADN'T KEPT TRACK OF HOW MUCH PROGRESS I WAS MAKING ON THAT DEBT.

MY MIND HAD BEEN SO PREOCCUPIED WITH THOUGHTS OF WRITING AND THE PENDING TRIP AND ALL. HERE IT WAS JUNE AND AS I WAS FIGURING OUT THE FINANCES AND WHAT I WOULD STILL NEED FOR THE TRIP AND MY TIME IN FIJI I HAD NOTICED I WAS ONLY 2000,00 IN DEBT NOW! YES!! YOU ARE READING THAT RIGHT!! I HAD COME 9,280.00 OUT OF DEBT IN ABOUT 5 1/2 MONTHS! GLORY TO GOD! I DIDN'T KNOW HOW. I MEAN JANUARY AND FEBRUARY WAS ROUGH MONTHS WITH THE MOVE AND CUSTOMERS BEING DOWN SO REALLY FROM MARCH TO JUNE GOD HAD MIRACULOUSLY CHANGED MY FINANCES AROUND AND I HADN'T MADE MUCH MORE THAT WHAT I HAD BEFORE, DIDN'T TAKE ON ANY EXTRA ROUTES OR ANYTHING, IT WAS ALL GOD!

MY FIRST BATTLE CAME AROUND THE 2ND WEEK OF JULY, WHEN I GOT A LETTER IN THE MAIL FROM THE AMERICAN EMBASSY HERE IN THE STATES. THEY TOLD ME IN THE LETTER THEY NEEDED A NEW BIRTH CERTIFICATE AS MINE HAD SOMEHOW BEEN DAMAGED WHEN THEY RECEIVED IT. I THOUGHT OH NO THIS CAN'T BE, MY APPLICATION HAD ALREADY BEEN IN 4 WEEKS, I WAS DUE TO LEAVE IN 4 WEEKS AND HAD SO MUCH TO DO YET, THAT I DIDN'T NEED TO DEAL WITH ANY DELAYS. BUT I DIDN'T LET IT GET ME DOWN, I NEVER GAVE UP HOPE THAT IT WOULDN'T ALL COME TOGETHER. GOD SHOWED ME WHAT TO DO, BUT I WOULD HAVE TO PUSH MY DATE BACK BY 2 WEEKS. INSTEAD OF LEAVING ON AUG 10TH IT WOULD NOW BE AUG 24TH, AND ALTHOUGH A LITTLE SAD, THERE WASN'T ANYTHING I COULD DO BUT TRUST GOD, I HAD TO HAVE THAT PASSPORT. BESIDES, BY CHNAGING THE

FLIGHT FOR 2 WEEKS LATER I ENDED UP SAVING 50.00 ON THE TICKETS.

YEEHAW! EVERY LITTLE BIT HELPED! THIS ONLY HAD ME PRAYING MORE FERVENTLY, TAKING AUTHORITY OVER THE ENEMY. IN FACT, EVER SINCE I HAD THE MEETING WITH MY PASTORS, TO THE TIME I GOT THE LETTER ABOUT MY BIRTH CERTIFICATE, I HAD BEEN COVERING THE TRIP IN PRAYER. THE FLIGHT, THE PILOT AND CO PILOT, TO MY SAFETY WHILE IN FIJI, ME STAYING HEALTHY, AND THAT I WOULD BE TAKEN CARE OF AS WELL AS THOSE THAT CROSSED MY PATH THAT I WOULD MINISTER TO, BUT NOW IT WAS TIME FOR WARFARE, I WOULD NOW BE STEPPIN UP MY PRAYER A BIT. WHAT THE ENEMY MEANS FOR HARM, GOD WILL TURN AROUND FOR GOOD! HOW? AT THIS POINT I WASN'T SURE, BUT FAITH IS THE EVIDENCE OF THINGS NOT SEEN, I HAD TO JUST TAKE IT DAY BY DAY.

I WENT THE SAME DAY TO THE HEALTH DEPARTMENT AND GOT A NEW COPY OF MY BIRTH CERTIFATE. THANKFULLY I WAS BORN IN THE CITY I NOW LIVED IN AND DIDN'T HAVE TO TRAVEL OUT OF TOWN TO GET ONE. I WENT TO THE POST OFFICE AND MAILED IT, PRAYING OVER IT AS I FILLED OUT THE SLIP THAT WOULD SEND IT BY PRIORITY MAIL SO THEY'D HAVE IT SOONER THAN BY STANDARD MAILING. I ALREADY INFORMED THE FAMILY AND PASTOR IN FIJI THAT I CHANGED MY FLIGHT DATE TO AUG 24TH DUE TO ISSUES WITH PASSPORT APPLICATION AND I DIDN'T WANT TO HAVE TO CHANGE IT AGAIN SO I PRAYED FOR PROTECTION AND THE ARRIVAL OF THE PASSPORT. THANKFULLY I HADN'T PURCHASED MY AIRLINE TICKETS YET OR I MAY HAVE HAD EXTRA EXPENSE IN

CHANGING MY TICKET. I RECEIVED ALL THE SHOTS I NEEDED BUT THE HEPATITIS WHICH WOULD BE ADMINISTERED BY MY FAMILY DOCTOR WHICH I HAD AN APPT AT THE END OF THE WEEK FOR THAT.

THAT FRIDAY WHEN I WENT TO THE DOCTOR I WAS PLEASED TO LEARN THERE WAS AN ACCELERATED VERSION OF THE HEPATITIS A&B SHOTS, ORIGINALLY THERE WAS A TIME FRAME YOU HAD TO GO BY AS THERE WAS 4 DOSES YOU HAD TO TAKE, BUT I DIDN'T HAVE TIME TO GO THRU THAT SO I PRAYED THERE WOULD BE SOMETHING THAT COULD BE DONE. SO WHAT THEY SAID I COULD DO WAS TAKE 3 DOSES ONE THAT DAY, ONE THE FOLLOWING WEEK, THEN ONE MONTH LATER BACK FOR THE THIRD ONE. THAT WAS CUTTING IT SO CLOSE AS THAT MADE IT THE 2OTH OF AUGUST FOR THE LAST AND I WAS TO FLY OUT THE 24TH, THEN WHEN I WOULD HAVE TO TAKE A BOOSTER WITHIN ONE YEAR. THAT WOULD BE NO ISSUE CAUSE I WAS PLANNING ON RETURNING HOME IN MAY OF 2011 SO I'D BE HOME IN PLENTY OF TIME! WOO HOO! GOD HAD IT ALL WORKED OUT! TEARS WELLED UP AS I REFLECTED ALL THAT HAD TAKEN PLACE THE LAST FEW MONTHS. MY MIND WANDERED OVER LAST YEAR SINCE BEING ON MY OWN, MY LIFE HAD BEEN TRANSFORMED, I WAS SO HUMBLED AND IN AWE AT HOW GOD HAD WORKED IN MY LIFE AND HEALED ME FROM THE AFFECTS OF THE ABUSE. I STILL BATTLED WITH ISSUES IN MY BODY AS A RESULT, BUT TO SEE WHERE GOD HAD BROUGHT ME AND THE MESS MY LIFE WAS, I KNEW HE COULD HEAL ME OF THESE ISSUES I FACED. THIS WAS JUST ICING ON THE CAKE!

IT WAS AUG 3RD 2010, JUST 3 WEEKS AWAY FROM THE DATE I WOULD TO FIJI. MY FLIGHT SCHEDULE WOULD TAKE ME FROM DAYTON TO DENVER, THEN A CONNECTING FLIGHT TO LA, THEN TAKING A BUS TO THE INTERNATIONAL AIRPORT WHERE I WOULD TAKE A FLIGHT TO FIJI AT A COST OF 1461.00 ROUND TRIP. PIECE OF CAKE RIGHT? YOU WOULD THINK SO ONLY THAT I HADN'T PURCHASED MY TICKET YET! TIME TO RECALCULATE MY MONEY LEFT OVER FROM PURCHASING THE PASSPORT, SHOTS, AND PAYING OFF SOME BILLS, AS WELL AS PAYING A FEW BILLS UP FOR A COUPLE MONTHS TILL MY BOYS GOT ADJUSTED TO ME BEING GONE. I DIDN'T WANT THEM TO WORRY, AS I HANDLED MOST OF THE BUDGET AND TOLD THEM WHAT NEEDED TO BE PAID AND HOW MUCH, THEN THEY GAVE THE MONEY TO ME TO GET PAID, SO NOW THEY HAD TO HANDLE THIS ON THEIR OWN WHILE I WAS GONE. MY YOUNGEST AGREED TO DO MY ROUTE FOR ME WHILE I WAS GONE SO WE DIDN'T LOSE MY INCOME AND THAT WOULD HELP ME IN CASE FUNDS RAN LOW WHILE I WAS IN FIJI TOO. AFTER ALL TOTALS WAS DONE I HAD 800.00 LEFT AND STILL HAD MY TICKET, TOILETRIES ITEMS TO GET, SOME CLOTHING ITEMS AND HAVE SPENDING MONEY TO LAST ALMOST 9 MOS. I HAD NO IDEA HOW MUCH THINGS COST IN FIJI, MOST TOURIST COUNTRIES CAN BE REAL EXPENSIVE. BUT I WAS SO GRATEFUL GOD CONNECTED ME WITH A FAMILY WHO COULD ASSIST ME ON WHERE THE BEST PLACES WERE TO SHOP ECONOMICALLY AND I WAS PRETTY THRIFTY TOO AND HANDLED MONEY WELL.

WHEN I TOTALED THE COST OF APPROXIMATELY WHAT I FELT WAS STILL NEEDED, IT WAS AN

ASTONISHING 2500.00. UGH! IN 3 WEEKS? WELL IT WAS TIME FOR SOME FASTING AND PRAYER, AND SOME SEED SOWING. I HAD COME TOO FAR TO BE DEFEATED NOW. I WASN'T GOING TO GIVE FEAR A FOOTHOLD! I BELIEVED IN SOWING AND REAPING. I REMEMBER WHEN WILLIE AND I HAD PURCHASED OUR HOUSE IN 2003 THE OWNERS WAS TO PAY CLOSING COST BUT SOMETHING HAPPENED AND THEY COULDN'T DO IT. WE WROTE A CHECK FOR 25.00 TO THE FORMER PASTORS OF THE CHURCH WE ATTENDED ON TROY. WE ASKED THEM TO WAIT TO CASH THE CHECK, PRAYING OVER IT EVERYDAY TILL WE HAD THE CLOSING, I BELIEVE IT WAS A 2 WEEK TIME FRAME. THEN WE TOLD THEM THAT ON THE MORNING OF THE CLOSING, THEY COULD CASH IT, BELIEVING THAT WHEN THEY DID WE WOULD HAVE NO CLOSING COST TO PAY.

ON THE DAY TO CLOSE ON THE HOUSE, WE GOT THERE AND LEARNED THERE WOULD BE NO CLOSING COSTS! THE SELLERS DECIDED TO PAY AFTER ALL! YIPPEE!! SO I KNEW THAT IS GOD DID IT ONCE, HE COULD DO IT AGAIN AND PROVIDE THE 2500.00 NEEDED. THAT'S FAITH! THE KIND OF FAITH THAT MOVES MOUNTAINS, AND I HAD A HUGE ONE STANDING IN MY WAY AT THE MOMENT! SO WHAT I DID WAS THE SAME THING, I WROTE A CHECK TO MY PASTOR'S FOR 25.00, PRAYED OVER IT AND WENT TO THEM THAT SUNDAY MORNING. I WASN'T SURE IF MY PASTORS BELIEVED IN SOWING SEEDS. WE WERE STILL A NEW CHURCH AND THEY WERE STILL NEW AT PASTORING. WHEN I TALKED TO THEM THAT MORNING HE SAID YES, WE BELIEVE IN SOWING SEEDS. I HANDED THEM THE CHECK AND EXPLAINED WHAT I NEEDED THEM TO DO, BELIEVING THAT WITHIN THE 2 WEEK TIME FRAME, I

WOULD RECEIVE THE 2500.00 I NEEDED FOR MY TRIP. THAT WOULD BE A 100 FOLD RETURN ON MY SEED. I NEEDED AT LEAST 1461.00 BY AUG 17 TH TO BOOK MY FLIGHT AND THE REST TO COME BY AUG 23 RD SO THEY COULD CASH THE CHECK ON AUG 17 TH.

WHEN I SHARED WITH OUR WORSHIP TEAM WHAT I WANTED THEM TO PRAY WITH ME ABOUT, ONE OF THE LADY'S ON THE TEAM SHARED ABOUT A FUNDRAISER SHE DID TO HELP WITH HOUSING COSTS FOR A HOUSE SHE OPENED FOR WOMEN TO GET THEM OFF THE STREET AND BACK ON THEIR FEET. SINCE MY TRIP WAS MISSIONS ORIENTED, SHE THOUGHT IT MAY HELP RAISE THE MONEY I NEEDED. I GOT SO EXCITED AND ASKED HER IF SHE WOULD BE WILLING TO HELP ME PUT SOMETHING TOGETHER AND SHE AGREED, AND AFTER SERVICE WE WENT TO THE PASTORS AND TALKED TO THEM ABOUT IT AND THEY AGREED! I WAS ESTACTIC AND AS TEARS WELLED UP, I THANKED GOD FOR BRINGING THESE WONDERFUL PEOPLE INTO MY LIFE! WHEN I GOT HOME I PUT SOME PLANS TOGETHER FOR A BENEFIT DINNER, AND SET THE DATE FOR THURS AUG 12 TH. THE MENU WOULD CONSIST OF SLOPPY JOES, MAC AND CHEESE, CHIPS, DESSERT AND DRINKS. THEN I DID RESEARCH ON FIJI AND PUT TOGETHER A BOOK REPORT WITH SOME PICTURES I HAD RECEIVED FROM THE PASTOR OVER IN FIJI. THE NEXT SUNDAY, AUGUST 1 ST, PASTORS ALLOWED ME TO MAKE AN ANNOUNCEMENT CONCERNING THE BENEFIT DIINER AND WHAT IT WAS FOR. I ALSO ASKED IF THERE WAS ANYONE THAT WANTED TO MAKE DONATIONS FOR THE DINNER OR MAKE A DISH TO BRING. I JUST COULDN'T CONTAIN THE JOY THAT WAS WELLING UP INSIDE AS MANY PEOPLE CAME FORWARD

AFTER SERVICE AND DONATED MONEY, OR SAID THEY WOULD BE HAPPY TO MAKE A DISH AND BRING.

THE NEXT WEEK WAS SO BUSY, I HAD A LITTLE OVER A WEEK TO PREPARE FOR THE BENEFIT DINNER ALL THE TIME STILL WORKING AND WHEN I WASN'T SLEEPING OR DOING HOUSE WORK, I WAS WORKING ON WHAT WAS STILL NEEDED FOR THE TRIP AND FINALIZING PLANS FOR THE BOYS. I HAD TAKEN THE MONEY THAT WAS DONATED AND BOUGHT THE PLATES, NAPKINS, CUTLERY, CUPS AND SOME DECORATIONS FOR THE DINNER. OUR ELDERS OF THE CHURCH PLAYED A GREAT ROLE IN SUPPORTING ME AND OFFERING THEIR SERVICES WHEREVER NEEDED AND I WAS SO THANKFUL. THAT WEEK SOMEONE HAD ALSO BROUGHT 2 BAGS OF LADIES CLOTHING AND DROPPED OFF TO ME TO GO THRU AND TAKE WHATEVER I COULD USE THEN DONATE THE REST. I WAS SO EXCITED AS I WENT THRU THE BAGS, THERE WAS ALOT I COULD USE, ALL I REALLY NEED TO BUY WAS A BATHING SUIT AND SOME UNDER GARMENTS! HALLELUJAH! THAT SAVED ALOT OF MONEY. I KEPT TRACK OF WHAT I THOUGHT THE CLOTHING ITEMS WAS WORTH AND I COUNTED IT IN THE RETURN FROM THE SEED I WAS BELIEVING FOR. I JUST COULDN'T BELIEVE THE BLESSINGS THAT WAS POURING IN. AMAZING HOW WHEN WE PUT OUR FAITH AND TRUST IN GOD, THE THINGS THAT CAN HAPPEN! HE TRULY DOES MEET ALL OF OUR NEEDS.

FINALLY THE DAY OF THE BENEFIT DINNER WAS HERE, I WAS PUMPED. EVERYTHING HAD COME TOGETHER BEAUTIFULLY. ONCE THE GUESTS ARRIVED, PASTOR PRAYED OVER THE MEAL AND WE ATE, THEN I

GAVE A SMALL PRESENTATION, EXPLAINING THE CALL I BELIEVED GOD PLACED ON MY HEART FOR MISSIONS. I SHARED HOW I HAD LEARNED ABOUT MISSIONARIES AS A TEENAGER, AND EVEN HELPED SUPPORT SOME WHEN I WAS IN MY LATE 20'S. I TOLD THEM I REMEMBERED MENTIONING TO GOD HOW I DIDN'T THINK I COULD DO WHAT THEY DID AND PLEASE DON'T CALL ME INTO MISSIONS, YET HERE I AM. I SHARED A FEW OF THE WORDS I HAD RECEIVED FROM GOD AND OTHER PEOPLE WHO I CAME IN CONTACT WITH, DOWN TO THE FAMILY I BECAME CONNECTED TO THRU FACEBOOK. I HAD SOME DISPLAYS SET UP OF PICTURES FROM FIJI AND THE FAMILY THAT WOULD BE MY HOSTS THERE AS WELL AS THE PASTORS OF THE CHURCH I WOULD BE ATTENDING WHILE IN FIJI AND I SHARED SOME INFORMATION ABOUT THEM. WE HAD SET UP A DONATION BOX TOO IF ANYONE WANTED TO SOW A SEED INTO MY TRIP THEY WAS WELCOMED TOO. AFTER THE DINNER, SOME HAD STAYED BEHIND TO HELP ME CLEAN UP. AS WE WERE FINISHING UP, I OPENED THE DONATION BOX, CURIOUS TO SEE HOW MUCH WAS RAISED. AS I COUNTED TEARS WERE WELLING UP, THE ELDERS CAME OVER WONDERING WHAT WAS WRONG. I SAID NOTHING AT ALL, I'M AMAZED AT THE AMOUNT RECEIVED AND WANT TO COUNT IT AGAIN TO MAKE SURE I DIDN'T MAKE AN ERROR IN COUNTING. SHE COUNTED WITH ME AND WE BROUGHT IN EXACTLY WHAT I COUNTED THE FIRST TIME, 866.00. THAT WAS A 30 FOLD RETURN SO FAR ON MY SEED I SOWED! GLORY TO GOD! BUT I KNEW GOD WASN'T FINISHED YET!

I COULD HARDLY SLEEP THAT NIGHT, I WAS SO IN AWE AT HOW GOD WAS MOVING, PUTTING EVERYTHING

INTO PLACE, INTO PERSPECTIVE, RIGHT DOWN TO THE FINEST DETAILS. AS I GOT UP TO GO DO MY ROUTE, GOD REMINDED ME OF THE SCRIPTURE, HE WHO HAS BEGUN A NEW WORK IN YOU, WILL BE FAITHFUL TO BRING TO COMPLETION ALL THINGS! YES SIREE! ONE NICE THING ABOUT MY ROUTES WAS I WORKED BY MYSELF, IT WAS THE WEE HOURS OF THE MORNING WHEN NO ONE WAS UP. I HAD A DELIVERY DEADLINE TO MEET AND COULD WORK AT MY OWN PACE AS LONG AS I MET THE DEADLINE. I WOULD OFTEN PRAY, TALKING TO GOD, LISTENING TO A CHRISTIAN RADIO STATION THAT HAD A TEACHING SEGMENT ON THERE THAT CAME ON AT 3 AM, THAT I ALWAYS ENJOYED. THAT MORNING I HAD LEFT NOTES WITH MY CUSTOMERS PAPER EXPLAINING ABOUT MY TRIP AND HOW LONG I'D BE GONE AND THAT MY SON WOULD BE SUBBING MY ROUTE FOR ME TILL I RETURNED AND LEFT HIS NUMBER WITH THEM. AS I FINISHED MY ROUTE THAT MORNING AND WAS MAKING THE TRIP HOME, I WENT OVER THINGS THAT I STILL NEEDED TO DO. IT WASN'T MUCH YET, BUT IT WAS ALREADY AUGUST 13 TH AND I HAD 4 DAYS TO GET THE MONEY FOR MY TICKET, I STILL NEEDED MY PASSPORT, HAD ONE LAST HEPITITIS A&B SHOT TO GET THE FOLLOWING WEEK AND I WANTED TO GET MY HAIR DONE. I BELIEVE THAT WAS IT. WOW, IT WAS ALL COMING TOGETHER!

THE WEEKEND FLEW BY AND IT WAS NOW MONDAY AUGUST 16 TH. JUST 8 DAYS BEFORE MY TRIP AND I WAS STILL SHORT. I HAD ONE DAY LEFT TO GET MY FLIGHT BOOKED. OH GOD, CAN YOU HEAR ME? AS I PRAYED. I DECIDED TO CALL THE AIRPORT AGAIN JUST TO CONFIRM HOW FAR IN ADVANCE THEY WOULD NEED

TO BOOK MY FLIGHT. MY MIND HAD BEEN SO OVERWHELMED WITH ALL THAT NEEDED DONE AND I WAS SURE IT WAS ONLY A WEEK, BUT YOU KNOW THE ENEMY. I STARTED TO HAVE DOUBTS AND SAID LORD WHAT IF IT'S 2 WEEKS THEY NEED OR EVEN LONGER? I ASKED HIM TO GO BEFORE ME AND WORK IT OUT, THAT WHEN I CALLED I WOULD GET GOOD NEWS. I BELIEVED IN THE POWER OF PRAYER! GOD WAS FAITHFUL, AND I STOOD ON HIS WORD THAT SAID, DO NOT BE ANXIOUS FOR ANYTHING, BUT BY PRAYER AND SUPPLICATION, WITH THANKSGIVING IN YOUR HEART, LET YOUR REQUESTS BE MADE KNOWN UNTO GOD, AND THATS JUST WHAT I HAD DONE! WHEN I CALLED THE AIRLINE, I COULDN'T BELIEVE WHAT THEY TOLD ME AND HAD TO HAVE THEM REPEAT IT TO ME.

THEY SAID THEY ONLY NEEDED A 1 TO 2 DAY NOTICE TO BOOK A FLIGHT. AND THE PRICE SHOULD BE AROUND THE SAME. ARE YOU SERIOUS? AFTER I HUNG UP I GAVE A SHOUT! MY SON COME RUNNING TO SEE WHAT WAS HAPPENING BUT I ASSURED HIM I WAS OK, THAT I RECEIVED SOME GOOD NEWS CONCERNING MY FLIGHT. I STILL HAD TIME TO BOOK THE FLIGHT, AND PEACE LIKE A RIVER IN MY HEART! MY SON HANDED ME THE MAIL THAT CAME AND THERE IN THE MIDST WAS MY PASSPORT. YEE HAW! IT CAME! I LAID DOWN FOR A NAP AND WHEN I WOKE DECIDED TO LOG INTO FACEBOOK AND TAKE A BREAK FOR A BIT.

I HAD A MESSAGE FROM PASTORS WIFE THAT SAID IN THE OFFERING THE DAY BEFORE, SOMEONE HAD MADE OUT SOME CHECKS TO THE CHURCH AND PUT IN THE MEMO IT WAS FOR MY TRIP. ALL TOTAL THERE WAS 155.00 WAITING FOR ME, I WAS SUPER

STOKED AND ADDED IT TO THE CHART I HAD MADE OF MONEY RAISED. I SAT THERE SORT OF IN A NUMB STATE, HOW I WAS FEELING AT THAT MOMENT, I NEVER WANTED TO END. GOD AT THAT MOMENT BROUGHT A WORD POSTED FROM A FRIEND, THAT SAID AS YOU DELIGHT YOURSELF IN ME, I GIVE YOU THE DESIRES OF YOUR HEART. LATER THAT EVENING I FINALIZED EVERYTHING WITH THE BOYS GIVING INSTRUCTIONS AS WHO WAS TO PAY WHAT, WHERE THE LANDLORD'S NUMBER WAS IN CASE OF ANY EMERGENCY WITH HOUSE THAT MAY COME UP. I LEFT A NUMBER OF WHERE I WOULD BE IN FIJI AND HOW TO CALL OVERSEAS IF NEED BE, BUT MOSTLY THEY WOULD BE ABLE TO CONTACT ME THRU FACEBOOK OR BY EMAIL.

A COUPLE DAYS WENT BY AND IT WAS NOW WEDNESDAY AUGUST 18 TH. I LEFT FOR WORK THINKING I HAD 6 DAYS LEFT BEFORE MY TRIP AND I WAS GETTING NERVOUS. AS I WAS DOING MY ROUTE, I REMEMBER LOOKING AT THE SKY AND SEEING A PLANE TRAVELING, AND SAID TO MYSELF, IT'S NOT THAT HIGH UP THERE, BUT IT'S STILL SCARY. THERE WAS A COUPLE HOUSES I DELIVERED TOO THAT HAD ENVELOPES ON THEIR DOORS WITH MY NAME ON IT TOO. SOMETIMES CUSTOMERS SAVED THEIR RUBBERBANDS AND BAGS FOR ME WHICH HELPED CUT DOWN ON MY SUPPLY COSTS AS WE HAD TO BUY OUR OWN BAGS AND RUBBERBANDS FOR OUR ROUTE. WHEN I OPENED THE ENVELOPE HOWEVER, THERE WAS MONEY IN THERE ALONG WITH A NOTE WISHING ME A SAFE TRIP. I WAS SO TOUCHED. THAT NIGHT WE HAD PRAISE AND WORSHIP PRACTICE.

I LOVED MUSIC AND SINGING AND BEING A PART OF THE TEAM. THAT NIGHT THERE WAS A LADY THERE THAT WAS THE SISTER OF ONE OF THE WORSHIP TEAM MEMBER. SHE WAS DIAGNOSED WITH CANCER AND DIDN'T HAVE MUCH TIME LEFT. WE HAD BEEN STANDING IN FAITH FOR HER HEALING AND SHE DECIDED SHE WANTED TO BE A PART OF THE TEAM. SHE CAME TO ME AND HANDED ME AN ENVELOPE AND SAID THE LORD PRESSED UPON HER TO SOW A SEED INTO MY TRIP. SHE WAS GIVEN AN AMOUNT BUT WAS A LITTLE SHORT ON THAT AND WOULD BRING IT SUNDAY. I TOLD HER THAT WAS OK AND THANKED HER AS I GAVE HER A HUG THEN PUT THE ENVELOPE INTO MY PURSE. I DIDN'T KNOW IF SHE WOULD FEEL AWKWARD ME OPENING IT IN FRONT OF THE OTHER MEMBERS, I WAITED TO OPEN IT AND WENT TO GET MY MIKE. I WAS TOUCHED BY HER GIFT AS I KNEW SHE WAS STRESSED AND STRUGGLING IN HER BODY AND NOT SURE HOW MUCH THE INSURANCE WAS COVERING HER EXPENSES. BUT SHE SAID GOD TOLD HER TO DO IT AND WAS WANTED TO BE OBEDIENT.

WHEN I ARRIVED HOME THAT NIGHT FROM PRACTICE, I WAS TALKING TO MY HOST FAMILY, GOING OVER THE FINAL DETAILS, AS TO WHO WOULD PICK ME UP AT AIRPORT. HE HAD A BROTHER WHO WORKED FOR THE AIRLINE AND SENT ME A PIC OF HIM SO I WOULD KNOW WHO TO LOOK FOR. HE WOULD HELP ME COLLECT MY BAGGAGE AND SHOW ME WHERE I COULD FIND HIM AND THE GIRLS. JUST THEN I REMEMBERED THE ENVELOPE IN MY PURSE AND WENT TO PULL IT OUT. AT THIS TIME WHEN I HAD DONE MY TOTALS OF WHAT CAME IN, I WAS AT A 60 FOLD RETURN ON THE 25.00 SEED I PLANTED. WHEN I PULLED THE MONEY

FROM THE ENVELOPE IT WAS A BRAND NEW CRISP 100.00 BILL. TEARS WELLED UP AS IT HAD BEEN A WHILE SINCE I SEEN A 100.00 BILL. MOSTLY MY CHECK WENT INTO BANK AND AFTER I PAID BILLS AND BOUGHT FOOD AND GAS, THERE WASN'T MUCH OF ANYTHING LEFT OVER. THANK GOODNESS I GOT PAID WEEKLY.

AS I WENT TO PUT THE MONEY WITH THE REST OF WHAT I HAD IN THE SAFE, THE BILLS SEPARATED. I THOUGHT WHAT? THERE'S ANOTHER? IT SEPARATED AGAIN AND THERE WAS A 3 RD 100.00 BILL,BUT IT WASN'T DONE YET. ALL TOTAL THERE WAS 900.00 IN THAT ENVELOPED AND I GASPED. IT MUST HAVE BEEN LOUD BECAUSE THE VOICE ON SKYPE ASKED ME WHAT WAS WRONG. WHEN I TOLD HIM HE WAS OVERJOYED AND ASKED IF HE COULD PRAY AND GIVE GOD THANKS, I SAID ABSOLUTELY. I NOW HAD ENOUGH MONEY TO PAY FOR MY FLIGHT AND WAS ONLY 275.00 AWAY FROM A 100 FOLD RETURN OFF MY 25.00 SEED. GLORY TO GOD! GOD WAS HONORING MY FAITH AND THOSE MOUNTAINS WERE MOVING!! THE BEST PART? AS IF THAT WASN'T GREAT ENOUGH! WHEN I LOOKED AT MY BILLS TO MAKE SURE I HAD EVERYTHING COVERED, I LOOKED AT MY TOTAL DEBT. NOW MIND YOU I SAID IN ANOTHER SECTION OF THIS BOOK THAT IN JAN I WAS 11,280.00 IN DEBT, IN JUNE I CAME 9,280.00 OUT OF DEBT LEAVING ME 2000.00 LEFT OF DEBT. AT THIS POINT. AUGUST 18 TH 2010 I HAD COME ANOTHER 1400.00 OUT OF DEBT AND WAS LEFT WITH ONLY 600.00 LEFT! ALL ON BEING A PAPERGIRL! ONLY GOD FOLKS! WHEN I HAD BEEN OBEDIENT AND INCREASED MY TITHE FROM 10% TO 15% IN JUST 8 MONTHS TIME I HAD COME 10,680.00 OUT OF DEBT! ONLY GOD HAS THE POWER TO WIPE OUT DEBT!

THE NEXT DAY I HAD A HAIR APPOINTMENT. THERE WAS A LADY IN OUR CHURCH THAT HAD HER OWN SALON. SHE COLORED MY HAIR AND CUT IT A TAD SHORTER THAN I NORMALLY GET IT SO IT WOULD LAST TILL I RETURNED HOME. I WAS SO PICKY ABOUT MY HAIR THAT I DIDN'T WANT JUST ANYONE TOUCHING IT. AFTER SHE HAD FINISHED, I WENT TO PICK UP SOME HAIR SPRAY SHE HAD FOR SALE AND ONLY CHARGED ME FOR THE PRODUCTS. SHE DID MY HAIR FOR FREE!! A 75.00 SEED!! THAT LEFT ME NEEDING JUST 200.00 AND I WOULD RECEIVE MY 100 FOLD RETURN ON MY SEED I SOWED. I WAS SO HUMBLED, I CRIED. AS I LEFT I SAT IN MY CAR FOR I DON'T KNOW HOW LONG. I HAD WONDERED WHY I WAITED SO LONG TO LEAVE AN ABUSIVE MARRIAGE, I WASTED SO MANY YEARS OF MY LIFE! BUT THERE IS A REASON FOR EVERYTHING AND GOD SHOWED ME IT WAS ALL STEPPING SOTNES TO GET ME TO THOSE HIGHER PLACES IN HIM. WHAT A JOURNEY AND LEARNING EXPERIENCE THIS WAS, BUT I ALSO PRAYED THAT I'D BE ABLE TO HANDLE THE MINISTRY GOD HAD FOR ME.

SUNDAY CAME AND I THRILLED, BUT YET KIND OF SAD AND NERVOUS AT THE SAME TIME. THIS WOULD BE MY LAST SERVICE BEFORE GOING TO FIJI AND I WAS TO GIVE A FAREWELL SPEECH. IT WAS A VERY EMOTIONAL TIME FOR ME AND I RECEIVED MANY WELL WISHES AND WAS PRAYED OVER BY MY PASTORS. WHAT WAS SO AMAZING WAS THE FACT THAT SOMEONE HAD GIVEN ME 200.00 THAT DAY. 200.00 WAS ALL I NEEDED TO RECEIVE THE 100 FOLD RETURN OFF MY 25.00 SEED!! GLORY TO GOD! I COULDN'T BELIEVE IT, BUT THERE IT WAS! IT WAS HARD TO GET THRU THE DAY, I FELT AS IF

I WAS RUNNING AROUND LIKE A CHICKEN WITH MY HEAD CUT OFF WHEN I SHOULD HAVE BEEN RELAXING, AND EVEN NAPPING AS THE NEXT 2 DAYS WAS GONNA BE SUPER BUSY. BUT WITH ME, I CAN'T LEAVE ONE STONE UNTURNED SO TO SPEAK, I HAD TO MAKE SURE EVERYTHING WAS IN ORDER, AFTER ALL I WOULD BE GONE FOR ABOUT 9 MONTHS. FIJI WAS A TROPICAL COUNTRY, SO I WAS LOOKING FORWARD TO NOT HAVING TO GO THRU ANOTHER WINTER IN OHIO AND PRAYED MY FAMILY HERE WOULD BE OK AND THAT THE WINTER WOULD BE MILD.

THE NEXT DAY I FINISHED MY SHOPPING AND GOT MY SUITCASES ALL PACKED. I MADE SURE I HAD EVERYTHING I NEEDED AND THEN I WAITED, WAITED, AND WAITED. THE WAITING WAS NERVE RACKING. I HAD BEEN SO BUSY THE LAST FEW MONTHS PREPARING FOR THE TRIP, I DIDN'T HAVE ALOT OF TIME TO REALLY LET IT SINK IN AS TO WHAT I WAS ABOUT TO DO. NOW THAT EVERYTHING WAS IN ORDER AND FINALIZED, IT WAS SINKING IN AND WAS GETTING A LITTLE SCARED. THIS WAS A HUGE STEP FOR ME AND FOR MY FAMILY TOO BEING WITHOUT ME, ESPECIALLY MY MOM. SHE WANTED ME TO MAKE SURE I WAS REALLY HEARING OF GOD, BUT I ASSURED HER I DID. I THOUGHT OF HER THAT DAY, WHAT SHE MUST BE FEELING. SHE'D LOST MY DAD MANY YEARS AGO, AND IT WAS JUST US KIDS, AND I'M SURE SHE WAS LONELY. ALTHOUGH SHE HAD FRIENDS, SHE NEVER REALLY GOT OUT MUCH.

WITH 20 HOURS LEFT BEFORE I WOULD NEED TO LEAVE FOR AIRPORT, ONE THING I FORGOT TO DO WAS GET A RIDE TO THE AIRPORT, GOODNESS HOW COULD I FORGET THAT? I DIDN'T WANT TO ASK FAMILY, AS IT

WAS HARD ENOUGH LEAVING THEM AS IT WAS. I KNOW THEY HAD MY BEST INTEREST AT HEART, I JUST WANTED A MORE PEACEFUL TRIP AND GO IN SILENCE AND I WOULD BE NERVOUS, AND PROBABLY CRY ANYWAY. TO RELAX SOME, I DECIDED TO LOG INTO FACEBOOK AND MESSAGE THE ELDERS. THEY SAID IF THERE WAS ANYTHING THEY COULD DO TO LET THEM KNOW, AND THEY JUST HAPPENED TO POP IN MY MIND SO I WAS GOING TO SEND THEM A MESSAGE, BUT I SEEN WHERE THERE WAS A MESSAGE FROM THEM ASKING ME IF EVERYTHING WAS ALL SET AND IF THERE WAS ANYTHING I NEEDED AND I TOLD THEM YES! CAN YOU GIVE ME A RIDE TO THE AIRPORT? THEY WERE ONLY TOO EXCITED TO HELP AND I BREATHED A SIGH OF RELIEF! NOW!! EVERYTHING WAS IN ORDER.

I TRIED TO GO TO BED EARLY THAT NIGHT TO REST UP FOR THE TRIP. I KNEW I HAD ALONG PLANE RIDE AHEAD OF ME AND MAY HAVE JET LAG. MY YOUNGEST SON WAS DOING MY ROUTE FOR ME, SO I DIDN'T HAVE TO WORRY ABOUT THAT AND GET A GOOD NIGHTS REST. HE IS SUCH AN AMAZING YOUNG MAN. ALL MY CHILDREN ARE A WONDERFUL GIFT FROM GOD! I AM SO BLESSED. NONE OF THEM HAD EVER BEEN IN ANY MAJOR TROUBLE WITH THE LAW. NONE OF THEM HAD GOTTEN INTO DRUGS OR HAD ALCOHOL ISSUES AND I WAS SO GRATEFUL. ALL FAMILIES HAVE ISSUES OR THINGS THEY COULD HAVE DONE BETTER. I KNOW I MADE MY SHARE OF MISTAKES, BUT IS THERE REALLY A MANUEL TO TELL YOU HOW TO DO THINGS? YOU GO ON INSTINCT, KNOWLEDGE, AND FOR ME PRAYER! WE'RE HUMAN, NOT PERFECT BY ANY MEANS AND WILL MAKE MISTAKES. WHAT YOU DO WITH THAT IS UP TO

YOU, BUT SHOULD TRY AND LEARN FROM THOSE MISTAKES, AND STRIVE TO MAKE THINGS BETTER!

FINALLY!! TUESDAY AUGUST 24 TH 2010 WAS HERE!! THE DAY I WAS TO LEAVE FOR FIJI! MY MOM HAD COME OVER TO WISH ME WELL AND HELP ME WITH ANY LAST MINUTE THINGS I MAY NEED HELP WITH. I KNEW THIS WAS HARD ON HER, ESPECIALLY BEING GONE 9 MOS BUT I PRAYED SHE WOULD HANG IN THERE. MY FLIGHT WOULD TAKE OFF AT 4 PM AND I WOULD GO FROM DAYTON TO DENVER COLORADO. MY RIDE WOULD BE HERE AT NOON TO TAKE ME TO THE AIRPORT, AS THEY WANTED YOU TO BE THERE ABOUT 2 HOURS BEFORE TAKE-OFF TO CHECK IN AND THE ELDERS WANTED TO GET ME SOME LUNCH TOO. IT WAS ABOUT 12:30 BEFORE THE ELDERS ARRIVED AND I WAS RUNNING BEHIND ANYWAY, AS I TALKED ALL MORNING WHILE GETTING READY TO GO.

I MADE ONE LAST CHECK, SAID MY GOODBYES, AND WE LOADED MY BAGS INTO THEIR SUV AND OFF WE WENT. WE STOPPED AND GRABBED A SANDWICH FOR THE ROAD AND ARRIVED AT THE AIRPORT A LITTLE EARLY. I LIKE BEING EARLY ANYWAY. IT GIVES ME MORE TIME TO JUST BREATHE AND RELAX. NORMALLY THEY DON'T ALLOW VISITORS IN THE BACK OF AIRPORT ONCE THE ONE'S FLYING WERE CHECKED IN, BUT WE ASKED GOD FOR FAVOR ASKING THAT THE ELDERS BE ALLOWED WITH ME SINCE THIS WAS TO BE MY FIRST MISSIONS TRIP AND NEVER BEING ON A PLANE BEFORE SO THEY COULD PRAY WITH ME BEFORE GETTING ON THE PLANE. THE ATTENDANT WAS SO GRACIOUS THAT HE GAVE BOTH THE ELDERS PASSES, TO GO BACK WITH ME AND I WAS SO THANKFUL TO HAVE SOMEONE

WITH ME AND TALK TO MAKE MY WAIT SEEM SHORTER. I'M ACTUALLY NOT SURE WHO WAS MORE EXCITED, THEM OR ME AND I WAS ESTACTIC! TO ME THIS WAS A TRIP OF A LIFETIME AND LIKE A VACATION TOO, AND IT HAD BEEN YEARS SINCE I HAD A TRUE VACATION. I'D USUALLY TAKE A DAY HERE OR A DAY THERE SO THEY LASTED LONGER AND WE CRAMMED SO MUCH INTO THE DAY IT'S HARD TO REMEBER ALL WE DID. THIS TRIP WOULD DEFINITELY BE ONE TO REMEMBER AND TREASURE FOR THE REST OF MY LIFE AND BE FULL OF PICTURES TOO.

FINALLY THE BOARDING CALL WAS ANNOUNCED. AS THEY PRAYED OVER ME AND GAVE ME HUGS AND SAID MY GOODBYES, TEARS WELLED UP INSIDE ME. THEY ASSURED ME EVERYTHING WAS GOING TO BE OK. THAT GOD WAS WITH ME AND THERE WAS NO TURNING BACK NOW. AS I BOARDED THE PLANE, I NOTICED IT WAS TINY INSIDE, THE AISLE SO SLIM YOU COULDN'T GET 2 PEOPLE SIDE BY SIDE. I SOMEHOW IMAGINED PLANES BEING BIGGER ON THE INSIDE AND I STARTED TO PANIC. BUT I SHOOK IT OFF AND ASKED GOD TO HELP CALM MY NERVES. I PRAYED FOR SAFETY AND THAT I WOULD STAY HEALTHY WHILE GONE. I DIDN'T WANT TO EXPERIENCE JET LAG OR MOTION SICKNESS AS YOU SOMETIMES HEAR ABOUT WITH FLYERS OR THOSE TRAVELING BY SEA AND I BROUGHT PLENTY OF GUM TO HELP WITH ANY EAR POPPING I MAY HAVE FROM THE ALTITUDE. THE FLIGHT WAS TO BE ABOUT AN HOUR AND 45 MINUTES TO DENVER, SO I SETTLED BACK AND READ A MAGAZINE THEN WORKED SOME PUZZLE BOOKS I HAD BROUGHT WITH ME. I WAS TO SCARED TO LOOK OUT THE WINDOW AT FIRST, BUT BRAVED IT AND TOOK A PEEK. I

WAS AMAZED TO SEE SO MANY CLOUDS OUT THERE AND SUCH A BEAUTIFUL SHAPE TO THEM.

IT REMINDED ME OF WHEN I WAS A GIRL, I'D BE PLAYING OUTSIDE AND REMEMBERED LOOKING AT HOW BLUE THE SKY WAS AND MAKING SHAPES OUT OF THE CLOUDS. I STILL DO THAT FROM TIME TO TIME. JUST THEN I WAS REMINDED OF A SCRIPTURE IN HEBREWS 12:1 THEREFORE, SINCE WE ARE SURROUNDED BY SUCH A GREAT CLOUD OF WITNESSES, LET US THROW OFF EVERYTHING THAT HINDERS AND THE SIN THAT SO EASILY ENTANGLES. LET US RUN WITH PERSERVERANCE THE RACE MARKED OUT FOR US. AT THAT MOMENT I FELT THE PRESENCE OF GOD AND AN OVERWHELMING CALM CAME OVER ME AND I KNEW EVERYTHING WAS GONNA BE ALRIGHT. THOSE CLOUDS WERE MINISTERING ANGELS, AND I FELT THE TENSION LEAVE MY BODY AND BE REPLACED WITH PEACE.

THE ANNOUNCEMENT CAME OVER THE SPEAKER TELLING US TO FASTEN OUR SEATBELTS, WE HAD ARRIVED IN DENVER AND WERE STARTING TO MAKE OUR DESCEND SO WE COULD LAND. WOO-HOO! IT WAS THE FIRST TIME BEING IN COLORADO. I HAD BEEN TO ALOT OF THE EASTERN STATES WHEN I WAS MARRIED TO GEORGE. GEORGE AND MY MOM WERE SPORT FANATICS AND WE TOOK HER TO COOPERSTOWN NEW YORK TO THE BASEBALL HALL OF FAME. SO WE WENT THRU PENNSYLVANIA,INTO NEW YORK, WALKED OVER THE BRIDGE FROM NIAGRA FALLS INTO CANADA WHICH WAS BEAUTIFUL. THE HALL OF FAME WAS AMAZING AND THE LOOK ON MY MOM'S FACE WAS PRICELESS. SHE HAD BEEN A BALL FAN SINCE SHE WAS A CHILD

AND NEVER REALLY GOT TO GO MANY PLACES. MY FATHER BARELY WORKED SO IT WAS MY MOM THAT HAD SUPPORTED THE FAMILY, SO IT WAS NICE SHE TOOK SOME TIME OFF TO MAKE THIS TRIP. AFTER WE WERE FINISHED AT THE HALL OF FAME, WE DECIDED TO TAKE A DIFFERENT ROUTE HOME AND VISIT SOME OTHER STATES. WE TRAVELED TO CONNECTICUT AND MASSECHUSETTS, STAYED THE NIGHT THERE. THE NEXT DAY AFTER HAVING BREAKFAST, WE SET OUT AND WENT TO NEW JERSEY AND DOWN INTO RHODE ISLAND AND SEEN THE ATLANTIC OCEAN. THAT PARTICULAR DAY THERE WERE LOTS OF SEAGULLS AROUND THE BEACH. IT WAS SO BEAUTIFUL AND WE TOOK LOTS OF PICTURES TOO EVERYWHERE WE VISITED. WHAT WAS FASCINATING TO ME WAS THE MOUNTAINS. HOW THEY SEEMED TO CUT OUT THE MOUNTAINS TO MAKE THE RODES, IT WAS SO FASCINATING. AT OTHER TIMES IN OUR LIFE WE HAD WENT TO KENTUCKY, TENNESSEE, THE OUTSKIRTS OF GEORGIA, MICHIGAN, INDIANA AND ILLINOIS. IT WAS EXCITING TO VISIT DIFFERENT AREAS ALTHOUGH THIS TIME I WAS ON A PLANE AND TRAVELING ALONE!

MY MIND WAS BROUGHT BACK WHEN WE FINALLY LANDED. IT WAS A SMOOTH LANDING, JUST AS I PRAYED IT WOULD BE AND I MUTTERED A THANK YOU TO GOD. AS I REACHED TO GET MY CARRYING ON BAG, MY MIND WENT TO THOUGHTS OF PLANE CRASHES, AND IT SCARES YOU TO THINK IT COULD HAPPEN TO YOU, BUT ACCIDENTS HAPPEN ANYWHERE, WHETHER A PLANE, CAR, WORK, OR EVEN IN YOUR OWN HOUSE. AS WE GOT OFF THE PLANE AND WALKED DOWN THE HALL INTO THE AIRPORT, I WAS MET WITH A CROWD OF PEOPLE. SOME SITTING, SOME BUZZING THRU FROM

ONE END TO OTHER WITH BAGS A TOW SEARCHING FOR THEIR GATE TO BOARD THEIR NEXT FLIGHT, YET DIDN'T APPEAR TO BE LONG LINES AT ANY OF THE TERMINALS, OR MANY SHOPS THEY HAD. I HAD MY TICKET IN HAND AND MADE MY WAY THRU THE HALLWAY IN SEARCH FOR THE NEXT GATE FOR MY FLIGHT TO LA, CALIFORNIA. WOW, LOS ANGELAS, I WONDERED IF I'D RUN INTO ANY CELEBRITIES, HOW AWESOME THAT WOULD BE! AS I WALKED AROUND TO KILL SOME TIME AS I HAD 2 HOURS BEFORE MY FLIGHT TO CALIFORNIA, I WAS DISAPPOINTED YOU COULDN'T SEE ALOT OF THE OUTSIDE SCENERY. MAYBE IT WAS THE PART OF THE AIRPORT I WAS IN, BUT I WAS AFRAID TO GO MUCH FARTHER FROM THE AREA I WAS IN FOR FEAR OF GETTING LOST AND MISSING MY FLIGHT. WOULDN'T THAT BE SOMETHING IF I MISSED MY FLIGHT. NO!

I WENT A GRABBED A BITE TO EAT AND WAS SHOCKED AT HOW HIGH THE AIRPORT PRICES WERE. I DIDN'T WANT TO EAT MUCH ANYWAY AS I WASN'T SURE HOW MY STOMACH WOULD HANDLE A HEAVY MEAL MIXED WITH THE ALTITUDE OF BEING HIGH IN THE AIR, AS IT WAS A 3 1/2 HOUR FLIGHT FROM DENVER TO LA COMPARED TO 1 HOUR 45 MIN FROM DAYTON TO LA, SO I OPTED FOR A SMALL SALAD NOT WANTING TO TAKE ANY CHANCES ON MOTION SICKNESS, AND MADE A CALL TO THE ELDERS OF OUR CHURCH TO LET THEM KNOW I LANDED SAFELY. THEY WERE SO GLAD TO HEAR FROM ME AND AFTER SHARING ABOUT THE FLIGHT HERE, WISHED ME WELL AND HUNG UP. I FOUND A PLACE TO SIT AT MY GATE AND TIME SEEMED TO DRAG BY.

I WORKED MY PUZZLE BOOK, READ MAGAZINES AND NEWSPAPERS AND WATCHED THE MANY PEOPLE COMING AND GOING. I NOTICED ALOT OF THEM IN BUSINESS SUITS OR DRESSED UP IN SOME FORM, AND MANY ON COMPUTERS OR PHONES AS IF PREPARING FOR SOME SORT OF BUSINESS MEETING. SOME WERE READING OR TALKING WITH FAMILY MEMBERS WHILE OTHERS STARED BLANKLY AT THE TELEVISION ANXIOUSLY AWAITING THE BOARDING CALL FOR THEIR FLIGHT. I ALWAYS GET A KICK OUT OF WATCHING PEOPLE, THEY CAN BE SO HILARIOUS. I FIND IT IRONIC HOW OUT OF ALL THE BILLIONS OF PEOPLE ON THIS EARTH, EVERYONES MAKE UP IS A LITTLE DIFFERENT, FROM HAIR, TO EYES, NOSES, HEAD SHAPE. ALL THE MARVELOUS CREATION OF GOD, EVERYTHING AND EVERYONE WONDERFULLY MADE TO PERFECTION BY A MIGHTY GOD WHO LOVES US ALL SO MUCH,YET PEOPLE WILL PURPOSELY ALTER THEIR APPEARANCE THRU PLASTIC SURGERY. NOT SAYING ANYTHING IS WRONG WITH PLASTIC SURGERY, IN SOME CASES IT BECOMES NECESSARY, WHEN IT COMES BY SICKNESS OR ACCIDENT OF SOME SORT, BUT IF IT IS DONE BECAUSE A PERSON DOESN'T LIKE THE WAY THEY WERE FORMED AND CREATED, THEN I THINK IT'S SORT OF A SLAP AGAINST GOD AS IF SAYING HE DID A BAD JOB. HE SAYS IN HIS WORD HE MAKES ALL THINGS BEAUTIFUL!

FINALLY THE ANNOUNCEMENT CAME OVER THE SPEAKER THAT IS WAS TIME TO BOARD THE FLIGHT TO LA. WE WERE AHEAD OF SCHEDULE WHICH WAS COOL WITH ME, BUT I STILL HAD A LONG FLIGHT SCHEDULE AHEAD OF ME. IT WAS 3 1/2 HOURS TO LA, THEN A 4 HOUR LAYOVER THERE, AND THEN A 10 1/2 HOUR

FLIGHT TO FIJI. THE PLANE INSIDE WAS MUCH BIGGER THAN THE ONE I WAS ON FROM DAYTON TO DENVER. I WAS IN A SIDE SEAT THAT I SHARED WITH ANOTHER LADY, I WAS OK WITH IT AS I SAT NEXT TO THE WINDOW AND COULD SIGHT SEE, WHAT LITTLE WE COULD SEE FROM SO HIGH UP. IT WAS STILL DAYLIGHT AND WITH NTHE SUN OUT THERE WAS A SLIGHT GLARE, AND MADE IT HARD TO MAKE SOME THINGS OUT, BUT I COULD SEE MOUNTAINS AND THE HILLS. EVERYTHING LOOKED SO MAJESTIC IN THEIR ARRAY OF COLORS THAT BLENDED TOGETHER SO WELL. THE CARS AND BUSES THAT ZOOMED DOWN THE ROADS THAT LOOKED LIKE ANTS FROM OVER 10,000 FEET IN THE AIR.

I'M NOT SURE HOW MANY STATES WE FLEW OR, OR IF I COULD EVEN SAY I WAS THERE, BUT I WAS THRILLED AT HAVING THIS OPPORTUNITY AND THANKED GOD FOR USING ME AND ALLOWING ME THIS PLEASURE TO SERVE HIM IN THIS CAPACITY. THIS WAS LIKE A MINI VACATION FOR ME, I WAS ALONE, NO ONE TO BOTHER ME, TELL ME HOW TO LIVE, WHAT TO WEAR, WHAT TO DO IN A CONTROLLING SENSE OF VIEW. WE WILL ALWAYS HAVE TO FOLLOW RULES AND STUFF BUT I WAS BECOMING MY OWN PERSON AND I WAS LOVING IT. SOON THE ANNOUNCEMENT CAME ACROSS THE P.A. SYSTEM THAT WE'D SOON BE LANDING AT LA AIRPORT. WE WERE AHEAD OF SCHEDULE, GIVING THE TIME AND THE WEATHER REPORT. WITH CALIFORNIA BEING 3 HOURS BEHIND OHIO, THERE WOULD STILL BE LOTS OF DAYLIGHT TIME LEFT AND SO MUCH SCENERY TO SEE. AS WE STARTED OUR DECENT INTO THE LANDING STRIP, I LOOKED OUT THE WINDOW AND MY MOUTH FELL OPEN. THE SIGHTS

WERE AMAZING. THE TALL BUILDINGS, MULTI LANED HIGHWAYS BUZZING WITH TRAFFIC AND THE ROWS OF BEAUTIFUL MANSIONS, SOME LOOKING SO BIG IT WAS LIKE A MINI TOWN WITHIN ITSELF.

THE LANDING WAS ANOTHER SMOOTH ONE AND I SMILED AS I THOUGHT TO MYSELF, I CAN DO THIS, I'M GETTING THE HANG OF THIS FLYING STUFF. THE DREAMS AND VISION GOD HAD PLACED IN MY HEART WAS BECOMING REALITY AND IN A LITTLE OVER 4 HOURS I WOULD BE FLYING TO FIJI. I KNEW WITH GOD ALL THINGS WERE POSSIBLE, SOMETIMES ALL IT TAKES IS A WILLING SPIRIT. SUBMISSION IS THE WORD I WANT HERE. SOMETIMES PEOPLE LOOK AT THAT WORD AS AN UGLY THING, SEEMS TO LOOK AT WANTING TO BE IN CONTROL AND THAT'S OK, BUT IT'S IMPORTANT TO KEEP GOD ON THE FORE FRONT. WE CAN BE IN CONTROL WITHOUT HAVING CONTROL IF THAT MAKES SENSE. NOW ANOTHER WAIT, WHAT WAS I GOING TO DO FOR THE NEXT 4 1/2 PLUS HOURS.

I PRAYED THAT THE FLIGHT WOULD BE EARLY AS OUR LAST 2 LANDINGS HAD BEEN. AS SOON AS I GOT OFF THE PLANE AND FOUND MY GATE, I CALLED MY ELDERS TO LET THEM KNOW I HAD LANDED. WE TALKED FOR A FEW MINUTES THEN AFTER HANGING UP I CALLED THE FAMILY IN FIJI TO LET THEM KNOW I HAD LANDED SAFELY IN CALIFORNIA AND WOULD BE ON MY WAY THERE IN A FEW HOURS. WE WENT OVER FINAL INSTRUCTIONS JUST SO I WAS CLEAR THAT HIS BROTHER WOULD STILL BE MEETING ME WHEN I GOT OFF THE PLANE AND HELP ME WITH MY BAGS. AFTER EVERYTHING WAS SITUATED I HUNG UP, THEN I LOOKED FOR A PLACE TO EAT. THE FLIGHT TO FIJI WAS

GOING TO BE MY LONGEST FLIGHT, BEING 10 HOURS AND 40 MINUTES. WE WOULD CROSS THE EQUATOR, 2 TIME ZONES AND THE DATE CENTER. ALL IN ALL ALTHOUGH IT WAS STILL TUES EVENING, IT WOULD BE THURS MORNING AT 5:30 AM BEFORE I WOULD ARRIVE IN FIJI. WHEN I CROSSED THE DATE LINE I WOULD SKIP A DAY ACTUALLY SPENDING WED ON THE PLANE EVEN THOUGH FOR ONLY A SHORT AMOUNT OF HOURS FLIGHT. WOW! GOING INTO THE FUTURE. IT REMINDED ME OF THE MOVIE I ONCE WATCHED BACK TO THE FUTURE ALTHOUGH I HAD NEVER BEEN TO THE FUTURE. WHAT A WILD EXPERIENCE TO ENCOUNTER.

AFTER I FINISHED EATING, I WENT TO CHECK IN AND LEARNED I HAD TO TAKE A SHUTTLE BUS OVER TO THE INTERNATIONAL AIRPORT IN ORDER TO CATCH FLIGHT OVERSEAS. THIS WAS A LITTLE SCARY STANDING ON THE STREETS OF LA WAITING FOR A BUS. HEAVY TRAFFIC FLEW BY, TAXI'S PULLING UP HERE AND THERE TO DROP OFF OR PICK UP PASSENGERS. SIDEWALKS CROWDED WITH PEOPLE COMING AND GOING, BUT THEY WERE ALL USED TO THE BUSYNESS, ME COMING FROM A SMALL TOWN THIS WAS ALMOST CLAUSTROPHOBIC. IT MADE ME THANKFUL FOR MY SMALL HOME TOWN THOUGH BUT IT WAS AWESOME THOUGH AND I TOOK IN EVERY MOVEMENT, THERE WAS DEFINITELY LOTS TO SEE. IT WAS HARD TO DESCRIBE INTO WORDS WHAT I WAS FEELING INSIDE, THE SITES WAS SO BREATHTAKING.

ONCE I ARRIVED AT THE INTERNATIONAL AIRPORT, DARKNESS HAD SETTLED IN. WHEN I GOT INSIDE THE PLACE WAS HUGE, LOTS OF DIFFERENT LANGUAGES ON THE BOARDS AND PEOPLE FROM

DIFFERENT CULTURES. I WENT TO CHECK IN AND THERE WAS 2 GATES TO FIJI, I THOUGHT I ARRIVED AT THE RIGHT GATE AND SAT DOWN AND GRABBED A MAGAZINE. TIME SEEM TO FLY AND SOON THE ANNOUNCEMENT OVER THE LOUD SPEAKER ANNOUNCED THAT THE PLANE COULD NOW BE BOARDED. I STOOD IN LINE AND WHEN IT CAME TIME TO BOARD, I HANDED MY TICKET TO THE ATTENDENT ONLY TO BE TOLD I WAS AT THE WRONG GATE. SHE TOLD ME I MHAD TO GO TO THE OTHER SIDE OF THE AIRPORT TO THE NEXT GATE. I GOT NERVOUDS AND SAID OH NO YOU ARE KIDDING ME RIGHT! SHE GAVE ME DIRECTIONS AND AS I SCURRIED ALONG I PRAYED I'D MAKE IT TO THE GATE BEFORE THE FLIGHT TOOK OFF. AFTER COMING ALL THIS WAY AND THEN TO MISS MY FLIGHT, IT WASN'T HAPPENING. I'M A FAST WALKER, BUT AT THIS TIME I DON'T THINK I EVER WALKED AS FAST AS I DID TO MAKE THAT GATE.

WHEN I ARRIVED AT THE RIGHT GATE, I WENT THRU CUSTOMS WITH JUST MINUTES TO SPARE, BUT THANK YOU LORD I MADE IT AND BREATHED A SIGH OF RELIEF, AS I BEGAN RUBBLING MY SORE LEGS. SOON IT WAS TIME TO BOARD AND AS I WENT OUT THE DOOR TO THE PLANE I TOOK NOTICE OF IT SIZE AND GASPED. IT WAS MONTROUS. I GOT INSIDE THE PLANE, HANDED MY TICKET TO THE ATTENDANT, AND AS SHE SHOWED ME WHERE MY SEAT WAS, TOOK NOTICE THAT THE INSIDE WAS EVEN BIGGER THAN THE LAST PLANE I WAS ON. I EVEN HEARD ONE OF THE ATTENDANTS DIRECTING PEOPLE TO AN UPSTAIRS. THEY HAD AN UPSTAIRS IN A PLANE? AS I GOT TO MY SEAT I NOTICED IT WAS A SIDE AISLE WHERE THE SEATS WERE ALOT SMALLER AND I HAD THE MIDDLE SEAT BETWEEN 2

311

LADIES. AS I PUT MY CARRYON BAG IN THE OVERHEAD COMPARTMENT, I TOOK A GLANCE AROUND TO SEE IF THERE WAS A SPARE SEAT AVAILABLE ELSEWHERE. I DIDN'T WANT TO BE CRAMMED IN THE MIDDLE OF PEOPLE, I WAS NERVOUS ENOUGH, THE FLIGHT LONG AND DIDN'T WANT SOMEONE CLIMBING OVER ME TO USE THE BATHROOM. NOR DID I WANT TO HAVE TO CLIMB OVER SOMEONE TO USE THE BATHROOM SINCE I SEEMED TO HAVE AN OVER ACTIVE BLADDER.

I SLID INTO AN EMPTY ROW AND PRAYED NO ONE HAD THAT SEAT. SOON I HEARD THE ENGINES START UP AND THEY WERE MASSIVE SOUNDING, AND FELT THE RUMBLING SOUND UNDER MY FEET. I SUPPOSE MY SECTION OF SEATS WAS RIGHT OVER THE ENGINE COMPARTMENT. SOON WE WERE IN THE AIR ON OUR WAY TO FIJI. I SORT OF REGRETTED NOT HAVING A WINDOW SEAT. SINCE IT WAS DARK, I WOULD HAVE LOVED TO SEE THE OCEAN UNDER THE LIGHTING FROM THE MOON, ESPECIALLY WHEN WE FLEW OVER THE EQUATOR. MY THOUGHTS WENT TO THOSE IN FIJI WAITING ON MY ARRIVAL, I PRAYED I WOULD BE WELCOMED. THE HOST FAMILY HAD TOLD ME STORIES ABOUT HOW FIJIANS LOOKED TO AMERICANS AS PEOPLE OF HONOR AND HELD THEM IN HIGH REGARDS. WOW, I WASN'T EVEN A CELEBRITY, BUT FELT LIKE ONE. EACH SEAT HAD THEIR OWN MINI TV AND HAD A FEATURE ON THERE WHERE YOU COULD TRACK THE PROGRESS OF THE PLANE AND WHERE YOU WERE. THAT WAS REALLY COOL. I SAT BACK AND WATCHED A PROGRAM AND THEN DOZED OFF. I SLEPT RESTLESSLY AND OFTEN CHECKED TO SEE WHERE WE WERE, THINKING WE WERE ON THERE WAY TOO LONG.

312

I FLIPPED THRU THE CHANNELS AGAIN, TO FIND SOMETHING TO WATCH AND SOON THE LIGHTS CAME ON AS THEY WERE PREPARING TO SERVE EVERYONE BREAKFAST. THEY HAD MENTIONED THAT WE WEOULD BE ARRIVING IN FIJI IN AN HOUR AND 20 MINUTES. YEE HAW! AS I GOT UP TO USE THE RESTROOM SOMEONE OPENED THE WINDOW SHADE AND I GOT A BRIEF LOOK AT THE OCEAN AND THE EQUATOR, IT WAS SO BEAUTIFUL.

SOON WE WERE LANDING AND I THOUGHT WOW, THAT WENT FAST. MAYBE IT WASN'T AS LONG AS THEY THOUGHT. AS WE MADE OUR DECENT, IT WAS JUST STARTING TO GET LIGHT. SOME BUILDINGS CAME INTO VIEW AND I MARVELED AT THE HILLS AND THE BEAUTY. I WAS SO IN AWE AND COULDN'T BELIEVE I WAS FINALLY HERE. I MADE MY WAY OFF THE PLANCE AND TO THE BAGGAGE CLAIN AREA. IT DIDN'T TAKE LONG FOR A MAN TO COME GREET ME, ASKING ME IF I WAS TERESA. I SAID YES AND LEARNED IT WAS THE BROTHER OF MY HOST FAMILY. HE SAID HIS BROTHER HAD GIVEN HIM A COPY OF MY PICTURE SO HE COULD FIND ME EASILY AND HE LED ME TO WHERE I COULD GET MY BAG. I HAD BUTTERFLIES IN MY STOMACH AS WE MADE OUR WAY TO THE FRONT OF THE AIRPORT WHERE HE SAID THE FAMILY WAS THERE WAITING FOR ME. I WAS SO EXCITED TO MEET EVERYONE AND FELT I ALREADY KNEW THEM MY WHOLE LIFE RATHER THAN THE LAST FEW MONTHS SINCE RECEIVING THE CALL OF GOD ON MY LIFE! I ALREADY KNEW WHAT THE FAMILY LOOKED LIKE FROM OUR VIDEO CHATS, SO THEY SHOULD BE EASY TO SPOT.

WHEN WE GOT TO THE FRONT OF THE AIRPORT I QUICKLY CAUGHT SITE OF AND WAS GREETED BY MY HOST FAMILY. WE SHOOK HANDS AND I INSTANTLY FELT THE ANNOINTING ON THIS FAMILY AND WHAT AN ADORABLE FAMILY THEY WERE. AS HE LOADED MY BAGS IN THE CAR, I WENT TO GET IN WHAT I THOUGHT WAS THE PASSENGER SIDE OF THE CAR. BUT THEIR CARS ARE BUILT DIFFERENT THERE AND IT WAS ACTUALLY THE DRIVER'S SIDE. HE JOKED ASKING ME IF I WAS GONNA DRIVE AND MY FACE BECAME RED AS I WENT AROUND THE OTHER SIDE OF THE CAR APOLOGIZING AND EXPLAINING THAT WHERE I'M FROM THE STEERING WHEEL IS ON THE OTHER SIDE. ALSO THEY DROVE ON THE OPPOSITE SIDE OF THE STREET TOO. I WAS ACTUALLY NERVOUS, ESPECIALLY WHEN I NOTICED THERE WASN'T ANY STOP SIGNS. PEOPLE PULLED UP TO AN OINTERSECTION AND IF NO TRAFFIC NEVER BOTHERED TO STOP AND JUST WENT ON. I JUST CLOSED MY EYES AND TOOK A DEEP BREATH, THIS WAS GOING TO TAKE SOME GETTING USED TO FOR SURE.

WE WENT TO THE FLAT WHERE I WOULD BE STAYING, AND WAS MET BY THE OLDER DAUGHTER AND THE STEP SON OF THE HOST FAMILY. THE CUSTOM THERE WAS TO TAKE OFF YOUR SHOES BEFORE ENTERING THE HOUSE, BUT I WAS ALREADY USED TO THIS AS BACK HOME WE HAD CARPETING AND I NEVER LIKED TO WALK WITH SIRTY SHOES ON IT, ESPECIALLY IN THE WINTER TIME AND THE CARPET WOULD BE WET AND YOU'D GET YOUR SOCKS WET. I PUT MY BAGS AWAY, THEN WE LEFT TO DO A LITTLE SIGHT SEEING. IT WAS A BEAUTIFUL TOWN WITH LOTS OF PALM TREES, AND THE SKY WAS SO LOW IT WAS

LIKE YOU COULD REACH OUT AND TOUCH IT. WE STOPPED TO A VENDOR ON THE SIDE OF THE ROAD SELLING COCONUT MILK AND I BOUGHT ONE. THEY WERE A REGULAR COCONUT AND HAD CHISELED A HOLE IN IT AND PUT A STRAW IN THE HOLE. I WASN'T A BIG FAN OF COCONUT, BUT THOUGHT I MWOULD TRY IT SINCE FRESH FROM THE COCONUT ITSELF AND NOT PROCESSED. I DIDN'T MUCH CARE FOR IT BUT DRANK IT ANYWAY AS NOT TO BE RUDE.

WE DROVE TO THE OCEAN AND IT WAS SO BREATHTAKING. I GOT OUT OF THE CAR, TOOK MY SHOES OFF AND WALKED THE BEACH LETTING THE SAND SQUISH BETWEEN MY TOES, LOOKING OUT OVER THE WATER SEEING ALL THE BOATS OUT THERE AND PEOPLE SWIMMING, THE PLANES FLYING OVER, I WAS SPEECHLESS. I COULD NOW SAY I HAD BEEN TO EACH OCEAN, AND DEFINITELY WANTED TO TAKE TIME, TO COME BACK FREQUENTLY AND DO SOME WRITING. WHAT A PEACEFUL PLACE THIS WAS. WE TALKED ABOUT MY FLIGHT AND THE DIFFERENT MINISTRY OPPORTUNITIES WE WERE LOOKING AT THEN WE HEADED BACK TO THE FLAT, TO GET READY FOR DINNER. WE WAS MEETING WITH THE PASTORS OF THE CHURCH I WOULD BE ATTENDING FOR DINNER AND I WAS LOOKING FORWARD TO FINALLY MEETING THEM.

WHEN WE ARRIVED AT THE RESTAURANT, THEY WERE ALREADY THERE AND SEATED. THEY WERE SUCH NICE PEOPLE AMND AFTER WE ORDERED, ENGAGED IN CONVERSATION, AND HIT IT OFF WELL, LIKE WE NEW EACH OTHER FOR YEARS. WHEN THEY BROUGHT THE FOOD, IT WAS SO FESTIVE LOOKING. RICE DISHES, COLORFUL VEGETABLES, FRESH FISH

AND CHICKEN. AS WE PRAYED OVER THE FOOD, I PRAYED I WOULD ADAPT TO THEIR FOOD AND CULTURE OK. ON THE WAY TO THE RESTAURANT, I NOTICED THAT THE FLATS WERE MADE OF CEMENT, I'M SURE TO ENDURE HURRICANE WEATHER, AND MOST OF THE WINDOWS HAD BARS ACROSS THEM. SOME AREAS SEEMED IMPOVERISHED, WITH THEIR VINYL FLOORING THAT LAID IN SHEETS ON THE FLOOR AND THEIR ROADS WERE MORE LIKE ALLEYS. BUT I KNEW I WAS SENT WITH A PURPOSE AND GOD WOULD BE WITH ME. WHAT AN HONOR TO SERVE HIM IN THIS CAPACITY.

THE FOOD WAS REALLY GOOD AND I GOT FULL FAST, WE HAD GREAT CONVERSATION, THEN LEFT AND RETURNED TO THE FLAT. I ASKED TO USE THE COMPUTER SO I COULD SEND A MESSAGE TO MY FAMILY LETTING THEM KNOW I ARRIVED SAFELY, AND CHATTED WITH MY SON FOR A BIT. IT WAS FUNNY TO SEE MY MOM NOW HAD A FACEBOOK PAGE, BUT CREATED IT TO COMMUNICATE WITH ME. AFTER I SIGNED OFF I WENT TO LAY DOWN FOR A BIT TO REST FROM MY TRIP. AS I LAID THERE RESTING, I WAS THINKING HOW FOR THE FIRST TIME IN A LONG TIME, MY LIFE WAS STARTING TO MAKE SENSE. MY KID'S MOVING HOME, MY FAILED MARRIAGES, THE ABUSE, EVERYTHING I'D BEEN THRU, GOD UNFOLDED BEFORE ME AND SHOWED ME THEY WERE STEPPING STONES, TO CLIMB TO WHERE HE WANTED ME TO BE. ALTHOUGH THE DESTINATION IS UNKNOWN AND EACH STEP UNSURE, IF YOU TAKE THE STEP ANYWAY, THINGS WILL SOON COME TO LIGHT AND MAKE SENSE. I THOUGHT OF THE LAST YEAR AND ALL THAT TRANSPIRED. I HAD DONE SOME SPONTANEOUS AND WILD THINGS FOR BEING 46. I GOT MY NOSE PIERCED,

MY HAIR CUT AND COLORED, NEW WARDROBE THAT WAS MORE UP TO DATE AND STYLISH, IT WAS A NEW ME! THERE SEEMED TO BE A WILD SIDE I NEVER KNEW EXISTED, NOT A BAD WILD SIDE, BUT A CONFIDENT SIDE. ONE OF DETERMINATION, AND RISK TAKING. TO GO WITH MY HEART AND IT WAS OK TO BE DIFFERENT.

WHEN I WOKE IT WAS 2 HOURS LATER, AND I SMELLED FOOD COOKING AND THOUGHT IT WAS ALMOST SUPPER TIME. AS WE SAT DOWN TO EAT AND PRAYED OVER THE FOOD, I WASN'T TOO SURE OF THE FOOD. I LEARNED IT WAS CALLED DAHL, WHICH IS SPLIT PEAS, SOAKED IN WATER AND COOKED IN I BELIEVE COCONUT MILK AND PUT OVER RICE. I TRIED IT AND FOUND I DIDN'T LIKE IT, SO JUST ATE THE RICE. I HAD NOTICED, THAT THEY SEEMED TO BE MORE OF A CALM AND LAID BACK COUNTRY. FUNNY HOW YOU CAN PICK UP ON THINGS LIKE THAT WHEN YOU COME FROM A COUNTRY THAT IS SO FAST PACED. I WONDERED HOW OUR 2 CULTURES WOULD MANAGE WHILE I WAS THERE. IN SOME WAYS WE WERE SIMILAR IN BELIEFS, BUT YET THERE WAS SO MANY MORE DIFFERENCES, BUT I HAD A PEACE THINGS WOULD ALL WORK OUT, GOD HAD ALREADY FORESEEN AND MADE ALLOWANCES AND PUT INTO MY SPIRIT THAT HE WORKS ALL THINGS OUT FOR GOOD TO THOSE WHO LOVE HIM AND ARE CALLED ACCORDING TO HIS PURPOSE. WHEN I WENT TO BED THAT NIGHT, I PRAYED AND TOLD THE LORD, THIS IS IT GOD, I AM HERE TO FULFILL WHATEVER PLAN YOU HAVE FOR ME, I AM HERE TO DO THE WORK OF THE MINISTRY.

THAT SUNDAY WE ATTENDED CHURCH WHERE I WAS MET BY THE MOST LOVING PEOPLE. THEY HELD

THEIR SERVICES IN A HALL THAT WAS RENTED OUT FOR DIFFERENT EVENTS. PLANS WERE BEING MADE TO BUILD THEIR OWN CHURCH, BUT TILL THE PERMIT AND FINANCES CAME THRU THEY RENTED THIS BUILDING FOR THEIR SERVICES. I WAS AMAZED HOW BIG THE CHURCH WAS AND MET PEOPLE FROM ALL DIFFERENT CULTURES. I WAS MET BY PHILLIPINO'S, CHINESE, KOREAN, ASIAN, INDIANS AND THEY ALL WERE WORSHIP TOGETHER AND SPOKE GOOD ENGLISH FOR THE MOST PART. I WASN'T SURE HOW I WOULD GET ALONG IN A FOREIGN COUNTRY FOR SO LONG, BUT I WAS THANKFUL I BECAME AQUAINTED WITH MY HOST FAMILY,SO THEY COULD HELP ME WITH THINGS I DIDN'T UNDERSTAND, ESPECIALLY THE LANGUAGE. IT WAS LIKE HAVING AN INTERPRETER OR TRAVEL AGENT WITH ME, I DEFINITELY FELT SPECIAL. THE WORSHIP SERVICE WAS GOOD, AND WHEN THE PASTOR GOT UP TO SPEAK, HE INTRODUCED ME TO THE CONGREGATION AND ASKED IF I WOULD COME UP AND GIVE A BRIEF TESTIMONY. I WAS SO HONORED AND WITH KNEES KNOCKING MADE MY WAY TO THE FRONT AND SHARED WHAT GOD HAD DONE AND PLACED IN MY HEART. THE PEOPLE INSTANTLY FELL IN LOVE WITH ME AND I WAS EXCITED TO SEE WHERE GOD WOULD TAKE THIS CHURCH! THE MESSAGE WAS GOOD AND I REMEMBER SAYING AMEN TO A STATEMENT HE HAD MADE. HE SPOKE UP AND SAID HE LIKED THAT, AND I FOUND MORE PEOPLE SPOKE UP AND AMENED HIM TOO. I REALLY FELT A SENSE OF FULFILLMENT AND PRAYED I WOULD MAKE A DIFFERENCE WHILE THERE.

AFTER SERVICE, WE WENT HOME TO A VERY NICE LUNCH ALREADY PREPARED FOR US. IT WAS WHAT THEY CALLED CURRY. IT CONSISTED OF CORNED

BEEF WHICH THEY CALLED TIN MEAT, VEGETABLES, POTATOES, COOKED WITH GARLIC AND CURRY POWDER AND SERVED OVER RICE. IT WAS REALLY GOOD QUICKLY BECAME A FAVORITE FOOD. THAT EVENING WE SAT TO PRAY TOGETHER, THEY HAD QUESTIONS CONCERNING OUR AMERICAN CULTURE. THEY WERE SHY GIRLS AND MAINLY KEPT TO THEMSELVES, SO I WAS GLAD THEY WERE BEING INQUISITIVE AND SHARED SOME THINGS WITH THEM. WE THEN PRAYED AND PUT IN A MOVIE TO WATCH AS DARKNESS WAS STARTING TO SET IN. SINCE WE WERE IN AN UPSTAIRS FLAT, IT WAS EASY TO GET A GOOD VIEW OF THE MOUNTAINS AND AS THE SUN WAS SETTING, THE SKY WAS SO COLORFUL OVER THE MOUNTAINS AND WAS SUCH A BREATHTAKING SIGHT. I WAS IN AWE OF THE GOD WHO CREATED THE UNIVERSE IN ALL OF IT'S SPLENDOR. HAD I NOT PINCHED MYSELF TO MAKE SURE I WAS REALLY THERE, I'D THINK I WAS DREAMING OF BEING IN SOME FAIRY TALE LAND.

IT WAS NOW THE END OF SEPTEMBER AND WE HAD LEARNED THRU A LETTER RECEIVED FROM THE IMMIGRATION DEPARTMENT THAT VISITORS STAYING LONGER THAN 4 MONTHS HAD TO FILL OUT AN APPLICATION REQUESTING TO STAY LONGER THAN THAT. SINCE I WAS TO BE THERE 9 MONTHS, WE WENT AND FILLED OUT THE APPLICATION REQUESTING A VISITOR PASS. ONCE WE FILLED IT OUT AND TURNED IT IN, THEY SAID IT WOULD TAKE ABOUT 2 WEEKS FOR PROCESSING AND I'D HAVE TO GO THRU AN INTERVIEW BEING ASKED WHY I WANTED TO REMAIN LONGER THAN 4 MONTHS. I REMEMBER PRAYING THAT I WOULD BE ALLOWED TO STAY KNOWING HOW THE ENEMY

WOULD LOVE NOTHING MORE THAN TO STOP THE THINGS OF GOD. I'D ALREADY BEEN WELL RECEIVED AND LOVED BY THE FIJIAN PEOPLE I CAME IN CONTACT WITH AND KNEW HE'D STOP AT NOTHING TO DETOUR THAT. BUT I WAS A DETERMINED WOMAN WHO WAS A FIGHTER AND BELIEVED IN THE POWER OF PRAYER. WHAT HE MEANT FOR HARM GOD WOULD TURN AROUND FOR GOOD. NO MISTAKE ABOUT IT!

THE NEXT DAY WE WAS TO START PRISON MINISTRY AND I WAS REALLY EXCITED. MINISTRY THERE WAS HELD FROM 1 TO 3 PM ON WEDNESDAY'S EACH WEEK. THIS FIRST WEEK WOULD TAKE ME TO THE MEN'S PRISON. IT WAS A 30 MINUTE DRIVE AND I JUST RODE SOAKING IN THE SURROUNDINGS. IT WAS EXPLAINED TO ME ON THE WAY THERE HOW THINGS WERE DONE IN THEIR PRISON SYSTEM. THEN I WOULD MEET THE OTHER MINISTRY TEAM MEMBERS, GET TO KNOW THE MALE INMATES AND GIVE MY TESTIMONY. THE LADY PLAYING GUITAR THIS WEEK AT THE MEN'S PRISON WAS A NEICE TO MY HOST FAMILY, AND ALSO IN CHARGE OF THE LADIES PRISON MINISTRY WHICH WAS LOCATED IN THE COUNTRY'S CAPITAL WHICH WAS A 3 1/2 TO 4 HOUR DRIVE. I WAS LOOKING FORWARD TO MEETING HER AND JOINING THEIR WOMEN'S MINISTRY TEAM. THE AWESOME THING WAS, AND I KNOW NOW IT WAS GOD ORDAINED COMING TO FIJI. MOST OF THE RELATIVES OF MY HOST FAMILY WERE PEOPLE IN SOME FORM OF A HIGH AUTHORITY POSITION. THEY HAD RELATIVES WHO WERE ATTORNEY'S, A POLICE COMMISSIONER, SOME WORKING AS HEADS IN THE IMMIGRATION DEPARTMENT,AND UNCLE WHO WORKED FOR THE AMERICAN EMBASSY IN FIJI. THE LIST GOES ON.

IT WAS A DEFINITE DIVINE CONNECTION IN HAVING THIS FAMILY TO WORK WITH. WHENEVER WE WOULD NEED ANYTHING THAT REQUIRE SPECIAL PERMISSION, WE HAD THEM AT OUR DISPOSAL, AND YOU NEVER KNOW WHEN YOU WOULD HAVE TO RELY ON ANY NUMBER OF THEM AND WOULD DEFINITELY HELP US WITH THE FINANCES SHOULD WE HAVE TO CALL ON THEM AND HAVE THEM IN OUR CORNER TO ADVISE US ANY WAY WE MAY NEED. WE SERVE A MIGHTY, MIGHTY GOD!

WHEN WE GOT THERE AND CHECKED IN, WE HAD TO WAIT IN A SHELTERED AREA FOR THE GUARD TO COME OPEN THE GATE. WE FOUND A BENCH TO SIT ON AS IT WAS CROWDED AND I FELT ALL EYES ON ME AS I SAT DOWN. I WAS GREETED AND LEARNED THAT THE WORD BULA MEANT HELLO, SO I QUICKLY PICKED UP ON THAT GREETING. I ALSO HEARD THE WORD MOTHEY AND VANAKA IN WHICH I ASKED WHAT THAT MEANT. MOTHEY MEANS GOOD BYE AND VINAKA MEANT THANK YOU. SO THE FIRST MONTH OF BEING IN FIJI I LEARNED 3 WORDS IN THEIR LANGUAGE SO I FREQUENTLY USED THESE WORDS. I FOUND THEY ALL SPOKE PRETTY GOOD ENGLISH APART FROM THEIR NATIVE LANGUAGE AND IT WAS GOOD I COULD UNDERSTAND SOME, IT WOULD HAVE BEEN AWKWARD FOR THEM TO SPEAK IN THEIR DIALECT AND NOT UNDERSTAND ANY OF IT, BUT THEN IT WAS NICE HAVING THE HOST FAMILY TOO TO HELP ME WITH THOSE LANGUAGE BARRIERS. I WAS ALSO TICKLED TO BE LEARNING SOME WORDS IN THEIR LANGUAGE TOO AND FEEL APART OF THEIR CULTURE. I DIDN'T WANT THEM TO FEEL AS IF I WAS SNOOTY OR BETTER THAN THEM JUST BECAUSE I WAS FROM

321

AMERICA WHEN THEY HELD AMERICANS IN SUCH HIGH REGARD!

I MET THE MINISTRY TEAM AND THEY WERE ALL SO NICE. THERE WAS ALSO SOME FAMILY MEMBERS OF THE INMATES IN WHICH WE INTRODUCED OURSELVES AND PASSED OUT TRACKS TO THEM. SOON WE WERE USHERED IN AND MET IN A SMALL ROOM. THE ROOM WAS CROWDED AND IT WAS SORT OF SAD SEEING SO MANY MEN WHO HAD OBVIOUSLY STEERED THEMSELVES IN THE WRONG DIRECTION IN LIFE. I HAD HOPED THAT BY SHARING WHAT GOD LAID ON MY HEART, PRAYING I DIDN'T BECOME NERVOUS BEING THE ONLY WHITE PERSON THERE AND START STUTTERING, THAT MY TESTIMONY WOULD ENCOURAGE THEM AND SHOW THEM THAT NO MATTER WHERE THEY WERE AT THIS POINT IN THEIR LIFE, GOD LOVED THEM. I CONSIDERED IT A GREAT HONOR TO COME HERE AND ENCOURAGE THEM. AS I OPENED MY MOUTH THE WORDS FLOWED AS THE SPIRIT OF GOD SPOKE THRU ME SO FREELY. THE GUYS STARED AND SEEMED TO HANG ON TO EVERY WORD THAT WAS BEING SPOKEN AND I WAS A LITTLE EMBARRASSED BY THE STARES, BUT NEW IT WAS JUST CAUSE I WAS A NEWBIE THAT CAME FROM AMERICA.

SOME OF THE GUYS GAVE THEIR TESTIMONY OF WHAT GOD HAD DONE FOR THEM SINCE BEING IN PRISON, MANY HAD TOLD OF THEIR STRUGGLES AND TIMES OF HARDSHIP AND I COULD CERTAINLY RELATE TO SOME OF WHAT THEY SHARED. AFTER THEY WERE FINISHED, SOMEONE GAVE AN ALTAR CALL IN WHICH, I BELIEVE 19 MEN GAVE THEIR HEARTS TO THE LORD. TEARS WELLED UP IN ME AND I THANKED GOD FOR THE

MOVING OF HIS SPIRIT AND TOUCHING THOSE MEN. I WAS THANKFUL FOR THE OPPORTUNITY TO BE THERE TO SHOW THEM THAT GOD CARED FOR THEM AND I CARED FOR THEM. ALTHOUGH I WAS THERE FROM AMERICA, I WAS JUST LIKE THEM, A PERSON THAT GOD SENT HIS SON TO DIE FOR. AFTERWARD, AS WE GOT READY TO LEAVE, MANY CAME AND THANKED ME FOR SHARING WITH THEM AND SHOOK MY HAND, IT MEANT SO MUCH AS I NORMALLY DIDN'T SPEAK MUCH IN FRONT OF PEOPLE OTHER THAN GIVING SOME ANNOUNCEMENTS. ONE PARTICULIAR GENTLEMAN CAME TO THE GATED ENTRANCE AND ASKED IF WE COULD VISIT HIS GIRLFRIEND WHO HAD JUST GIVEN BIRTH, AND TELL HER HE LOVED HER AND WOULD BE OUT SOON. I ASSURED HIM WE WOULD DO THAT FOR HIM AS WE GOT IN THE CAR TO LEAVE.

WHILE ON THE DRIVE HOME, I WAS A REGUALR CHATTERBOX, ASKING ALL SORTS OF QUESTIONS. THEY WERE EXCITED OVER MY ENTHUSIASM AS WE TALKED ABOUT THE VISIT WITH THE INMATES AND THEY SAID THE MEN WERE IN AW THAT SOMEONE COMING ALL THE WAY FROM AMERICA WOULD TAKE TIME OUT OF HER SCHEDULE TO COME AND DELIVER A WORD FROM THE LORD. I WAS TOUCHED. I KNEW GOD HAD SHAPED MY LIFE FOR THIS PARTICULAR TIME. EACH ARE GIVEN GIFTS TO BE USED FOR THE GLORY OF GOD, WHETHER PASTORING, TEACHING, MUSIC, OR ANY OTHER NUMBER OF FIELDS. NOT MANY ARE CALLED OR EQUIPPED FOR THIS TYPE OF MINISTRY AND I KNEW GOD HAD SHAPED MY LIFE AND PREPARED ME AHEAD OF TIME, GIVEN ME KNOWLEDGE OF SOME THINGS I MAY FACE AS TO NOT HAVE ANY SURPRISES. I ALWAYS FELT IT BEST TO BE PREPARED, EVEN IF WHAT

YOU PREPARE FOR DOESN'T HAPPEN. IT'S NOT EXPECTING A WORSE CASE SCENERIO OR WANTING ANYTHING NEGATIVE TO HAPPEN , BUT YET NOT TO HAVE EXPECTATIONS TO HIGH SO YOU ARE NOT LET DOWN. YOU NEED BALANCE.

WE TALKED ABOUT OTHER THINGS LIKE CHILDREN, CHURCH, THINGS I MAY FACE WHILE IN FIJI AND SOME OF THE AREAS WE WOULD BE VISITING. I KNEW I WAS IN FOR A VERY BUSY TIME, BUT WOULD TAKE TIME FOR MORE SIGHT SEEING AND RELAXATION TOO TO REFRESH MYSELF. WE TALKED ABOUT THE WEATHER AND I LEARNED THAT FIJI HAS JUST 2 SEASONS. ONE IS THEIR COOLER AND DRYER SEASON THAT RUNS FROM APRIL TO SEPTEMBER, THEN THEIR HOT AND WET SEASON WAS OCTOBER TO MARCH. OCTOBER TO MARCH WAS ALSO THEIR CYCLONE SEASON AND I PRAYED THERE WOULD BE NONE AS LONG AS I WAS THERE. HERE IN THE STATES WE EXPERIENCE 4 SEASONS, AND HAD SNOW, THERE WASN'T SNOW IN FIJI, YEE HAW! THEY WERE ALSO ON DAYLIGHT SAVINGS TIME BUT THE OPPOSITE OF THE STATES. WHEN WE WENT FORWARD AND HOUR THEY WENT BACK AND VISE VERSA. THEY ALSO HAD QUITE A TIME DIFFERENCE RANGING FROM 16 HOURS AHEAD IN THE COOL AND DRY SEASON TO 18 HOURS AHEAD OF OHIO IN THE HOT AND WET SEASON. DEFINITELY SOMETHING MY FAMILY HAD TO GET USED TOO WHILE WAITING FOR A MESSAGE FROM ME. I ALSO LEARNED THAT FIJI WAS AN IDOL WORSHIPPING COUNTRY TO, MADE UP OF MAINLY HINDUS AND MUSLIMS. THERE WERE ALOT OF CHRISTIANS THERE AND THEY DEFINITELY HAD THEIR WORK CUT OUT FOR THEM, BUT WE BELIEVED IN THE KING OF KINGS, THE ONE TRUE

GOD WHO WE KNEW WOULD BRING RESTORATION AND HEALING TO THIS COUNTRY.

WHEN WE ARRIVED BACK AT THE FLAT, THERE WAS A CALL FROM THE IMMIGRATION DEPARTMENT TO COME IN THE NEXT DAY FOR MY INTERVIEW. I THOUGHT ALREADY? WE THOUGHT IT WOULD BE ANOTHER 2 WEEKS YET, BUT EAGER TO GET IT OVER WITH HOPING IT WENT WELL AND I WOULD BE ABLE TO STAY THE FULL 9 MONTHS I FELT I WAS TO STAY. AFTER SUPPER I SPOKE WITH MY FAMILY BACK HOME. THINGS WERE GOING WELL AND I THANKED THE LORD FOR PROTECTING THEM AND HELPING THEM THRU WHILE I WAS AWAY. ONCE OUR CONVERSATION WAS FINISHED, WE SAT DOWN FOR DEVOTIONS AND PRAYER, THEN A MOVIE.

AFTERWARD WE HEADED TO BED, WHICH I WELCOMED AFTER OUR EXCITING DAY. IT WAS NICE AND COOL THAT NIGHT, WHICH MADE FOR NICE SLEEPING WEATHER. AS I LAID DOWN I WAS MET WITH THE SOUND OF THE CRICKETS CHIRPING AND THOUGHT HOW NICE TO BE SERENADED TO SLEEP. THEY NEVER SEEMED THAT LOUD BACK HOME, LIKE THEY WERE HERE. THEN I HEARD WHAT I THOUGHT WAS CATS SCREECHING, AND WHEN I LEFT MY ROOM TO CHECK IT OUT WAS TOLD IT WAS BATS. UGH! BATS? I WAS TOLD THAT THERE WERE BREAD FRUIT TREES THAT GREW IN FIJI AND THAT WAS BATS FAVORITE FOOD. JUST GREAT, I THOUGHT, WELL, AS LONG AS THEY DON'T FLY THIS WAY, EVERYTHING WOULD BE FINE. ONE THING I WAS A LITTLE SQUEEMISH OF WAS THE COCKROACHES. THESE ROACHES WERE NOT ONLY HUGE, BUT FLEW! I SAID NO WAY DO THEY FLY

BUT SURE ENOUGH, WHEN I WAS SITTING IN THE CHAIR TALKING ABOUT THE BATS, ONE FLEW PAST MY HEAD AND LANDED ON THE TABLE, AND IT'S WINGS FELL OFF AND IT BEGAN CRAWLING.

I JUMPED ABOUT 2 FEET IN THE AIR AND FLED BACK TO MY ROOM AND SHUT THE DOOR PRAYING NONE WOULD CRAWL IN THERE. I HAD NEVER SEEN ROACHES SO BIG. YUCK! THERE WERE A LOT OF DOGS IN THE AREA THAT ROAMED FREE TOO, THEY OWNERS DIDN'T SEEM TO NEED A DOG LICENSE LIKE WE DID BACK HOME AND NO ONE HAD THEIR DOGS PENNED UP EITHER. THEY SEEMED TO PROWL AROUND AS IF ON PATROL, BARKING FURIOUSLY AT ANYONE WHO CAME ALONG, ALERTING THE NEIGHBORHOOD OF STRANGERS. SOMETIMES THIS GOT A LITTLE ANNOYING, AS IT WAS HARD TO SLEEP WITH DOGS BARKING HALF THE NIGHT. SOMETIMES THE GENTLEMAN OF THE HOUSE WHO I LEARNED STAYED UP LATE AT NIGHT PRAYING OVER THE FAMILY AND THE HOUSE WOULD OPEN THE DOOR AND TOSS STONES AT THEM TO QUIET THEM DOWN, IF THEY BARKED TO LONG. I WAS SO REFRESHING TO KNOW THAT THE FAMILY I STAYED WITH LOVED GOD JUST AS MUCH AND CARED ABOUT THE WELFARE OF THE OTHER MEMBERS TO STAY UP AT NIGHT WHILE OTHERS SLEPT, PRAYING AND INTERCEDING FOR THE NEEDS OF THE FAMILY AND OF THE COUNTRY. THEN I FELL OFF TO SLEEP.

THE NEXT DAY I HAD MY INTERVIEW WITH IMMIGRATION AND I THINK IT WENT REALLY WELL. THEY TOLD ME THEY WOULD LOOK OVER THE APPLICATION AND RENDER THEIR DECISION WITHIN A COUPLE

WEEKS AND WE LEFT. WE DIDN'T HAVE MUCH PLANNED FOR THE REST OF THE DAY AND DECIDED TO DO SOME SHOPPING IN TOWN. THEIR DOWNTOWN WAS SORT OF COMPACTED ALMOST LIKE AN OUTSIDE MALL AREA SIMILAR TO THE GREENE BACK IN OHIO. WE WALKED THE STREETS, LISTENING TO MUSIC PLAYING AS WE PEERED THRU THE WINDOWS OF THE DIFFERENT SHOPS AND I MARVELED AT ALL THE BEAUTIFUL FIJIAN DRESSES THAT HUNG IN THE WINDOWS. I MENTIONED THE IDEA OF HAVING ONE FOR MYSELF AND THEY TOOK ME TO A SHOP THAT WAS REASONABLE TO MAKE ME ONE OF MY OWN.

I WAS SO TICKLED TO HAVE A FIJIAN DRESS TO TAKE HOME WITH ME AS A REMINDER OF MY TRIP AND EVEN FOUND SOME THINGS FOR THE GIRLS THAT THEY HAD BEEN IN NEED OF, AS THEIR FATHER WAS NOW RETIRED AND FINANCES WERE TIGHT AS THEY DIDN'T REALLY HAVE A RETIREMENT INCOME FROM WHERE HE WORKED. THEIR MOTHER HAD PASSED THE YEAR BEFORE FROM BREAST CANCER, AND OTHER FAMILY MEMBERS STAYED TO HELP WITH THEM WHILE THE FATHER HAD WORKED. FROM THERE WE FOUND A BARGAIN BOX STORE THAT HAD JUST OPENED APPARENTLY, SO WE WENT IN THERE TO CHECK IT OUT. I FOUND THAT MOST ITEMS WERE FAIRLY REASONABLE LIKE BACK IN THE STATES, AND I BOUGHT SOME SOUVENIERS FOR MY FAMILY BACK HOME, THEN WE LEFT TO HEAD BACK OURSELVES AND GET SUPPER.

THE NEXT COUPLE OF MONTHS FLEW BY AS WE BUSIED OURSELVES WITH PRAYER MEETINGS, DOOR TO DOOR VISITING, JAIL MINISTRY AND CELL GROUPS.

THE CELL GROUP WE HAD LEADERSHIP OVER WAS HELD AT THEIR HOME ON SATURDAY NIGHTS. THE FAMILY WAS VERY NICE AND RECEIVED ME WELL. THEY WAS A HINDU FAMILY THAT HAD CONVERTED TO CHRISTIANITY THE YEAR BEFORE. THE LADY OF THE HOUSE HAD BATTLED WITH MANY HEALTH ISSUES, WE WERE PRAYING OVER HER FOR. WHENEVER WE HAD OUR CELL GROUP THEY INSISTED ON COOKING FOR US, SO WE HAD TO MAKE SURE WE WERE HUNGRY. IT WAS AN USUAL CUSTOM OF FIJI THAT WHEN YOU VISITED SOMEONE'S HOME YOU BROUGHT A GIFT OFFERING, WHETHER IT BE A LOAF OF BREAD, CHICKEN, FLOUR, RICE. SOMETIMES ONE OF THE GIRLS WOULD BAKE A PIE TO TAKE AND BLESS THE FAMILY WITH. SOWING SEEDS IS WHAT THEY CALLED IT AND I KNOW I WAS A FIRM BELIEVER IN SOWING SEEDS. I LOVED TO GIVE AND BLESS OTHERS, I ADAPTED WELL TO THIS FIJIAN TRADITION. I WAS USUALLY POKED FUN OF BACK HOME BY CERTAIN PEOPLE IN MY LIFE FOR BEING SUCH A GIVER, SOMETIMES GIVING UP THINGS OF MINE, I KNOW IT WAS JUST A LACK OF UNDERSTANDING WHERE GOD WAS CONCERNED. MANY I BELIEVE LACKED KNOWLEDGE AS TO HOW GOD MOVES WHEN WE PUT OUR FAITH AND TRUST IN HIM.

IT WAS NOW THE MIDDLE OF NOV 2010. THINGS HAD BEEN SO BUSY, THAT WE DECIDED TO TAKE A DAY OF REST AND HAVE SOME FUN. I ASKED IF WE COULD GO TO THE BEACH, AS I WANTED TO SIT THERE, LOOKING OUT OVER THE OCEAN AND GET WITH GOD, AND MAYBE DO SOME WRITING. JUST SOUNDED SO REFRESHING! WE GATHERED SOME GEAR AND HEADED OUT FOR THE BEACH AFTER LUNCH. THAT PARTICULIAR DAY THE TIDE WAS DOWN AND YOU

COULD WALK OUT ON THE PIER. THE LAST TIME I WAS THERE THE TIDE WAS UP AND THE PIER HAD BEEN BURIED UNDERWATER. IT WAS COOL TO WALK OUT ON THE PIER, LOOKING OUT OVER THE OCEAN, IT WAS SO BEAUTIFUL AND PEACEFUL. THERE WAS WHAT SEEMED TO BE A HUNDRED SEA SHELLS THAT HAD BEEN WASHED UP ON THE PIER WHEN THE WATER RECEDED, DIFFERENT SHAPES AND SIZES, AND I PICKED UP A COUPLE FOR SOUVENIERS. I EVEN SAW A JELLY FISH, AND A CRAB SCRAMBLING BACK TO IT'S HABITAT OF WATER, AND OF COURSE SEAWEED AND SLIME SO YOU HAD TO BE CAREFUL WHEN YOU WALKED AS NOT TO SLIP AND FALL. THE TIDE WAS STARTING TO RISE SO WE HEADED BACK FOR SHORE, AND SAT ON THE BEACH FOR A BIT WATCHING OTHERS SWIM, AND THE LORD GAVE ME 2 POEMS THAT I WROTE DOWN. SUCH AN AWESOME TIME WE HAD THERE, AND A MUCH NEEDED TIME TO REFUEL AND BE FILLED WITH THE PRESENCE OF GOD!

AFTER WE WAS FINISHED AT THE BEACH WE DECIDED TO GO INTO TOWN AND OPEN UP THE POSTAL BOX AS IT HAD BEEN A COUPLE DAYS SINCE THE FAMILY CHECKED THEIR MAIL. ALTHOUGH IN THE STATES WE HAD POST OFFICE BOXES, MOST OF OUR MAIL WAS DELIVERED TO OUR HOUSE. THEY DIDN'T HAVE THIS IN FIJI. EVERYONE HAD A POST OFFICE BOX AND HAD TO PICK UP THEIR MAIL THEMSELVES. WHEN HE OPENED HIS BOX THERE WAS A LETTER FROM THE IMMIGRATION DEPARTMENT. I WAS EXCITED TO FINALLY HEAR FROM THEM, YET NERVOUS TO OPEN IT. I MEAN WHAT IF THEY SAID I HAD TO LEAVE AFTER 4 MONTHS, YET MY TICKET HOME WAS FOR 9.

WE PRAYED OVER THE LETTER BEFORE OPENING AND ASKED THE LORD TO LET IT BE GOOD NEWS, REMINDING HIM OF THE CALL HE PLACED ON MY LIFE. WHEN I OPENED IT AND READ WHAT IT SAID, I GAVE OUT A SHOUT OF PRAISE! THE WHOLE CAR WAS LIKE WHAT? I HAD BEEN APPROVED FOR AN EXTENDED STAY IN FIJI UP TO ONE YEAR!! AND WHENEVER I RETURNED FOR A VISIT OR MISSIONS WORK, I WOULDN'T HAVE TO PURCHASE A RETURN TICKET. I COULD NOW COME AND GO AS I PLEASED! WHAT AWESOME NEWS THIS WAS AND WE GAVE GOD THANKIS FOR IT! ALTHOUGH I COULD HAVE STAYED TILL THE END OF AUGUST 2011, MY TICKET WAS ALREADY PAID FOR TO LEAVE IN MAY 2011, I COULD HAVE SWITCHED IT OUT FOR ONLY 250.00 AND STAYED IN FIJI, BUT I TOLD MY FAMILY I WOULD BE BACK, AND NEEDED TO TAKE CARE OF THINGS BACK HOME.

TO CELEBRATE WE WENT OUT THAT NIGHT FOR PIZZA, WHICH WAS A NICE CHANGE FROM THE NORMAL RICE, GREENS AND VEGI'S, FISH, CHICKEN AND CORNED BEEF. WE DIDN'T HAVE ALOT OF VARIETY. SOMETIMES WHEN MONEY WAS SCARCE, WE HAD JUST BISQUITS AND TEA, EVEN WAS A DAY HERE OR THERE WHEN THERE WAS NOTHING TO EAT, BUT I DIDN'T COMPLAIN. I KNEW THERE MAY BE TIMES LIKE THIS AND WAS ALREADY PREPARED FOR WHAT MAY COME. I KNEW THERE WOULD BE SOME IMPERFECTIONS, AND I WOULD MORE THAN LIKELY NOT HAVE SOME OF THE LUXERIES I WAS ACCUSTOMED TO BACK HOME IN AMERICA. SOMETHING I CAN ALWAYS SAY ABOUT MYSELF, AND IT'S NOT BEING PRIDEFUL OR HAUGHTY AT ALL IS THE FACT I HAVE ALWAYS BEEN ABLE TO ADAPT TO MY SURROUNDINGS.

WHATEVER SITUATION, OR CIRCUMSTANCE CAME MY WAY, I WAS ALWAYS THINKING ABOUT HOW TO GET THRU RATHER THAN WALLOW IN SELF PITY AND LET IT GET ME DOWN! I ALWAYS LOOKED OUT FOR THE INTEREST OF OTHERS RATHER THAN MYSELF, AND ALTHOUGH I WAS OFTEN TAKEN FOR GRANTED, I THANKED GOD FOR CREATING ME JUST THE WAY I WAS. THERE ARE MANY WHO HAVE COPING ISSUES AND DON'T MAKE IT WELL THRU SITUATIONS LIKE ONES I HAVE FACED. MANY SHRINK BACK AND BECOME DEPRESSED AND LIVE LIVES OF SOLITUDE, SHUTTING THEMSELVES OFF FROM THE WORLD. SOME HAVE NERVOUS BREAK DOWNS OR EVEN COMMIT SUICIDE AND IT'S SO TRAGIC. THE POWER OF THE ENEMY IS JUST AS REAL AS THE POWER OF GOD, BUT WHAT YOU HAVE TO UNDERSTAND IS THE ENEMY HAS BEEN DEFEATED! GOD SUPERCEDES OVER THE ENEMY, AND WE WIN!

GOD THRU JESUS HAS GIVEN US POWER AND AUTHORITY TO OVER COME THE ENEMY AND EVEN SAID IN HIS WORD THAT GREATER THINGS WE WILL DO IN HIS NAME BECAUSE HE GOES TO HIS FATHER! THE ENEMY HAS A FIELD DAY WITH PEOPLE WHO WALLOW IN SELF PITY AND WALK IN SELF DEFEAT. THAT'S WHY WE MUST RESIST THE ENEMY AND PUT ON THE FULL ARMOR OF GOD DAILY, TO WARD OF THE FIREY ATTACKS OF THE ENEMY. WE WILL NEVER BE TOTALLY EXEMPT FROM THE ATTACKS OF THE ENEMY, BUT WITH GOD FOR US, NO ONE CAN STAND AGAINST US AND WE'LL GET THRU IS EASIER AND COME OUT STRONGER WHEN WE PUT GOD ON THE FOREFRONT OF OUR LIVES! I THANK GOD HE'S MADE ME A STRONG,

RESILIENT WOMAN WITH ALL I'VE BEEN THRU. I HAVE STOOD, PERSEVERED, PRESSED THRU, HAD NOW I STAND HAVING CONQUERED AND OVERCOME WHAT THE ENEMY MEANT FOR HARM. GOD BY NO MEANS IS A RESPECTOR OF PERSONS. WHAT HE'S DONE FOR ME, HE CAN DO FOR ANYONE THAT BELIEVES HE CAN AND PUTS THEIR TRUST IN HIM! ALL IT TAKES, IS CALLING ON THE NAME OF JESUS! HE SAYS IN HIS WORD THAT IF YOU DON'T KNOW WHERE TO START, JUST CALL ON THE NAME OF JESUS AND YOU SHALL BE SAVED!

THAT'S ALL IT TAKES TO START TURNING THINGS AROUND IN YOUR LIFE. YOU JUST NEED TO BELIEVE IN YOURSELF! AND IF YOU ALLOW GOD TO HE WILL GUIDE EACH STEP YOU TAKE ON THIS JOURNEY OF LIFE THAT YOU WILL NEVER FORGET!

IT WAS SOON THANKSGIVING IN THE STATES, AND I WAS A LITTLE SAD. THIS WAS MY FIRST THANSGIVING AWAY FROM HOME AND I WAS FEELING SAD. THE HOLIDAYS MEANT SO MUCH TO MY FAMILY AND I. FIJI DIDN'T CELEBRATE THANKSGIVING AS THAT WAS MAINLY AN AMERICAN TRADITION, BUT I WAS HOPING TO SHARE WITH MY HOST FAMILY OUR FAMILY TRADTIONS BACK HOME. WE WENT SHOPPING TO LOOK FOR TURKEY, AND CRANBERRY SAUCE. WE ALREADY HAD THE POTATOES AND THE SWEET POTATOES AND VEGIS, AND SINCE THEY DID LOT OF THEIR OWN BAKING FROM SCRATCH THEY COULD MAKE OUR OWN ROLLS. HOWEVER WE FOUND THAT TURKEY THERE WAS VERY EXPENSIVE, AND WE WERE GOING THRU SOME FINANCIAL DIFFICULTY AT THE MOMENT, SO I MADE ANOTHER AMERICAN DISH FOR THEM WHICH WAS TUNA CASSEROLE, AND THEY ENJOYED IT. I GOT

TO SPEAK TO MY FAMILY BACK HOME OVER SKYPE, AND THAT MEANT THE WORLD TO US. I THANKED THE LORD FOR SEEING THEM THRU AND PROTECTING THEM. IT WAS THE FALL SEASON IN THE STATES, AND THEY HAD ALREADY HAD SOME SNOW FALL, SO I PRAYED AN EXTRA PRAYER FOR MY SON WHO WAS DOING MY PAPER ROUTE.

THE NEXT COUPLE WEEKS WAS BUSY FOR US AS WE ENTERED INTO THE CHRISTMAS SEASON. I LOVED CHRISTMAS AND WAS A LITTLE SAD I WOULDN'T BE HOME WITH MY FAMILY, BUT I HAD A PURPOSE TO FULFILL AND I WOULD MAKE THE BEST OF IT. I LEARNED THAT IN THE PRISON MINISTRY THEY TOO DID ANGEL TREE AND I WAS EXCITED AND HOPED TO BE A PART OF IT. WE SEEN OUR FIRST MIRACLE OF DEBT CANCELATION FOR THE HOST FAMILY I STAYED WITH WHEN HE HAD BEEN BLESSED WITH MONEY FROM HIS WORKPLACE AS PART OF A RETIREMENT BENEFIT. HE WENT TO PAY A BILL THAT WAS 185.00 AND LEARNED THAT THEY HAD NO RECORD OF HIM OWING THAT BILL. HE STOOD THERE HE SAID ABOUT 15 MINUTES, NOT WANTING TO ARGUE THE POINT BUT MAKING SURE THEY DIDN'T MAKE AN ERROR. THINGS CHECKED OUT AND IT HIT HIM THAT IT WAS GOD WHO HAD CANCELED THIS DEBT! GLORY! HE WAS SO ESTACTIC OVER THIS AND USED IT TO CATCH UP ON OTHERS THINGS HE HAD FALLEN BEHIND ON.

MY FAMILY HAD SENT A CARE PACKAGE FROM OVERSEAS AND IT FINALLY ARRIVED AFTER SENDING THE MONTH BEFORE. IT TAKES SO LONG FOR THINGS TO TRAVEL OVERSEAS, BUT I WAS GRATEFUL IT CAME AND IT EVEN INCLUDED SOME TREATS FOR THE GIRLS.

THEY LOVED JELLY BEANS AND WERE A LITTLE HARD TO COME BY IN FIJI, SO I HAD 2 BAGS SENT OVER FROM THE STATES ALONG WITH SOME OTHER ITEMS NEEDED AND A LITTLE CASH TO HELP OUT TOO. WITH FIJI THEIR CURRENCY ISN'T WORTH AS MUCH AS WHAT U.S. CURRENCY IS, SO WHEN MONEY IS GOTTEN FROM THE STATES, IT'S ALMOST DOUBLE IN FIJI. THEY WERE SO HAPPY, THE SMILES WAS PRICELESS, AND IT WARMED MY HEART TO BE ABLE TO BLESS THEM AFTER ALL THEY DID FOR ME.

WHEN IT WAS TIME FOR BED, I WAS READY. I WAS WORN OUT FROM THE EVENTS OF THE PAST COUPLE WEEKS, AND LOOKING FORWARD TO TAKING THE NEXT DAY OFF FOR REST. HOWEVER, AS I LAID THERE, I HAD TROUBLE FALLING ASLEEP. I TOSSED AND TURNED ALL NIGHT AND WHEN THE ALARM WENT OFF AT 5 AM, I DIDN'T WANT TO GET UP. I LAID THERE ANOTHER 10 MINUTES THEN GOT UP TO GO TO THE BATHROOM AND CAME BACK TO LAY DOWN, FIGURING I WOULD JUST SKIP MY MORNING WALK AND SLEEP A BIT BEFORE BREAKFAST. HOWEVER I WAS WIDE AWAKE, ALTHOUGH TIRED AND DECIDED TO GET UP AND GO FOR THE WALK ANYWAY. I COME TO LOVE THESE MORNING WALKS. MY ROUTE TOOK ME PAST A HINDU TEMPLE AND I OFTEN CARRIED TRACKS WITH ME IN CASE I PASSED PEOPLE AT THE BUS STOP WAITING FOR THE BUS THAT WOULD TAKE THEM TO THEIR JOBS. AS I WALKED BY THE TEMPLE, I WOULD PRAY AND SLIDE A TRACK UNDER THE GATE.

I DIDN'T USUALLY SEE ALOT OF PEOPLE WALKING AROUND UNTIL I GOT CLOSER TO THE BUS STOP, SO IN THE DESERTED SPOTS I WOULD PRAY, OUT LOUD BUT

TO MYSELF, PRAYING FOR ALL THE HOUSES I WALKED BY. WHAT WAS SO BEAUTIFUL ABOUT THE NIGHT TIME OR MORNING ESPECIALLY WAS THE STARS. BEING ON THE UNDERSIDE OF THE WORLD AS FIJI WAS, THE SKY SEEMED TO BE ON TOP OF YOU. YOU COULD SEE WHAT SEEMED LIKE HUNDREDS OF STARS, SOME CLUSTERED TOGETHER AND IT WAS AF IF YOU COULD REACH UP AND TOUCH THEM. IT WAS THE MOST AWESOME THING TO SEE. I REMEMBER THE FIRST TIME SEEING IT I EXCLAIMED A WOW, AND A COUPLE WAS WALKING BY AND JUST GIGGLED. I WAS A LITTLE EMBARRASSED, BUT WHAT COULD I DO. A LITTLE LATER, AS I WAS ON MY WAY BACK TO THE FLAT, THERE HAD BEEN NO SIGN OF LIGHTNING, THUNDER OR ANYTHING WHEN I STARTED ON MY WALK. ALL OF A SUDDEN THE RAIN CAME DOWN IN TORRENTS. I WASN'T FAR FROM THE FLAT SO I RAN BACK, BUT I WAS STILL SOAKED. I GUESS WITH THE SKY SEEMING SO CLOSE TO THE GROUND, THE RAIN FELL HARDER HERE. I WENT IN AND GRABBED A TOWEL, AND CHANGED MY CLOTHES. IT WAS STILL A LITTLE EARLY FOR BREAKFAST, SO I LAID DOWN TO SEE IF I COULD TAKE A SMALL CAT NAP.

THE NEXT WEEK THE GIRLS FOR OUT FOR THEIR SCHOOL HOLIDAY, AS THEY CALLED IT. THEIR SCHOOL YEAR RAN DIFFERENT, GOING ALL YEAR ROUND FROM THE END OF JANUARY TO AROUND THE MIDDLE OF DECEMBER. THEY WOULD GO TO SCHOOL FOR 8 OR 9 WEEKS, HAVE 2 WEEKS OFF, GO BACK FOR 8 OR 9 WEEKS WITH 2 WEEKS OFF AND GETTING JUST A LITTLE OVER A MONTH OFF FOR CHRISTMAS AND NEW YEARS. WHEREAS IN THE STATES, THE KIDS WENT FROM THE END OF AUGUST TO THE END OF MAY, FIRST WEEK OF JUNE, THEN HAVING 2 1/2 MONTHS OFF, AND

OF COURSE TIME OFF FOR HOLIDAYS AND SPRING BREAK. EVEN WITH THEM SPEAKING GOOD ENGLISH, THEIR SPELLING OF WORDS WAS DIFFERENT FROM OURS AS WELL. THE WAY WE SPELL TIRE, THEY SPELL TYRE, AMERICANS SPELL GOOD THIS WAY BUT FIJIANS SPELL IT GUD. THEY ALSO HAVE A DIFFERENT METRIC SYSTEM THAN WE HAVE. THEY GO ON THE BRITISH METRIC SYSTEM, MEASURING IN LITERS, METERS, KG'S, WHERE AS US AMERICANS, USE POUNDS, CUPS, INCHES AND MILES AND SO FORTH. THE SPELLING I COULD MANAGE OK BUT THE METRIC SYSTEM? I HAD TO REALLY RACK MY BRAIN TO CONVERT OUR SYSTEM INTO THEIRS WHEN HELPING TO COOK, OR EVEN WEIGH MYSELF. I REMEMBER ONE TIME THE LADIES GROUP AT GOTTEN TOGETHER TO HELP ANOTHER LADY PACK AS SHE WAS MOVING. THEY GOT OUT A SCALE JUST FOR FUN AND WE TOOK TURNS WEIGHING OURSELF. NOT THINKING ABOUT THE METRIC SYSTEM THEY USED, I STOOD ON THE SCALE AND IT SAID 70. I GREW CONCERNED AND THOUGHT WHAT? I KNEW I HAD DROPPED SOME WEIGHT FROM THE BUSYNESS OF OUR SCHEDULE BUT TO 70 POUNDS? THEN I THOUGHT, I BETTER ASK. WHEN I DID THEY SAID IT WAS KG'S NOT POUNDS AS I HAD THOUGHT. SO I HAD TO CONVERT 70 KG'S INTO POUNDS SO I KNEW WHAT I ACTUALLY WEIGHED. SO 70 KG'S WAS ABOUT 154 LBS. THAT WAS MORE LIKE IT! THAT WAS THE HARDEST THING FOR ME TO GET. EVEN WHEN I MADE A COUPLE OF AMERICAN DISHES FOR THEM, I HAD TO CONVERT MY RECIPE INTO THEIR METRIC SYSTEM AND PRAYED I'D GET IT RIGHT AND NOT RUIN THE MEAL FOR THEM.

I LEARNED THAT THEY DID ALOT OF THEIR OWN GARDENING THERE TOO, MANY HAD PARCELS OF LAND

THAT THEY TOOK CARE OF AND PLANTED THEIR OWN FOOD, OTHERS WOULD RENT A SPOT AND EITHER PAY IN CASH FOR IT OR USE PART OF THEIR PRODUCE AS PAYMENT. MANY SOLD THEIR PRODUCTS IN MARKETS THAT WERE SET UP AT A COUPLE DIFFERENT POINTS IN THE CITY, AND SOME WOULD SET A TABLE UP AT THE SIDE OF THE ROAD AND SELL THEIR ITEMS. I NOTICED THE FEW TIMES WE WENT TO THE BEACH THAT SOME WOULD HAVE NETS AND FISH, THEN DRIVE THRU NEIGHBORHOODS WITH COOLERS ON THE BACK OF TRUCKS THEY STORED THE FISH IN AND SELL THEM. A COOL WAY TO MAKE A LIVING, ESPECIALLY IF RETIRED. THEY PLANTED THINGS LIKE EGG PLANT AND CASSAVA, GREENS, CARROTS ALL SORTS OF THINGS. BEFORE COMING TO FIJI, I HAD NOT HAD EGGPLANT AND TRYING IT THERE, I FOUND IT WASN'T TOO BAD. THEN I TRIED OYSTERS FOR THE FIRST TIME. YUCK! THEY WERE SLIMY AS THEY WENT DOWN, BUT AT LEAST I COULD SAY I TRIED THEM. THE LONGER I WAS IN FIJI, THE MORE I COME TO KNOW THAT THEY ARE VERY LOVING AND CARING PEOPLE. SURE THEY HAVE THEIR CRIME SPREES, BUT FOR THE MOST PART MOST OF THE FAMILIES WERE ALWAYS BAKING OR COOKING SOMETHING AND MAKING EXTRA TO SOW IN THE LIFE OF SOMEONE ELSE. MANY TIMES WHEN WE WERE NOT SURE WHAT WE OURSELVES WOULD EAT, SOMEONE WOULD KNOCK AT THE DOOR AND BLESS US WITH A MEAL.

WITH THE GIRLS BEING OUT OF SCHOOL FOR THE HOLIDAYS, IT WAS A LITTLE EASIER TO PLAN OUR VISITING TIMES WITHOUT HAVING TO RUSH BACK HOME TO GREET THEM. IT ALWAYS BROUGHT ME GREAT JOY TO OFFER LOVE AND COMFORT DURING THIS TIME OF

YEAR THAT MAY BE TOUGHER FOR SOME, WHETHER, HAVING LOST JOBS, OR LOST LOVED ONES OR EVEN HAVE FAMILY INCARCERATED, OR WHO MAY HAVE MOVED AWAY AND NOT ABLE TO KEEP IN TOUCH. MY HEART ACHED FOR THEM AND MANY TIMES I WOULD TEAR UP, TO SEE THEIR SMILES AND GRATEFULNESS AT HAVING SOMEONE WHO SEEMED TO CARE ABOUT THEM. I WAS SO HONORED TO BE CHOSEN TO BE THE BLESSING!

CHRISTMAS BEING A WEEK AWAY, I WANTED TO DO SOMETHING SPECIAL FOR THE GIRLS. WHILE DOING OUR MORNING CHORES, ONE OF THE GIRLS OPENED A TRUNK TO GET SOMETHING OUT WHEN I NOTICED SOME EXTRA MATERIAL IN THERE. I ASKED IF I COULD SEE IT AND THEY GOT IT OUT FOR ME. AS I LOOKED THRU IT, I GOT SOME IDEAS, OF WHAT I COULD DO FOR THEM. THERE WAS ALOT OF MATERIAL THERE AND ASKED THE GENTLEMAN IF I COULD HAVE IT, TO HAVE SOMETHING MADE FOR THE GIRLS FOR CHRISTMAS AND HE AGREED. HE SAID IT WASN'T DOING HIM ANY GOOD JUST LAYING IN THE TRUNK. I WAS EXCITED AND WENT AND GOT A DRESS OF THEIRS, THEY DIDN'T WEAR OFTEN, THAT I WOULDN'T THINK THEY'D MISS AT THE TIME AND WENT TO TOWN AND HAD IT MEASURED, TELLING THE SEAMSTRESS WHAT I WANTED DONE. ALL TOTAL THERE WOULD BE A NEW PAIR OF PJ'S FOR EACH GIRL AND ONE NEW OUTFIT, ON WHAT THEY CALLED A CHAMBA. ALL TOTAL I WOULD GET IT ALL FOR 64.00, NOT BAD AT ALL. THEN I SET ASIDE MONEY FOR THE OLDER GIRL AND FOR THE STEP SON.

IT WAS CHRISTMAS EVE AND I WAS SORT OF HOMESICK. I WOULD MISS SHOPPING FOR EVERYONE

338

AND WATCHING MY GRANDKIDS OPEN THEIR GIFTS. THIS YEAR THOUGH MY YOUNGEST SON WAS HANDLED ALL THE SHOPPING FOR ME AND I WAS SO GRATEFUL, THAT ALTHOUGH I WASN'T THERE, THEY WOULD STILL GET A PRESENT FROM ME. I WAS SO PROUD OF HOW WELL HE HANDLED EVERYTHING WITH HAVING HIS OWN JOB AND SCHOOLING HE WAS TAKING. I HAD MADE HIM POA FOR ME SO HE COULD HANDLE MY CHECKS, BANK ACCOUNTS AND WHATEVER ELSE WAS NEEDED. I ALSO THOUGHT OF HOW WE WERE USED TO A COLDER CLIMATE. NORMALLY WE HAD SNOW FOR CHRISTMAS, YET THIS YEAR AT CHRISTMAS WAS FIJI'S HOT SEASON, WHAT WE AMERICAN'S CALLED SUMMER.

WOULD CHRISTMAS EVEN SEEM THE SAME FOR ME? BUT I WAS GOING TO MAKE THE BEST OF IT, IT WAS ALL ABOUT THE BIRTH OF JESUS ANYWAY. I ASKED THE GIRLS IF THEY HAD A CHRISTMAS TREE. THEY SAID YES ALTHOUGH THEY DIDN'T USUALLY PUT IT UP. I ASKED IF I COULD PUT IT UP AND EVERYONE AGREED, SO THEY GOT OUT WHAT DECORATIONS THEY HAD, AND I PURCHASED 2 SETS OF LIGHTS. THEN WE TOOK A PAPER CUP AND MADE AN ANGEL FOR A TREE TOPPER. WE ALSO MADE SOME GARLAND OUT OF HEAVY THREAD AND BEADS THAT THE GIRLS HAD. WE HAD CHRISTMAS MUSIC PLAYING AND ENJOYED A SNACK OF FRESH BAKED COOKIES AND HOT CHOCOLATE. THEY USUALLY DRANK TEA AND COFFEE BUT MANAGED TO FIND SOME COCOA FOR THE HOT CHOCOLATE TO MAKE IT A VERY SPECIAL TIME. WE SAT DOWN FOR DEVOTIONS AND A MOVIE THEN HEADED OFF TO BED.

THE NEXT DAY WAS CHRISTMAS MORNING. AS I WOKE I SMELLED PANCAKES COOKING AND AS I DRESSED, I NOTICED HOW PARTICULARLY CHILLY IT WAS FOR THE SEASON FIJI WAS IN. WHEN I LOOKED OUT THE WINDOW, I NOTICED IT WAS OVERCAST AND HAD BEGUN TO RAIN AND I THOUGHT OF HOW STRANGE IT WAS. AS I WAS SAYING MY PRAYERS AND WISHING JESUS A VERY HAPPY BIRTHDAY THE PRESENCE OF GOD FELL IN THE ROOM AND I WAS OVERCOME WITH EMOTION. THEN IT HIT ME, GOD KNEW HOW MUCH CHRISTMAS MEANT TO ME AND BEING AWAY FROM HOME ALTHOUGH DIFFERENT HERE, HE HAD BROUGHT A CHILLY DAY TO FIJI SO I WOULDN'T BE SO HOMESICK. IT WAS THE MOST MEMORABLE MOMENT I WILL NEVER FORGET AND SHOWS THAT GOD INDEED CARES ABOUT EVEN THE SMALLEST DETAILS OF YOUR LIFE! I WAS SO IN AWE AS I SHARED THIS WITH THE FAMILY OVER BREAKFAST AND THEY WERE DELIGHTED TOO.

AFTER BREAKFAST WE ALL GATHERED IN THE LIVING ROOM WHERE I GAVE THE GIRLS THEIR GIFTS AND THE OLDER ADULT CHILDREN, THEIR FACES LIT UP AS THEY OPENED THEIR PACKAGES. THE LAST COUPLE YEARS THERE WASN'T MUCH TO BE GIVEN AT CHRISTMAS DUE TO THEIR MOM BEING ILL AND EVENTUALLY PASSING AWAY. I DIDN'T REALIZE THE FINANCIAL STATE OF THE FAMILY, BUT MORE AND MORE WAS COMING TO LIGHT AS TIME WENT ON AND LEARNED THEY REALLY STRUGGLED ON A ONE PARENT INCOME. LATER THAT NIGHT AFTER CALCULATING THE TIME CHANGE, I SIGNED INTO SKYPE WHERE I GOT TO SEE MY FAMILY VIA WEB CAM! ALTHOUGH IT WASN'T THE SAME, I STILL WATCHED AS

THEY OPENED THEIR GIFTS AND ALL SCREAMING IN DELIGHT AT WHAT THEY GOT. ALL I COULD DO WAS STAND IN AWE OF SUCH AN AMAZING LORD WE HAD. A DEFINITE CHRISTMAS TO REMEMBER!

THE NEXT WEEK, WHEN WE WENT FOR PRISON MINISTRY, IT WAS TO BE A TESTIMONY SERVICE. I WAS ANXIOUS TO HEAR HOW THE ANGEL TREE PROGRAM WENT AND HOW MANY WERE BLESSED. IT WASN'T ABOUT NUMBERS EXACTLY, I MEAN HEAVEN REJOICES WHEN JUST ONE COMES TO KNOW CHRIST AS SAVIOR, BUT IT WAS EXCITING TO HEAR HOW MANY LIVES WERE TOUCHED BUT THE GRACE OF GOD. SOME OF THE GENTLEMAN HAD A HARD TIME SPEAKING, SO THEY APPOINTED ONE SPOKESPERSON TO SHARE ABOUT WHAT THEY DID OVER CHRISTMAS. THEY SAID THAT 8 OF THE MEN WERE ALLOWED TO LEAVE THE PRISON FOR THE FIRST TIME IN THE HISTORY OF FIJI AND GO TO CHURCH WITH THE WARDENS THAT PAST SUNDAY AND GIVE THEIR TESTIMONYS AS TO WHERE THEIR LIFE WAS AND HOW THEIR LIVES HAD CHANGED WHILE IN PRISON DUE TO THE LOVE AND MINISTRY SHOWED TO THEM BY THOSE WHO CAME IN TO SHARE THE LOVE OF GOD WITH THEM EACH WEEK! IT LOOKED AS IF THIS COULD BE A CONTINUAL THING FOR THE INMATES AS WELL!!

GLORY TO GOD! AFTER SHOUTING AND GIVING THANKS TO GOD, HE SPOKE AGAIN AND SAID THAT THE SAME 8 MEN WERE EVEN ALLOWED TO GO CHRISTMAS CAROLING AT SOME OF THE AREA BUSINESSES. WHAT AN INSPIRATION IT WAS FOR THESE MEN, TO SEE GOD MOVING IN THEIR MIDST, SHOWING THEM THAT NOTHING IS IMPOSSIBLE FOR THOSE THAT BELIEVE!

THEY NEVER TRIED TO RUN OFF OR ANYTHING, BUT GAVE GOD GLORY, THAT EVEN IN THE FACT OF THEM BEING IN PRISON, THEY WERE MAKING AN IMPACT IN THE LIVES OF OTHERS AND BRING HOPE! HALLELUJAH. I WAS SO EXCITED AND HONORED TO BE HERE AT THIS APPOINTED TIME TO SHARE IN THE CHANGES GOD WAS MAKING IN THIS COUNTRY. TO SEE GOVERNMENT POLICIES CHANGING RIGHT BEFORE OUR EYES, WAS NOTHING SHORT OF A MIRACLE. AND I WAS THERE TO WITNESS THIS AWESOME CHANGE WE WERE SEEING!

SOON THE NEW YEAR WAS UPON US, AND WAS GOING TO BE A BUSY YEAR. WE HAD BEEN TALKING OF STARTING A STREET PASTORS MINISTRY, THIS WOULD BE DONE AT CERTAIN TIMES OF THE DAY, BUT MAINLY AT NIGHT TO HELP GET YOUNG PEOPLE OFF THE STREET AND MINISTER TO THOSE COMING OUT OF THE BARS. I WAS ALSO GETTING READY TO START BIBLE COLLEGE THAT THE PASTOR OF THE CHURCH I ATTENDED WAS GOING TO BE TEACHING! ALTHOUGH IT WAS A YEAR PROGRAM AND I WOULD BE LEAVING IN A BOUT 4 MONTHS TIME, HE SAID I COULD STILL ATTEND AND FINISH VIA EMAIL WHEN I RETURNED HOME. THEN WHEN I CAME BACK TO FIJI AT SOME POINT I COULD FINISH THE COURSE. I WAS PUMPED, WOW, ME TAKING A COLLEGE COURSE! YEE-HAW!

FOR NOW THOUGH WE HAD THE MONTH OF JANUARY OFF FROM THE MINISTRY TEAMS DUE TO THE HOLIDAYS AND KID'S STILL BE HOME FROM SCHOOL AND NOT GOING BACK TILL THE END OF THE MONTH. I HAD SPENT ANOTHER DAY AT THE BEACH, HOW WEIRD IT WAS FOR ME IN JANUARY TO BE AT THE BEACH. AS I SAT ON THE SAND AND TOOK MY SHOES OFF LETTING

MY TOES RUN THRU THE SAND, I THOUGHT OF THE SCRIPTURE THAT GOD KNOWS THE VERY NUMBER OF THE HAIRS ON OUR HEAD. AS I LOOKED AT THE SAND I WONDERED HOW MANY GRAINS OF SAND THERE WAS ON THE BEACH, YET GOD KNEW. I COULDN'T WRAP MY MIND AROUND THE AWESOMENESS OF GOD AND THE BEAUTY OF ALL HE CREATED JUST FOR OUR ENJOYMENT. IN THE 6 DAYS OF CREATION WHEN HE FORMED THE EARTH. HE SPOKE INTO EXISTANCE ALL THAT HE WANTED. HE SPOKE TO THE MOON AND THE STARS, THE SUN AND THE WATER AND TOLD THEM EXACTLY WHERE HE WANTED THEM AND HOW THEY WOULD FUNCTION. HE MADE THE FISH AND ALL THE ANIMALS, THE TREES AND THE LAND. WHAT A MIGHTY GOD HE WAS. I REFELCTED OVER MY LIFE AND WHERE HE HAD BROUGHT ME TO THIS POINT. I THOUGHT OF THE LAST YEAR AND ALL THAT TRANSPIRED AND WAS JUST SPEECHLESS, IT WAS AMAZING.

THE HOST FAMILY SAID THIS WAS THE BEST CHRISTMAS THEY EXPERIENCED IN A WHILE AND IT MEANT SO MUCH TO THEM AND THEY THANKED ME FOR BEING A PART OF THEIR LIVES. I WAS SO HUMBLED! A CATALYST I WAS! LATER THE EVENING WE DID MAKE A COUPLE HOUSE VISITS TO CHECK ON FAMILES OF A COUPLE OF THE INMATES FROM THE PRISON. THEY'D HAD SOME HEALTH ISSUES WE WAS PRAYING OVER AND WENT TO CHECK TO SEE HOW THEY WERE DOING SINCE SEEING THE DOCTOR. WE LEARNED THAT THEY WERE DOING MUCH BETTER, ONE LADY BEING HEALED FROM A SKIN IRRITATION SHE HAD BEEN DEALING WITH FOR A FEW MONTHS. WE WERE DELIGHTED AT THEIR NEWS, PRAYED FOR THEM AND LEFT.

IT WAS NOW THE END OF JANUARY AND THE KIDS WERE BACK IN SCHOOL. THE LAST 3 WEEKS SINCE THE NEW YEAR HAD REALLY FLOWN BY AND WE WEREN'T REALLY BUSY WITH ANY SORT OF MINISTRY. I REALLY ENJOYED GETTING TO KNOW THE GIRLS MORE, AND I'M SURE IT WAS NICE FOR THEM HAVING A SORT OF MOTHER FIGURE AROUND. I COULDN'T WAIT FOR GROUPS AND MINISTRY TEAMS TO GET UP AND RUNNING AGAIN. I ESPECIALLY ENJOYED THE MID WEEK PRAYER MEETING WHERE WE GATHERED AT A HOME AT 10 PM FOR PRAYER AND SOMETIMES STAYED TILL WELL AFTER MIDNIGHT. ALWAYS A GREAT TIME OF SINGING AND SHARING, AS WELL AS PRAYING OVER DIFFERENT REQUESTS THAT COME INTO THE CHURCH. THE NEXT WEEK BIBLE SCHOOL STARTED AND I WAS SO EXCITED TO BE ATTENDING.

THEY WERE HELD EVERY SAT FOR A COUPLE HOURS IN THE AFTERNOON AT THE HOME OF ONE OF THE CELL GROUPS. WE WERE GOING TO STUDY THE BOOK OF GALATIANS AND DISCUSS THE GOSPELS WHICH I WAS EAGER TO LEARN ALL ABOUT IT. I EVEN EMAILED MY PASTORS AS I'D DONE OFF AND ON DURING MY STAY HERE, AND SHARED THE NEWS WITH THEM, THEY WERE ALWAYS SO SUPPORTIVE AND I WAS THANKFUL FOR THEM AND THEIR ENCOURAGING WORDS AND PRAYERS!

THE NEXT FEW MONTHS FLEW BY AND NOW IT WAS FINALLY TIME TO RETURN HOME. I WAS THRILLED, YET SAD AT THE SAME TIME THAT MY MINISTRY IN FIJI HAD COME TO AN END. GOING OVER IN MY MIND THE THINGS GOD HAD DONE WHILE I WAS THERE WAS

NOTHING SHORT OF A MIRACLE. WE SEEN PEOPLE HEALED AND TOUCHED, LIVES RESTORED. WE SEEN GOVERNMENT POLICIES CHANGED, AND PEOPLE SAVED AND TRANSFORMED BY THE POWER OF GOD'S HAND! I ENJOYED BEING A PART OF THE BIBLE SCHOOL AND HOW WELL I HAD DONE, AND BEING A PART OF THE WORSHIP TEAM. THEY LOVED MY ZEAL AND MY FIRE AND IT WAS CONTAGIOUS AND SEEMED TO SPREAD.

I REMEMBER MY FAREWELL SPEECH THAT LAST SUNDAY AT CHURCH, I WANTED TO DO SOMETHING SPECIAL FOR THE PASTORS, AND I REMEMBER THAT WHEN I FIRST LEFT FOR FIJI, MY HAIRDRESSER, WHO WAS ALSO A PART OF OUR CHURCH, HAD MADE FOR ME A TABERET. IT WAS A HAND HELD PIECE THAT HAD STREAMERS, THAT SOMETIMES DANCERS WOULD USE TO WAVE AS A SIGN OF WORSHIP UNTO THE LORD. A VERY BEAUTIFUL MINISTRY TOOL THAT I HAD BROUGHT TO FIJI FOR ME. I HAD DECIDED TO GIVE IT TO THE PASTORS AND THE CONGREGATION THERE. I THANKED EVERYONE FOR THE LOVE AND THE ACCEPTANCE THEY HAD SHOWN TO ME DURING MY STAY THERE AND SHARED SOME OF WHAT GOD HAD DONE THRU THE MINISTRY I WAS A PART OF. AT THE END OF THE SERVICE, MANY GREETED ME AND GAVE HUGS WISHING ME WELL AND HOPING ONE DAY I WOULD RETURN. MANY HAD GIVEN MONEY AND GIFTS IN WHICH THE GIFTS I KEPT BUT THE MONEY I SOWED TO THE FAMILY I STAYED WITH WHILE THERE.

THE NEXT DAY WAS MONDAY, AND ONE DAY BEFORE I WAS DUE TO DEPART FOR HOME. WE DID SOME MORE SIGHT SEEING TO DIFFERENT PARTS OF

THE COUNTRY. ONE THING THAT FASCIANTED ME WAS THE MOUNTAIN THEY CALLED THE SLEEPING GIANT. THE FORMATION OF IT WAS THAT OF A GIANT PERSON. YOU COULD SEE THE HEAD, MAKE OUT PART OF A FACE, BODY AND LEGS. IT WAS THE MOST AMAZING THING I HAD SEEN IN MY LIFE. IN ONE PART OF THE CITY, THEY WERE BUILDING SOMETHING AND WHEN THEY HAD DUG THE EARTH IT WAS THE REDDEST EARTH I HAD EVER SEEN. THEN I WAS SHOWN A PINE FACTORY WHERE THERE WAS HUGE MOUNDS OF PINE PIECES AND THE SMELL OF PINE WAS HEAVENLY. NEXT WE WENT TO THE SUGAR CANE FACTORY WHERE WE GET OUR SUGAR FROM AND ACTUALLY SEEN THE TRAIN GOING AS THEY BROUGHT SUPPLIES AND OTHER THINGS UP TO THE FACTORY. IT WAS SO COOL. WE HEADED BACK TO THE FLAT TO PREPARE FOR DINNER, THEN WATCH A MOVIE AND HOPEFULLY HEAD TO BED EARLY TO REST FOR MY TRIP HOME.

FINALLY, THE DAY OF MY DEPARTURE HAD ARRIVED. WE MADE A FEW LAST VISITS, AND THEN I CAME BACK TO PACK. I WAS DUE TO BE AT THE AIRPORT AT 7:30 PM THAT NIGHT AND I KNEW I WOULD MISS IT THERE, BUT EXCITED TO GET HOME TO MY FAMILY. THE GIRLS CAME IN FROM SCHOOL AND WE VISITED, THEN ATE AN EARLY SUPPER. BEFORE LONG IT WAS TIME TO HEAD TO THE AIRPORT FOR CHECK IN. THE PASTORS HAD COME TO SEE ME OFF AS WELL AS THE HOST FAMILY AND HIS BROTHER WHO WOULD ESCORT ME BACK TO BOARD THEN PLANE. WHEN THE TIME HAD COME TO BOARD, THEY GAVE ME HUGS AND PRAYED OVER ME AND I WAS GONE. AS I BOARDED THE PLANE AND GOT READY FOR TAKE OFF, I WAS THINKING HOW I WOULD BE GOING BACK IN TIME.

ALTHOUGH IT WAS TUES NIGHT IN FIJI WHEN I BOARDED THE PLANE, ONCE I CROSSED THE DATELINE AT THE EQUATOR, I WOULD ARRIVE IN CALIFORNIA TUESDAY AFTERNOON.

I THOUGHT HMMM, NOW WOULD BE A GOOD TIME, TO PULL A PRANK, CAUSE ONCE I GOT TO CALIFORNIA AND WENT BACK IN TIME, IT WOULD BE AS IF I HAD NEVER PULLED THE PRANK. I LAUGHED AT MYSELF, FOR MY GOOFINESS. SOON WE LANDED IN CALIFORNIA, AND I THOUGHT WOW, THE TRIP HERE DIDN'T SEEM SO LONG AS IT DID WHEN I WAS FLYING TO FIJI. BUT I WAS WEARY. I HAD A 9 HOUR LAYOVER BEFORE I CAUGHT THE FLIGHT FROM CALIFORNIA TO CHICAGO. WHAT WOULD I DO FOR 9 HOURS? I THOUGHT OF SITE SEEING BUT WASN'T SURE I WOULDN'T GET LOST IN SUCH A BIG CITY. I COULDN'T FIND A SHUTTLE BUS SO I WALKED FROM THE INTERNATIONAL AIRPORT TO LA AIRPORT. IT WASN'T TOO BAD OF A WALK, AND WHEN I WENT THRU CUSTOMS, WAS GREETED AND WELCOMED BACK TO THE U.S. IT WAS GOOD TO BE BACK.

AFTER CALLING MY MOM TO LET HER KNOW I WAS IN CALIFORNIA AND WHEN I WOULD ARRIVE IN DAYTON AS LONG AS NO DELAYS. I WENT TO GET A BITE TO EAT AND WAIT. FINALLY IT WAS TIME TO BOARD THE PLANE AND WHILE STOPPING IN CHICAGO AND WAITING FOR 2 HOURS BEFORE FLYING TO OHIO, AFTER 12 HOURS I WAS NOW AT THE DAYTON AIRPORT AND GREETED BY MY MOM AND HER FRIEND. SHE WAS SO EXCITED TO SEE ME AS I WAS HER. I WAS A CHATTERBOX ALL THE WAY HOME AS I SHARED MY EXPERIENCES FROM THE LAST 9 MONTHS. MY KIDS

HAD A WELCOME HOME PARTY FOR ME, AND MY SON WAS SO GRACIOUS AS TO DO MY ROUTE THE NEXT DAY SO I COULD RECOVER FROM MY FLIGHT. I WAS TRULY A BLESSED WOMAN!

IT HAS NOW BEEN ALMOST 5 YEARS SINCE MY RETURN FROM FIJI. I CAN'T BEGIN TO DESCRIBE THE TRANSFORMATION MY LIFE HAD TAKEN SINCE SEPT OF 2009 WHEN I BROKE FREE FROM THE CHAINS OF AN ABUSIVE LIFE STYLE AND RECEIVED THE CALL TO WRITE THIS BOOK. THE OPPORTUNITIES THAT CAME MY WAY, WAS UNBELIEVABLE TO SAY THE LEAST AND RESULTED OUT OF FAITH AND TRUST IN MY HEAVENLY FATHER AND BEING ABLE TO LET GO OF THOSE THINGS THAT HAD ME BOUND, AND HEEDING THE CALL HE PLACED ON MY LIFE. IT WAS BY NO MEANS AN EASY PROCESS. I HAD ALOT TO WORK THRU ESPECIALLY WITH MY KIDS. BUT I COULD FINALLY BE MYSELF, AND SOMETIMES I DIDN'T KNOW HOW TO ACT.

JANUARY 2014 I HAD THE OPPORTUNITY TO BRING OVER FROM FIJI THE 3 DAUGHTERS OF THE HOST FAMILY WHO I STAYED WITH WHILE IN FIJI. WHAT AN HONOR IT WAS TO BE USED OF GOD IN THIS CAPACITY AND GIVE THEM A CHANCE AT A BETTER LIFE IN AMERICA. DIVINE CONNECTION IS WHAT COMES TO MIND. GOD PLACED SO MANY WONDERFUL PEOPLE IN MY LIFE THAT HELPED WITH FUNDRAISERS AND A BENEFIT DINNER TO RAISE THE FUNDS WE NEEDED FOR THEIR VISA'S, MEDICAL EXAMS AND POLICE CLEARANCE. A DEAR FRIEND AND HER HUSBAND STEPPED FORTH TO BE THEIR AFFIDAVIT OF SUPPORT SINCE MY INCOME FELL JUST BELOW THEIR INCOME STANDARD. AN AUNT HAD PAID FOR THEIR GREEN

CARDS AND A STEP BROTHER PAID THEIR AIRFARE OVER. IT WAS A MIRACLE IN THE MAKING AND YOU JUST KNEW IT WAS GOD THAT WORKED EVERYTHING OUT.

THE DAY THEY ARRIVED WE WERE HAVING SNOW FALL. THEY FLEW FROM CALIFORNIA TO PHILADELPHIA, PENNSYLVANIA AND THEY WERE HAVING A BLIZZARD. WE PRAYED THE AIRPORT WOULDN'T CLOSE, AS I WASN'T SURE WHERE THE GIRLS WOULD GO AT THAT POINT. THEY DIDN'T GET SNOW IN FIJI SO THIS WAS DEFINITELY A NEW EXPERIENCE FOR THEM. GOD AGAIN MOVED AND JUST WHEN THEY WERE DUE TO LAND THE STORM ENDED AND THINGS WERE GETTING CLEARED. 2 HOURS LATER THEY WERE ON THE PLANE FOR DAYTON, OHIO. I HAVE COME TO LOVE THESE GIRLS AS IF MY OWN. THEY HAVE BEEN A JOY AND A BLESSING AND ALTHOUGH THERE ARE CULTURAL DIFFERENCES, WHICH WAS TO BE EXPECTED AND HAS TAKEN THEM SOME TIME TO LEARN SOME OF THE AMERICAN CULTURE AND OUR WAYS OF DOING THINGS, THEY HAVE ADJUSTED RATHER WELL WITH THEIR NEW LIFE HERE IN AMERICA! YES, WE HAVE STRUGGLES, BUT WHO DOESN'T?

BEING ALL THIS WAY WITHOUT THEIR FRIENDS, DAD AND OTHER FAMILY MEMBERS WAS SCARY FOR THEM. AFTER ALL I WAS ONLY IN FIJI FOR 9 MONTHS. NOT REALLY THAT LONG TO GET TO KNOW SOMEONE, BUT AGAIN, GOD HAD A PLAN FOR OUR LIVES AND IT WAS UNFOLDED BEFORE US. WE FOUGHT THE SCHOOL SYSTEM TO GET THE TWINS IN SCHOOL, TAKING A YEAR TO DO SO, WE HAD SOME DENTAL ISSUES GOING ON AND NOT ABLE TO GET INSURANCE

FOR THEM JUST YET, AND SINCE STARTING SCHOOL ONE OF THE TWINS HAD SOME MEDICAL ISSUES, BUT GOD MET EVERY NEED!! I HAVE LEARNED THAT GROWTH MAINLY COMES OUTSIDE OF WHAT WE CONSIDER TO BE OUR COMFORT ZONE.

EVERY STRUGGLE I WENT THRU, WAS FOR SUCH A TIME AS THIS. I BEING ONE OF PERSISTANCE, AND DETERMINATION, BELIEVES THAT NO MATTER WHAT THE CIRCUMSTANCE, WE HAVE THE POWER TO CHANGE IT IF WE SET OUR MIND TO IT. SOMETIMES WE GET BLINDSIDED AND OFF COURSE AS I HAD DONE OVER THE COURSE OF MY LIFE. BUT THE BEAUTY OF IT IS GOD WAS ALWAYS THERE, AND HE NEVER QUIT KNOCKING, NEVER GAVE UP ON ME, AND HE STILL DOESN'T. HE IS THERE TO LOVE US AND HELP US PICK UP THE PIECES OF THE BROKEN PARTS OF OUR LIFE. EVERYTHING YOU MAY BE GOING THRU OR HAVE GONE THRU IS TRAINING YOU FOR SOMETHING FAR GREATER THAN YOU COULD EVER IMAGINE. TRUST ME, I KNOW FIRST HAND. I DEFINITELY LEARNED OVER THE LAST 6 YEARS TO GIVE THANKS IN "ALL" THINGS!

TO SEE AND EXPERIENCE ALL THAT I DID WHILE IN FIJI AND SEE LIVES TOUCHED MADE ME SEE THAT ALL I WENT THRU WAS TRAINING GROUND, AS IF A SOLDIER, WHICH THAT IS WHAT WE ARE IN A SENSE. OUR LIFE FROM THE MOMENT WE ARE BORN IS ALL ABOUT TRAINING AND LEARNING EACH AND EVERY DAY. THE BIBLE SAYS IN JOHN 16:33 THAT IN THIS WORLD WE WILL HAVE TROUBLE, BUT TO TAKE HEART BECAUSE JESUS OVERCAME THE WORLD! HE SAID TO CONSIDER IT A JOY WHEN WE GO THRU THINGS BECAUSE ONCE WE ARE THRU IT, IT MAKES US SO

MUCH STRONGER, AND GIVES US INSIGHT TO HELP OTHERS. WE ARE IN A BATTLE FOR OUR LIFE FROM AN ADVERSARY THAT DOESN'T WANT TO SEE THE KINGDOM OF GOD ADVANCE.

BUT WE ARE THE VOICE, HANDS AND FEET OF GOD. WE ARE THE CHOSEN ONES TO SPREAD THE GOSPEL OF CHRIST TO A LOST AND DYING WORLD. MANY FEEL LOST AND HOPELESS, AND FEEL AS THOUGH THEIR LIFE HAS LOST MEANING AND HAS NO PURPOSE. THAT IS THE VERY REASON FOR THIS BOOK, TO SHARE MY EXPERIENCES, MY FAITH, AND HOW THRU GOD, AND THRU THE PEOPLE GOD PLACED IN MY LIFE FOR SUCH A TIME AS THIS, HAS HELPED ALONG WITH ME AS WELL, TO MAKE ME THE WOMAN I AM TODAY, FULL OF LIFE, AND SPUNK, FUNNY, VIBRANT, ONE WHO IS STRONG AND CONFIDENT IN WHO SHE IS AND WAS CREATED TO BE! I HAVE STARTED MY OWN BUSINESS AND BECOME INDEPENDANT. I HAVE TIMES WHERE I GET DOWN, BUT HAVE LEARNED THAT IS WHATSOEVER STATE I AM IN TO BE CONTENT AND PRESS THRU.

MAY YOUR LIFE BE TOUCHED, AND ENCOURAGED BY READING THIS BOOK! MAY YOU ALLOW THE WORDS SPOKEN TO PENETRATE YOUR HEART AND GIVE YOU THE HOPE, AND DRIVE YOU ARE SEARCHING FOR AND MOST OF ALL BRING YOU TO THE UNDERSTANDING OF WHO GOD IS AND WHO YOU ARE IN HIM! YOU ARE THE RIGHTEOUSNESS OF CHRIST! YOUR LIFE HAS PURPOSE AND MEANING! NOTHING IS TOO HARD FOR HIM! LEARN TO GIVE THANKS IN ALL THINGS, THAT WHATEVER STATE YOU FIND YOURSELF IN, BE CONTENT. YOU DO THIS THRU PRAYER, AND FAITH AND TRUST. FAITH IS

THE SUBSTANCE OF THINGS HOPED FOR THE EVIDENCE OF THINGS "NOT" SEEN. DON'T LOOK AT YOUR CIRCUMSTANCES. YOU MAY SEE NEGATIVE THINGS ALL AROUND YOU, BUT IF YOU CHANGE YOUR MINDSET TOWARDS THAT NEGATIVE OR HOPELESS SITUATION AND THINK WHAT THE POSITIVE RESULT MAY BE FROM IT HAPPENING. YOU CAN TRULY OVERCOME IT.

YOU SEE, WHEN YOU STOP LIVING IN THE PROBLEM, WHATEVER IT MAY BE, THE ANSWER MAY BE STARING YOU IN THE FACE. OR THE ANSWER MAY BE SOMETHING THAT HASN'T EVEN HAPPENED YET, IT'S A DEFINITE WALK OF FAITH, BUT WHEN YOU WALK IN THE ANSWER INSTEAD OF YOUR PROBLEM, THE PROBLEM WILL GO AWAY! BUT THE CHOICE IS YOURS! GOD WILL NOT FORCE HIS WILL UPON ANYONE. HE HAS GIVEN US THE POWER TO CHOOSE AND KNOW THIS, SOMETHING I TOLD MY KIDS ALL THE TIME GROWING UP. THERE ARE CONSEQUENCES FOR EVERY CHOICE YOU MAKE WHETHER GOOD OR BAD. YOU WILL REAP WHAT YOU SOW, WHETHER GOOD OR BAD.

LET ME GIVE YOU AN EXAMPLE OF FAITH FOR THOSE THAT MAY FEEL THEY DON'T KNOW WHAT FAITH IS. YOU PAY YOUR ELECTRICITY BILL TO KEEP THE LIGHTS ON, YOU GO TO THE LIGHT SWITCH TO TURN IT ON. NOW YOU DON'T STAND THERE AND THINK OH I WONDER IF IT WILL COME ON. RIGHT? MOST PEOPLE JUST GO AND FLIP IT EXPECTING IT TO COME ON. SAME WAY WITH YOUR CAR, YOU GO OUT EVERYDAY TURN THE KEY AND START IT UP. YOU DON'T THINK WHEN YOU GET READY TO LEAVE OH I BETTER HEAD OUT EARLY IN CASE THE CAR DON'T TURN OVER. YOU GO

TO WORK AND CLOCK IN, KNOWING THAT AT THE END OF THE WEEK YOU WILL BE PAID FOR THE TIME YOU PUT IN. THAT IS WHAT FAITH IS! BELIEVING!

THE BIBLE SAYS NOT TO BE CONFORMED TO THE WAYS OF THE WORLD. THIS MEANS THE ISSUES, THE WAY THE WORLD DOES THINGS, THIS DOESN'T MEAN WE DON'T FOLLOW RULES. WE HAVE RULES AND LAWS FOR A REASON. BUT THIS MEANS HAVING THE NEED TO FIT IN WITH THE CROWD, SO WE LOWER OUR MORALS AND STANDARDS TO BE POPULAR. TRANSFORM YOUR MIND BY RENEWING IT BY THINKING POSITIVE THOUGHTS. WE DO THIS THRU MUSIC, READING THE WORD OF GOD OR OTHER ENCOURAGING BOOKS, LISTENING TO MESSAGES, WRITING AND KEEPING A JOURNAL, SURROUNDING OURSELVES WITH POSITIVE PEOPLE. MAYBE YOU NEED TO WEED NEGATIVE PEOPLE FROM YOUR LIFE. I'M NOT AN ADVOCATE FOR DIVORCE, BUT IF YOU ARE IN AN UNHEALTHY AND ABUSIVE SITUATION, OR A RELATIONSHIP WHERE YOU ARE BEING NEGLECTED IN SOME WAY, GOD DOESN'T WANT THAT FOR YOU. SURROUND YOURSELF WITH THOSE WHO NO MATTER WHAT KIND OF DAY YOU HAVE, THEY WILL UPLIFT YOU AND ENCOURAGE YOU. EVEN WHEN YOU FAIL, AND YOU WILL FAIL AND MAKE MISTAKES THEN THEY WILL BE A FRIEND WHO STICKS CLOSER THAN A BROTHER, JUST AS OUR HEAVENLY FATHER IS! THEY WILL TELL YOU TO GET UP AND TAKE ANOTHER STEP, TO PUSH THRU. DON'T BE DISCOURAGED IN TRYING ANYTHING AND FINDING YOU ARE STILL STRUGGLING. IT TAKES TIME AND EVEN IF YOU TAKE 3 STEPS FORWARD AND 2 STEPS BACK. DON'T LOOK AT THE GOING BACKWARDS, BUT LOOK AT

THE FACT YOU ARE STILL 1 STEP AHEAD AND YOU'LL
MAKE IT!

*I LOVE YOU! THIS BOOK WILL BE COVERED IN PRAYER
FOR EACH THAT HAVE PURCHASED IT AND I WILL
CONTINE TO PRAY THAT YOUR LIFE WILL BE TOUCHED
AND BLESSED JUST BY READING IT! HERE IS TO NEW
BEGINNINGS! GOD BLESS YOU!*

Bibliography

The following is a list of invaluable resources for abuse victims or those seeking more information. By providing links to other sites, this author does not pledge, support, or endorse the information or products available on these sites.

Domestic Violence and Abuse: Signs of Abuse and Abusive Relationships. HelpGuide.org, Updated Mar. 2016. Web. <http://www.helpguide.org/articles/abuse/domestic-violence-and-abuse.htm>. This page has an abundance of resources on discovering abuse, links to appropriate resources, and other helpful information on victims of abuse. Authors: Melinda Smith, M.A., and Jeanne Segal, Ph.D.

HOTLINES FOR WOMEN AND MEN:

- **US**: National Domestic Violence Hotline at 1-800-799-SAFE (7233) -- Also reference other resources: http://www.ncadv.org/need-help/resources
  - State Coalitions: http://www.ncadv.org/need-help/state-coalitions
- **UK**: Women's Aid at 0808 2000 247 – or for Men mainly: ManKind Initiative at 01823 334244
- **AUS**: 1800RESPECT at 1800 737 732 -- Other information for Men: http://www.oneinthree.com.au/servicesandresources/
- **INT'L**: see: http://www.hotpeachpages.net/

www.ingramcontent.com/pod-product-compliance
Lightning Source LLC
LaVergne TN
LVHW051540080426
835510LV00020B/2795